William J Fay

The Epistles of St. John

Alfred Plummer

BAKER BOOK HOUSE
Grand Rapids, Michigan

Reprinted 1980 by
Baker Book House Company
from the edition published by
Cambridge University Press
First published in 1886
ISBN: 0-8010-7058-9

PHOTOLITHOPRINTED BY CUSHING - MALLOY, INC.
ANN ARBOR, MICHIGAN, UNITED STATES OF AMERICA

PREFACE
BY THE GENERAL EDITOR

THE General Editor of *The Cambridge Bible for Schools* thinks it right to say that he does not hold himself responsible either for the interpretation of particular passages which the Editors of the several Books have adopted, or for any opinion on points of doctrine that they may have expressed. In the New Testament more especially questions arise of the deepest theological import, on which the ablest and most conscientious interpreters have differed and always will differ. His aim has been in all such cases to leave each Contributor to the unfettered exercise of his own judgment, only taking care that mere controversy should as far as possible be avoided. He has contented himself chiefly with a careful revision of the notes, with pointing out omissions, with suggesting occasionally a reconsideration of some question, or a fuller treatment of difficult passages, and the like.

Beyond this he has not attempted to interfere, feeling it better that each Commentary should have its own individual character, and being convinced that freshness and variety of treatment are more than a compensation for any lack of uniformity in the Series.

ON THE GREEK TEXT

IN undertaking an edition of the Greek text of the New Testament with English notes for the use of Schools, the Syndics of the Cambridge University Press have not thought it desirable to reprint the text in common use*. To have done this would have been to set aside all the materials that have since been accumulated towards the formation of a correct text, and to disregard the results of textual criticism in its application to MSS., Versions and Fathers. It was felt that a text more in accordance with the present state of our knowledge was desirable. On the other hand the Syndics were unable to adopt one of the more recent critical texts, and they were not disposed to make themselves responsible for the preparation of an

---

* The form of this text most used in England, and adopted in Dr Scrivener's edition, is that of the third edition of Robert Stephens (1550). The name "Received Text" is popularly given to the Elzevir edition of 1633, which is based on this edition of Stephens, and the name is borrowed from a phrase in the Preface, "Textum ergo habes nunc ab omnibus receptum."

entirely new and independent text: at the same time it would have been obviously impossible to leave it to the judgment of each individual contributor to frame his own text, as this would have been fatal to anything like uniformity or consistency. They believed however that a good text might be constructed by simply taking the consent of the two most recent critical editions, those of Tischendorf and Tregelles, as a basis. The same principle of consent could be applied to places where the two critical editions were at variance, by allowing a determining voice to the text of Stephens where it agreed with either of their readings, and to a third critical text, that of Lachmann, where the text of Stephens differed from both. In this manner readings peculiar to one or other of the two editions would be passed over as not being supported by sufficient critical consent; while readings having the double authority would be treated as possessing an adequate title to confidence.

A few words will suffice to explain the manner in which this design has been carried out.

In the *Acts*, the *Epistles*, and the *Revelation*, wherever the texts of Tischendorf and Tregelles agree, their joint readings are followed without any deviation. Where they differ from each other, but neither of them agrees with the text of Stephens as printed in Dr Scrivener's edition, the consensus of Lachmann with either is taken in preference to the text of Stephens. In all other cases the text of Stephens as represented in Dr Scrivener's edition has been followed.

In the *Gospels*, a single modification of this plan has been rendered necessary by the importance of the Sinai MS. (א), which was discovered too late to be used by Tregelles except in the last chapter of St John's Gospel and in the following books. Accordingly, if a reading which Tregelles has put in his margin agrees with א, it is considered as of the same authority as a reading which he has adopted in his text; and if any words which Tregelles has bracketed are omitted by א, these words are here dealt with as if rejected from his text.

In order to secure uniformity, the spelling and the accentuation of Tischendorf have been adopted where he differs from other Editors. His practice has likewise been followed as regards the insertion or omission of Iota subscript in infinitives (as ζῆν, ἐπιτιμᾶν), and adverbs (as κρυφῇ, λάθρα), and the mode of printing such composite forms as διαπαντός, διατί, τουτέστι, and the like.

The punctuation of Tischendorf in his eighth edition has usually been adopted : where it is departed from, the deviation, together with the reasons that have led to it, will be found mentioned in the Notes. Quotations are indicated by a capital letter at the beginning of the sentence. Where a whole verse is omitted, its omission is noted in the margin (*e.g.* Matt. xvii. 21 ; xxiii. 12).

The text is printed in paragraphs corresponding to those of the English Edition.

Although it was necessary that the text of all the portions of the New Testament should be uniformly constructed in accordance with these general rules, each editor has been left at perfect liberty to express his preference for other readings in the Notes.

It is hoped that a text formed on these principles will fairly represent the results of modern criticism, and will at least be accepted as preferable to "the Received Text" for use in Schools.

J. J. STEWART PEROWNE

CONTENTS

INTRODUCTION

CHAPTER I

THE LAST YEARS OF S. JOHN

A SKETCH of the life of S. John as a whole has been given in the Introduction to the Fourth Gospel. Here it will not be necessary to do more than retouch and somewhat enlarge what was there said respecting the closing years of his life, in which period, according to all probability, whether derived from direct or indirect evidence, our three Epistles were written. In order to understand the motive and tone of the Epistles, it is requisite to have some clear idea of the circumstances, local, moral, and intellectual, in the midst of which they were written.

(1) *The Local Surroundings—Ephesus.*

Unless the whole history of the century which followed upon the destruction of Jerusalem is to be abandoned as chimerical and untrustworthy, we must continue to believe the almost universally accepted statement that S. John spent the last portion of his life in Asia Minor, and chiefly at Ephesus. The sceptical spirit which insists upon the truism that well-attested facts have nevertheless not been demonstrated with all the certainty of a proposition in Euclid, and contends that it is therefore right to doubt them, and lawful to dispute them, renders history impossible. The evidence of S. John's residence at Ephesus is too strong to be shaken by conjectures. It will be worth while to state the main elements of it.

(1) The opening chapters of the Book of Revelation are written in the character of the Metropolitan of the Churches of

Asia Minor. Even if we admit that the Book is possibly not written by S. John, at least it is written by some one who knows that S. John held that position. Had S. John never lived in Asia Minor, the writer of the Apocalypse would at once have been detected as personating an Apostle of whose abode and position he was ignorant.

(2) Justin Martyr (c. A.D. 150) probably within fifty years of S. John's death writes : "*Among us* also a certain man named John, one of the Apostles of Christ, prophesied in a Revelation made to him, that the believers of our Christ shall spend a thousand years in Jerusalem." These words occur in the *Dialogue with Trypho* (LXXXI.), which Eusebius tells us was held at Ephesus : so that ' among us' naturally means at or near Ephesus, though it might mean ' in our time.'

(3) Irenaeus, the disciple of Polycarp, the disciple of S. John, writes thus (c. A.D. 190) in the celebrated Epistle to his fellow-pupil, the heretically inclined Florinus, of which a portion has been preserved by Eusebius (*H. E.* v. xx. 4, 5); "These views (δόγματα) those elders who preceded us, who also were conversant with the Apostles, did not hand down to thee. For I saw thee when I was yet a lad in lower Asia with Polycarp, distinguishing thyself in the royal court, and endeavouring to have his approbation. For I remember what happened then more clearly than recent occurrences. For the experiences of childhood, growing up along with the soul, become part and parcel of it : so that I can describe the very place in which the blessed Polycarp used to sit and discourse, and his goings out and his comings in, the character of his life and the appearance of his person, and the discourses which he used to deliver to the multitude ; and how he recounted *his close intercourse with John* (τὴν μετὰ 'Ι. συναναστροφήν), and with the rest of those who had seen the Lord[1]").

---

[1] Lipsius (*Dict. of Christ. Biogr.* III. 263) shews that the letter to Florinus must be later in date than the work on Heresies. Bishop Lightfoot, who once thought otherwise (*Contemp. Rev.* May, 1875, 834), now accepts this view (*S. Ignatius and S. Polycarp* I. 429). Florinus was a presbyter at Rome under Eleutherius and Victor, and seems to have been deposed for accepting Valentinian Gnosticism (Eus. *H. E.* v. xv.).

That Polycarp was Bishop of Smyrna, where he spent most of his life and suffered martyrdom, is well known. And this again proves S. John's residence in Asia Minor. Still more plainly Irenaeus says elsewhere (*Haer.* III. i. 1); "Then John, the disciple of the Lord, who also leaned back on His breast, he too published a gospel *during his residence at Ephesus* in Asia."

(4) Polycrates, Bishop of Ephesus, in his Epistle to Victor Bishop of Rome (A. D. 189—199) says; "And moreover John also that leaned back upon the Lord's breast, who was a priest bearing the plate of gold, and a martyr and a teacher,—he lies asleep *at Ephesus*" (Eus. *H. E.* v. xxiv. 3.

(5) Apollonius, sometimes said to have been Presbyter of Ephesus, wrote a treatise against Montanism (c. A.D. 200), which Tertullian answered; and Eusebius tells us that Apollonius related the raising of a dead man to life by S. John *at Ephesus* (*H. E.* v. xviii. 14).

There is no need to multiply witnesses. That S. John ended his days in Asia Minor, ruling 'the Churches of Asia' from Ephesus as his usual abode, was the uniform belief of Christendom in the second and third centuries, and there is no sufficient reason for doubting its truth[1]. We shall find that S. John's residence there harmonizes admirably with the tone and contents of these Epistles; as also with the importance assigned to these Churches in the Revelation and in several of the Epistles of S. Paul.

Ephesus was situated on high ground in the midst of a fertile plain, not far from the mouth of the Cayster. As a centre of commerce its position was magnificent. Three rivers drain

[1] The silence of the Ignatian Epistles presents some difficulty, but not a serious one. It is certainly remarkable that in writing to the Ephesians Ignatius alludes to S. Paul and not to S. John (xii.). But Ignatius is writing of *martyrs* connected with Ephesus. The parallel between himself and S. Paul was exact; each visiting Ephesus before going to a martyr's death at Rome. There was no parallel between Ignatius and S. John. See Lightfoot *in loco* I. 64; also II. 390. A few lines above (xi) Ignatius speaks of those Ephesians who had "ever been of one mind with *the Apostles*," which probably means S. Paul and S. John. The interpolator expands "the Apostles" into "Paul and John and Timothy."

western Asia Minor, the Maeander, the Cayster, and the Hermes, and of these three the Cayster is the central one, and its valley is connected by passes with the valleys of the other two. The trade of the eastern Aegean was concentrated in its port. Through Ephesus flowed the chief of the trade between Asia Minor and the West. Strabo, the geographer, who was still living when S. John was a young man, had visited Ephesus, and as a native of Asia Minor must have known the city well from reputation. Writing of it in the time of Augustus he says; "Owing to its favourable situation, the city is in all other respects increasing daily, for it is the greatest place of trade of all the cities of Asia west of the Taurus." The vermilion trade of Cappadocia, which used to find a port at Sinope, now passed through Ephesus. What Corinth was to Greece and the Adriatic, and Marseilles to Gaul and the Western Mediterranean, that Ephesus was to Asia Minor and the Aegean. And its home products were considerable: corn in abundance grew in its plains, and wine and oil on its surrounding hills. Patmos, the scene of the Revelation, is only a day's sail from Ephesus, and it has been reasonably conjectured that the gorgeous description of the merchandise of 'Babylon,' given in the Apocalypse (xviii. 12, 13) is derived from S. John's own experiences in Ephesus; 'Merchandise of gold, and silver, and precious stone, and pearls, and fine linen, and purple, and silk, and scarlet; and all thyine wood, and every vessel of ivory, and every vessel made of most precious wood, and of brass, and iron, and marble; and cinnamon, and spice, and incense, and ointment, and frankincense, and wine and oil, and fine flour, and wheat, and cattle, and sheep; and merchandise of horses and chariots and slaves; and souls of men.' The last two items give us in terrible simplicity the traffic in human beings which treated them as body and soul the property of their purchaser. Ephesus was the place at which Romans visiting the East commonly landed. Among all the cities of the Roman province of Asia it ranked as 'first of all and greatest,' and was called 'the Metropolis of Asia.' In his Natural History Pliny speaks of it as *Asiae lumen*. It is quite in harmony with this that it should after Jerusalem and Antioch become the third great home of Christianity, and after the death of S. Paul be chosen by S. John as the centre whence he would direct the Churches of Asia. It is the first Church addressed in the Apocalypse (i. 11; ii. 1). If we had been entirely without information respecting S. John's life subsequent to the destruction of Jerusalem, the conjecture that he had moved to Asia Minor and taken up his abode in Ephesus would have been one of the most reasonable that could have been formed. With its mingled population of Asiatics and Greeks it combined more completely than any other city the characteristics of both East and West. With the exception of Rome, and perhaps of Alexandria, no more important centre could have been found for the work of the last surviving Apostle. There is nothing either in his writings or in traditions respecting him to connect S. John with Alexandria; and not much, excepting the tradition about the martyrdom near the Porta Latina (see p. xxx), to connect him with Rome. If S. John ever was in Rome, it was probably with S. Peter at the time of S. Peter's death. Some have thought that Rev. xiii. and xviii. are influenced by recollections of the horrors of the persecution in which S. Peter suffered. It is not improbable that the death of his companion Apostle (Luke xxii. 8; John xx. 2; Acts iii. 1, iv. 13, viii. 14) may have been one of the circumstances which led to S. John's settling in Asia Minor. The older friend, whose destiny it was to wander and to suffer, was dead; the younger friend, whose lot was 'that he abide,' was therefore free to choose the place where his abiding would be of most use to the Churches of Asia, which had lost their first guide and protector, S. Paul. While the activity of other Apostles was devoted to extending the borders of the Church, S. John directed his energies towards consolidating and purifying it. They 'lengthened the cords,' he 'strengthened the stakes' (Is. liv. 2), contending with internal corruptions in the doctrine and conduct of its converts, building up and completing its theology.

But there is no local colouring in S. John's Epistles. For him everything local or national has passed away. His images are drawn, not from the scenery or customs of Ephesus, but from facts and feelings that are as universal as humanity and as old as creation itself: light and darkness, life and death, love and hate.

The Church of Ephesus had been founded by S. Paul about A.D. 55, and some eight years later he had written the Epistle which now bears the name of the Ephesians, but which was apparently a circular letter addressed to other Churches as well as to that at Ephesus. Timothy was left there by S. Paul, when the latter went on to Macedonia (1 Tim. i. 3) to endeavour to keep in check the presumptuous and even heretical theories in which some members of the Ephesian Church had begun to indulge. Timothy was probably at Rome at the time of S. Paul's death (2 Tim. iv. 9, 21), and then returned to Ephesus, where, according to tradition, he suffered martyrdom during one of the great festivals in honour of 'the great goddess Artemis,' under Domitian or Nerva[1]. It is not impossible that 'the angel of the Church of Ephesus' praised and blamed in Rev. ii. 1—7 is Timothy, although Timothy is often supposed to have died before the Apocalypse was written. He was succeeded, according to Dorotheus of Tyre (c. A.D. 300), by Gaius (Rom. xvi. 23; 1 Cor. i. 14); but Origen mentions a tradition that this Gaius became Bishop of Thessalonica.

These particulars warrant us in believing that by the time that S. John settled in Ephesus there must have been a considerable number of Christians there. The labours of Aquila and Priscilla (Acts xviii. 19; 2 Tim. iv. 19), of S. Paul for more than two years (Acts xix. 8—10), of Trophimus (Acts xxi. 29), of the family of Onesiphorus (2 Tim. i. 16—18, iv. 9), and of Timothy for a considerable number of years, must have resulted in the conversion of many Jews and heathen. Besides which after the destruction of Jerusalem not a few Christians would be likely to settle there from Palestine. Between the downfall of Jerusalem and the rise of Rome as a Christian community, Ephesus

---

[1] The *Apostolical Constitutions* (vii. 46) give a double succession at Ephesus, Timothy ordained by S. Paul and John ordained by S. John; just as at Rome they give Linus ordained by S. Paul and Clement by S. Peter, and at Antioch Euodius ordained by S. Peter and Ignatius by S. Paul.

becomes the centre of Christendom. Among those who came hither, if the tradition preserved in the Muratorian Canon may be trusted (p. xlix), was John's fellow townsman and fellow Apostle, Andrew. And Philip, who died at Hierapolis, was possibly for a time at Ephesus: his third daughter was buried there (Eus. *H. E.* III. xxxi. 3). A Church which was already organized under presbyters in S. Paul's day, as his own speech to them and his letters to Timothy shew, must have been scandalously mismanaged and neglected, if in such a centre as Ephesus it had not largely increased in the interval between S. Paul's departure and S. John's arrival. For that interval was probably considerable. No mention of S. John is made when S. Paul takes leave of the Ephesian elders at Miletus, nor in the Epistle to the Ephesians. The obvious conclusion is that S. John was not yet there, nor even expected. In the Epistles to the Ephesians, Colossians, and Timothy, there is no hint that the Churches of Asia Minor have any other Apostolic overseer but S. Paul.

(ii) *The Moral Surroundings—Idolatry.*

If there was one thing for which the Metropolis of Asia was more celebrated than another in the apostolic age, it was for the magnificence of its idolatrous worship. The temple of Artemis, its tutelary deity, which crowned the head of its harbour, was one of the wonders of the world. Its 127 columns, 60 feet high, were each one the gift of a people or a prince. In area it was considerably larger than Durham Cathedral and nearly as large as S. Paul's; and its magnificence had become a proverb. 'The gods had one house on earth, and that was at Ephesus.' The architectural imagery of S. Paul in the First Epistle to the Corinthians (iii. 9—17), which was written at Ephesus, and in the Epistles to the Ephesians (ii. 19—22) and to Timothy (1 Tim. iii. 15, vi. 19; 2 Tim. ii. 19, 20), may well have been suggested by it. The city was proud of the title 'Temple-keeper of the great Artemis' (Acts xix. 35), and the wealthy vied with one another in lavishing gifts upon the shrine. The temple thus became a vast treasure-house of gold and silver vessels and works of art. It was served by a college of priestesses and of priests. "Besides these there was a vast throng of dependents, who lived by the temple and its services,—*theologi*, who may have expounded sacred legends, *hymnodi*, who composed hymns in honour of the deity, and others, together with a great crowd of *hierodulae*, who performed more menial offices. The making of shrines and images of the goddess occupied many hands.... But perhaps the most important of all the privileges possessed by the goddess and her priests was that of *asylum*. Fugitives from justice or vengeance who reached her precincts were perfectly safe from all pursuit and arrest. The boundaries of the space possessing such virtue were from time to time enlarged. Mark Antony imprudently allowed them to take in part of the city, which part thus became free of all law, and a haunt of thieves and villains....Besides being a place of worship, a museum, and a sanctuary, the Ephesian temple was a great bank. Nowhere in Asia could money be more safely bestowed than here" (P. Gardner). S. Paul's advice to Timothy to 'charge them that are rich' not to amass, but to 'distribute' and 'communicate' their wealth, 'laying up in store for themselves a good foundation,' for 'the life which is life indeed' (1 Tim. vi. 17—19), acquires fresh meaning when we remember this last fact. In short, what S. Peter's and the Vatican have been to Rome, that the temple of Artemis was to Ephesus in S. John's day.

It was in consequence of the scandals arising out of the abuse of sanctuary, that certain states were ordered to submit their charters to the Roman Senate (A.D. 22). As Tacitus remarks, no authority was strong enough to keep in check the turbulence of a people which protected the crimes of men as worship of the gods. The first to bring and defend their claims were the Ephesians. They represented "that Diana and Apollo were not born at Delos, as was commonly supposed; the Ephesians possessed the Cenchrean stream and the Ortygian grove where Latona, in the hour of travail, had reposed against an olive-tree, still in existence, and given birth to those deities; and it was by the gods' command that the grove had been consecrated. It was there that Apollo himself, after slaying the Cyclops, had escaped the wrath of Jupiter: and again that father Bacchus in his victory had spared the suppliant Amazons who had occupied his shrine" (Tac. *Ann.* III. 61).

We have only to read the first chapter of the Epistle to the Romans (21—32), or the catalogue of vices in the Epistles to the Galatians (v. 19—21) and Colossians (iii. 5—8) to know enough of the kind of morality which commonly accompanied Greek and Roman idolatry in the first century of the Christian era; especially when, as in Ephesus, it was mixed up with the wilder rites of Oriental polytheism, amid all the seductiveness of Ionian luxury, and in a climate which, while it enflamed the passions, unnerved the will. Was it not with the idolatry of Ephesus and all its attendant abominations in his mind that the Apostle of the Gentiles wrote Eph. v. 1—21?

A few words must be said of one particular phase of superstition, closely connected with idolatry, for which Ephesus was famous;—its magic. "It was preeminently the city of astrology, sorcery, incantations, amulets, exorcisms, and every form of magical imposture." About the statue of the Ephesian Artemis were written unintelligible inscriptions to which mysterious efficacy was attributed. 'Ephesian writings,' or charms ('Εφέσια γράμματα) were much sought after, and seem to have been about as senseless as Abracadabra. In the epistles of the pseudo-Heraclitus the unknown writer explains why Heraclitus of Ephesus was called "the weeping philosopher." It was because of the monstrous idiotcy and vice of the Ephesian people. Who would not weep to see religion made the vehicle of brutal superstition and nameless abominations? There was not a man in Ephesus who did not deserve hanging. (See Farrar's *Life of S. Paul*, vol. II. p. 18.) Wicked folly of this kind had tainted the earliest Christian community at Ephesus. They had accepted the Gospel and still secretly held fast their magic. Hence the bonfire of costly books of charms and incantations which followed upon the defeat of the sons of Sceva when they attempted to use the name of Jesus as a magical form of exorcism (Acts xix. 13—20). Timothy at Ephesus is warned against impostors (γόητες) of this kind, half knaves, half dupes (2 Tim. iii. 13).

It was at Ephesus that Apollonius of Tyana is said by some to
have ended his days: and it is not improbable that he was
teaching there simultaneously with S. John. In the Epistle of
Ignatius to the *Ephesians* (XIX) he mentions first among the
consequences of the Nativity that "every sorcery and every spell
was undone" (ἐλύετο πᾶσα μαγεία καὶ πᾶς δεσμός).

Facts such as these place in a very vivid light S. John's
stern insistence upon the necessity of holding stedfastly the
true faith in the Father and the incarnate Son, of keeping oneself
pure, of avoiding the world and the things in the world, of being
on one's guard against lying spirits, and especially the sharp
final admonition, 'Guard yourselves from the idols.'

(iii)   *The Intellectual Surroundings—Gnosticism.*

It is common to speak of the Gnostic heresy or the Gnostic
heresies; but such language, though correct enough, is apt to
be misleading. We commonly think of heresy as a corrupt
growth out of Christian truth, or a deflection from it; as when we
call Unitarianism, which so insists upon the Unity of God as to
deny the Trinity, or Arianism, which so insists upon the Primacy
of the Father as to deny the true Divinity of the Son, heretical
systems or heresies. These and many other corruptions of the
truth grew up inside the bosom of the Church. They are one-
sided and exaggerated developments of Christian doctrines.
But corruption may come from without as well as from within.
It may be the result of impure elements imported into the
system, contaminating and poisoning it. It was in this way
that the Gnostic heresies found their way into the Church. The
germs of Gnosticism in various stages of development were in
the very air in which Christianity was born. They had influenced
Judaism; they had influenced the religions of Greece and of the
East: and the Christian Church had not advanced beyond its
infancy when they began to shew their influence there also.
While professing to have no hostility to the Gospel, Gnosticism
proved one of the subtlest and most dangerous enemies which

it has ever encountered. On the plea of interpreting Christian doctrines from a higher standpoint it really disintegrated and demolished them; in explaining them it explained them away. With a promise of giving to the Gospel a broader and more catholic basis, it cut away the very foundations on which it rested—the reality of sin, and the reality of redemption.

It is not easy to define Gnosticism. Its name is Greek, and so were many of its elements ; but there was much also that was Oriental in its composition ; and before long, first Jewish, and then Christian elements were added to the compound. It has been called a 'philosophy of religion.' It would be more true perhaps to call it a philosophy of being or of existence; an attempt to explain the seen and the unseen universe. But this again would be misleading to the learner. Philosophy with us presupposes a patient investigation of facts ; it is an attempt to rise from facts to explanations of their relations to one another, and their causes, efficient and final. In Gnosticism we look almost in vain for any appeal to facts. Imagination takes the place of investigation, and what may be conceived is made the test, and sometimes almost the only test, of what is. Gnosticism, though eminently philosophic in its aims and professions, was yet in its method more closely akin to poetry and fiction than to philosophy. If on the one hand it was intended as a contrast to the πίστις of the Christian, on the other it was meant to supersede the φιλοσοφία of the heathen. While it professed to appeal to the intellect, and in modern language would have called itself rationalistic, yet it perpetually set intelligence at defiance, both in its premises and in its conclusions. We may describe it as a series of imaginative speculations respecting the origin of the universe and its relation to the Supreme Being. In reference to man its problem was, How can the human spirit be freed from the trammels of matter ? And this led to the further question, How came the human spirit under such trammels ? In other words, What is the origin of evil ?

Gnosticism had in the main two ground principles which run through all the bewildering varieties of Gnostic systems. A. The supremacy of the intellect and the superiority of enlightenment to faith and conduct. This is the *Greek* element in Gnosticism. B. The absolutely evil character of matter and everything material. This is the *Oriental* element.

A. In N. T. *knowledge* or *gnosis* means the profound apprehension of Christian truth. Christianity is not the Gospel of stupidity. It offers the highest satisfaction to the intellectual powers in the study of revealed truth ; and theology in all its branches is the fruit of such study. But this is a very different thing from saying that the intellectual appreciation of truth is the main thing. Theology exists for religion and not religion for theology. The Gnostics made knowledge the main thing, indeed the only thing of real value. Moreover, as the knowledge was difficult of attainment, they completely reversed the principle of the Gospel and made 'the Truth' the possession of the privileged few, instead of being open to the simplest. The historical and moral character of the Gospel, which brings it within the reach of the humblest intellectual power, was set on one side as valueless, or fantastically explained away. Spiritual excellence was made to consist, not in a holy life, but in knowledge of an esoteric kind open only to the initiated, who "knew the depths" (Hippol. *Ref. Haer.* v. vi. 1) and could say " this is profound." (Tert. *Adv. Valent.* i.) In the fragment of a letter of Valentinus preserved by Epiphanius this Gnostic teacher says ; " I come to speak to you of things ineffable, secret, higher than the heavens, which cannot be understood by principalities or powers, nor by anything beneath, nor by any creature, unless it be by those whose intelligence can know no change" (Epiph. *Contra Haer. adv. Valent.* i. 31). This doctrine contained three or four errors in one. (1) Knowledge was placed above virtue. (2) This knowledge treated the facts and morality of the Gospel as matter which the ordinary Christian might understand literally, but which the Gnostic knew to mean something very different. Besides which, there was a great deal of the highest value that was not contained in the Scriptures at all. (3) The true meaning of Scripture and this knowledge over and above Scripture being hard to attain, the benefits of Revelation were the exclusive property of a select band of philosophers. (4) To the poor, therefore, the Gospel (in its reality and fulness) could *not* be preached.

B.   That the material universe is utterly evil and impure in character is a doctrine which has its source in Oriental Dualism, which teaches that there are two independent Principles of existence, one good and the other bad, which are respectively the origin of all the good and all the evil that exists.   The material world, on account of the manifest imperfections and evils which it contains, is assumed to be evil and to be the product of an evil power.   This doctrine runs through almost all Gnostic teaching.   It involves the following consequences. (1) The world being evil, a limitless gulf lies between it and the Supreme God.   He cannot have created it.   Therefore (2) the God of the O. T., who created the world, is not the Supreme God, but an inferior, if not an evil power.   (3) The Incarnation is incredible ; for how could the Divine Word consent to be united with an impure material body ?   This last difficulty drove many Gnostics into what is called Docetism, i.e. the theory that Christ's humanity was not real, but only *apparent* (δοκεῖν). In S. John's time there were two forms of Docetism.   (*a*) Some maintained that Christ's body from His infancy to His Ascension was a phantom.   This seems to have been the view of Simon Magus and of Saturninus.   (β) Others allowed reality to the body of Jesus, but said that the Christ only seemed to be born and to suffer, for the Christ did not unite Himself with Jesus until the Baptism, and departed before the Passion.   This was the teaching of Cerinthus.   S. John seems to attack both forms : Ignatius specially the more thoroughgoing and simpler.   Other modifications were invented later on by Basilides and Valentinus[1].   (4) There can be no resurrection of the flesh : the redeemed will be freed from the calamity of having bodies.

The first of these four consequences opened the door to boundless imaginations.   The gulf between the material world and the Supreme God was commonly filled by Gnostic speculators with a series of beings or aeons emanating from the

[1] Lightfoot's *S. Ignatius and S. Polycarp* I. 365.

Supreme God and generating one another, in bewildering profusion and intricacy. It is this portion of the Gnostic theories which is so repugnant to the modern student. It seems more like a night-mare than sober speculation ; and one feels that to call such things 'fables and endless genealogies, the which minister questionings rather than a dispensation of God' (1 Tim. i. 4; comp. iv. 7; 2 Tim. iv. 4) is very gentle condemnation. But we must remember (1) that these were not mere wanton flights of an unbridled imagination. They were attempts to bridge the chasm between the finite and the Infinite, between the evil world and the Supreme God, attempts to explain the origin of the universe and with it the origin of evil. We must remember (2) that in those days any hypothesis was admissible which might conceivably account for the facts. The scientific principles, that hypotheses must be *capable* of verification, that existences must not rashly be multiplied, that imaginary causes are unphilosophical, and the like, were utterly unknown. The unseen world might be peopled with any number of mysterious beings ; and if their existence helped to explain the world of sense and thought, then their existence might be asserted. If the Supreme God generated an aeon inferior to Himself, and that aeon other inferior aeons, we might at last arrive at a being so far removed from the excellence of God, that his creation of this evil world would not be inconceivable. Thus the Gnostic cosmogony was evolution inverted : it was not an ascent from good to better, but a descent from best to bad. And the whole was expressed in chaotic imagery, in which allegory, symbolism, mythology and astronomy were mixed up in a way that sets reason at defiance.

These two great Gnostic principles, the supremacy of knowledge, and the impurity of matter, produced opposite results in ethical teaching ; asceticism, and antinomian profligacy. If knowledge is everything, and if the body is worthless, then the body must be beaten down and crushed in order that the emancipated soul may rise to the knowledge of higher things : "the soul must live by ecstasy, as the cicada feeds on dew." On the other hand, if knowledge is everything and the body worthless, the body may rightly be made to undergo every kind of experience, no matter how shameless and impure, in order that the soul may increase its store of knowledge. The body cannot be made more vile than it is, and the soul of the enlightened is incapable of pollution.

Speculations such as these were rife in Asia Minor, both among Jews and Christians. They were foretold by S. Paul when he bade farewell to the Ephesian Elders at Miletus (Acts xx. 29, 30). They were already troubling the Churches when S. Paul wrote his letters to Timothy (1 Tim. i. 7—11, vi. 3—10; 2 Tim. ii. 16, iii. 2—5, iv. 34). And when S. John wrote the Revelation they were rampant (ii. 6, 14, 15, 20, 24). They are among the many proofs that we have that the Apostolic Church had blemishes both in thought and practice as serious as those which disfigure our own. 'The gates of hell' did not prevail then; nor will they now, if the Apostolic example in contending with such things be followed. That S. John would offer the most uncompromising opposition to them is only what we should expect. While professing to be Christian and to be a sublime interpretation of the Gospel, they struck at the very root of all Christian doctrine and Christian morality. They contradicted the O. T., for they asserted that all things were made, not 'very good,' but very evil, and that the Maker of them was not God. They contradicted the N. T., for they denied the reality of the Incarnation and the sinfulness of sin. Morality was undermined when knowledge was made of far more importance than conduct; it was turned upside down when men were taught that crimes which enlarged experience were a duty.

The classification of the Gnostic teachers and sects is a problem of well-known difficulty, which fortunately does not lie within the scope of our inquiry. But a rough table, based partly on local, partly on chronological considerations, will be of service to the student, in helping to shew the relation of the errors combated by S. John to the flood of wild speculation which passed over the Church in the century and a half that followed his death. The chronology in some cases is only tentative.

xxvi INTRODUCTION.

The Germs of Gnosticism. A. D. 30—70.

Samaritan.

Dositheus.

Simon Magus, said to be a pupil of Dositheus.

Menander, pupil and successor of Simon.

These early teachers cannot in any proper sense be called heretics. They did not deprave the Gospel, but simply opposed it. Their doctrine was thoroughly antichristian, not only in tendency, but in form. Simon Magus, though baptized, was not converted. He probably did not understand Christianity: he certainly never embraced it.

Early Gnosticism. A. D. 70—100.

Jewish or Ebionite.

The Ophite sects; the earliest Gnostic systems.

Cerinthus, contemporary with S. John.

Carpocrates, placed sometimes before, sometimes after Cerinthus.

In this group Gnosticism has not fully entered within the pale of the Church, but it is far less distinctly antichristian. Cerinthus and Carpocrates have a similar and well-defined Christology, against the errors of which S. John contends with all the intensity of his nature. In other respects Carpocrates was pagan rather than Jewish in his sympathies, and his moral teaching was utterly antinomian and licentious.

Fully developed Gnosticism. A. D. 100—250.

Syrian.

Saturninus or Saturnilus (c. A. D. 100—120): ascetic.

Tatian, converted to Christianity by Justin Martyr, after whose death he became a Gnostic (c. A. D. 160): ascetic.

Bardaisan or Bardesanes, born A. D. 155, died 223.

Alexandrian.

Basilides, flourished under Hadrian (A. D. 117—138): he made a great impression, became widely known, but founded no school.

Valentinus, came to Rome and taught in the time of Hyginus, Pius, and Anicetus (c. A. D. 140—160) : he was the most success-ful of all Gnostic teachers in gaining able disciples.

Heracleon, pupil of Valentinus (c. A. D. 160—180): the earliest known commentator on S. John's Gospel[1].

Asiatic or Anti-Judaic.

Cerdon, came to Rome c. A. D. 135.

Marcion, taught at Rome simultaneously with Valentinus (c. A. D. 140—165): perhaps the most permanently influential and least Gnostic of all the Gnostic leaders: ascetic.

Apelles, chief disciple of Marcion (c. A. D. 150—190).

Almost all these teachers held Docetic views of Christ's body, and therefore denied the Incarnation. The Syrian school was more Oriental and dualistic, the Alexandrian more Greek and pantheistic. It was mainly the heresy of Valentinus, as taught by his brilliant pupil Ptolemaeus, which occasioned the great work of Irenaeus on Heresies. The Asiatic school contended for a distorted and mutilated Christianity in opposition to both Jewish and pagan philosophy. All of them are condemned by anticipa-tion by S. John no less than those who were his contemporaries. He mentions no one by name: it is not a personal or a local controversy. And he does not pause to go into details. He goes at once to first principles of faith and of morals, and with uncompromising sternness condemns all tampering with either. Thus, while guarding against the special errors of his own age, he taught how further developments of them must be met, and left to the Church of all ages a storehouse of truth that can never be exhausted or become inapplicable[2].

---

[1] The use made by Basilides and the Valentinians of the Fourth Gospel is an important element in the evidence for its authenticity. They equally with the orthodox recognised its authority ; which implies that it was fully accepted before they separated from the Church.

[2] "The Epistles are, humanly speaking, the result of the very

INTRODUCTION.

His unflinching severity seems to have anticipated the magnitude of the evil that was coming. The swiftness with which Gnosticism overtook (or even outran) Christianity, is without a parallel in the history of human thought. Even German philosophy since Kant has not developed systems with the rapidity with which new Gnostic schemes sprang up and spread between A.D. 100 and 250. In rather high-flown language Eusebius tells us that "when the sacred choir of Apostles had taken its departure from life, and when the generation of those who were privileged to hear with their own ears their inspired wisdom had passed away, then the conspiracy of godless error took its rise through the deceit of false teachers, who, now that none of the Apostles was any longer left, henceforth endeavoured with brazen face to preach their 'knowledge falsely so called' in opposition to the preaching of the truth" (*H. E.* VI. xxxii. 8). From Edessa to Lyons there was probably not a single educated congregation that was not more or less tainted with some form of this plague.

The result was by no means unmixed evil. These varying and often antagonistic speculations stimulated thought, broke down the barriers of formalism and literalism, forced upon the Church the necessity of clear ideas about fundamental doctrines, and promoted the study of Scripture. We have a close parallel in our own day. "The Gnostic heresy, with all its destructive tendency, had an important mission as a propelling force in the ancient Church, and left its effects upon patristic theology. So also this modern gnosticism [of the Tübingen school, Renan, &c.] must be allowed to have done great service to biblical and historical learning by removing old prejudices, opening new avenues of thought, bringing to light the immense fermentation of the first century, stimulating research, and compelling an entire

conflict between the good and evil elements which existed together in the bosom of the early Christian society. As they exhibit the principles afterwards to be unfolded into all truth and good, so the heresies which they attack exhibit the principles which were afterwards to grow up into all the various forms of errors and wickedness" (Stanley, *Apostolic Age*, 193).

scientific reconstruction of the history of the origin of Christianity and of the Church. The result will be a deeper and fuller knowledge, not to the weakening, but to the strengthening of our faith" (Schaff).

The fantastic speculations of the Gnostics as to the origin of the universe have long since perished, and cannot be revived. Nor is their tenet as to the evil nature of everything material much in harmony with modern thought. With us the danger is the other way;—of deifying matter, or materialising God. But the heresy of the supremacy of knowledge is as prevalent as ever. We still need an Apostle to teach us that mere knowledge will not raise the quality of men's moral natures any more than light without food and warmth will raise the quality of their bodies. We still need a Bishop Butler to assure us that information is "really the least part" of education, and that religion "does not consist in the knowledge and belief even of fundamental truth," but rather in our being brought "to a certain temper and behaviour." The philosophic Apostle of the first century and the philosophic Bishop of the eighteenth alike contend, that light without love is moral darkness, and that not he that can 'know all mysteries and all knowledge,' but only 'he who *doeth* righteousness is righteous.' If the *Sermons* of the one have not become obsolete, still less have the Epistles of the other.

(iv) *The Traditions respecting S. John.*

The century succeeding the persecution under Nero (A.D. 65 —165) is a period that is exceedingly tantalising to the ecclesiastical historian and exceedingly perplexing to the chronologer. The historian finds a very meagre supply of materials: facts are neither abundant nor, as a rule, very substantial. And when the historian has gleaned together every available fact, the chronologer finds his ingenuity taxed to the utmost to arrange these facts in a manner that is at once harmonious with itself and with the evidence of the principal witnesses.

The traditions respecting S. John share the general character of the period. They are very fragmentary and not always trustworthy; and they cannot with any certainty be put into chronological order. The following sketch is offered as a tentative arrangement, in the belief that a clear idea, even if wrong in details, is a great deal better than bewildering confusion. The roughest map gives unity and intelligibility to inadequate and piecemeal description.

S. John was present at the Council of Jerusalem (Acts xv.), which settled for the time the controversy between Jewish and Gentile Christians. And here, as in the opening chapters of the Acts (i. 15, ii. 14, 38, iii. 4, 12, v. 3, 8), his retiring character is seen, in that he is quite in the background, while Peter and James take the lead. He was at Jerusalem as one of the 'pillars' of the Church (Gal. ii. 6), and in all probability Jerusalem had been his usual abode from the Ascension until this date (A.D. 50) and for some time longer[1]. It is by no means improbable that he was with S. Peter during the last portion of his great friend's life and was in Rome when he was martyred (A.D. 64). Here will come in the well-known story, which rests upon the early testimony of Tertullian (*Praescr. Haer.* XXXVI.), and perhaps the still earlier testimony of Leucius, that S. John was thrown into boiling oil near the site of the Porta Latina and was preserved unhurt. Two churches in Rome and a festival in the Calendar (May 6th) perpetuate the tradition. The story, if untrue, may have grown out of the fact that S. John was in Rome during the Neronian persecution. The similar story, that he was offered poison and that the drink became harmless in his hands, may have had a similar origin. In paintings S. John is often represented with a cup from which poison in the form of a viper is departing.

It is perhaps too soon to take S. John to Ephesus immediately

---

[1] An ancient tradition, quoted by Clement of Alexandria (*Strom.* VI. v. *sub fin.*) from the *Preaching of Peter*, states that Christ commanded the Apostles, "After twelve years go forth into the world; lest any one say, We have not heard." So also Apollonius, according to Eusebius (*H. E.* v. xviii. 14). The *Clementine Recognitions* (I. xliii.) give seven years instead of twelve; "A week of years was completed from the Passion of the Lord."

after S. Peter's death[1]. Let us suppose that he returned to
Jerusalem (if he had ever left it) and remained there until A.D. 67,
when large numbers of people left the city just before the siege.
If the very questionable tradition be accepted, that after leaving
Jerusalem he preached to the Parthians, we must place the
departure from Judaea somewhat earlier. Somewhere in the
next two years (A.D. 67—69) we may perhaps place the Revelation, written during the exile, enforced or voluntary, in Patmos.
This exile over, S. John went, or more probably returned, to
Ephesus, which henceforth becomes his chief place of abode
until his death in or near the year A.D. 100.

Most of the traditions respecting him are connected with this
last portion of his life, and with his government of the Churches
of Asia as Metropolitan Bishop. Irenaeus, the disciple of
Polycarp, the disciple of S. John, says; "All the presbyters,
who met John the disciple of the Lord in Asia, bear witness that
John has handed on to them this tradition. For he continued
with them until the times of Trajan" (A.D. 98—117). And
again; "Then John, the disciple of the Lord, who also leaned
back on His breast, he too published a gospel during his residence at Ephesus." And again; "The Church in Ephesus
founded by Paul, and having John continuing with them until
the times of Trajan, is a truthful witness of the tradition of
Apostles" (*Haer.* II. xxii. 5; III. i. 1, iii. 4). Here, therefore, he
remained "a priest," as his successor Polycrates tells us, "wear-
ing the plate of gold;" an expression which some people consider to be merely figurative. "John, the last survivor of the
Apostolate, had left on the Church of Asia the impression of a
pontiff from whose forehead shone the spiritual splendour of the

---

[1] Bishop Lightfoot thinks otherwise. " The most probable chronology makes his withdrawal from Palestine to Asia Minor coincide very
nearly with the martyrdom of these two Apostles (Peter and Paul)....
This epoch divides his life into two distinct periods : hitherto he had
lived as a Jew among Jews ; henceforth he will be as a Gentile among
Gentiles. The writings of S. John in the Canon probably mark the
close of each period. The Apocalypse winds up his career in the
Church of the Circumcision ; the Gospel and the Epistles are the
crowning result of a long residence in the heart of Gentile Christendom " (*S. Paul and the Three, Galatians,* 360).

holiness of Christ" (Godet). And here, according to the anti-
Montanist writer Apollonius, he raised a dead man to life (Eus.
H.E. v. xviii. 14).

It would be in connexion with his journeys through the
Churches of Asia that the beautiful episode commonly known as
'S. John and the Robber' took place. The Apostle had commended a noble-looking lad to the local Bishop, who had instructed and baptized him. After a while the lad fell away and
became a bandit-chief. S. John on his next visit astounded the
Bishop by asking for his 'deposit;' for the Apostle had left no
money in his care. "I demand the young man, the soul of a
brother:" and then the sad tale had to be told. The Apostle
called for a horse and rode away to the haunts of the banditti.
The chief recognised him and fled. But S. John went after
him, and by his loving entreaties induced him to return to his
old home and a holy life (Clement of Alexandria in Eus. *H. E.*
III. xxxiii.).

The incident of S. John's rushing out of a public bath, at the
sight of Cerinthus, crying, "Let us fly, lest even the bath fall on
us, because Cerinthus, the enemy of the truth, is within,"
took place at Ephesus. Doubt has been thrown on the story
because of the improbability of the Apostle visiting a public
bath, and because Epiphanius, in his version of the matter, substitutes Ebion for Cerinthus. But Irenaeus gives us the story
on the authority of those *who had heard it from Polycarp:* and
it must be admitted that such evidence is somewhat strong. If
Christians of the second century saw nothing incredible in an
Apostle resorting to a public bath, we cannot safely dogmatize on
the point. The incident may doubtless be taken as no more
than "a strong metaphor by way of expressing marked disap-
proval." But at any rate, when we remember the downright
wickedness involved in the teaching of Cerinthus, we may with
Dean Stanley regard the story "as a living exemplification of
the possibility of uniting the deepest love and gentleness with
the sternest denunciation of moral evil;" or with Dean Plumptre
as evidence of "the ardent spirit that alike loves strongly and
strongly hates." The charge given to the elect lady (2 John 10,

11) is a strong corroboration of the story. Late versions of it end with the sensational additioh that when the Apostle had gone out, the bath fell in ruins, and Cerinthus was killed.

Another and far less credible story comes to us through Irenaeus (*Haer.* v. xxxiii. 3) on the authority of the uncritical and (if Eusebius is to be believed) not very intelligent Papias, the companion of Polycarp.—The elders who had seen John, the disciple of the Lord, relate that they heard from him how the Lord used to teach about those times and say, "The days will come in which vines shall grow, each having 10,000 stems, and on each stem 10,000 branches, and on each branch 10,000 shoots, and on each shoot 10,000 clusters, and on each cluster 10,000 grapes, and each grape when pressed shall give 25 firkins of wine. And when any saint shall have seized one cluster, another shall cry, I am a better cluster, take me; through me bless the Lord." In like manner that a grain of wheat would produce 10,000 ears, and each ear would have 10,000 grains, and each grain 5 double pounds of clear, pure flour : and all other fruit-trees, and seeds, and grass, in like proportion. And all animals feeding on the products of the earth would become peaceful and harmonious one with another, subject to man with all subjection." And he added these words; "These things are believable to believers." And he says that when Judas the traitor did not believe and asked, "How then shall such production be accomplished by the Lord?" the Lord said, "They shall see who come to those [times]."

This extraordinary narrative is of great value as shewing the kind of discourse which pious Christians of the second century attributed to Christ, when they came to inventing such things. Can we believe that those who credited the Lord with millenarian utterances of this kind, could have written a single chapter of the Gospels with nothing but their own imagination to draw upon. Even with the Gospels before them they can do no better than this. Possibly the whole is only a grotesque enlargement of Matt. xxvi. 29. For the apocryphal correspondence between S. Ignatius and S. John and the Virgin, which again illustrates the character of fictitious Christian documents, see Appendix I.

Of S. John's manner of life nothing trustworthy has come down to us. That he never married may be mere conjecture; but it looks like history. S. Paul certainly implies that most, if not all, of the Apostles did 'lead about a wife' (1 Cor. ix. 5). But the tradition respecting S. John's virginity is early and general. In a Leucian fragment (Zahn, *Acta Johannis*, p. 248) the Lord is represented as thrice interposing to prevent John from marrying. We find the tradition in Tertullian (*De Monog.* XVII.); in Ambrosiaster (*ad* 2 *Cor.* xi. 2); in Augustine (*Tract.* CXXIV.), who quotes Jerome (*Contra Jovinianum* I.) as declaring that John was specially loved by Christ, because he never married, but adds, *Hoc quidem in Scripturis non evidenter apparet;* and in Epiphanius. See below, p. xliii. It may well be true that (as Jerome expresses it) to a virgin son the Virgin Mother was committed: ut hereditatem virginis Domini, virginem matrem filius virgo susciperet (*Ep. ad Principiam*). But Epiphanius (A.D. 357) is much too late to be good authority for S. John's rigid asceticism. It is mentioned by no earlier writer, and would be likely enough to be assumed; especially as S. James, brother of the Lord and Bishop of Jerusalem, was known to have led a life of great rigour. The story of S. John's entering a public bath for the purpose of bathing is against any extreme asceticism.

We may conclude with two stories of late authority, but possibly true. Internal evidence is strongly in favour of the second. Cassian (A.D. 420) tells us that S. John used sometimes to amuse himself with a tame partridge. A hunter expressed surprise at an occupation which seemed frivolous. The Apostle in reply reminded him that hunters do not keep their bows always bent, as his own weapon at that moment shewed. It is not improbable that Cassian obtained this story from the writings of Leucius, which he seems to have known. In this case the authority for the story becomes some 250 years earlier. In a Greek fragment it is an old priest who is scandalized at finding the Apostle gazing with interest on a partridge which is rolling in the dust before him (Zahn, p. 190).

The other story is told by Jerome (*In Gal.* vi. 10). When the Apostle became so infirm that he could not preach he used to be carried to church and content himself with the exhortation, "Little children, love one another." And when his hearers wearied of it and asked him, "Master, why dost thou always speak thus?" "Because it is the Lord's command," he said, "and if only this be done, it is enough."

Of his death nothing is known; but the Leucian fragments contain a remarkable story respecting it, to which Augustine also alludes as "found in certain apocryphal scriptures" (*Tract.* cxxiv. in Johan. xxi. 19). On the Lord's Day, the last Sunday of the Apostle's life, "after the celebration of the divine and awful mysteries and the breaking of the bread," S. John told some of his disciples to take spades and follow him. Having led them out to a certain place he told them to dig a grave, in which, after prayer, he placed himself, and they buried him up to the neck. He then told them to place a cloth over his face and complete the burial. They wept much but obeyed him and returned home to tell the others what had taken place. Next day they all went out in prayer to translate the body to the great Church. But when they had opened the grave they found nothing therein. And they called to mind the words of Christ to Peter, 'If I will that he abide till I come, what is that to thee?' (Zahn, p. 191; comp. p. 162). The still stranger story, which S. Augustine seems almost disposed to believe[1], that the earth over his grave moved with his breathing and shewed that he was not dead but sleeping,—is another, and probably a later outgrowth, of the misunderstood saying of Christ respecting S. John. Yet another legend represents John as dying, but being immediately raised from the dead, and then translated, like Enoch and Elijah, to reappear on earth as the herald of the Christ and the opponent of the Antichrist[2]. Such legends testify to the estimation in

---

[1] Viderint enim qui locum sciunt, utrum hoc ibi faciat vel patiatur terra quod dicitur, quia et re vera non a levibus hominibus id audivimus (*Tract.* cxxiv. in Johann. xxi. 19).

[2] John Malalas, a Greek writer of about A.D. 570, says; "Now unto the second year of his reign [Trajan's] there was appearing and teaching in Ephesus, being Bishop and Patriarch, Saint John the

which the last man living who had seen the Lord was held. After he had passed away people refused to believe that no such person remained alive. The expectations respecting Antichrist helped to strengthen such ideas. If Nero was not dead, but had merely passed out of sight for a time, so also had the beloved Apostle. If the one was to return as Antichrist to vex the Church, so also would the other to defend her. (See Appendix B.)

One point in the above sketch requires a few words of explanation,—the early date assigned to the Book of Revelation. This sets at defiance the express statement of Irenaeus, that the vision "was seen almost in our own days, at the end of the reign of Domitian" (*Haer.* v. xxx. 1), who was killed A.D. 97. The discussion of this point belongs to the commentary on Revelation. Suffice to say that the present writer shares the opinion which seems to be gaining ground among students, that only on one hypothesis can one believe that the Fourth Gospel, First Epistle, and Apocalypse are all by the same author; viz., that the Apocalypse was written first, and that a good many years elapsed before the Gospel and Epistle were written. (1) The writer of the Apocalypse has not yet learned to write Greek. The writer of the Gospel and Epistle writes Greek, not indeed elegantly, but with ease and correctness. (2) The antinomian licentiousness condemned in the Revelation (ii. 6, 14, 15, 20) is of a crude and less philosophic kind than that which is opposed in the Epistle. (3) The Revelation is still fully under the influence of Judaism : its language and imagery are

---

Apostle and Divine: and he made himself vanish and was no more seen by any one, and no man knows what became of him unto this day, even as Africanus and Irenaeus, most able (writers), have related" (*Chronographia* xi. *sub init.* p. 269 ed. Bonn.). What Africanus said we do not know ; but Irenaeus confirms no more of this than that John lived on at Ephesus into the reign of Trajan (*Haer.* ii. xxii. 5 ; iii. iii. 3). See Lightfoot's *S. Ignatius and S. Polycarp* ii. 437. One of the Vienna MSS. of the *Apostolical Constitutions* (viii. 16) has this note : "John the Evangelist, brother of James, was banished by Domitian to the island of Patmos, and there composed the Gospel according to him. He died a natural death, in the third year of Trajan's reign, in Ephesus. His remains were sought, but have not been found." Book viii. is probably of the sixth century.

intensely Jewish. The Gospel and Epistle are much more free from such influence. "The Apocalypse winds up St John's career in the church of the circumcision; the Gospel and the Epistles are the crowning result of a long residence in the heart of Gentile Christendom" (Bishop Lightfoot).

CHAPTER II.

THE FIRST EPISTLE OF S. JOHN.

THE First Epistle of S. John has an interest which is unique. In all probability, as we shall hereafter find reason for believing, it contains the last exhortations of that Apostle to the Church of Christ. And as he long outlived all the rest of the Apostles, and as this Epistle was written near the end of his long life, we may regard it as the farewell of the Apostolic body to the whole company of believers who survived them or have been born since their time. The Second and Third Epistles may indeed have been written later, and probably were so, but they are addressed to individuals and not to the Church at large. "If it were not for the writings of S. John the last thirty years of the first century would be almost a blank. They resemble that mysterious period of forty days between the resurrection and the ascension, when the Lord hovered, as it were, between heaven and earth, barely touching the earth beneath, and appearing to the disciples like a spirit from the other world. But the theology of the second and third centuries evidently presupposes the writings of John, and starts from his Christology" (Schaff). An Introduction to this unique Epistle requires the discussion of a variety of questions, which can most conveniently be taken separately, each under a heading of its own. The first which confronts us is that of its genuineness. Is the Epistle the work of the Apostle whose name it bears?

(i) The Authority of the Epistle.

Eusebius (*H. E.* III. xxv.) is fully justified in reckoning our Epistle among those canonical books of N. T. which had been universally received (ὁμολογούμενα) by the Churches. The obscure sect, whom Epiphanius with a scornful *double entendre* calls the Alogi ('devoid of [the doctrine of] the Logos,' or 'devoid of reason') probably rejected it, for the same reason as they rejected the Fourth Gospel; because they distrusted S. John's teaching respecting the Word or Logos. And Marcion rejected it, as he rejected all the Gospels, excepting an expurgated S. Luke, and all the Epistles, excepting those of S. Paul; not because he believed the books which he discarded to be spurious, but because they contradicted his peculiar views. Neither of these rejections, therefore, need have any weight with us. The objectors did not contend that the Epistle was not written by an Apostle, but that some of its contents were doctrinally objectionable.

On the other hand, the evidence that the Epistle was received as Apostolic from the earliest times is abundant and satisfactory. It begins with those who knew S. John himself and goes on in an unbroken stream which soon becomes full and strong. See Professor Charteris, *Canonicity*, 319—326.

Whether the recently discovered DOCTRINE OF THE TWELVE APOSTLES indicates that the author knew S. John's writings, is disputed. If this question is answered in the affirmative, then we have evidence which is probably even earlier than that of Polycarp. See Appendix F.

POLYCARP, the disciple of S. John, in his Epistle to the Philippians writes in a way which needs only to be placed side by side with the similar passage in our Epistle to convince any unprejudiced mind that the two passages cannot have become so like one another accidentally, and that of the two writers it is Polycarp who borrows from S. John and not *vice versâ*.

1 John.	Polycarp, *Phil.* vii.
Every spirit which confesseth Jesus Christ as come in the flesh is of God : and every spirit which confesseth not Jesus is not of God : and this is the spirit of Antichrist (iv. 2, 3). He that doeth sin is of the devil (iii. 8).	Every one that shall not confess that Jesus Christ is come in the flesh is Antichrist : and whosoever shall not confess the witness of the Cross is of the devil.

When we remember that the expression 'Antichrist' in N. T. is peculiar to S. John's Epistles, that it is not common in the literature of the sub-Apostolic age, and that 'confess,' 'witness,' and 'to be of the devil' are also expressions which are very characteristic of S. John, the supposition that Polycarp knew and accepted our Epistle seems to be placed beyond reasonable doubt. Therefore about thirty years[1] after the date at which the Epistle, if genuine, was written we have a quotation of it by a man who was the friend and pupil of its reputed author. Could Polycarp have been ignorant of the authorship, and would he have made use of it if he had doubted its genuineness? Would he not have denounced it as an impudent forgery?

Eusebius tells us (*H. E.* III. xxxix. 16) that PAPIAS (c. A. D. 140) "made use of testimonies from the first epistle of John." S. Irenaeus tells us that Papias was "a disciple of John and a companion of Polycarp." Thus we have a second Christian writer among the generation which knew S. John, making use of this Epistle. When we consider how little of the literature of that age has come down to us, and how short this Epistle is, we may well be surprised at having two such early witnesses.

---

[1] S. John's Epistle cannot well have been written much before A.D. 90 (see p. xliv.). Polycarp's Epistle was written about the time of the martyrdom of Ignatius : Ignatius had already left Asia Minor, but Polycarp has not yet heard of his death (xiii). Ignatius suffered at Rome, probably in the reign of Trajan (A.D. 98–117), and perhaps at the time when, as we know from Pliny, a persecution was going on in Bithynia (A.D. 112). Polycarp's letter, therefore, may be placed A.D. 112–118. See Lightfoot's *S. Ignatius and S. Polycarp*, I. 567.

Eusebius also states (*H. E.* v. viii. 7) that IRENAEUS (c. A.D. 140—202) "mentions the first epistle of John, citing very many testimonies from it." In the great work of Irenaeus on Heresies, which has come down to us, he quotes it twice. In III. xvi. 5 he quotes 1 John ii. 18—22, expressly stating that it comes from the Epistle of S. John. In III. xvi. 8 he quotes 2 John 7, 8, and by a slip of memory says that it comes from "the epistle before mentioned" (*praedictâ epistolâ*). He then goes on to quote 1 John iv. 1—3. This evidence is strengthened by two facts. 1. Irenaeus, being the disciple of Polycarp, is in a direct line of tradition from S. John. 2. Irenaeus gives abundant testimony to the authenticity of the Fourth Gospel; and it is so generally admitted by critics of all schools that the Fourth Gospel and our Epistle are by the same hand, that evidence to the genuineness of the one may be used as evidence to the genuineness of the other.

CLEMENT OF ALEXANDRIA (fl. A.D. 185—210) makes repeated use of the Epistle and in several places mentions it as S. John's.

TERTULLIAN (fl. 195—215) quotes it 40 or 50 times, repeatedly stating that the words he quotes are S. John's.

The MURATORIAN FRAGMENT is a portion of the earliest attempt known to us to catalogue those books of N. T. which were recognised by the Church. Its date is commonly given as c. A.D. 170—180; but some now prefer to say A.D. 200—215. It is written in barbarous and sometimes scarcely intelligible Latin, having been copied by an ignorant and very careless scribe. It says; "The Epistle of Jude however and two Epistles of the John who has been mentioned above are received in the Catholic (Church)," or "are reckoned among the Catholic (Epistles)." It is uncertain what 'two Epistles' means. But if, as is probably the case (see p. lxix.), the Second and Third are meant, we may be confident that the First was accepted also and included in the catalogue. The opening words of the Epistle are quoted in the Fragment in connexion with the Fourth Gospel, and this quotation from it seems to be intended as equivalent to mention of it. The writer apparently regarded the First Epistle as a kind of postscript to the Gospel. See Light-

foot, *Contemp. Rev.* Oct. 1875, p. 835.   We know of no person or
sect that accepted the Second and Third Epistles and yet rejected
the First.

ORIGEN (fl. A.D. 220—250) frequently cites the Epistle as
S. John's.   DIONYSIUS OF ALEXANDRIA, his pupil (fl. A.D. 235
—265), in his masterly discussion of the authenticity of the
Apocalypse argues that, as the Fourth Gospel and First Epistle
are by S. John, the Apocalypse (on account of its very different
style) cannot be by him (Eus. *H. E.* VII. xxv).   CYPRIAN,
ATHANASIUS, EPIPHANIUS, JEROME, and in short all Fathers,
Greek and Latin, accept the Epistle as S. John's.

The Epistle is found in the Old Syriac Version, which omits
the Second and Third as well as other Epistles.

In the face of such evidence as this, the suspicion that the
Epistle may have been written by some careful imitator of the
Fourth Gospel does not seem to need serious consideration.   A
guess, not supported by any evidence, has no claim to be
admitted as a rival to a sober theory, which is supported by
all the evidence that is available, that being both plentiful and
trustworthy.

The student must, however, be on his guard against uncritical
overstatements of the case in favour of the Epistle.   Some
commentators put forward an imposing array of references to
Justin Martyr, the Epistle of Barnabas, the Shepherd of
Hermas, and the Ignatian Epistles.   This is altogether misleading.   All that such references prove is that early Christian
writers to a large extent used similar language in speaking of
spiritual truths, and that this language was influenced by the
writers (not necessarily the *writings*) of N. T.

Where the resemblance to passages in N. T. is very slight
and indistinct (as will be found to be the case in these references), it is at least as possible that the language comes from
the oral teaching of Apostles and Apostolic men as from the
writings contained in N. T.

The author of the Epistle to Diognetus knew our Epistle;
but the date of that perplexing treatise, though probably ante-
Nicene, is uncertain.   "Notwithstanding all that has been said

to the contrary, the Epistle of Diognetus may, I think, with fair confidence be placed during the period with which we are concerned (A.D. 117—180), and not improbably in the earlier years of it" (Lightfoot, *S. Ignatius and S. Polycarp*, I. 517).

That the *internal* evidence in favour of the Apostolic authorship of the Epistle is also very strong, will be seen when we consider in sections iv. and v. its *relation to the Gospel* and its *characteristics.*

"The traces of Montanism which some have attempted to find (the sacredness of Christianity, χρῖσμα, distinction between mortal and other sins) depend upon exegetical extravagance, and overlook the parallels in the Gospels and Epistles; Matt. xii. 31; 2 Cor. i. 22; &c..... The circumstance that destructive criticism should fix now upon the Gospel and now upon the Epistle as representing the higher stage of development is not calculated to arouse great confidence in its arguments" (Reuss).

(ii)   *The Persons addressed.*

The Epistle is rightly called *catholic* or *general*, as being addressed to the Church at large. It was probably written with special reference to the Church of Ephesus and the other Churches of Asia, to which it would be sent as a circular letter. The fact of its containing no quotations from the O. T. and not many allusions to it, as also the warning against idolatry (v. 21), would lead us to suppose that the writer had converts from heathenism specially in his mind. But it has more the form of a homily than of a letter. There is no address or salutation at the beginning; no farewell or benediction at the close. Nevertheless, the frequent use of γράφω (ii. 1, 7, 8, 12, 13,) and ἔγραψα (ii. [13, 14, 21] 26; v. 13), with γράφομεν at the very outset (i. 4), quite justify the appellation universally given to it of Epistle. It is a Pastoral Epistle, to be read aloud to those to whom it is addressed.

S. Augustine in the ·heading[1] to his ten homilies on the Epistle styles it 'the Epistle of John to the Parthians' (*ad Parthos*), and

---

[1] This heading is by some considered not to be original : it occurs in the *Indiculus Operum S. Augustini* of his pupil Possidius.

he elsewhere (*Quaest. Evang.* II. xxxix.) gives it the same title. In this he has been followed by other writers in the Latin Church. The title occurs in some MSS. of the Vulgate. The Venerable Bede states that "Many ecclesiastical writers, and among them Athanasius, Bishop of the Church of Alexandria, witness that the first Epistle of S. John was written to the Parthians" (Cave, *Script. Eccles. Hist. Lit.* ann. 701). But not all editions of Bede contain the statement; and Athanasius and the Greek Church generally seem to be wholly ignorant of this superscription, although in a few modern Greek MSS. 'to the Parthians' occurs in the subscription of the *second* Epistle. Whether the tradition that S. John once preached in Parthia grew out of this Latin superscription, or the latter produced the tradition, is uncertain. More probably the title originated in a mistake and then gave birth to the tradition. Gieseler's conjecture respecting the mistake seems to be reasonable, that it arose from a Latin writer finding the letter designated 'the Epistle of John *the Virgin*' (τοῦ παρθένου) and supposing that this meant 'the Epistle of John *to the Parthians*' (πρὸς πάρθους). From very early times S. John was called 'virgin' from the belief that he never married. *Johannes aliqui Christi spado*, says Tertullian (*De Monogam.* XVII.). In the longer and interpolated form of the Ignatian Epistles (*Philad.* IV.) we read "Virgins, have Christ alone before your eyes, and His Father in your prayers, being enlightened by the Spirit. May I have pleasure in your purity as that of Elijah......as of *the beloved disciple*, as of Timothy......who departed this life in chastity." So also the Pseudo-Clement *De Virgin.* i. 6, quoted by Lightfoot *in loco* (II. 792). See above, p. xxxiv. But there is reason for believing that *Ad Virgines* (πρὸς παρθένους) was an early superscription for the *second* Epistle. Some transcriber, thinking this very inappropriate for a letter addressed to a lady with children, may have transferred the heading to the first Epistle, and then the corruption from 'virgins' (παρθένους) to 'Parthians' (πάρθους) would be easy enough.

Other variations or conjectures are *Ad Spartos, Ad Pathmios*, and *Ad sparsos*. None are worth much consideration.

(iii) *The Place and Date.*

Neither of these can be determined with any certainty, the
Epistle itself containing no intimations on either point. Irenaeus tells us that the Fourth Gospel was written in Ephesus,
and Jerome writes to the same effect. In all probability the
Epistle was written at the same place. Excepting Alexandria,
no place was so distinctly the home of that Gnosticism, which
S. John opposes in both Gospel and Epistle, as Asia Minor, and
in particular Ephesus. We know of no tradition connecting S.
John with Alexandria, whereas tradition is unanimous in connecting him with Ephesus. In the next section we shall find
reason for believing that Gospel and Epistle were written near
about the same time; and this in itself is good reason for
believing that they were written at the same place. Excepting
occasional visits to the other Churches of Asia, S. John probably
rarely moved from Ephesus.

As to the date also we cannot do more than attain to probability. (1) Reason has been given above why as long an interval
as possible ought to be placed between the Apocalypse on the
one hand and the Gospel and Epistle on the other. If then the
Apocalypse was written about A.D. 68, and S. John died about
A.D. 100, we may place Gospel and Epistle between A.D. 85 and
95. (2) Moreover, the later we place these two writings in S.
John's lifetime, the more intelligible does the uncompromising
and explicit position, which characterizes both of them in reference to Gnosticism, become. (3) Again, the tone of the Epistles
is that of an old man, writing to a younger generation. We can
scarcely fancy an Apostle still in the prime of life, writing thus
to men of his own age. But those who see in this forcible and
out-spoken letter, with its marvellous combination of love and
sternness, signs of senility and failing powers, have read either
without care or with prejudice. 'The eye' of the Eagle Apostle
is 'not dim, nor his natural force abated.' (4) The contents lead
us to suppose that it was written at a time when the Church
was free from persecution : therefore before the persecution
under Domitian (A.D. 95). Later than that S. John would be

too old to write. (5) No inference can be drawn from 'it is the last hour' (ii. 18): these words cannot refer to the destruction of Jerusalem (see note *in loco*). And perhaps it is not wise to dwell much on the fact that the introductory verses seem to imply that the seeing, hearing, and handling of the Word of Life took place in the remote past. This will not help us to determine whether S. John wrote the Epistle forty or sixty years after the Ascension.

(iv) *The Object of the Epistle: its Relation to the Gospel.*

The Epistle appears to have been intended as a *companion to the Gospel.* No more definite word than 'companion' seems to be applicable, without going beyond the truth. We may call it "a preface and introduction to the Gospel," or a "second part" and "supplement" to it; but this is only to a very limited extent true. The Gospel has its proper introduction in its first eighteen verses, and its supplement in its last chapter. It is nearer the truth to speak of the Epistle as a comment on the Gospel, "a sermon with the Gospel for its text." It is "a practical application of the lessons of the life of Christ to the wants of the Church at the close of the first century" (Schaff). References to the Gospel are scattered thickly over the whole Epistle.

If this theory respecting its connexion with the Gospel be correct, we shall expect to find that the object of Gospel and Epistle is to a large extent one and the same. This is amply borne out by the facts. The object of the Gospel S. John tells us himself; 'these have been written *that ye may believe that Jesus is the Christ, the Son of God, and that believing ye may have life in His name*' (xx. 31). The object of the Epistle he tells us also; 'These things have I written unto you, *that ye may know that ye have eternal life*, even *unto you that believe on the name of the Son of God*' (v. 13). The Gospel is written to shew the way to eternal life through belief in the incarnate Son. The Epistle is written to confirm and enforce the Gospel; to assure those who believe in the incarnate Son that they *have* eternal life. The one is an historical, the other an ethical statement of the truth. The one sets forth the acts and words which prove that Jesus is the Christ, the Son of God; the other sets forth the acts and words which are obligatory upon those who believe this great truth. Of necessity both writings in stating the truth oppose error: but with this difference. In the Gospel S. John simply states the truth and leaves it: in the Epistle he commonly over against the truth places the error to which it is opposed. The Epistle is often directly polemical: the Gospel is never more than indirectly so.

S. John's Gospel has been called a summary of *Christian Theology*, his first Epistle a summary of *Christian Ethics*, and his Apocalypse a summary of *Christian Politics*. There is much truth in this classification, especially as regards the first two members of it. It will help us to give definiteness to the statement that the Epistle was written to be a companion to the Gospel. They both supply us with the fundamental doctrines of Christianity. But in the Gospel these are given as the foundations of the Christian's *faith;* in the Epistle they are given as the foundation of the Christian's *life.* The one answers the question, 'What must I believe about God and Jesus Christ?' The other answers the question, 'What is the believer's duty towards God and towards man?' It is obvious that in the latter case the direct treatment of error is much more in place than in the former. If we know clearly what to believe, we may leave on one side the consideration of what *not* to believe. But inasmuch as the world contains many who assert what is false and do what is wrong, we cannot know our duty to God and man, without learning how we are to bear ourselves in reference to falsehood and wrong.

Again, it has been said that in his three works S. John has given us three pictures of the *Divine life* or *life in God.* In the Gospel he sets forth the Divine life as it is exhibited in *the person of Christ.* In his Epistle he sets forth that life as it is exhibited in *the individual Christian.* And in the Apocalypse he sets forth that life as it is exhibited in *the Church.* This again is true, especially as regards the Gospel and Epistle. It is between these two that the comparison and contrast are closest.

The Church is the Body of Christ, and it is also the collective body of individual Christians. So far as it comes up to its ideal, it will present the life in God as it is exhibited in Christ Himself. So far as it falls short of it, it will present the Divine life as it is exhibited in the ordinary Christian. It is therefore in the field occupied by the Gospel and Epistle respectively that we find the largest amount both of similarity and difference. In the one we have the perfect life in God as it was realised in an historical Person. In the other we have the directions for reproducing that life as it might be realised by an earnest but necessarily imperfect Christian.

To sum up the relations of the Gospel to the Epistle, we may say that the Gospel is objective, the Epistle subjective; the one is historical, the other moral; the one gives us the theology of the Christ, the other the ethics of the Christian; the one is didactic, the other polemical; the one states the truth as a thesis, the other as an antithesis; the one starts from the human side, the other from the divine; the one proves that the Man Jesus is the Son of God, the other insists that the Son of God is come in the flesh. But the connexion between the two is intimate and organic throughout. The Gospel suggests principles of conduct which the Epistle lays down explicitly; the Epistle implies facts which the Gospel states as historically true.

It would perhaps be too much to say that the Epistle "was written designedly as the supplement to all extant New Testament Scripture, as, in fact, the final treatise of inspired revelation." But it will be well to remember in studying it that as a matter of fact the letter is that final treatise. We can hardly venture to say that in penning it S. John was consciously putting the coping stone on the edifice of the New Testament and closing the Canon. But in it the leading doctrines of Christianity are stated in their final form. The teaching of S. Paul and that of S. James are restated, no longer in apparent opposition, but in intimate and inseparable harmony. They are but two sides of the same truth. And just as the different forms of truth are blended, so also are the different forms of error. S. Paul constantly reminds us that the believer has to meet the xlviii *INTRODUCTION.*

hostility both of the Jew and of the Pagan. In this Epistle neither Jew nor Pagan is even named : "Their distinctive hostility to the Church has melted into the one dark background of 'the world'" (Farrar).

But though S. John's hand was thus guided to gather up and consummate the whole body of evangelical truth, it seems evident that this was not his own intention in writing the Epistle. The letter, like most of the Epistles in N. T., is an *occasional* one. It is written for a special occasion; to meet a definite crisis in the Church. It is a solemn warning against the seductive assumptions and deductions of various forms of Gnostic error; an emphatic protest against anything like a compromise where Christian truth is in question. The nature of God, so far as it can be grasped by man; the nature of Christ; the relation of man to God, to the world, and to the evil one; are stated with a firm hand to meet the shifty theories of false teachers. 'I have been very jealous for the Lord God of hosts' (1 Kings xix. 10) is the mental attitude of this polemical element in the Epistle. "We hear again the voice of the 'son of thunder,' still vehement against every insult to the majesty of his Lord." But it is a thunder which is not simply destructive. It clears the air and prepares the way for the sunshine. Thus, he who professes knowledge of God without holiness of life, is a liar (i. 6; ii. 4): he who hates his brother is a murderer (iii. 15): he who habitually sins is a child of the devil (iii. 8): he who denies the Incarnation is a liar, and a deceiver, and an Antichrist (ii. 22: 2 John 7). But, on the other hand, if any man sin we have an Advocate, a propitiation for the sins of the whole world (ii. 1, 2): he that doeth the will of God abideth for ever (ii. 17): we are in Him that is true, in His Son Jesus Christ (v. 20). The intensity of his severity grows out of the intensity of his love; and both reflect that union of the two which is so conspicuous in the life of his Lord and Master.

The connexion between Gospel and Epistle is recognised by the writer of the Muratorian Canon, who probably lived within a century of the writing of both. We have no means of verifying his narrative, but must take it or leave it as it stands.

"Of the fourth of the Gospels, John one of the disciples [is the author]. When his fellow-disciples and bishops[1] exhorted him [to write it], he said; 'Fast with me for three days from to-day, and let us relate to each other whatever shall be revealed to each.' On the same night it was revealed to Andrew[2], one of the Apostles, that, though all should revise, John should write down everything in his own name. And therefore, though various principles are taught in the separate books of the Gospels, yet it makes no difference to the faith of believers, seeing that by one supreme Spirit there are declared in all all things concerning the Birth, the Passion, the Resurrection, the life with His disciples, and His double Advent; the first in humility, despised, which is past; the second glorious in kingly power, which is to come. What wonder, therefore, is it, if John so constantly in his Epistles also puts forward particular [phrases], saying in his own person, *what we have seen with our eyes and heard with our ears, and our hands have handled, these things have we written to you.*" Bishop Lightfoot conjectures that the author of the Canon, or some earlier authority whom he copied, had a MS. in which the First Epistle of S. John was placed immediately after his Gospel.

The following table of parallels between the Gospel and the Epistle will go far to convince anyone; (1) that the two writings are by one and the same hand; (2) that the passages in the Gospel are the originals to which the parallels in the Epistle have been consciously or unconsciously adapted; (3) that in a number of cases the reference to the Gospel is conscious and intentional.

---

[1] *Cohortantibus condiscipulis et episcopis suis.* This evidence of bishops in the lifetime of S. John is important. ' His bishops ' means bishops appointed by him. Clement of Alexandria in his μῦθος οὐ μῦθος of S. John and the Robber represents S. John as going about Asia Minor ἐπισκόπους καταστήσων (Eus. *H. E.* iii. xxiii. 6).

[2] It is scarcely probable that S. Andrew was living when S. John wrote his Gospel: but this may be accepted as evidence that for a time he lived at Ephesus with S. John.

Gospel.	Epistle.
i. 1. In the beginning was the Word.	i. 1. That which was from the beginning...concerning the Word of life.
i. 14. We beheld His glory.	That which we beheld.
xx. 27. Reach hither thy hand, and put it into My side.	And our hands handled.
iii. 11. We speak that we do know, and bear witness of that we have seen.	i. 2. We have seen, and bear witness, and declare unto you.
xix. 35. He that hath seen hath borne witness.	
i. 1. The Word was with God.	The eternal life, which was with the Father.
xvii. 21. That they may all be one ; even as Thou, Father, art in Me, and I in Thee, that they also may be in Us.	i. 3. Our fellowship is with the Father, and with His Son Jesus Christ.
xvi. 24. That your joy may be fulfilled.	i. 4. That our joy may be fulfilled.
i. 19. And this is the witness of John.	i. 5. And this is the message which we have heard from Him. God is light, and in Him is no darkness at all.
i. 5. The light shineth in the darkness ; and the darkness apprehended it not.	
viii. 12. He that followeth Me shall not walk in darkness, but shall have that light of life.	i. 6. If we say that we have fellowship with Him, and walk in darkness we lie, and do not the truth ; but if we walk in light, as He is in the light...
iii. 21. He that doeth the truth, cometh to the light.	
xiv. 16. I will pray the Father and He shall give you another Advocate.	ii. 1. We have an Advocate with the Father, Jesus Christ the righteous.
i. 29. Behold, the Lamb of God, which taketh away the sin of the world.	ii. 1. And not for ours only, but also for the whole world.
iv. 24. The Saviour of the world.	
xiv. 15. If ye love Me, ye will keep my commandments.	ii. 3. Hereby know we that we know Him, if we keep His commandments.

Gospel.	Epistle.
xiv. 21. He that hath My commandments and keepeth them, he it is that loveth Me.	**ii. 5.** Whoso keepeth His word, in Him verily hath the love of God been perfected.
xv. 5. He that abideth in Me, and I in him, the same beareth much fruit.	**ii. 6.** He that saith he abideth in Him ought himself also to walk even as He walked.
xiii. 34. A new commandment I give unto you.	**ii. 8.** A new commandment write I unto you.
i. 9. There was the true light.	The true light already shineth.
v. 17. Even until now.	**ii. 9.** Even until now.
xi. 9. If a man walk in the day, he stumbleth not, because he seeth the light of this world.	**ii. 10.** He that loveth his brother abideth in the light, and there is none occasion of stumbling in him.
xii. 35. He that walketh in the darkness knoweth not whither he goeth.	**ii. 11.** He that hateth his brother is in the darkness, and walketh in the darkness, and knoweth not whither he goeth, because the darkness hath blinded his eyes.
xii. 40. He hath blinded their eyes.	
xiii. 33. Little children (τεκνία).	**ii. 1,12,28.** Little children (τεκνία).
i. 1. In the beginning was the Word.	**ii. 13.** Ye know Him which is from the beginning.
v. 38. Ye have not His word abiding in you.	**ii. 14.** The word of God abideth in you.
viii. 35. Abideth for ever.	**ii. 17.** Abideth for ever.
xxi. 5. Children (παιδία).	**ii. 18.** Little children (παιδία).
vi. 39. This is the will of Him that sent Me, that of all which He hath given Me I should lose nothing.	**ii. 19.** If they had been of us, they would have abided with us.
vi. 69. The Holy One of God (Christ).	**ii. 20.** The Holy One (Christ).
xvi. 13. When He, the Spirit of truth, is come, He shall guide you into all truth.	Ye have an anointing from the Holy One, and ye know all things.
xv. 23. He that hateth Me hateth My Father also.	**ii. 23.** Whosoever denieth the Son, the same hath not the Father.
xiv. 9. He that hath seen Me hath seen the Father.	He that confesseth the Son, hath the Father also.

s. JOHN (EP.)

Gospel.	Epistle.
xiv. 23. If a man love Me, he will keep My word ; and My Father will love him, and We will come unto him, and make Our abode with him.	ii. 24. If that which ye heard from the beginning abide in you, ye also shall abide in the Son, and in the Father.
xvii. 2. That whatsoever Thou hast given Him, to them He should give eternal life.	ii. 25. And this is the promise which He promised us, even eternal life.
xvi. 13. When He, the Spirit of truth, is come, He shall guide you into all truth.	ii. 27. As His anointing teacheth you concerning all things.

These are but gleanings out of a couple of chapters[1], but they are sufficient to shew the relation between the two writings. Some of them are mere reminiscences of particular modes of expressions. But in other cases the passage in the Epistle is a deduction from the passage in the Gospel, or an illustration of it, or a development in accordance with the Apostle's experience in the half century which had elapsed since the Ascension. But the fact that the Epistle at every turn presupposes the Gospel, does not prove beyond all question that the Gospel was *written* first. S. John had delivered his Gospel orally over and over again before writing it : and it is possible, though hardly probable, that the Epistle was written before the Gospel.

In this abundance of parallels between the two writings, especially between the discourses of the Lord in the Gospel and the Apostle's teaching in the Epistle, "it is most worthy of notice that no use is made in the Epistle of the language of the discourses in John iii. and vi."

"Generally it will be found on a comparison of the closest parallels, that the Apostle's own words are more formal in expression than the words of the Lord which he records. The Lord's words have been moulded by the disciple into aphorisms in the Epistle."—Westcott.

[1] Dr Farrar is far below the mark when he writes, "There are fully thirty-five parallel passages in the Gospel and the Epistle" (*Messages of the Books*, 475).

(v) *The Plan of the Epistle.*

That S. John had a plan, and a very carefully arranged plan, in writing his Gospel, those who have studied its structure will scarcely be able to doubt. It is far otherwise with the Epistle. Here we may reasonably doubt whether the Apostle had any systematic arrangement of his thoughts in his mind when he wrote the letter. Indeed some commentators have regarded it as the rambling prattle of an old man, "an unmethodised effusion of pious sentiments and reflections." Others, without going quite these lengths, have concluded that the contemplative and undialectical temper of S. John has caused him to pour forth his thoughts in a series of aphorisms without much sequence or logical connexion.

Both these opinions are erroneous. It is quite true to say with Calvin that the Epistle is a compound of doctrine and exhortation: what Epistle in N.T. is not? But it is a mistake to suppose with him that the composition is confused. Again, it is quite true to say that the Apostle's method is not dialectical. But it cannot follow from this that he has no method at all. He seldom argues; one who sees the truth, and believes that every sincere believer will see it also, has not much need to argue: he merely states the truth and leaves it to exercise its legitimate power over every truth-loving heart. But in thus simply affirming what is true and denying what is false he does not allow his thoughts to come out hap-hazard. Each one as it comes before us may be complete in itself; but it is linked on to what precedes and what follows. The links are often subtle, and sometimes we cannot be sure that we have detected them; but they are seldom entirely absent. This peculiarity brings with it the further characteristic, that the transitions from one section of the subject to another, and even from one main division of it to another, are for the most part very gradual. They are like the changes in dissolving views. We know that we have passed on to something new, but we hardly know how the change has come about. And in addition to this there is the peculiarity

that subjects touched upon and left are frequently reappearing
further on for development and fresh treatment. The *spiral
movement*, which is so conspicuous in the Prologue to the Gospel
and in Christ's Farewell Discourses, is apparent in the Epistle
also. See Notes on the Gospel, pp. 75, 273.

A writing of this kind is exceedingly difficult to analyse. We
feel that there are divisions ; but we are by no means sure where
to make them, or how to name them. We are conscious that
the separate thoughts are intimately connected one with another;
but we cannot satisfy ourselves that we have discovered the
exact lines of connexion. At times we hardly know whether we
are moving forwards or backwards, whether we are returning to
an old subject or passing onwards to a new one, when in truth
we are doing both and neither ; for the old material is recast and
made new, and the new material is shewn to have been involved
in the old. Probably few commentators have satisfied themselves with their own analysis of this Epistle : still fewer have
satisfied other people. Only those who have seriously attempted
it know the real difficulties of the problem. It is like analysing
the face of the sky or of the sea. There is contrast, and yet
harmony; variety and yet order; fixedness, and yet ceaseless
change; a monotony which soothes without wearying us, because the frequent repetitions come to us as things that are both
new and old. But about one point most students of the Epistle
will agree ; that it is better to read it under the guidance of any
scheme that will at all coincide with its contents, than with no
guidance whatever. Jewels, it is true, remain jewels, even when
piled confusedly into a heap : but they are then seen to the very
least advantage. Any arrangement is better than that. So also
with S. John's utterances in this Epistle. They are robbed of
more than half their power if they are regarded as a string of
detached aphorisms, with no more organic unity than a collection of proverbs. It is in the conviction of the truth of this
opinion that the following analysis is offered for consideration.
It is, of course, to a considerable extent based upon previous
attempts, and possibly it is no great improvement upon any of
them. It has, however, been of service to the writer in studying

the Epistle, and if it helps any other student to frame a better analysis for himself, it will have served its purpose.

One or two divisions may be asserted with confidence. Beyond all question the first four verses are introductory, and are analogous to the first eighteen verses of the Gospel. Equally beyond question the last four verses, and probably the last eight verses, form the summary and conclusion. This leaves the intermediate portion from i. 5 to v. 12 or v. 17 as the main body of the Epistle : and it is about the divisions and subdivisions of this portion that so much difference of opinion exists.

Again, nearly every commentator seems to have felt that a division must be made somewhere near the end of the second chapter. In the following analysis this generally recognised landmark has been adopted as central. Logically as well as locally it divides the main body of the Epistle into two fairly equal halves. And these two halves may be conveniently designated by the great statement which each contains respecting the Divine Nature—'God is Light' and 'God is Love.' These headings are not merely convenient; they correspond to a very considerable extent with the contents of each half. The first half, especially in its earlier portions, is dominated by the idea of 'light': the second half is still more clearly and thoroughly dominated by the idea of 'love.'

As regards the subdivisions and the titles given to them, all that it would be safe to affirm is this ;—that, like trees in a well-wooded landscape, the Apostle's thoughts evidently fall into groups, and that it conduces to clearness to distinguish the groups. But it may easily be the case that what to one eye is only one cluster, to another eye is two or three clusters, and that there may also be a difference of opinion as to where each cluster begins and ends. Moreover the description of a particular group which satisfies one mind will seem inaccurate to another. The following scheme will do excellent service if it provokes the student to challenge its correctness and to correct it, if necessary, throughout.

INTRODUCTION.

An Analysis of the Epistle.

i. 1—4. INTRODUCTION.

1. The Subject-Matter of the Gospel employed in the Epistle (i. 1—3).
2. The Purpose of the Epistle (i. 4).

i. 5—ii. 28. GOD IS LIGHT.

a. i. 5—ii. 11. **What Walking in the Light involves: the Condition and Conduct of the Believer.**

1. Fellowship with God and with the Brethren (i. 5—7).
2. Consciousness and Confession of Sin (i. 8—10).
3. Obedience to God by Imitation of Christ (ii. 1—6).
4. Love of the Brethren (ii. 7—11).

b. ii. 12—28. **What Walking in the Light excludes: the Things and Persons to be avoided.**

1. Threefold statement of Reasons for Writing (ii. 12—14).
2. The Things to be avoided;—the World and its Ways (ii. 15—17).
3. The Persons to be avoided;—Antichrists (ii. 18—26).
4. (Transitional) The Place of safety;—Christ (ii. 27, 28).

ii. 29—v. 12. GOD IS LOVE.

c. ii. 29—iii. 24. **The Evidence of Sonship;—Deeds of righteousness before God.**

1. The Children of God and the Children of the Devil (ii. 29—iii. 12).
2. Love and Hate; Life and Death (iii. 13—24).

d. iv. 1—v. 12. **The Source of Sonship;—Possession of the Spirit as shewn by Confession of the Incarnation.**

1. The Spirit of Truth and the Spirit of Error (iv. 1—6).
2. Love is the Mark of the Children of Him who is Love (iv. 7—21).
3 Faith is the Source of Love, the Victory over the World, and the Possession of Life (v. 1—12).

v. 13—21. CONCLUSION.

1. Intercessory Love the Fruit of Faith (v. 13—17).
2. The Sum of the Christian's Knowledge (v. 18—20).
3. Final Injunction (v. 21).

Perhaps our first impression on looking at the headings of the smaller sections would be that these subjects have not much connexion with one another, and that the order in which they come is more or less a matter of accident. This impression would be erroneous. *Fellowship with God* involves *consciousness of sin,* and its *confession* with a view to its removal. This implies *obedience to God,* which finds its highest expression in *love. Love of God and of the brethren* excludes love of the *world,* which is passing away, as is shewn by the appearance of *antichrists.* He who would not pass away must *abide in Christ.* With the idea of *sonship,* introduced by the expression 'begotten of God,' the Epistle takes a fresh start. This Divine sonship implies *mutual love* among God's children and the *indwelling of Christ* to which the Spirit testifies. The mention of the Spirit leads on to the distinction between *true and false spirits.* By a rather subtle connexion (see on iv. 7) this once more leads to the topic of *mutual love,* and to *faith as the source of love,* especially as shewn in *intercessory prayer.* The whole closes with a *summary of the knowledge* on which the moral principles inculcated in the Epistle are based, and with a warning against idols.

The omissions are as remarkable as the contents. Unlike the Gospel, the Epistle contains no quotations from the O.T. It tells us nothing about the government, ministry, sacraments, or worship of the Apostolic Church. The word ἐκκλησία does not occur in it. There is no mention of bishop, presbyter, or deacon, of Baptism or the Eucharist Not that the Apostle is indifferent to these things, but that they are no part of his subject. He has to tell, not of the structure or discipline of the community, but of its spiritual life and organism :—the fellowship of believers with the Father and the Son and their consequent fellowship with one another.

(vi.) *The Characteristics of the Epistle.*

"In reading John it is always with me as though I saw him before me, lying on the bosom of his Master at the last supper : as though his angel were holding the light for me, and in certain passages would fall upon my neck and whisper something in

mine ear. I am far from understanding all I read, but it often
seems to me as if what John meant were floating before me in
the distance; and even when I look into a passage altogether
dark, I have a foretaste of some great, glorious meaning, which
I shall one day understand" (Claudius).

Dante expresses the same feeling still more strongly when he
represents himself as blinded by the radiance of the beloved
disciple (*Paradiso* xxv. 136—xxvi. 6).

> "Ah, how much in my mind was I disturbed,
>   When I turned round to look on Beatrice,
>   That her I could not see, although I was
> Close at her side and in the Happy World!
> While I was doubting for my vision quenched,
>   Out of the flame refulgent that had quenched it
>   Issued a breathing, that attentive made me,
> Saying—'Whilst thou recoverest the sense
>   Of seeing which in me thou hast consumed,
>   'Tis well that speaking thou should'st compensate it.' "
>   (Longfellow's Translation: see notes.)

Two characteristics of this Epistle will strike every serious
reader; the almost oppressive *majesty of the thoughts* which are
put before us, and the extreme *simplicity of the language* in
which they are expressed. The most profound mysteries in the
Divine scheme of Redemption, the spiritual and moral relations
between God, the human soul, the world, and the evil one, and
the fundamental principles of Christian Ethics, are all stated in
words which any intelligent child can understand. They are
the words of one who has 'received the kingdom' of heaven
into his inmost soul, and received it 'as a little child.' They are
the foolish things of the world putting to shame them that are
wise. "They are still waters, which run deep." Their ease, and
simplicity, and repose irresistibly attract us. Even the unwilling
ear is arrested and listens. We are held as by a spell. And as
we listen, and stop, and ponder, we find that the simple words,
which at first seemed to convey a meaning as simple as themselves, are charged with truths which are not of this world, but
have their roots in the Infinite and Eternal. S. John has been

so long on the mount in communion with God that his very words, when the veil is taken off them, shine: and, as Dante intimates, to be brought suddenly face to face with his spirit is well-nigh too much for mortal eyes.

Another characteristic of the Epistle, less conspicuous perhaps, but indisputable, is its *finality*. As S. John's Gospel, not merely in time, but in conception and form and point of view, is the last of the Gospels, so this is the last of the Epistles. It rises above and consummates all the rest. It is in a sphere in which the difficulties between Jewish Christian and Gentile Christian, and the apparent discords between S. Paul and S. James, are harmonized and cease to exist. It is indeed no handbook or summary of Christian doctrine; for it is written expressly for those who 'know the truth'; and therefore much is left unstated, because it may be taken for granted. But in no other book in the Bible are so many cardinal doctrines touched, or with so firm a hand. And each point is laid before us with the awe-inspiring solemnity of one who writes under the profound conviction that 'it is the last hour.'

Closely connected with this characteristic of finality is another which it shares with the Gospel;—the tone of *magisterial authority* which pervades the whole. None but an Apostle, perhaps we may almost venture to say, none but the last surviving Apostle, could write like this. There is no passionate claim to authority, as of one who feels compelled to assert himself and ask, 'Am I not an Apostle?' There is no fierce denunciation of those who are opposed to him, no attempt at a compromise, no anxiety about the result. He will not argue the point; he states the truth and leaves it. Every sentence seems to tell of the conscious authority and resistless though unexerted strength of one who has 'seen, and heard, and handled' the Eternal Word, and who 'knows that his witness is true.'

Once more, there is throughout the Epistle a *love of moral and spiritual antitheses*. Over against each thought there is constantly placed in sharp contrast its opposite. Thus light and darkness, truth and falsehood, love and hate, life and death, love of the Father and love of the world, the children of God and the children of the devil, the spirit of truth and the spirit of error, sin unto death and sin not unto death, to do righteousness and to do sin, follow one another in impressive alternation. The movement of the Epistle largely consists of progress from one opposite to another. And it will nearly always be found that the antithesis is not exact, but an advance beyond the original statement or else an expansion of it. 'He that believeth on the Son of God hath the witness in him : he that believeth not God hath made Him a liar' (v. 10). The antithetical structure and rhythmical cadence of the sentences would do much to commend them "to the ear and to the memory of the hearers. To Greek readers, familiar with the lyrical arrangements of the Greek Drama, this mode of writing would have a peculiar charm ; and Jewish readers would recognise in it a correspondence to the style and diction of their own Prophetical Books" (Wordsworth).

> If we say we have no sin,
> We deceive ourselves,
> And the truth is not in us.

> If we confess our sins,
> He is faithful and righteous to forgive us our sins,
> And to cleanse us from all unrighteousness.

> If we say that we have not sinned,
> We make Him a liar ;
> And His word is not in us.

In this instance it will be noticed that we pass from one opposite to another and back again : but that to which we return covers more ground than the original position and is a distinct advance upon it. This progress by means of alternating statements is still more apparent in the following example.

> He that saith he is in the light,
> And hateth his brother,
> Is in the darkness even until now.

> He that loveth his brother
> Abideth in the light,
> And there is none occasion of stumbling in him.

But he that hateth his brother
Is in the darkness,
And walketh in the darkness,
And knoweth not whither he goeth,
Because the darkness hath blinded his eyes.

For other characteristics of S. John's style which are common
to both Gospel and Epistle see the Introduction to the Gospel,
chapter v. Many of these are pointed out in the notes on these
Epistles: see in particular the notes on 1 John i. 2, 4, 5, 8, ii. 1,
3, 8, 24, iii. 9, 15, 17, iv. 9, v. 9, 10.

"Every reader feels the calmness and the serenity which pervade this book. It tells of a soul that has reached peace, of the
serenity of an aged man; and the very reading of it puts us in
the rest, the quiet, the tranquillity of peace. He likes to dwell
upon a great thought; he turns it this way and that, and sinks
his soul into it. He ever leads us back to the same thoughts
and gladly repeats them to us, so as to send them deep into the
soul and make them stay there....

This calmness of lingering contemplation, and this passive,
peaceful tranquillity, is, however, not nature. It is command of
the mind. For we can still discover in him the fiery, violent
character of the youth. If the hasty glow of earlier days is no
longer there, still a reminiscence of it is always at hand. We
can see his natural character in his short decisive sentences, his
emphatic way of building sentences, the want of connexion in
his array of sentences, and in the use of contrasts in his speech.
His nature is not destroyed. It is purified, brightened, raised
to the truth, and so taken into the service of the loved Master....
The fire of youth has left its calm light and its warm enthusiasm.
It breathes through the most quiet speech, and raises the language to the rhythmical beauty of Hebrew poetry, and to a very
hymn of praise."

These words, though written by Luthardt of the Gospel of
S. John (Introduction II. 5, § 2), may be applied, without the
alteration of a single sentence, to the Epistles.

The following characteristic words and phrases are common to

S. John's Gospel and one or more of his Epistles, those printed in thick type being found in the Apocalypse also :—

ἀγαπᾶν, ἀγάπη, ἁγνίζειν ἑαυτόν, ἀλήθεια, ἀληθής, **ἀληθινός**, ἀληθινὸς Θεός (comp. Rev. vi. 10), ἀληθῶς, ἀλλ' ἵνα (see on 1 John ii. 19), ἁμαρτίαν ἔχειν, ἀνθρωποκτόνος, γινώσκειν, γεννηθῆναι ἐκ, **εἶναι ἐκ,** εἶναι ἐκ τῆς ἀληθείας, εἶναι ἐκ τοῦ Θεοῦ, εἶναι ἐκ τοῦ κόσμου, ἐντολὴ καινή, ζωή, ζωὴ αἰώνιος, θεᾶσθαι, **θεωρεῖν**, ἵνα in unusual constructions (see on 1 John i. 9), καινός in a good sense, **κόσμος, Λόγος,** μαρτυρεῖν, μαρτυρία, μένειν, μεταβαίνειν ἐκ τοῦ θανάτου εἰς τὴν ζωήν, μονογενής (of the Son of God), **νικᾶν**, νικᾶν τὸν κόσμον, ὁρᾶν in the perfect tense, παιδία, παράκλητος, περιπατεῖν ἐν τῇ σκοτίᾳ, πιστεύειν εἰς, παρρησία, **πλανᾶν**, τὸ πνεῦμα τῆς ἀληθείας, ποιεῖν τὴν ἀλήθειαν, ποιεῖν τὴν ἁμαρτίαν, ὁ πονηρός, σκοτία, σωτὴρ τοῦ κόσμου, **τέκνα Θεοῦ, τεκνία, τηρεῖν τὰς ἐντολάς, τηρεῖν τὸν λόγον,** τιθέναι τὴν ψυχὴν αὐτοῦ, **φαίνειν**, φανεροῦν, φῶς, χαρὰ πεπληρωμένη.

The following expressions occur in one or more of the Epistles, but not in the Gospel :—

ἀγγελία, ἁμαρτία πρὸς θάνατον, ἀντίχριστος, ἐπιθυμία τῶν ὀφθαλμῶν, ἐπιθυμία τῆς σαρκός, ἐν σαρκὶ ἔρχεσθαι, ἐν ἀληθείᾳ περιπατεῖν, ἐν τῷ φωτὶ περιπατεῖν, ἱλασμός, κοινωνία, παρουσία (of the Second Advent), πλάνος, ποιεῖν τὴν ἀνομίαν, ποιεῖν δικαιοσύνην (Rev.), χρῖσμα.

(vii) *Its relation to the Teaching of S. Paul.*

"John and Paul have depth of knowledge in common. They are the two apostles who have left us the most complete systems of doctrine. But they know in different ways. Paul, educated in the schools of the Pharisees, is an exceedingly acute thinker and an accomplished dialectician. He sets forth the doctrines of Christianity in a systematic scheme, proceeding from cause to effect, from the general to the particular, from premise to conclusion, with logical clearness and precision. He is a representative of genuine *scholasticism* in the best sense of the term. John's knowledge is that of intuition and contemplation. He gazes with his whole soul upon the object before him, surveys all as in one picture, and thus presents the profoundest truths as an eye-witness, not by a course of logical demonstration, but immediately as they lie in reality before him. His knowledge of divine things is the deep insight of love, which ever fixes itself at the centre, and thence surveys all points of the circumference at once. He is the representative of all true *mysticism*.... Paul and John, in their two grand systems, have laid the eternal foundations of all true theology and philosophy; and their writings, now after eighteen centuries of study, are still unfathomed" (Schaff).

The theory that S. John "came to Ephesus with a view to upholding the principles of the Christianity of Jerusalem against the encroachments of the Christianity of S. Paul," and that "John, the writer of the Apocalypse, as superintendent of the Churches of Asia Minor, made war upon Pauline Christianity," would be sufficiently untenable even if S. John had written nothing but the Apocalypse. But this Epistle contains the most ample refutation of it. F. C. Baur, the great upholder of the theory, can make it look plausible only by attributing the Fourth Gospel, and with it of course this Epistle, to some unknown evangelist who assumed S. John's personality. He admits that "inner points of connexion between the Apocalypse and the Gospel are not wanting." But "the author of the Gospel felt his standpoint to be a new and peculiar one, and essentially distinct, both from the Pauline and the Jewish Christian: but this very fact forced upon him the necessity of giving a genuinely apostolic expression to the new form of Christian consciousness."

This view has recently been elaborated afresh by Dr Pfleiderer in the Hibbert Lectures. He holds that Baur has proved "how profound was the antagonism between Paul and the first Apostles," and with Baur he maintains that the Revelation is an attack on S. Paul by S. John. He goes on to suggest that the Gospel of S. Mark is a Pauline rejoinder to the Revelation, and that of S. Matthew a Judaic reply to S. Mark. Then comes the Third Gospel as a partial attempt at a reconciliation, an end which is ultimately reached by the writer of the Fourth.

We are asked, therefore, to believe that the first age of the Church was spent in a pamphlet war between the representatives

of three totally different forms of Christianity. (1) The Gospel
of S. Paul; (2) that of S. John, who in the Apocalypse "made
war upon Pauline Christianity;" (3) that of the Fourth Evangelist, who usurped the name of S. John in order to take up a
position "essentially distinct" both from that of S. John and of
S. Paul. The theory that the Revelation is an attack on S. Paul
has been sufficiently answered by Bishop Lightfoot in his Essay on
S. Paul and the Three (*Galatians*, 6th ed. pp. 308—311, 346—
364), in which he points out the fundamental agreement between
S. Paul's Epistles and the Apocalypse on the one hand, and
between the Apocalypse and the Fourth Gospel with our Epistle
on the other. It remains to compare the last member in this
series with the first. An examination of the following passages
will enable the reader to judge whether in this Epistle the author
of the Fourth Gospel teaches a Christianity "essentially distinct"
from that of S. Paul. And it should be observed that in almost
all cases the references are taken exclusively, or at least partly,
from the four great Epistles on which even Baur admits "there
has never been cast the slightest suspicion of unauthenticity,"—
Romans, 1 and 2 Corinthians, and Galatians. In addition to
these Dr Pfleiderer accepts as genuine 1 Thessalonians, Philippians,
and Philemon; and as partly genuine 2 Thessalonians and Colossians.

(1)   The manifestation of the Eternal Son: i. 2, iii. 5; Rom.
xvi. 26; 1 Tim. iii. 16.

(2)   Our fellowship with the Son: i. 3, ii. 24; 1 Cor. i. 9.

(3)   No fellowship between light and darkness: i. 6; 2 Cor. vi. 15.

(4)   Redemption through Christ's blood: i. 7; Rom. v. 9;
Eph. i. 7.

(5)   Christ our Advocate with the Father: ii. 1; Rom. viii. 34;
1 Tim. ii. 5.

(6)   Christ a propitiation: ii. 2, iv. 10; Rom. iii. 25; 2 Cor. v. 18.

(7)   Obedience the test of a true Christian: ii. 4, iii. 24; 1 Cor.
vii. 19.   Imitation of Christ: ii. 6; Eph. v.

(8)   Darkness yielding to light: ii. 8; Rom. xiii. 12; Eph. v. 8.

(9)   Enlightenment worthless without love: ii. 9; 1 Cor. xiii. 2.

(10)   The world passing away: ii. 17; 1 Cor. vii. 31.

INTRODUCTION.

(11) The end close at hand : ii. 18; 1 Cor. vii. 29; x. 11.

(12) Antichrists a sign of the end : ii. 18; 1 Tim. iv. 1.

(13) The use of heresies in sifting faithful from unfaithful Christians : ii. 19; 1 Cor. xi. 19.

(14) The unction of the Spirit : ii. 20; 2 Cor. i. 21, 22.

(15) The fulness of the Christian's knowledge : ii. 20, 21; Rom. xv. 14.

(16) The Divine gift of sonship : ii. 1, 2; Rom. viii. 15; Gal. iii. 26.

(17) The beatific vision : iii. 2; 1 Cor. xiii. 12.

(18) The Christian's hope an incentive to self-purification : iii. 3; 2 Cor. vii. 1.

(19) Our future glory not yet revealed : iii. 2; Rom. viii. 18.

(20) The relation of sin to law : iii. 4; Rom. iv. 15, v. 13.

(21) The sinlessness of Christ : iii. 5; 2 Cor. v. 21.

(22) Conduct more important than knowledge : iii. 7; Rom. ii. 13.

(23) The world's hatred of Christians natural : iii. 13; 2 Tim. iii. 12.

(24) The Divine love exhibited in the work of redemption : iii. 16, iv. 9; Rom. v. 8; Eph. v. 2, 25.

(25) Love without hypocrisy : iii. 18; Rom. xii. 9.

(26) Conscience not infallible : iii. 20; 1 Cor. iv. 4.

(27) Mutual indwelling of the Divine and the human : iii. 24; Rom. viii. 9.

(28) Possession of the Spirit a proof of union with God : iii. 24, iv. 13; Rom. viii. 9; Gal. iv. 6.

(29) Prophets must be tested : iv. 1; 1 Cor. iv. 29, xii. 10, xiv. 32.

(30) Belief in the Incarnation a sure test : iv. 2, 15, v. i; Rom. x. 9; 1 Cor. xii. 3.

(31) The spirit of Antichrist already in the world : iv. 3 2 Thess. ii. 7.

(32) God the source of the Christian's victory : iv. 4, v. 4; Rom. viii. 37; 1 Cor. xv. 57.

(33) Submission to Apostolic authority : iv. 6; 1 Cor. xiv. 37.

(34) God invisible : iv. 12; 1 Tim. vi. 16.

(35)   Fear giving place to love; iv. 18; Rom. viii. 15; 2 Tim. i. 7.
(36)   The whole world evil: v. 19; 1 Cor. v. 10; Gal. i. 4.
(37)   Idolatry to be shunned: v. 21; 1 Cor. x. 14.

The coincidences of *doctrine* rarely extend to *language:* but κοινωνία, περιπατεῖν (in the figurative sense) and ἐπιθ. τῆς σαρκός are almost peculiar to S. Paul and S. John. Some remarks of the late Professor Shirley respecting these theories of Baur and others may be added with profit. " Such views are only possible where the history of doctrine is extensively studied apart from the general history of the Church; and they stand as a warning against all that handling of history which reduces it to a branch of literary criticism. The relations in which the Apostles actually stood to each other are in fact to be ascertained far less by framing a theology out of the extant writings of each, than by considering how they must have been affected by the mode of their training and appointment, by the nature of their powers, and by the links which bound together the society of which they were the rulers. In point of fact the writings even of St Paul and St John are inadequate to express their whole theology. Each has contributed to the Canon not his whole system, but that special side of his teaching of which he seemed to the Holy Spirit to be the most appropriate organ; and the account of their opinions, based simply on an analysis of their writings, however perfect and however free from colouring such an analysis may be, must always exaggerate what is distinctive of the individual, and throw into the shade what belongs to the Christian and the apostle" (*Apostolic Age*, 79, 80).

CHAPTER III.

The Second Epistle.

Short as this letter is, and having more than half of its contents common to either the First or the Second Epistle, our loss would have been great had it been refused a place in the Canon, and in consequence been allowed to perish. It gives us a new

aspect of the Apostle: it shews him to us as the shepherd of individual souls. In the First Epistle he addresses the Church at
large. In this Epistle, whether it be addressed to a local
Church, or (as we shall find reason to believe) to a Christian
lady, it is certain definite individuals that he has in his mind as
he writes. It is for the sake of particular persons about whom
he is greatly interested that he sends the letter, rather than for
the sake of Christians in general. It is a less formal and less
public utterance than the First Epistle. We see the Apostle at
home rather than in the Church, and hear him speaking as a
friend rather than as a Metropolitan. The Apostolic authority
is there, but it is in the background. The letter beseeches and
warns more than it commands.

i. *The Authorship of the Epistle.*

Just as nearly all critics allow that the Fourth Gospel and the
First Epistle are by one hand, so it is generally admitted that
the Second and Third Epistle are by one hand. The question
is whether *all four* writings are by the same person; whether
'the Elder' of the two short Epistles is the beloved disciple of
the Gospel, the author of the First Epistle. If this question is
answered in the negative, then only two alternatives remain;
either these twin Epistles were written by a person commonly
known as 'John the Elder' or 'the Presbyter John,' a contemporary of the Apostle sometimes confused with him; or they
were written by some Elder entirely unknown to us. In either
case he is a person who has studiously and with very great
success imitated the style of the Apostle.

The External Evidence.

The voice of antiquity is strongly in favour of the first and
simplest hypothesis; that all four writings are the work of the
Apostle S. John. The evidence is not so full or so indisputably
unanimous as for the Apostolicity of the First Epistle; but,
when we take into account the brevity and comparative unimportance of these two letters, the amount is considerable. See
Charteris, *Canonicity*, 327—330.

IRENAEUS, the disciple of Polycarp, the disciple of S. John, says; "*John, the disciple of the Lord,* intensified their condemnation by desiring that not even a 'God-speed' should be bid to them by us; *For,* says he, *he that biddeth him, God speed, partaketh in his evil works*" (*Haer.* I. xvi. 3). And again, after quoting 1 John ii. 18, he resumes a little further on; "These are they against whom the Lord warned us beforehand; and *His disciple,* in his Epistle already mentioned, commands us to avoid them, when he says; *Many deceivers are gone forth into this world, who confess not that Jesus Christ is come in the flesh. This is the deceiver and the Antichrist. Look to them, that ye lose not that which ye have wrought*" (III. xvi. 8). In one or two respects, it will be observed, Irenaeus must have had a different text from ours: but these quotations shew that he was well acquainted with the Second Epistle and believed it to be by the beloved disciple. And though in the second passage he makes the slip of quoting the Second Epistle and calling it the First, yet this only shews all the more plainly how remote from his mind was the idea that the one Epistle might be by S. John and the other not.

CLEMENT OF ALEXANDRIA, and indeed the Alexandrian school generally (A.D. 200—300), testify to the belief that the second letter is by the Apostle. He quotes 1 John v. 16 with the introductory words; "John in his longer Epistle (ἐν τῇ μείζονι ἐπιστολῇ) seems to teach &c." (*Strom.* II. xv.), which shews that he knows of at least one other and shorter Epistle by the same John. In a fragment of a Latin translation of one of his works we read; "The second Epistle of John, which is written to virgins, is very simple: it is written indeed to a certain Babylonian lady, Electa by name; but it signifies the election of the holy Church." Eusebius (*H. E.* VI. xiv. 1) tells us that Clement in his *Hypotyposes* or *Outlines* commented on the 'disputed' books in N. T. viz. "the Epistle of Jude and the other Catholic Epistles."

DIONYSIUS OF ALEXANDRIA in his famous criticism (Eus. *H. E.* VII. xxv.) so far from thinking 'the Elder' an unlikely title to be taken by S. John, thinks that his not naming himself is like the Apostle's usual manner.

Thus we have witnesses from two very different centres, Irenaeus in Gaul, Clement and Dionysius in Alexandria.

CYPRIAN in his account of a Council at Carthage, A.D. 256, gives us what we may fairly consider to be evidence as to the belief of the North African Church. He says that Aurelius, Bishop of Chullabi, quoted 2 John 10, 11 with the observation; *Johannes apostolus in epistula sua posuit:* "Si quis ad vos venit et doctrinam Christi non habet, nolite eum admittere in domum vestram et ave illi ne dixeritis . qui enim dixerit illi ave communicat factis ejus malis." This quotation exhibits no less than ten differences from the Vulgate of Jerome (*Cod. Am.*) and proves the existence of an early African text of this Epistle. But Cyprian frequently quotes the First Epistle and several times with the formula *Johannes in epistola sua,* or *in epistola:* he nowhere adds *prima* or *maxima* any more than he here adds *secunda.*

The evidence of the MURATORIAN FRAGMENT is by no means clear. We have seen (p. xl.) that the writer quotes the First Epistle in his account of the Fourth Gospel, and later on speaks of "two Epistles of the John who has been mentioned before." This has been interpreted in various ways. (1) That these 'two Epistles' are the Second and Third, the First being omitted by the copyist (who evidently was a very inaccurate and incompetent person), or being counted as part of the Gospel. (2) That these two are the First and the Second, the Third being omitted. (3) That the First and the Second are taken together as one Epistle and the Third as a second. And it is remarkable that Eusebius twice speaks of the First Epistle as "the *former* Epistle of John" (*H. E.* III. xxv. 2, xxxix. 16), just as Clement speaks of "the *longer* Epistle," as if in some arrangements there were only two Epistles. But in spite of this the first of these three explanations is to be preferred. The context in the Fragment decidedly favours it.

ORIGEN knows of the two shorter letters, but says that "not all admit that these are genuine" (Eus. *H. E.* VI. xxv. 10). Yet he expresses no opinion of his own, and never quotes them. On the other hand he quotes the First Epistle "in such a manner as at least to shew that the other Epistles were not familiarly known" (Westcott).

Eusebius, who was possibly influenced by Origen, classes these two Epistles among the 'disputed' books of the Canon, and suggests (without giving his own view) that they may be the work of a namesake of the Evangelist. "Among the *disputed* (ἀντιλεγόμενα) books, which, however, are well known and recognised by most, we class the Epistle circulated under the name of James, and that of Jude, as well as the second of Peter, and the so-called second and third of John, whether they belong to the Evangelist, or possibly to another of the same name as he" (*H. E.* iii. xxv. 3). Elsewhere he speaks in a way which leaves one less in doubt as to his own opinion (*Dem. Evan.* iii. iii. again p. 120), which appears to be favourable to the Apostolic authorship; he speaks of them without qualification as S. John's.

The school of Antioch seems to have rejected these two 'disputed' Epistles, together with Jude and 2 Peter.

Jerome (*Vir. Illust.* ix.) says that, while the First Epistle is approved by all Churches and scholars, the two others are ascribed to John the Presbyter, whose tomb was still shewn at Ephesus as well as that of the Apostle.

The Middle Ages attributed all three to S. John.

From this summary of the external evidence it is apparent that precisely those witnesses who are nearest to S. John in time are favourable to the Apostolic authorship and seem to know of no other view. Doubts are first indicated by Origen, although we need not suppose that they were first propounded by him. Probably the belief that there had been another John at Ephesus, and that he had been known as 'John the Presbyter' or 'the Elder,' first made people think that these two comparatively insignificant Epistles, written by some one who calls himself 'the Elder,' were not the work of the Apostle. But, as is shewn in Appendix E., *it is doubtful, whether any such person as John the Elder, as distinct from the Apostle and Evangelist, ever existed.* In all probability those writers who attribute the two shorter letters to John the Presbyter, whether they know it or not, are really attributing them to S. John.

The Internal Evidence.

The internal is hardly less strong than the external evidence in favour of the Apostolic authorship of the Second, and therefore of the Third Epistle: for no one can reasonably doubt that the writer of the one is the writer of the other. The argument is parallel to that respecting the Pastoral Epistles. There is much in these Epistles that cannot reasonably be ascribed to anyone but S. Paul: these portions cannot be severed from the rest: therefore those portions which are not in his usual style were nevertheless written by him. So here; the Second Epistle has so much that is similar to the First, that common authorship is highly probable: and the Third Epistle has so much that is similar to the Second, that common authorship is practically certain. Therefore the Third Epistle, though not like the First, is nevertheless by the same hand. We have seen in the preceding sections that Apostles were sometimes called Elders. This humbler title would not be likely to be assumed by one who wished to pass himself off as an Apostle; all the less so, because no Apostolic writing in N. T. begins with this appellation, except the Epistles in question. Therefore these Epistles are not like the work of a forger imitating S. John in order to be taken for S. John. On the other hand an ordinary Presbyter or Elder, writing in his own person without any wish to mislead, would hardly style himself '*The* Elder.' 'John the Elder,' if he ever existed, would have given his name. Had he been so important a person as to be able to style himself 'The Elder,' we should find clearer traces of him in history. Assume, however, that S. John wrote the Epistles, and the title seems to be very appropriate. The oldest member of the Christian Church and the last surviving Apostle might well be called, and call himself, with simple dignity, 'The Elder.' " Nothing is more welcome to persons of simple character who are in high office than an opportunity of laying its formalities aside ; they like to address others and to be themselves addressed in their personal capacity, or by a title in which there is more affection than form...Just as we might speak of some one person as 'the

Vicar,' or 'the Colonel,' as if there were no one else in the world who held those offices, so St John was known in the family to which he writes by the affectionately familiar title of 'the Presbyter'" (Liddon).

The following table will help us to judge whether the similarities between the four writings are not most naturally and reasonably explained by accepting the primitive (though not universal) tradition, that all four proceeded from one and the same author.

Gospel and First Epistle.	Second Epistle.	Third Epistle.
1 John iii. 18. Let us not love in word, neither in tongue, but in deed and truth. John viii. 31. If ye abide in My word... ye shall know the truth.	1. The Elder unto the elect lady...whom I love in truth: and not I only, but also all they that know the truth.	1. The Elder unto Gaius the beloved, whom I love in truth.
x. 18. This commandment received I from My Father. 1 John iv. 21. This commandment have we from Him.	4. I rejoiced greatly that I have found of thy children walking in truth, even as we received commandment from the Father.	3. I rejoiced greatly when brethren came and bare witness unto thy truth, even as thou walkest in truth.
ii. 7. No new commandment write I unto you, but an old commandment which ye had from the beginning. John xiii. 34. A new commandment I give unto you, that ye love one another.	5. And now I beseech thee, lady, not as though I wrote to thee a new commandment, but that which we had from the beginning, that we love one another.	
xiv. 21. He that hath My commandments,	6. And this is love, that we should walk	

Gospel and First Epistle.	Second Epistle.	Third Epistle.
and keepeth them, he it is that loveth Me. 1 John v. 3. This is the love of God, that we keep His commandments. ii. 24. Let that abide in you which ye heard from the beginning.	after His commandments. This is the commandment, even as ye heard from the beginning, that ye should walk in it.	
iv. 1—3. Many false prophets are gone out into the world. Hereby know ye the Spirit of God: every spirit which confesseth that Jesus Christ is come in the flesh is of God: and every spirit which confesseth not Jesus is not of God: and this is the spirit of the Antichrist.	7. For many deceivers are gone forth into the world, even they that confess not that Jesus Christ cometh in the flesh. This is the deceiver and the Antichrist.	
ii. 23. Whosoever denieth the Son, the same hath not the Father: he that confesseth the Son hath the Father also.	9. Whosoever goeth onward and abideth not in the doctrine of Christ, hath not God: he that abideth in the doctrine, the same hath both the Father and the Son.	
ii. 29. Every one that doeth righteousness is begotten of Him. iii. 6. Whosoever sinneth hath not seen Him, neither knoweth Him.		11. He that doeth good is of God: he that doeth evil hath not seen God.

INTRODUCTION.

Gospel and First Epistle.	Second Epistle.	Third Epistle.
John xxi. 24. This is the disciple which beareth witness of these things : and we know that his witness is true.		12. Yea, we also bear witness ; and thou knowest that our witness is true.
xv. 11. That your joy may be fulfilled. 1 John i. 4. That our joy may be fulfilled.	12, 13. Having many things to write unto you, I would not write them with paper and ink: but I hope to come unto you, and to speak face to face that your joy may be fulfilled. The children of thine elect sister salute thee.	13, 14. I had many things to write unto thee, but I am unwilling to write them to thee with ink and pen : but I hope shortly to see thee, and we shall speak face to face. Peace be unto thee. The friends salute thee. Salute the friends by name.

The brevity and comparative unimportance of the two letters is another point in favour of their Apostolicity. "Under such intimate personal relations forgery is out of the question" (Reuss). What motive could there be for attempting to pass such letters off as the work of an Apostle? Those were not days in which the excitement of duping the literary world would induce anyone to make the experiment. Some years ago the present writer was disposed to think the authorship of these two Epistles very doubtful. Further study has led him to believe that the balance of probability is very greatly in favour of their being the writings, and probably the last writings, of the Apostle S. John.

ii. *The Person or Persons addressed.*

It seems to be impossible to determine with anything like certainty whether the Second Epistle is addressed to *a com-*

munity, i.e. a particular Church, or the Church at large, or to *an individual,* i.e. some lady personally known to the Apostle.

In favour of the former hypothesis it is argued as follows : "There is no individual reference to one person ; on the contrary, the children 'walk in truth' ; mutual love is enjoined ; there is an admonition, 'look to yourselves'; and 'the bringing of doctrine' is mentioned. Besides, it is improbable that 'the children of an elect sister' would send a greeting by the writer to an 'elect Kyria and her children.' A sister Church might naturally salute another" (Davidson).

In favour of the latter hypothesis : "There is no sufficient reason for supposing that by 'elect lady' St John is personifying a particular Christian Church. He is writing to an actual individual...She was an elderly person, probably a widow, living with her grown-up children. When St John says that she was loved by 'all them that knew the truth,' he makes it plain that her name was at least well known in the Asiatic Churches, and that she was a person of real and high excellence. There were many such good women in the Apostolic age" (Liddon).

A very great deal will depend upon the translation of the opening words (ἐκλεκτῇ κυρίᾳ), which may mean : (1) *To the elect lady:* (2) *To an elect lady;* (3) *To the elect Kyria;* (4) *To the lady Electa;* (5) *To Electa Kyria.* The first two renderings leave the question respecting a community or an individual open : the last three close it in favour of an individual. But the fourth rendering, though supported by the Latin translation of some fragments of Clement of Alexandria (see p. lxviii), is untenable on account of *v.* 13. It is incredible that there were *two sisters* each bearing the very unusual name of Electa. The name is possible (for Electus occurs as a man's name, e.g. the chamberlain of Commodus), but it has not been found. The third rendering is more admissible, and S. Athanasius seems to have adopted it. The proper name Kyria occurs in ancient documents : Lücke quotes examples. Like Martha in Hebrew, it is the feminine of the common word for 'Lord'; and some have conjectured that the letter is addressed to Martha of Bethany. But, had Kyria been a proper name, S. John would probably (though not necessarily) have written Κυρίᾳ τῇ ἐκλεκτῇ like Γαίῳ τῷ ἀγαπητῷ. Moreover, to insist on this third rendering is to assume as certain two things which are uncertain: (1) That the letter is addressed to an individual; (2) that the individual's name was Kyria. These two objections apply to the fifth rendering also. Besides which, the combination of two uncommon names is improbable. We therefore fall back upon one of the first two renderings; and of the two the first seems preferable. The omission of the Greek definite article is quite intelligible, and may be compared with ΑΓΝΩΣΤΩ ΘΕΩ in Acts xvii. 23, which may quite correctly be rendered, 'To *the* unknown God,' in spite of the absence of the article in the original. "The delicate suppression of the individual name in a letter which might probably be read aloud in the Christian assembly is perfectly explicable" (Farrar).

That 'the elect lady' *may* be a figurative name for a Church, or for *the* Church, must at once be admitted: and perhaps we may go further and say that such a figure would not be unlikely in the case of a writer so fond of symbolism as S. John. But is a sustained allegory of this kind likely in the case of so slight a letter? Is not the form of the First Epistle against it! Is there any parallel case in the literature of the first three centuries? And if 'the elect lady' be the Church universal, as Jerome suggests, what possible meaning is to be found for the elect lady's *sister?* The common sense canon, that where the literal meaning makes good sense the literal meaning is right, seems applicable here. No one doubts that the twin Epistle is addressed to an individual. *In letters so similar it is scarcely probable that in the one case the person addressed is to be taken literally, while in the other the person addressed is to be taken as the allegorical representative of a Church.* It seems more reasonable to suppose that in both Epistles, as in the Epistle to Philemon, we have precious specimens of the private correspondence of an Apostle. We are allowed to see how the beloved Disciple at the close of his life could write to a Christian lady and to a Christian gentleman respecting their personal conduct.

Adopting, therefore, the literal interpretation as not only

tenable but probable, we must be content to remain in ignorance who 'the elect lady' is. That she is Mary the Mother of the Lord is not merely a gratuitous but an incredible conjecture. The Mother of the Lord, during S. John's later years, would be from a hundred and twenty to a hundred and forty years old. But it is not impossible that 'the elect lady' may be one who helped, if not to fill the place of the Virgin Mother, at any rate "to brighten with human affection the later years of the aged Saint, who had thus outlived all his contemporaries."

iii. *Place, Date and Contents.*

We can do no more than frame probable hypotheses with regard to place and date. The Epistle itself gives us vague outlines; and these outlines are all that is certain. But it will give reality and life to the letter if we fill in these outlines with details which may be true, which are probably like the truth, and which though confessedly conjectural make the drift of the letter more intelligible.

The Apostle, towards the close of his life—for the letter presupposes both Gospel and First Epistle—has been engaged upon his usual work of supervision and direction among the Churches of Asia. In the course of it he has seen some children of the lady to whom the letter is addressed, and has found that they are living Christian lives, steadfast in the faith. But there are other members of her family of whom this cannot be said. And on his return to Ephesus the Apostle, in expressing his joy respecting the faithful children, conveys a warning respecting their less steadfast brothers. 'Has their mother been as watchful as she might have been to keep them from pernicious influences? Her hospitality must be exercised with discretion; for her guests may contaminate her household. There is no real progress in advancing beyond the limits of Christian truth. There is no real charity in helping workers of evil to work successfully. On his next Apostolic journey he hopes to see her.' Near the Apostle's abode are some nephews of the lady addressed, but their mother, her sister, is dead, or is living elsewhere. These nephews send their greeting in his letter, and thus shew that they share his loving anxiety respecting the elect lady's household. It was very possibly from them that he had heard that all was not well there.

The letter may be subdivided thus :

    1—3. **Address and Greeting.**
    4—11. **Main Body of the Epistle.**
        1. Occasion of the Letter (4).
        2. Exhortation to Love and Obedience (5, 6).
        3. Warnings against False Doctrine (7—9).
        4. Warnings against False Charity (10, 11).
  12, 13. **Conclusion.**

CHAPTER IV.

The Third Epistle.

In this we have another sample of the private correspondence of an Apostle. For beyond all question, whatever we may think of the Second Epistle, this letter is addressed to an individual. And it is not an official letter, like the Epistles to Timothy and Titus, but a private one, like that to Philemon. While the Second Epistle is mainly one of warning, the Third is one of encouragement. As in the former case, we are conscious of the writer's authority in the tone of the letter ; which, however, is friendly rather than official.

i. *The Authorship of the Epistle.*

On this point very little need be added to what has been said respecting the authorship of the Second Epistle. The two Epistles are universally admitted to be by one and the same person. But it must be pointed out that, if the Second Epistle did not exist, the claims of the Third to be Apostolic would be more disputable. Neither the external nor the internal evidence is so strongly in its favour. It is neither quoted nor mentioned so early or so frequently as the Second. It is not nearly so closely akin to the First Epistle and the Gospel. It labours under the difficulty involved in the conduct of Diotrephes : for it must be admitted that "there is something astonishing in the notion that the prominent Christian Presbyter of an Asiatic Church should not only repudiate the authority of St John, and not only refuse to receive his travelling missionary, and prevent others from doing so, but should even excommunicate or try to excommunicate those who did so" (Farrar). Nevertheless, it is impossible to separate these two twin letters, and assign them to different authors. And, as has been seen already, the balance of evidence, both external and internal, strongly favours the Apostolicity of the Second ; and this, notwithstanding the difficulty about Diotrephes, carries with it the Apostolicity of the Third. That difficulty only forces on us once more the conviction that the Church in the Apostolic age was not, any more than in our age, an untroubled community of saints. The ideal primitive Church, bright in the unbroken possession of truth and holiness, is unknown to the historian. The First and Second Epistles of St John tell us of gross corruptions in doctrine and practice. The Third tells of open rebellion against an Apostle's commands.

ii. *The Person addressed.*

The name Gaius was so common throughout the Roman Empire that to identify any person of this name with any other of the same name requires specially clear evidence. In N.T. there are probably at least three Christians who are thus called. 1. *Gaius of Corinth*, in whose house S. Paul was staying when he wrote the Epistle to the Romans (Rom. xvi. 23), who is probably the same as he whom S. Paul baptized (1 Cor. i. 14). 2. *Gaius of Macedonia*, who was S. Paul's travelling companion at the time of the uproar at Ephesus, and was seized by the mob (Acts xix. 29). 3. *Gaius of Derbe*, who with Timothy and others left Greece before S. Paul and waited for him at Troas (Acts xx. 4, 5). But these three may be reduced to two, for 1 and 3 may possibly be the same person. It is possible, but nothing more, that the Gaius of our Epistle may be one of these.

Origen says that the first of these three became Bishop of Thessalonica. The Apostolical Constitutions (vii. 46) mention a Gaius, Bishop of Pergamos, and the context implies that he was the first Bishop, or at least one of the earliest Bishops, of that city. Here again we can only say that he may be the Gaius of S. John. The Epistle leaves us in doubt whether Gaius is at this time a Presbyter or not. Apparently he is a well-to-do layman.

iii. *Place, Date, and Contents.*

The place may with probability be supposed to be Ephesus: the letter has the tone of being written from head-quarters. Its strong resemblance, especially in its opening and conclusion, inclines us to believe that it was written about the same time as the Second Epistle, i.e. after the Gospel and First Epistle, and therefore towards the end of S. John's life. The unwillingness to write a long letter which appears in both Epistles (*vv.* 12, 13) would be natural in an old man to whom correspondence is a burden.

The contents speak for themselves. Gaius is commended for his hospitality, in which he resembles his namesake of Corinth (Rom. xvi. 23); is warned against imitating the factious and intolerant Diotrephes; and in contrast to him is told of the excellence of Demetrius, who is perhaps the bearer of the letter. These two opposite characters are sketched "in a few words with the same masterly psychological skill which we see in the Gospel." In his next Apostolic journey S. John hopes to visit him. Meanwhile he and 'the friends' with him send a salutation to Gaius and 'the friends' with him.

The Epistle may be thus analysed.

1. **Address.**
2—12. **Main Body of the Epistle.**
    1. Personal Good Wishes and Sentiments (2—4).
    2. Gaius commended for his Hospitality (5—8).
    3. Diotrephes condemned for his Hostility (9, 10).
    4. The Moral (11, 12).
13, 14. **Conclusion.**

"The Second and Third Epistles of S. John occupy their own place in the sacred Canon, and contribute their own peculiar element to the stock of Christian truth and practice. They lead us from the region of miracle and prophecy, out of an atmosphere charged with the supernatural, to the more average every-day life of Christendom, with its regular paths and unexciting air. There is no hint in these short notes of extraordinary *charismata*. The tone of their Christianity is deep, earnest, severe, devout, but has the quiet of the Christian Church and home very much as at present constituted. The religion which pervades them is simple, unexaggerated, and practical. The writer is grave and reserved. Evidently in the possession of the fulness of the Christian faith, he is content to rest upon it with a calm consciousness of strength....By the conception of the Incarnate Lord, the Creator and Light of all men, and of the universality of Redemption, which the Gospel and the First Epistle did so much to bring home to all who received Christ, germs were deposited in the soil of Christianity which necessarily grew from an abstract idea into the great reality of the Catholic Church. In these two short occasional letters S. John provided two safeguards for that great institution. Heresy and schism are the dangers to which it is perpetually exposed. S. John's condemnation of the spirit of *heresy* is recorded in the Second Epistle; his condemnation of the spirit of *schism* is written in the Third Epistle. Every age of Christendom up to the present has rather exaggerated than dwarfed the significance of this condemnation" (Bishop Alexander).

CHAPTER V.

THE TEXT OF THE EPISTLES.

i. *The Greek Text.*

OUR authorities for determining the Greek which S. John wrote, though far less numerous than in the case of the Gospel, are various and abundant. They consist of Greek MSS., Ancient lxxxii *INTRODUCTION.*

Versions, and quotations from the Epistles in Christian writers of the second, third and fourth centuries. The Apostolic autographs were evidently lost at a very early date. Irenaeus, in arguing as to the true reading of the mystical number in Rev. xiii. 18, cannot appeal to S. John's own MS., which would have been decisive (*Haer.* v. xxx. 1); and Origen knew no older copy of S. John's Gospel than that of Heracleon. Papyrus is very perishable, and this was the material commonly employed (2 John 12: comp. 2 Tim. iv. 13).

It will be worth while to specify a few of the principal MSS. and Versions which contain these Epistles or portions of them.

Greek Manuscripts.

Primary Uncials.

CODEX SINAITICUS (ℵ). 4th century. Discovered by Tischendorf in 1859 at the monastery of S. Catherine on Mount Sinai, and now at Petersburg. All three Epistles.

CODEX ALEXANDRINUS (A). 5th century. Brought by Cyril Lucar, Patriarch of Constantinople, from Alexandria, and afterwards presented by him to Charles I. in 1628. In the British Museum. All three Epistles.

CODEX VATICANUS (B). 4th century. Brought to Rome about 1460. It is entered in the earliest catalogue of the Vatican Library, 1475. All three Epistles.

CODEX EPHRAEMI (C). 5th century. A palimpsest: the original writing has been partially rubbed out and the works of Ephraem the Syrian have been written over it. In the National Library at Paris. Part of the First and Third Epistles; 1 John i. 1—iv. 2; 3 John 3—15. Of the whole N. T. the only Books entirely missing are 2 John and 2 Thessalonians.

The fifth great Uncial, Codex Bezae (D), has lost the leaves in which all three Epistles were undoubtedly contained. Only the servile Latin translation of 3 John 11—15 remains.

Secondary Uncials.

CODEX MOSQUENSIS (K). 9th century. All three Epistles.
CODEX ANGELICUS (L). 9th century. All three Epistles.

CODEX PORPHYRIANUS (P). 9th century. A palimpsest. All three Epistles excepting 1 John iii. 19—v. 1. There is a fac-simile of a portion in Hammond's *Outlines of Textual Criticism* showing the late leaning uncial letters of the 9th century (Acts iv. 10—15), with cursives of the 13th (Heb. vii. 17—25) written over them.

Besides these four primary and three secondary Uncial MSS., more than two hundred Cursives contain the Epistles. These range from the 10th to the 15th centuries, and are of every degree of value, from the excellent Codex Colbert (13, or 33 in the Gospels) of the 11th century, and Codex Leicestrensis (31, or 69 in the Gospels) of the 14th century, to the worthless Codex Mont-fortianus (34, or 61 in the Gospels), of the 15th or 16th century, famous as the "Codex Britannicus" which induced Erasmus, in consequence of his unfortunate promise to yield to the evidence of a single Greek Codex, to insert the spurious text about the Heavenly Witnesses into his third edition (A.D. 1522).

But it cannot be too carefully remembered that the date of a document is a very different thing from the date of the text which it contains. Obviously the text must be at least as old as the document which contains it. But it may be centuries older, or it may be only a few years older. Comparison with readings in the Fathers of the second, third, and fourth centuries proves that while Codex B and Codex א are of the fourth century, yet they represent a text which can be traced to the second, whereas Codex A, which is of the fifth century, represents a text which is no older than the fourth, at any rate as regards the Gospels. The scribe of A had evidently purer texts to copy when he transcribed the Epistles. We might arrange these witnesses roughly as follows.

Text of B, early and very pure.

Text of א, early, but somewhat mixed.

Text of A in the Epistles, fairly early, but mixed.

Text of A in the Gospels, late and very mixed.

Ancient Versions.

VULGATE SYRIAC. (Peschito='simple' meaning perhaps 'faithful'). 3rd century. The First Epistle.

PHILOXENIAN SYRIAC. "Probably the most servile version of Scripture ever made." 6th century. All three Epistles.

OLD LATIN. 2nd century. Nearly the whole of an Old Latin text of 1 John i. 1—v. 3 can be constructed from Augustine's Homilies on the Epistle: but Augustine's text is of a mixed character, somewhat remote from the original. Another Old Latin text of 1 John iii. 8—v. 21 exists in a Munich MS. of the 7th century (Scrivener, 339, 346). See W. and H. small ed., 1885, p. 571.

VULGATE LATIN (mainly the Old Latin revised by Jerome, A.D. 383—385). All three Epistles.

THEBAIC or SAHIDIC (Egyptian). 3rd century. All three Epistles.

MEMPHITIC or BAHIRIC (Egyptian, but independent of the Thebaic). Most of it 3rd century. All three Epistles.

ARMENIAN. 5th century. All three Epistles.

AETHIOPIC. 4th or 5th century. All three Epistles.

To these Greek MSS. and ancient Versions must be added the evidence of the *Fathers* who comment upon or quote these Epistles. The Greek commentaries of Clement of Alexandria, of Didymus, and of Diodorus of Tarsus, are unhappily lost: but portions of the two former survive in translations. Considerable quotations, however, especially from the First Epistle, exist in various Greek and Latin writers from the second to the fourth centuries. Quotations by writers later than the fourth century are of little value. By that time the corruption of the text was complete. The Diocletian persecution had caused the destruction of most of the ancient MSS., and a composite text, formed with very imperfect knowledge, and emanating mainly from Constantinople, gradually took their place.

In examining the text of S. John's Epistles, which is more free from corruption than perhaps that of any other book in N.T., the great excellence of the text found in B is again conspicuous[1]. There are very few cases in which it gives an unquestionably corrupt reading. And this is the test of excellence in a witness :—To what extent does it give evidence which is obviously false? Tried by this test B stands easily first, and ℵ second, though considerably behind B. Codex A, though inferior to the other two, is found to give a purer text here than in the Gospels. A few of the indefensible readings in each of these three great authorities are worth noting.

False readings in B.

1 John i. 2.   ὃ ἑοράκαμεν for ἑωράκαμεν.
    ii. 14.   τὸ ἀπ᾽ ἀρχῆς for τὸν ἀπ᾽ ἀρχῆς.
    ii. 27.   χάρισμα for χρῖσμα.
3 John 9.   ἔγραψας for ἔγραψα.

False readings in ℵ.

1 John ii. 4.   ἡ ἀλήθεια τοῦ Θεοῦ οὐκ ἔστιν for ἐν τούτῳ ἡ ἀλήθεια οὐκ ἔστιν.
    ii. 9.   ψεύστης ἐστὶν καὶ ἐν τῇ σκοτίᾳ ἐστίν for ἐν τῇ σκοτίᾳ ἐστίν.
    iii. 5.   οἴδαμεν for οἴδατε.
    iii. 14.   μεταβέβηκεν for μεταβεβήκαμεν.

[1] See Introduction to S. John's Gospel lvi.—lviii. "We accord to Codex B *at least* as much weight as to *any single document in existence.*"—"Cod. B is a document of such value, that it grows by experience *even upon those who may have been a little prejudiced against it.*"—"Notice especially those instances in the Catholic Epistles, wherein the primary authorities are comparatively few, in which Cod. B accords with the later copies against Codd. ℵAC, and is supported by internal evidence; e.g. 1 Pet. iii. 18; iv. 14; v. 2; 2 Pet. ii. 20; 1 John ii. 10; iii. 23, &c. In 1 John iii. 21, where the first ἡμῶν is omitted by A and others, the second by C almost alone, B seems right in rejecting the word in both places. So in other cases *internal probabilities occasionally plead strongly in favour of* B, *when it has little other support.*" Those who have followed recent controversy on the subject will find the above remarks all the more interesting when they know that they are taken, not from Westcott, or Westcott and Hort, or the Revisers, or Dr Sanday, but from Dr Scrivener's latest edition of the *Introduction to the Criticism of N. T.* (1883), pp. 116, 552 and note. The italics are not Dr Scrivener's.

1 John iii. 21. ἀδελφοί for ἀγαπητοί.

    iv. 10. ἡ ἀγάπη τοῦ Θεοῦ for ἡ ἀγάπη.

          ἠγάπησεν (ℵ¹) for ἠγαπήσαμεν (ℵ³).

    iv. 17. μεθ' ἡμῶν ἐν ἡμῖν for μεθ' ἡμῶν.

          ἔχομεν for ἔχωμεν.

          τῇ ἀγάπῃ τῆς κρίσεως for τῇ ἡμέρᾳ τῆς κρίσεως.

          ἐσόμεθα for ἐσμέν.

2 John 4. ἔλαβον for ἐλάβομεν.

3 John 8. τῇ ἐκκλησίᾳ for τῇ ἀληθείᾳ.

False readings in A.

1 John i. 6. ἐὰν γὰρ εἴπωμεν for ἐὰν εἴπωμεν.

    ii. 8. ἡ σκιά for ἡ σκοτία.

    ii. 27. τὸ αὐτὸ χρῖσμα for τὸ αὐτοῦ χρῖσμα.

          καθὼς ἐδίδαξεν for καὶ καθὼς ἐδίδαξεν.

    iv. 7. ὁ ἀγαπῶν τὸν Θεόν for ὁ ἀγαπῶν.

    iv. 8. οὐ γινώσκει for οὐκ ἔγνω.

    iv. 10. ἐκεῖνος for αὐτός.

    v. 6. πνεύματι for αἵματι.

    v. 14. ὄνομα for θέλημα.

2 John 3. omits ἔσται μεθ' ἡμῶν.

In a good many of its peculiar readings A is supported by the Vulgate. This fact is significant. "By a curious and apparently unnoticed coincidence the text of A in several books agrees with the Latin Vulgate in so many peculiar readings devoid of Old Latin attestation, as to leave little doubt that a Greek MS. largely employed by Jerome in his revision of the Latin Version must have had to a great extent a common original with A. Apart from this individual affinity, A both in the Gospels and elsewhere may serve as a fair example of MSS. that, to judge by patristic quotations, were commonest in the fourth century" (Westcott and Hort, II. 152).

False readings in which A *unites with the Vulgate.*

1 John iv. 19. ἡμεῖς οὖν ἀγαπῶμεν τὸν Θεόν, ὅτι ὁ Θεός for ἡμεῖς
          ἀγαπῶμεν, ὅτι αὐτός.

    iv. 21. ἔχομεν ἀπὸ τοῦ Θεοῦ for ἔχομεν ἀπ' αὐτοῦ.

1 John v. 10. τὴν μαρτυρίαν τοῦ Θεοῦ for τὴν μαρτυρίαν.
τῷ υἱῷ for τῷ Θεῷ.

v. 20. τὸν ἀληθινὸν Θεόν for τὸν ἀληθινόν.
omits Ἰησοῦ Χριστῷ.

2 John 9. τὸν υἱὸν καὶ τὸν πατέρα for τὸν πατέρα καὶ τὸν υἱόν.

In Westcott's *Epistles of St John* much more complete lists are
given; and from them nearly all of these instances have been
taken. But these suffice as examples. In all of them the
balance of evidence is conclusive against the rejected reading;
and in most cases it is much easier to understand how the
reading of B became corrupted into that of ℵ, or of A, or of C, than
the converse process would be. *That reading is most likely to be
original which best explains the origin of the other readings.*

The superiority of B may be exhibited in another way from
the text of these Epistles. As we have seen, B is *occasionally* in
error when it stands *alone* among the primary authorities. *It is
very rarely in error when it is united with any one of them.* It
would be difficult to find a reading supported by ℵB, or AB, or
BC, or even BP, or B with any Version, which is certainly false.
In the following instances the original text seems to have been
preserved by B and some one other authority : 1 John ii. 14, 20
(B, Thebaic); iii. 21 (AB, BC); iv. 12 (ℵB); iv. 15 (B, Armenian);
v. 13 (ℵB). The other three Uncials not unfrequently go wrong
in pairs, and sometimes all three of them go wrong together :
e.g. 1 John iii. 21; v. 6; 2 John 6, 12 (ℵA):—i. 9; ii. 6; iii. 5, 11,
13, 19, 21 (ℵC):—i. 4; ii. 15; iii. 7, 10 (AC):—ii. 5 and possibly
ii. 10; ii. 29; iii. 23 (ℵAC). Various instances have been given
above in which A and the Vulgate are both at fault. In the
following passages ℵ is in error in company with one or more
Versions: ii. 4, 9, 24, 26, 27; iii. 18, 24; iv. 3, 19; 3 John 3.
And almost as often (making allowance for what is missing) C
goes wrong with the support of one or more Versions:—i. 5;
3 John 4, 6, 10, 12.

In the two instances of *conflate readings* which these Epistles
supply, ℵB are among those authorities which preserve the original
text.

1 John ii. 15.   ἡ ἀγάπη τοῦ πατρός (אB, and Versions).

   ἡ ἀγάπη τοῦ Θεοῦ (AC).

   ἡ ἀγάπη τοῦ Θεοῦ καὶ πατρός.

3 John 12.   ὑπὸ αὐτῆς τῆς ἀληθείας (אB and Versions).

   ὑπὸ αὐτῆς τῆς ἐκκλησίας (A¹?).

   ὑπὸ αὐτ. τ. ἐκκλησίας καὶ ἀληθείας (C).

Only one case of *omission through homoeoteleuton* occurs in B, and there the omitted words are inserted in the margin, perhaps by the original scribe.

1 John iv. 21.   [τὸν Θεὸν ἀγαπᾷ καὶ] τὸν κ.τ.λ. (A¹B¹).

Other instances of *homoeoteleuton* are

ii. 27, 28.   ἐν αὐτῷ [καὶ νῦν τεκνία, μένετε ἐν αὐτῷ,] ἵνα κ.τ.λ. (א).

iv. 6.   ἀκούει ἡμῶν· [ὃς οὐκ ἔστιν ἐκ τοῦ Θεοῦ οὐκ ἀκούει ἡμῶν.] ἐκ or ἐν κ.τ.λ. (AL).

iv. 7, 8.   τὸν Θεόν. [ὁ μὴ ἀγαπῶν οὐκ ἔγνω τὸν Θεόν,] ὅτι κ.τ.λ. (א¹)

v. 2, 3.   τὰς ἐντολὰς αὐτοῦ [ποιῶμεν. αὕτη γάρ ἐστιν ἡ ἀγάπη τοῦ Θεοῦ, ἵνα τὰς ἐντολὰς αὐτοῦ] τηρῶμεν. (A)

v. 14, 15.   ακούει ἡμῶν. [καὶ ἐὰν οἴδαμεν ὅτι ἀκούει ἡμῶν] ὃ ἂν κ.τ.λ. (א¹A)

One important omission through *homoeoteleuton* has found its way into the *Textus Receptus* and thence into A. V., where the translation of the omitted words is in italics, implying that the passage is wanting in the original. The italics come from the Great Bible of 1539. But the passage is in all the primary Uncials and Versions.

ii. 23.   τὸν πατέρα ἔχει· [ὁ ὁμολογῶν τὸν υἱὸν καὶ τὸν πατέρα ἔχει.] ὑμεῖς κ.τ.λ.   (KL)

Thus out of seven cases of omission through *homoeoteleuton* only one is found in B, while א and A each admit four. And though frequent cases of omission through this cause prove nothing as to the purity of the text, they do prove something as to the accuracy of the scribe. The scribe of B was evidently a more careful worker than the scribes of א and A.

Whatever reasonable test we select, the preeminence of B as an authority becomes conspicuous: but the superiority of ℵ to A is not nearly so apparent as in the Gospels, where the scribe of A must have used inferior copies. The absence of C in so much of the First Epistle (iv. 2 to the end) and the whole of the Second makes comparison less easy: but "the peculiar readings of C have no appearance of genuineness" (Westcott).

From the notes on the text at the head of the notes on each chapter the student may collect many more instances, all tending to show that where the *Textus Receptus* needs revision (1) B is almost always among the authorities which preserve the original reading, and that (2) the combination ℵB is practically conclusive —at any rate in these Epistles: e.g. 1 John v. 13. The *apparatus criticus* in Alford will supply facts for still further inductions. Any analysis of the evidence supplied there will lead to the conclusion that B is a preeminently trustworthy witness.

In conclusion it may be worth while to repeat a caution already given in the volume on S. John's Gospel. The sight of a large collection of various readings is apt to produce a very erroneous impression. It may lead to very exaggerated ideas as to the amount of uncertainty which exists with regard to the Greek text of N. T. "If comparative trivialities, such as changes of order, the insertion or omission of the article with proper names, and the like, are set aside, the words in our opinion still subject to doubt *can hardly amount to more than* A THOUSANDTH PART of the N. T." (Westcott and Hort, *The N. T. in Greek*, Macmillan, 1881, I. p. 561). Every student of the Greek Testament who can afford the time should study the work just quoted. Those who cannot, should at least read the Appendix to the small edition in one volume, Macmillan, 1885. Schaff's *Companion to the Greek Testament and the English Versions*, Harper, New York, 1883, will by many readers be found more useful than the larger edition of Westcott and Hort. Hammond's *Outlines of Textual Criticism*, Clarendon Press, is a clear, interesting and inexpensive manual. Scrivener's *Introduction to the Criticism of N. T.* contains an immense store of information not easily accessible elsewhere. The latest edition (1883) is somewhat disappointing in being not quite up to date in its statement of facts : and the conclusions drawn from the facts are in some cases to be accepted with caution.

ii. *The English Versions.*

The earliest translation of the N. T. into English of which we have any knowledge is the translation of the Gospel of S. John made by the VENERABLE BEDE, in completing which he died (A. D. 735). It must have been almost the earliest piece of prose literature written in the English language. Unfortunately it has long since disappeared; and two or more centuries elapsed before anything of the same kind which has come down to us was attempted[1]. WICLIF began his work of translating the Scriptures into the vulgar tongue with parts of the Apocalypse. So that for a second time in history S. John was the first N. T. writer made known to the English people. In the *Last Age of the Church* (A.D. 1356) there is a translation and explanation of the portion of the Revelation which Wiclif believed to be applicable to his own age. Whether Wiclif completed his translation of the Apocalypse at this time or not seems to be uncertain. A version of the Gospels with a commentary was given next; and then the rest of the N. T. A complete N. T. in English was finished about 1380. This, therefore, we may take as the date at which our Epistle first appeared in the English language. While the O. T. of Wiclif's Bible was by various hands, the N. T. seems to have been mainly, if not entirely, the work of Wiclif himself. The whole was revised by JOHN PURVEY about 1388. Specimens of both will be found in Appendix H.

But these early English Versions, made from a late and corrupt text of the Latin Vulgate, exercised little or no influence on the later Versions of Tyndale and others, which were made

---

[1] The earliest prose translations extant are Psalms i.—l., attributed to S. Aldhelm and preserved in the National Library at Paris. The famous Lindisfarne Gospels written in Latin by Eadfrith (c. A.D. 680) have interlinear English glosses, forming a word by word translation, added by Ealdred (c. A.D. 950). They are now in the British Museum. The earliest extant version of a complete book is the Psalter of William de Schorham, who became Vicar of Chart-Sutton in Kent A. D. 1320.

from late and corrupt Greek texts. TYNDALE translated direct
from the Greek, checking himself by the Vulgate, the Latin
of Erasmus, and the German of Luther. Dr Westcott in his
most valuable work on the *History of the English Bible*, from
which the material for this section has been largely taken, often
takes the First Epistle of S. John as an illustration of the variations between different versions and editions. The present writer
gratefully borrows his statements. Tyndale published his first
edition in 1525, his second in 1534, and his third in 1535; each
time, especially in 1534 making many alterations and corrections. "Of the thirty-one changes which I have noticed in the
later (1534) version of 1 John, about a third are closer approximations to the Greek: rather more are variations in connecting
particles or the like designed to bring out the argument of the
original more clearly; three new readings are adopted; and in
one passage it appears that Luther's rendering has been substi-
tuted for an awkward paraphrase. Yet it must be remarked
that even in this revision the changes are far more frequently at
variance with Luther's renderings than in accordance with them"
(p. 185). "In his Preface to the edition of 1534, Tyndale had
expressed his readiness to revise his work and adopt any changes
in it which might be shewn to be improvements. The edition
of 1535, however enigmatic it may be in other respects, is a proof
of his sincerity. The text of this exhibits a true revision and
differs from that of 1534, though considerably less than the text
of 1534 from that of 1525. In 1 John I have noted sixteen
variations from the text of 1534 as against thirty-two (thirty-
one?) in that of 1534 from the original text" (p. 190). But for the
ordinary student the differences between the three editions of
Tyndale are less interesting than the differences between Tyndale
and the A. V. How much we owe to him appears from the fact
that "about *nine-tenths* of the A. V. of the first Epistle of S. John
are retained from Tyndale" (p. 211). Tyndale places the three
Epistles of S. John between those of S. Peter and that to the
Hebrews, S. James being placed between Hebrews and S. Jude.
This is the order of Luther's translation, of Coverdale's Bible
(1535), of Matthew's Bible (1537), and also of Taverner's (1539).

The GREAT BIBLE, which exists in three typical editions (Cromwell's, April, 1539; Cranmer's, April, 1540; Tunstall's and Heath's, Nov. 1540) is in the N. T. "based upon a careful use of the Vulgate and of Erasmus' Latin Version. An analysis of the variations in the first Epistle of S. John may furnish a type of its general character. As nearly as I can reckon there are seventy-one differences between Tyndale's text (1534) and that of the Great Bible: of these forty-three come directly from Coverdale's earlier revision (and in a great measure indirectly from the Latin): seventeen from the Vulgate where Coverdale before had not followed it: the remaining eleven variations are from other sources. Some of the new readings from the Vulgate are important, as for example the additions in i. 4, 'that *ye may rejoice and that* your joy may be full.' ii. 23, '*he that knowledgeth the Son hath the Father also.*' iii. 1, 'that we should be called *and be indeed* the sons of God.' v. 9, 'this is the witness of God *that is greater.*' All these editions (like v. 7) are marked distinctly as *Latin* readings: of the renderings adopted from Coverdale one is very important and holds its place in our present version. iii. 24, '*Hereby* we know that *he* abideth in us, *even by* the Spirit which he *hath given* us,' for which Tyndale reads: '*thereby* we know that *there* abideth in us *of* the Spirit which he *gave* us.' One strange blunder also is corrected; 'that old commandment which ye *heard*' (as it was in the earlier text) is replaced by the true reading: 'that old commandment which ye have *had*' (ii. 7). No one of the new renderings is of any moment" (pp. 257, 258).

The revision made by TAVERNER, though superficial as regards the O. T., has important alterations in the N. T. He shews an improved appreciation of the Greek article. "Two consecutive verses of the first Epistle of S. John furnish good examples of his endeavour to find English equivalents for the terms before him. All the other versions adopt the Latin '*advocate*' in 1 John ii. 1, for which Taverner substitutes the Saxon '*spokesman.*' Tyndale, followed by Coverdale, the Great Bible, &c. strives after an adequate rendering of ἱλασμός (1 John ii. 2) in the awkward periphrasis 'he *it is that obtaineth grace* for our sins: Taverner boldly coins a word which if insufficient is yet worthy of notice: 'he is *a mercystock* for our sins'" (p. 271).

The history of the GENEVA N. T. "is little more than the record of the application of Beza's translation and commentary to Tyndale's Testament......An analysis of the changes in one short Epistle will render this plain. Thus according to as accurate a calculation as I can make more than two-thirds of the new renderings in 1 John introduced into the revision of 1560 are derived from Beza, and two-thirds of these then for the first time. The rest are due to the revisers themselves, and of these only two are found in the revision of 1557" (pp. 287, 288).

The RHEMISH BIBLE, like Wiclif's, is a translation of a translation, being based upon the Vulgate. It furnished the revisers of 1611 with a great many of the words of Latin origin which they employ. It is "simply the ordinary, and not pure, Latin text of Jerome in an English dress. Its merits, and they are considerable, lie in its vocabulary. The style, so far as it has a style, is unnatural, the phrasing is most unrhythmical, but the language is enriched by the bold reduction of innumerable Latin words to English service" (p. 328). Dr Westcott gives no examples from these Epistles, but the following may serve as such.

In a few instances the Rhemish has given to the A. V. a word not previously used in English Versions. 'And he is the *propitiation* for our sins' (ii. 2). 'And sent his son a *propitiation* for our sins' (iv. 10). 'These things have I written to you concerning them that *seduce* you' (ii. 26).

In some cases the Rhemish is superior to the A. V. '*Every one that* committeth sin, *committeth* also *iniquity: and* sin is *iniquity*' (iii. 4). The following also are worthy of notice. 'We *seduce* ourselves' (i. 8). 'Let no man *seduce* you' (ii. 6). 'Because many *seducers* are *gone out* into the world' (2 John 7).

But we may be thankful that King James's revisers did not adopt such renderings as these. 'That you also may have *society* with us, and our *society may be* with the Father and with his Son' (i. 3). 'And this is the *annuntiation*' (i. 5, iii. 11). 'That he might *dissolve* the works of the devil' (iii. 8). '*The generation* of God *preserveth* him' (v. 18). 'The *Senior* to the lady elect' (2 John 1). 'The *Senior* to Gaius the *dearest*' (3 John 1). 'Greater *thanke* have I not *of them*' (3 John 4). 'That we may be *coadjutors* of the truth' (3 John 8)[1].

This is not the place to discuss the REVISED VERSION of 1881. When it appeared the present writer had the satisfaction of finding that a very large proportion of the alterations which he had suggested in notes on S. John's Gospel in 1880 were sanctioned by alterations actually made by the Revisers. In the notes on these Epistles it will be found that in a large number of cases he has followed the R. V., of the merits of which he has a high opinion. Those merits seem to consist not so much in skilful and happy treatment of very difficult passages as in careful correction of an enormous number of small errors and inaccuracies. Of the Revisers, even their most severe and most unreasonable critic has said, "that their work bears mark of conscientious labour which those only can fully appreciate who have made the same province of study to some extent their own." The late Dr Routh of Magdalen College, Oxford, when asked what he considered to be the best commentary on the N. T., is said to have replied, 'The Vulgate.' If by that he meant that in the Vulgate we have a faithful translation made from a good Greek text, we may say in a similar spirit that the best commentary on the N. T. is now the Revised Version. The A. V. is a sufficiently faithful translation of a corrupt Greek text. The R. V. is a very faithful translation of an excellent Greek text. It is in the latter particular that its great value lies. The corrections made through revision of the Greek are far more important than the corrections made through revision of the renderings. Tastes may continue to differ respecting the Revisers' merits as translators. Scientific criticism will in the large majority of cases confirm their decisions as to the Greek to be trans-

---

[1] For further information respecting early English Versions see Scrivener's *Cambridge Paragraph Bible*, 1873; Eadie's *The English Bible: an External and Critical History*, 1876; Stevens' *The Bibles in the Caxton Exhibition*, 1878; and the article on the 'English Bible' in *Encyclopædia Britannica* VIII., 1878.

lated. The rules laid down for determining the text in the *Cambridge Greek Testament* have resulted in producing a text very similar to that of the Revisers. Out of about seventy-three corrections made by them in these Epistles all but four or five are adopted in this edition: and in these four or five cases and a few more the reading must remain a little doubtful[1].

CHAPTER VI.

THE LITERATURE OF THE EPISTLES.

Although not so voluminous as that of the Gospel of S. John, the literature of the Epistles is nevertheless very abundant. It would be simply confusing to give anything approaching to an exhaustive list of the numerous works on the subject. All that will be attempted here will be to give the more advanced student some information as to where he may look for greater help than can be given in a handbook for the use of schools.

Of ancient commentaries not a very great deal remains. In his *Outlines* ('Υποτυπώσεις) CLEMENT OF ALEXANDRIA (c. A. D. 200) commented on detached verses of the First and Second Epistles, and of these comments a valuable fragment in a Latin translation is extant. DIDYMUS, who was placed by S. Athanasius in the catechetical chair of Clement at Alexandria a century and a half later (c. A.D. 360), commented on all the Catholic Epistles; and his notes as translated by Epiphanius Scholasticus survive, together with some fragments of the Greek original. Specimens of each are given by Lücke. "The chief features of his remarks on S. John's three Epistles are (1) the earnestness against Docetism, Valentinianism, all speculations injurious to the Maker of the world, (2) the assertion that a

[1] Comp. 1 John ii. 20 ; iii. 15, 19, 23 ; 2 John 8.

true knowledge of God is possible without a knowledge of His essence, (3) care to urge the necessity of combining orthodoxy with right action" (W. Bright). The commentary of DIODORUS OF TARSUS (c. A.D. 380) on the First Epistle is lost. S. CHRYSOSTOM is said to have commented on the whole of the N. T., and Oecumenius and Theophylact appeal to him in discussing the Catholic Epistles. But his commentary exists no longer. We have ten Homilies by S. AUGUSTINE on the First Epistle; but the series ends abruptly in the tenth Homily at 1 John v. 3. They are translated in the *Library of the Fathers*, vol. 29, Oxford 1849. In our own country the earliest commentary is that of the VENERABLE BEDE (c. A.D. 720), written in Latin. Like S. Augustine's, it is doctrinal and hortatory: quotations from both will be found in the notes. It is possible that we have the substance of Augustine's commentary on 1 John v. 3—21 in Bede, who elsewhere sometimes adopts Augustine *verbatim*. If so, we have further evidence that Augustine knew nothing of the spurious passage 1 John v. 7, for Bede omits it. Bede's notes on the Second and Third Epistles are very slight and are perhaps wholly his own. In the tenth and eleventh centuries we have the Greek commentaries of OECUMENIUS and THEOPHYLACT. The former is highly praised by Lücke, who quotes a good deal of it.

Of the reformers, Beza, Bullinger, Calvin, Erasmus, Luther, and Zwingli have all left commentaries on one or more of these Epistles. Besides these we have the frequently quoted works of Grotius (c. A.D. 1550), of his critic Calovius (c. A.D. 1650), and of Bengel (c. A.D. 1750). Bengel's *Gnomon N. T.* has been translated into English; but those who can read Latin will prefer the epigrammatic terseness of the original.

Among original English commentaries those of Bishop Alexander (in the Speaker's Commentary), Alford, Blunt, Jelf, Pope (in Schaff's Commentary), Sinclair (in Bishop Ellicott's Commentary), and of Bishop Chr. Wordsworth are easily accessible. But superior to all these is that of Canon Westcott, Macmillan, 1883.

Neander's work on the First Epistle has been translated by Mrs Conant, New York, 1853. The commentaries of Braune,

Ebrard, Haupt, Huther, and Lücke have been published in an English form by T. and T. Clark, Edinburgh. Of these that of Haupt on the First Epistle may be specially commended. Among untranslated foreign commentaries may be mentioned those of Düsterdieck, 1852; Rothe, 1879; C. A. Wolf, 1881: Erdmann, 1855; Luthardt, 1860; Stockmeyer, 1873. The last three are chiefly concerned with the structure of the First Epistle.

Other works which give valuable assistance are Cox's *Private Letters of S. Paul and S. John*, F. W. Farrar's *Early Days of Christianity*, several of Liddon's *Easter Sermons*, Macdonald's *Life and Writings of S. John* with Introduction by Dean Howson, F. D. Maurice's *Epistles of S. John*, Schaff's *History of the Church* vols. I. and II. (1883), Stanley's *Sermons and Essays on the Apostolic Age*, with various articles in the *Dictionary of Christian Biography* edited by Smith and Wace, in the *Religious Encyclopaedia* edited by Schaff, and in the *Real-Encyklopädie* edited by Herzog, Plitt, and Hauck.

The references to Winer's *Grammar of N. T. Greek* in this volume are from the second English edition by Moulton: those to Cremer's *Lexicon of N. T. Greek* are from the English edition by Urwick. The latter volume has by no means superseded the similar work by Archbishop Trench, *The Synonyms of the N. T.*, the references to which are from the edition of 1865.

The present writer desires to express his obligations, which in some cases are very great, to many of the works mentioned above, as well as to others. Almost all that can be said with truth about S. John's writings has already been said, and well said, by some one. The most that a new commentator can hope to do is to collect together what seems to him to be best in other writers, to think it out afresh, and recoin it for his own and others' use. What might have remained unknown, or unintelligible, or unattractive to many, if left in the original author and language, may possibly become better known and more intelligible when reduced to a smaller compass and placed in a new light and in new surroundings. Be this as it may, the writer who undertakes, even with all the helps available, to interpret S. John to others, must know that he incurs serious responsibility. He will not be anxious to be original. He will not be eager to insist upon views which have found no favour among previous workers in the same field. He will not regret that his conclusions should be questioned and his mistakes exposed. He will be content that a dirge should be sung over the results of his own work, if only what is true may prevail.

αἴλινον αἴλινον εἰπὲ, τὸ δ' εὖ νικάτω.

ΙΩΑΝΝΟΥ Α

1 ¹Ὃ ἦν ἀπ' ἀρχῆς, ὃ ἀκηκόαμεν, ὃ ἑωράκαμεν τοῖς ὀφθαλμοῖς ἡμῶν, ὃ ἐθεασάμεθα, καὶ αἱ χεῖρες ἡμῶν ἐψηλάφησαν, περὶ τοῦ λόγου τῆς ζωῆς ²(καὶ ἡ ζωὴ ἐφανερώθη, καὶ ἑωράκαμεν, καὶ μαρτυροῦμεν, καὶ ἀπαγγέλλομεν ὑμῖν τὴν ζωὴν τὴν αἰώνιον, ἥτις ἦν πρὸς τὸν πατέρα, καὶ ἐφανερώθη ἡμῖν), ³ὃ ἑωράκαμεν καὶ ἀκηκόαμεν, ἀπαγγέλλομεν καὶ ὑμῖν, ἵνα καὶ ὑμεῖς κοινωνίαν ἔχητε μεθ' ἡμῶν· καὶ ἡ κοινωνία δὲ ἡ ἡμετέρα μετὰ τοῦ πατρὸς καὶ μετὰ τοῦ υἱοῦ αὐτοῦ Ἰησοῦ Χριστοῦ· ⁴καὶ ταῦτα γράφομεν ἡμεῖς, ἵνα ἡ χαρὰ ἡμῶν ᾖ πεπληρωμένη.

⁵Καὶ ἔστιν αὕτη ἡ ἀγγελία ἣν ἀκηκόαμεν ἀπ' αὐτοῦ καὶ ἀναγγέλλομεν ὑμῖν, ὅτι ὁ θεὸς φῶς ἐστὶν καὶ σκοτία οὐκ ἔστιν ἐν αὐτῷ οὐδεμία. ⁶Ἐὰν εἴπωμεν ὅτι κοινωνίαν ἔχομεν μετ' αὐτοῦ, καὶ ἐν τῷ σκότει περιπατῶμεν, ψευδόμεθα καὶ οὐ ποιοῦμεν τὴν ἀλήθειαν· ⁷ἐὰν δὲ ἐν τῷ φωτὶ περιπατῶμεν, ὡς αὐτός ἐστιν ἐν τῷ φωτί, κοινωνίαν ἔχομεν μετ' ἀλλήλων, καὶ τὸ αἷμα Ἰησοῦ τοῦ υἱοῦ αὐτοῦ καθαρίζει ἡμᾶς ἀπὸ πάσης ἁμαρτίας. ⁸Ἐὰν εἴπωμεν ὅτι ἁμαρτίαν οὐκ ἔχομεν, ἑαυτοὺς πλανῶμεν, καὶ ἡ ἀλήθεια ἐν ἡμῖν οὐκ ἔστιν. ⁹ἐὰν ὁμολογῶμεν τὰς

ἁμαρτίας ἡμῶν, πιστός ἐστιν καὶ δίκαιος, ἵνα ἀφῇ ἡμῖν
τὰς ἁμαρτίας, καὶ καθαρίσῃ ἡμᾶς ἀπὸ πάσης ἀδικίας.
¹⁰ ἐὰν εἴπωμεν ὅτι οὐχ ἡμαρτήκαμεν, ψεύστην ποιοῦμεν
αὐτόν, καὶ ὁ λόγος αὐτοῦ οὐκ ἔστιν ἐν ἡμῖν.

2 ¹ Τεκνία μου, ταῦτα γράφω ὑμῖν, ἵνα μὴ ἁμάρτητε.
καὶ ἐάν τις ἁμάρτῃ, παράκλητον ἔχομεν πρὸς τὸν πατέρα,
Ἰησοῦν Χριστὸν δίκαιον· ² καὶ αὐτὸς ἱλασμός ἐστιν περὶ
τῶν ἁμαρτιῶν ἡμῶν, οὐ περὶ τῶν ἡμετέρων δὲ μόνον,
ἀλλὰ καὶ περὶ ὅλου τοῦ κόσμου. ³ καὶ ἐν τούτῳ γινώσκομεν ὅτι ἐγνώκαμεν αὐτόν, ἐὰν τὰς ἐντολὰς αὐτοῦ
τηρῶμεν. ⁴ ὁ λέγων ὅτι Ἔγνωκα αὐτόν, καὶ τὰς ἐντολὰς
αὐτοῦ μὴ τηρῶν, ψεύστης ἐστίν, καὶ ἐν τούτῳ ἡ ἀλήθεια
οὐκ ἔστιν· ⁵ ὃς δ' ἂν τηρῇ αὐτοῦ τὸν λόγον, ἀληθῶς ἐν
τούτῳ ἡ ἀγάπη τοῦ θεοῦ τετελείωται. ἐν τούτῳ γινώσκομεν ὅτι ἐν αὐτῷ ἐσμέν· ⁶ ὁ λέγων ἐν αὐτῷ μένειν
ὀφείλει καθὼς ἐκεῖνος περιεπάτησεν καὶ αὐτὸς περιπατεῖν.

⁷ Ἀγαπητοί, οὐκ ἐντολὴν καινὴν γράφω ὑμῖν, ἀλλ'
ἐντολὴν παλαιάν, ἣν εἴχετε ἀπ' ἀρχῆς· ἡ ἐντολὴ ἡ
παλαιά ἐστιν ὁ λόγος ὃν ἠκούσατε. ⁸ πάλιν ἐντολὴν
καινὴν γράφω ὑμῖν, ὅ ἐστιν ἀληθὲς ἐν αὐτῷ καὶ ἐν
ὑμῖν· ὅτι ἡ σκοτία παράγεται, καὶ τὸ φῶς τὸ ἀληθινὸν
ἤδη φαίνει. ⁹ ὁ λέγων ἐν τῷ φωτὶ εἶναι καὶ τὸν ἀδελφὸν
αὐτοῦ μισῶν ἐν τῇ σκοτίᾳ ἐστὶν ἕως ἄρτι. ¹⁰ ὁ ἀγαπῶν
τὸν ἀδελφὸν αὐτοῦ ἐν τῷ φωτὶ μένει, καὶ σκάνδαλον οὐκ
ἔστιν ἐν αὐτῷ. ¹¹ ὁ δὲ μισῶν τὸν ἀδελφὸν αὐτοῦ ἐν τῇ σκοτίᾳ ἐστίν, καὶ ἐν τῇ σκοτίᾳ περιπατεῖ, καὶ οὐκ οἶδεν ποῦ
ὑπάγει, ὅτι ἡ σκοτία ἐτύφλωσεν τοὺς ὀφθαλμοὺς αὐτοῦ.

¹² Γράφω ὑμῖν, τεκνία, ὅτι ἀφέωνται ὑμῖν αἱ ἁμαρτίαι
διὰ τὸ ὄνομα αὐτοῦ. ¹³ γράφω ὑμῖν, πατέρες, ὅτι ἐγνώκατε τὸν ἀπ' ἀρχῆς. γράφω ὑμῖν, νεανίσκοι, ὅτι νενική-

κατε τὸν πονηρόν. ἔγραψα ὑμῖν, παιδία, ὅτι ἐγνώκατε τὸν πατέρα. ¹⁴ἔγραψα ὑμῖν, πατέρες, ὅτι ἐγνώκατε τὸν ἀπ᾽ ἀρχῆς. ἔγραψα ὑμῖν, νεανίσκοι, ὅτι ἰσχυροί ἐστε, καὶ ὁ λόγος τοῦ θεοῦ ἐν ὑμῖν μένει, καὶ νενικήκατε τὸν πονηρόν. ¹⁵Μὴ ἀγαπᾶτε τὸν κόσμον, μηδὲ τὰ ἐν τῷ κόσμῳ. ἐάν τις ἀγαπᾷ τὸν κόσμον, οὐκ ἔστιν ἡ ἀγάπη τοῦ πατρὸς ἐν αὐτῷ. ¹⁶ὅτι πᾶν τὸ ἐν τῷ κόσμῳ, ἡ ἐπιθυμία τῆς σαρκός, καὶ ἡ ἐπιθυμία τῶν ὀφθαλμῶν, καὶ ἡ ἀλαζονεία τοῦ βίου, οὐκ ἔστιν ἐκ τοῦ πατρός, ἀλλὰ ἐκ τοῦ κόσμου ἐστίν. ¹⁷καὶ ὁ κόσμος παράγεται, καὶ ἡ ἐπιθυμία αὐτοῦ· ὁ δὲ ποιῶν τὸ θέλημα τοῦ θεοῦ μένει εἰς τὸν αἰῶνα.

¹⁸Παιδία, ἐσχάτη ὥρα ἐστίν· καὶ καθὼς ἠκούσατε ὅτι ἀντίχριστος ἔρχεται, καὶ νῦν ἀντίχριστοι πολλοὶ γεγόνασιν· ὅθεν γινώσκομεν ὅτι ἐσχάτη ὥρα ἐστίν. ¹⁹ἐξ ἡμῶν ἐξῆλθαν, ἀλλ᾽ οὐκ ἦσαν ἐξ ἡμῶν· εἰ γὰρ ἦσαν ἐξ ἡμῶν, μεμενήκεισαν ἂν μεθ᾽ ἡμῶν· ἀλλ᾽ ἵνα φανερωθῶσιν ὅτι οὐκ εἰσὶν πάντες ἐξ ἡμῶν. ²⁰καὶ ὑμεῖς χρῖσμα ἔχετε ἀπὸ τοῦ ἁγίου, καὶ οἴδατε πάντα. ²¹οὐκ ἔγραψα ὑμῖν, ὅτι οὐκ οἴδατε τὴν ἀλήθειαν, ἀλλ᾽ ὅτι οἴδατε αὐτήν, καὶ ὅτι πᾶν ψεῦδος ἐκ τῆς ἀληθείας οὐκ ἔστιν. ²²τίς ἐστιν ὁ ψεύστης, εἰ μὴ ὁ ἀρνούμενος ὅτι Ἰησοῦς οὐκ ἔστιν ὁ Χριστός; οὗτός ἐστιν ὁ ἀντίχριστος, ὁ ἀρνούμενος τὸν πατέρα καὶ τὸν υἱόν. ²³πᾶς ὁ ἀρνούμενος τὸν υἱὸν οὐδὲ τὸν πατέρα ἔχει· ὁ ὁμολογῶν τὸν υἱὸν καὶ τὸν πατέρα ἔχει. ²⁴ὑμεῖς ὃ ἠκούσατε ἀπ᾽ ἀρχῆς, ἐν ὑμῖν μενέτω. ἐὰν ἐν ὑμῖν μείνῃ ὃ ἀπ᾽ ἀρχῆς ἠκούσατε, καὶ ὑμεῖς ἐν τῷ υἱῷ καὶ ἐν τῷ πατρὶ μενεῖτε. ²⁵καὶ αὕτη ἐστὶν ἡ ἐπαγγελία, ἣν αὐτὸς ἐπηγγείλατο ἡμῖν, τὴν ζωὴν τὴν αἰώνιον. ²⁶ταῦτα ἔγραψα ὑμῖν περὶ τῶν πλανώντων ὑμᾶς. ²⁷καὶ ὑμεῖς τὸ χρῖσμα ὃ ἐλάβετε ἀπ᾽

αὐτοῦ, μένει ἐν ὑμῖν, καὶ οὐ χρείαν ἔχετε ἵνα τις διδάσκῃ
ὑμᾶς· ἀλλ᾽ ὡς τὸ αὐτοῦ χρῖσμα διδάσκει ὑμᾶς περὶ
πάντων, καὶ ἀληθές ἐστιν, καὶ οὐκ ἔστιν ψεῦδος, καὶ
καθὼς ἐδίδαξεν ὑμᾶς, μένετε ἐν αὐτῷ. ²⁸ καὶ νῦν, τεκνία,
μένετε ἐν αὐτῷ· ἵνα ἐὰν φανερωθῇ, σχῶμεν παρρησίαν,
καὶ μὴ αἰσχυνθῶμεν ἀπ᾽ αὐτοῦ ἐν τῇ παρουσίᾳ αὐτοῦ.
²⁹ Ἐὰν εἰδῆτε ὅτι δίκαιός ἐστιν, γινώσκετε ὅτι καὶ πᾶς ὁ
ποιῶν τὴν δικαιοσύνην ἐξ αὐτοῦ γεγέννηται.

3 ¹ Ἴδετε, ποταπὴν ἀγάπην δέδωκεν ἡμῖν ὁ πατήρ,
ἵνα τέκνα θεοῦ κληθῶμεν· καὶ ἐσμέν. διὰ τοῦτο ὁ
κόσμος οὐ γινώσκει ἡμᾶς, ὅτι οὐκ ἔγνω αὐτόν. ² ἀγαπητοί, νῦν τέκνα θεοῦ ἐσμέν, καὶ οὔπω ἐφανερώθη τί
ἐσόμεθα. οἴδαμεν ὅτι ἐὰν φανερωθῇ, ὅμοιοι αὐτῷ ἐσόμεθα, ὅτι ὀψόμεθα αὐτὸν καθώς ἐστιν. ³ καὶ πᾶς ὁ ἔχων
τὴν ἐλπίδα ταύτην ἐπ᾽ αὐτῷ ἁγνίζει ἑαυτόν, καθὼς
ἐκεῖνος ἁγνός ἐστιν. ⁴ πᾶς ὁ ποιῶν τὴν ἁμαρτίαν καὶ
τὴν ἀνομίαν ποιεῖ, καὶ ἡ ἁμαρτία ἐστὶν ἡ ἀνομία. ⁵ καὶ
οἴδατε ὅτι ἐκεῖνος ἐφανερώθη, ἵνα τὰς ἁμαρτίας ἄρῃ, καὶ
ἁμαρτία ἐν αὐτῷ οὐκ ἔστιν. ⁶ πᾶς ὁ ἐν αὐτῷ μένων οὐχ
ἁμαρτάνει· πᾶς ὁ ἁμαρτάνων οὐχ ἑώρακεν αὐτόν, οὐδὲ
ἔγνωκεν αὐτόν. ⁷ τεκνία, μηδεὶς πλανάτω ὑμᾶς· ὁ ποιῶν
τὴν δικαιοσύνην δίκαιός ἐστιν, καθὼς ἐκεῖνος δίκαιός ἐστιν·
⁸ ὁ ποιῶν τὴν ἁμαρτίαν ἐκ τοῦ διαβόλου ἐστίν, ὅτι ἀπ᾽
ἀρχῆς ὁ διάβολος ἁμαρτάνει. εἰς τοῦτο ἐφανερώθη ὁ
υἱὸς τοῦ θεοῦ, ἵνα λύσῃ τὰ ἔργα τοῦ διαβόλου. ⁹ πᾶς
ὁ γεγεννημένος ἐκ τοῦ θεοῦ ἁμαρτίαν οὐ ποιεῖ, ὅτι
σπέρμα αὐτοῦ ἐν αὐτῷ μένει· καὶ οὐ δύναται ἁμαρτάνειν, ὅτι ἐκ τοῦ θεοῦ γεγέννηται. ¹⁰ ἐν τούτῳ φανερά
ἐστιν τὰ τέκνα τοῦ θεοῦ καὶ τὰ τέκνα τοῦ διαβόλου·
πᾶς ὁ μὴ ποιῶν δικαιοσύνην οὐκ ἔστιν ἐκ τοῦ θεοῦ, καὶ
ὁ μὴ ἀγαπῶν τὸν ἀδελφὸν αὐτοῦ. ¹¹ ὅτι αὕτη ἐστὶν ἡ

ἀγγελία ἣν ἠκούσατε ἀπ᾽ ἀρχῆς, ἵνα ἀγαπῶμεν ἀλλή-
λους· ¹² οὐ καθὼς Κάϊν ἐκ τοῦ πονηροῦ ἦν, καὶ ἔσφαξεν
τὸν ἀδελφὸν αὐτοῦ. καὶ χάριν τίνος ἔσφαξεν αὐτόν ;
ὅτι τὰ ἔργα αὐτοῦ πονηρὰ ἦν, τὰ δὲ τοῦ ἀδελφοῦ αὐτοῦ
δίκαια. ¹³ Μὴ θαυμάζετε, ἀδελφοί, εἰ μισεῖ ὑμᾶς ὁ κόσμος.
¹⁴ ἡμεῖς οἴδαμεν ὅτι μεταβεβήκαμεν ἐκ τοῦ θανάτου εἰς
τὴν ζωήν, ὅτι ἀγαπῶμεν τοὺς ἀδελφούς. ὁ μὴ ἀγαπῶν
μένει ἐν τῷ θανάτῳ. ¹⁵ πᾶς ὁ μισῶν τὸν ἀδελφὸν αὐτοῦ
ἀνθρωποκτόνος ἐστίν· καὶ οἴδατε ὅτι πᾶς ἀνθρωποκτόνος
οὐκ ἔχει ζωὴν αἰώνιον ἐν αὐτῷ μένουσαν. ¹⁶ ἐν τούτῳ
ἐγνώκαμεν τὴν ἀγάπην, ὅτι ἐκεῖνος ὑπὲρ ἡμῶν τὴν
ψυχὴν αὐτοῦ ἔθηκεν· καὶ ἡμεῖς ὀφείλομεν ὑπὲρ τῶν
ἀδελφῶν τὰς ψυχὰς θεῖναι. ¹⁷ ὃς δ᾽ ἂν ἔχῃ τὸν βίον τοῦ
κόσμου, καὶ θεωρῇ τὸν ἀδελφὸν αὐτοῦ χρείαν ἔχοντα, καὶ
κλείσῃ τὰ σπλάγχνα αὐτοῦ ἀπ᾽ αὐτοῦ, πῶς ἡ ἀγάπη τοῦ
θεοῦ μένει ἐν αὐτῷ ; ¹⁸ τεκνία, μὴ ἀγαπῶμεν λόγῳ μηδὲ
τῇ γλώσσῃ, ἀλλὰ ἐν ἔργῳ καὶ ἀληθείᾳ. ¹⁹ καὶ ἐν τούτῳ
γνωσόμεθα ὅτι ἐκ τῆς ἀληθείας ἐσμέν, καὶ ἔμπροσθεν
αὐτοῦ πείσομεν τὰς καρδίας ἡμῶν, ²⁰ ὅτι ἐὰν καταγινώσκῃ
ἡμῶν ἡ καρδία, ὅτι μείζων ἐστὶν ὁ θεὸς τῆς καρδίας
ἡμῶν, καὶ γινώσκει πάντα. ²¹ ἀγαπητοί, ἐὰν ἡ καρδία
μὴ καταγινώσκῃ ἡμῶν, παρρησίαν ἔχομεν πρὸς τὸν
θεόν, ²² καὶ ὃ ἐὰν αἰτῶμεν, λαμβάνομεν ἀπ᾽ αὐτοῦ, ὅτι
τὰς ἐντολὰς αὐτοῦ τηροῦμεν, καὶ τὰ ἀρεστὰ ἐνώπιον
αὐτοῦ ποιοῦμεν. ²³ καὶ αὕτη ἐστὶν ἡ ἐντολὴ αὐτοῦ, ἵνα
πιστεύωμεν τῷ ὀνόματι τοῦ υἱοῦ αὐτοῦ Ἰησοῦ Χριστοῦ,
καὶ ἀγαπῶμεν ἀλλήλους, καθὼς ἔδωκεν ἐντολὴν ἡμῖν.
²⁴ καὶ ὁ τηρῶν τὰς ἐντολὰς αὐτοῦ ἐν αὐτῷ μένει, καὶ
αὐτὸς ἐν αὐτῷ. καὶ ἐν τούτῳ γινώσκομεν ὅτι μένει ἐν
ἡμῖν, ἐκ τοῦ πνεύματος οὗ ἡμῖν ἔδωκεν.

4 ¹ Ἀγαπητοί, μὴ παντὶ πνεύματι πιστεύετε, ἀλλὰ δοκιμάζετε τὰ πνεύματα, εἰ ἐκ τοῦ θεοῦ ἐστίν· ὅτι πολλοὶ ψευδοπροφῆται ἐξεληλύθασιν εἰς τὸν κόσμον. ² ἐν τούτῳ γινώσκετε τὸ πνεῦμα τοῦ θεοῦ· πᾶν πνεῦμα ὃ ὁμολογεῖ Ἰησοῦν Χριστὸν ἐν σαρκὶ ἐληλυθότα ἐκ τοῦ θεοῦ ἐστίν· ³ καὶ πᾶν πνεῦμα ὃ μὴ ὁμολογεῖ τὸν Ἰησοῦν ἐκ τοῦ θεοῦ οὐκ ἔστιν· καὶ τοῦτό ἐστιν τὸ τοῦ ἀντι- χρίστου, ὃ ἀκηκόατε ὅτι ἔρχεται, καὶ νῦν ἐν τῷ κόσμῳ ἐστὶν ἤδη. ⁴ ὑμεῖς ἐκ τοῦ θεοῦ ἐστέ, τεκνία, καὶ νενική- κατε αὐτούς· ὅτι μείζων ἐστὶν ὁ ἐν ὑμῖν ἢ ὁ ἐν τῷ κόσμῳ. ⁵ αὐτοὶ ἐκ τοῦ κόσμου εἰσίν· διὰ τοῦτο ἐκ τοῦ κόσμου λαλοῦσιν, καὶ ὁ κόσμος αὐτῶν ἀκούει. ⁶ ἡμεῖς ἐκ τοῦ θεοῦ ἐσμέν· ὁ γινώσκων τὸν θεὸν ἀκούει ἡμῶν· ὃς οὐκ ἔστιν ἐκ τοῦ θεοῦ, οὐκ ἀκούει ἡμῶν. ἐκ τούτου γινώ- σκομεν τὸ πνεῦμα τῆς ἀληθείας καὶ τὸ πνεῦμα τῆς πλάνης.

⁷ Ἀγαπητοί, ἀγαπῶμεν ἀλλήλους· ὅτι ἡ ἀγάπη ἐκ τοῦ θεοῦ ἐστίν, καὶ πᾶς ὁ ἀγαπῶν ἐκ τοῦ θεοῦ γεγέν- νηται καὶ γινώσκει τὸν θεόν. ⁸ ὁ μὴ ἀγαπῶν οὐκ ἔγνω τὸν θεόν· ὅτι ὁ θεὸς ἀγάπη ἐστίν. ⁹ ἐν τούτῳ ἐφανε- ρώθη ἡ ἀγάπη τοῦ θεοῦ ἐν ἡμῖν, ὅτι τὸν υἱὸν αὐτοῦ τὸν μονογενῆ ἀπέσταλκεν ὁ θεὸς εἰς τὸν κόσμον, ἵνα ζήσω- μεν δι' αὐτοῦ. ¹⁰ ἐν τούτῳ ἐστὶν ἡ ἀγάπη, οὐχ ὅτι ἡμεῖς ἠγαπήσαμεν τὸν θεόν, ἀλλ' ὅτι αὐτὸς ἠγάπησεν ἡμᾶς, καὶ ἀπέστειλεν τὸν υἱὸν αὐτοῦ ἱλασμὸν περὶ τῶν ἁμαρ- τιῶν ἡμῶν. ¹¹ ἀγαπητοί, εἰ οὕτως ὁ θεὸς ἠγάπησεν ἡμᾶς, καὶ ἡμεῖς ὀφείλομεν ἀλλήλους ἀγαπᾶν. ¹² θεὸν οὐδεὶς πώποτε τεθέαται· ἐὰν ἀγαπῶμεν ἀλλήλους, ὁ θεὸς ἐν ἡμῖν μένει, καὶ ἡ ἀγάπη αὐτοῦ τετελειωμένη ἐν ἡμῖν ἐστίν· ¹³ ἐν τούτῳ γινώσκομεν ὅτι ἐν αὐτῷ μένομεν, καὶ αὐτὸς ἐν ἡμῖν, ὅτι ἐκ τοῦ πνεύματος αὐτοῦ

δέδωκεν ἡμῖν. ¹⁴ καὶ ἡμεῖς τεθεάμεθα καὶ μαρτυροῦμεν ὅτι ὁ πατὴρ ἀπέσταλκεν τὸν υἱὸν σωτῆρα τοῦ κόσμου. ¹⁵ ὃς ἂν ὁμολογήσῃ ὅτι Ἰησοῦς ἐστιν ὁ υἱὸς τοῦ θεοῦ, ὁ θεὸς ἐν αὐτῷ μένει, καὶ αὐτὸς ἐν τῷ θεῷ. ¹⁶ καὶ ἡμεῖς ἐγνώκαμεν καὶ πεπιστεύκαμεν τὴν ἀγάπην ἣν ἔχει ὁ θεὸς ἐν ἡμῖν. ὁ θεὸς ἀγάπη ἐστίν, καὶ ὁ μένων ἐν τῇ ἀγάπῃ ἐν τῷ θεῷ μένει, καὶ ὁ θεὸς ἐν αὐτῷ [μένει]. ¹⁷ ἐν τούτῳ τετελείωται ἡ ἀγάπη μεθ᾽ ἡμῶν, ἵνα παρρησίαν ἔχωμεν ἐν τῇ ἡμέρᾳ τῆς κρίσεως, ὅτι καθὼς ἐκεῖνός ἐστιν καὶ ἡμεῖς ἐσμὲν ἐν τῷ κόσμῳ τούτῳ. ¹⁸ φόβος οὐκ ἔστιν ἐν τῇ ἀγάπῃ· ἀλλ᾽ ἡ τελεία ἀγάπη ἔξω βάλλει τὸν φόβον, ὅτι ὁ φόβος κόλασιν ἔχει, ὁ δὲ φοβούμενος οὐ τετελείωται ἐν τῇ ἀγάπῃ. ¹⁹ ἡμεῖς ἀγαπῶμεν, ὅτι αὐτὸς πρῶτος ἠγάπησεν ἡμᾶς. ²⁰ ἐάν τις εἴπῃ ὅτι Ἀγαπῶ τὸν θεόν, καὶ τὸν ἀδελφὸν αὐτοῦ μισῇ, ψεύστης ἐστίν· ὁ γὰρ μὴ ἀγαπῶν τὸν ἀδελφὸν αὐτοῦ, ὃν ἑώρακεν, τὸν θεόν, ὃν οὐχ ἑώρακεν, οὐ δύναται ἀγαπᾶν. ²¹ καὶ ταύτην τὴν ἐντολὴν ἔχομεν ἀπ᾽ αὐτοῦ, ἵνα ὁ ἀγαπῶν τὸν θεὸν ἀγαπᾷ καὶ τὸν ἀδελφὸν αὐτοῦ.

5 ¹ Πᾶς ὁ πιστεύων ὅτι Ἰησοῦς ἐστιν ὁ Χριστὸς ἐκ τοῦ θεοῦ γεγέννηται· καὶ πᾶς ὁ ἀγαπῶν τὸν γεννήσαντα ἀγαπᾷ [καὶ] τὸν γεγεννημένον ἐξ αὐτοῦ. ² ἐν τούτῳ γινώσκομεν ὅτι ἀγαπῶμεν τὰ τέκνα τοῦ θεοῦ, ὅταν τὸν θεὸν ἀγαπῶμεν, καὶ τὰς ἐντολὰς αὐτοῦ ποιῶμεν. ³ αὕτη γάρ ἐστιν ἡ ἀγάπη τοῦ θεοῦ, ἵνα τὰς ἐντολὰς αὐτοῦ τηρῶμεν· καὶ αἱ ἐντολαὶ αὐτοῦ βαρεῖαι οὐκ εἰσίν. ⁴ ὅτι πᾶν τὸ γεγεννημένον ἐκ τοῦ θεοῦ νικᾷ τὸν κόσμον· καὶ αὕτη ἐστὶν ἡ νίκη ἡ νικήσασα τὸν κόσμον, ἡ πίστις ἡμῶν. ⁵ τίς ἐστιν ὁ νικῶν τὸν κόσμον, εἰ μὴ ὁ πιστεύων ὅτι Ἰησοῦς ἐστιν ὁ υἱὸς τοῦ θεοῦ; ⁶ οὗτός ἐστιν ὁ ἐλθὼν δι᾽ ὕδατος καὶ αἵματος, Ἰησοῦς Χριστός· οὐκ ἐν τῷ

ὕδατι μόνον, ἀλλ᾽ ἐν τῷ ὕδατι καὶ ἐν τῷ αἵματι. καὶ τὸ
πνεῦμά ἐστιν τὸ μαρτυροῦν, ὅτι τὸ πνεῦμά ἐστιν ἡ
ἀλήθεια. ⁷ὅτι τρεῖς εἰσὶν οἱ μαρτυροῦντες, ⁸τὸ πνεῦμα,
καὶ τὸ ὕδωρ, καὶ τὸ αἷμα· καὶ οἱ τρεῖς εἰς τὸ ἕν εἰσιν.
⁹εἰ τὴν μαρτυρίαν τῶν ἀνθρώπων λαμβάνομεν, ἡ μαρτυρία
τοῦ θεοῦ μείζων ἐστίν· ὅτι αὕτη ἐστὶν ἡ μαρτυρία τοῦ
θεοῦ, ὅτι μεμαρτύρηκεν περὶ τοῦ υἱοῦ αὐτοῦ. ¹⁰ὁ πιστεύων εἰς τὸν υἱὸν τοῦ θεοῦ ἔχει τὴν μαρτυρίαν ἐν αὐτῷ·
ὁ μὴ πιστεύων τῷ θεῷ ψεύστην πεποίηκεν αὐτόν, ὅτι
οὐ πεπίστευκεν εἰς τὴν μαρτυρίαν, ἣν μεμαρτύρηκεν ὁ
θεὸς περὶ τοῦ υἱοῦ αὐτοῦ. ¹¹καὶ αὕτη ἐστὶν ἡ μαρτυρία,
ὅτι ζωὴν αἰώνιον ἔδωκεν ἡμῖν ὁ θεός, καὶ αὕτη ἡ ζωὴ ἐν
τῷ υἱῷ αὐτοῦ ἐστίν. ¹²ὁ ἔχων τὸν υἱὸν ἔχει τὴν ζωήν·
ὁ μὴ ἔχων τὸν υἱὸν τοῦ θεοῦ τὴν ζωὴν οὐκ ἔχει.
¹³Ταῦτα ἔγραψα ὑμῖν, ἵνα εἰδῆτε ὅτι ζωὴν ἔχετε
αἰώνιον, τοῖς πιστεύουσιν εἰς τὸ ὄνομα τοῦ υἱοῦ τοῦ θεοῦ.
¹⁴καὶ αὕτη ἐστὶν ἡ παρρησία ἣν ἔχομεν πρὸς αὐτόν, ὅτι
ἐάν τι αἰτώμεθα κατὰ τὸ θέλημα αὐτοῦ, ἀκούει ἡμῶν·
¹⁵καὶ ἐὰν οἴδαμεν ὅτι ἀκούει ἡμῶν ὃ ἂν αἰτώμεθα, οἴδαμεν
ὅτι ἔχομεν τὰ αἰτήματα ἃ ᾐτήκαμεν ἀπ᾽ αὐτοῦ. ¹⁶ἐάν
τις ἴδῃ τὸν ἀδελφὸν αὐτοῦ ἁμαρτάνοντα ἁμαρτίαν μὴ
πρὸς θάνατον, αἰτήσει, καὶ δώσει αὐτῷ ζωὴν τοῖς ἁμαρτάνουσιν μὴ πρὸς θάνατον. ἔστιν ἁμαρτία πρὸς θάνατον·
οὐ περὶ ἐκείνης λέγω ἵνα ἐρωτήσῃ. ¹⁷πᾶσα ἀδικία ἁμαρτία ἐστίν· καὶ ἔστιν ἁμαρτία οὐ πρὸς θάνατον.
¹⁸Οἴδαμεν ὅτι πᾶς ὁ γεγεννημένος ἐκ τοῦ θεοῦ οὐχ
ἁμαρτάνει, ἀλλ᾽ ὁ γεννηθεὶς ἐκ τοῦ θεοῦ τηρεῖ αὐτόν,
καὶ ὁ πονηρὸς οὐχ ἅπτεται αὐτοῦ. ¹⁹οἴδαμεν ὅτι ἐκ τοῦ
θεοῦ ἐσμέν, καὶ ὁ κόσμος ὅλος ἐν τῷ πονηρῷ κεῖται.
²⁰οἴδαμεν δὲ ὅτι ὁ υἱὸς τοῦ θεοῦ ἥκει, καὶ δέδωκεν ἡμῖν
διάνοιαν, ἵνα γινώσκομεν τὸν ἀληθινόν, καί ἐσμεν ἐν τῷ

ἀληθινῷ, ἐν τῷ υἱῷ αὐτοῦ Ἰησοῦ Χριστῷ. οὗτός ἐστιν ὁ ἀληθινὸς θεὸς καὶ ζωὴ αἰώνιος. ²¹Τεκνία, φυλάξατε ἑαυτὰ ἀπὸ τῶν εἰδώλων.

ΙΩΑΝΝΟΥ Β

¹Ὁ πρεσβύτερος ἐκλεκτῇ κυρίᾳ καὶ τοῖς τέκνοις αὐτῆς, οὓς ἐγὼ ἀγαπῶ ἐν ἀληθείᾳ, καὶ οὐκ ἐγὼ μόνος ἀλλὰ καὶ πάντες οἱ ἐγνωκότες τὴν ἀλήθειαν, ²διὰ τὴν ἀλήθειαν τὴν μένουσαν ἐν ἡμῖν, καὶ μεθ᾽ ἡμῶν ἔσται εἰς τὸν αἰῶνα· ³ἔσται μεθ᾽ ἡμῶν χάρις, ἔλεος, εἰρήνη παρὰ θεοῦ πατρός, καὶ παρὰ Ἰησοῦ Χριστοῦ τοῦ υἱοῦ τοῦ πατρός, ἐν ἀληθείᾳ καὶ ἀγάπῃ.

⁴Ἐχάρην λίαν ὅτι εὕρηκα ἐκ τῶν τέκνων σου περιπατοῦντας ἐν ἀληθείᾳ, καθὼς ἐντολὴν ἐλάβομεν παρὰ τοῦ πατρός. ⁵Καὶ νῦν ἐρωτῶ σε, κυρία, οὐχ ὡς ἐντολὴν καινὴν γράφων σοι, ἀλλὰ ἣν εἴχαμεν ἀπ᾽ ἀρχῆς, ἵνα ἀγαπῶμεν ἀλλήλους. ⁶καὶ αὕτη ἐστὶν ἡ ἀγάπη, ἵνα περιπατῶμεν κατὰ τὰς ἐντολὰς αὐτοῦ. αὕτη ἡ ἐντολή ἐστιν, καθὼς ἠκούσατε ἀπ᾽ ἀρχῆς, ἵνα ἐν αὐτῇ περιπατῆτε. ⁷ὅτι πολλοὶ πλάνοι ἐξῆλθαν εἰς τὸν κόσμον, οἱ μὴ ὁμολογοῦντες Ἰησοῦν Χριστὸν ἐρχόμενον ἐν σαρκί. οὗτός ἐστιν ὁ πλάνος καὶ ὁ ἀντίχριστος. ⁸βλέπετε ἑαυτούς, ἵνα μὴ ἀπολέσητε ἃ εἰργάσασθε, ἀλλὰ μισθὸν πλήρη ἀπολάβητε. ⁹πᾶς ὁ προάγων καὶ μὴ μένων ἐν τῇ διδαχῇ τοῦ Χριστοῦ θεὸν οὐκ ἔχει· ὁ μένων ἐν τῇ διδαχῇ, οὗτος καὶ τὸν πατέρα καὶ τὸν υἱὸν ἔχει. ¹⁰Εἴ τις ἔρχεται πρὸς ὑμᾶς, καὶ ταύτην τὴν διδαχὴν οὐ φέρει,

μὴ λαμβάνετε αὐτὸν εἰς οἰκίαν, καὶ χαίρειν αὐτῷ μὴ λέγετε· ¹¹ ὁ λέγων γὰρ αὐτῷ χαίρειν κοινωνεῖ τοῖς ἔργοις αὐτοῦ τοῖς πονηροῖς.

¹² Πολλὰ ἔχων ὑμῖν γράφειν οὐκ ἐβουλήθην διὰ χάρτου καὶ μέλανος· ἀλλὰ ἐλπίζω γενέσθαι πρὸς ὑμᾶς, καὶ στόμα πρὸς στόμα λαλῆσαι, ἵνα ἡ χαρὰ ὑμῶν ᾖ πεπληρωμένη. ¹³ Ἀσπάζεταί σε τὰ τέκνα τῆς ἀδελφῆς σου τῆς ἐκλεκτῆς.

ΙΩΑΝΝΟΥ Γ

¹ Ὁ πρεσβύτερος Γαΐῳ τῷ ἀγαπητῷ, ὃν ἐγὼ ἀγαπῶ ἐν ἀληθείᾳ.

² Ἀγαπητέ, περὶ πάντων εὔχομαί σε εὐοδοῦσθαι καὶ ὑγιαίνειν, καθὼς εὐοδοῦταί σου ἡ ψυχή. ³ ἐχάρην [γὰρ] λίαν ἐρχομένων ἀδελφῶν καὶ μαρτυρούντων σου τῇ ἀληθείᾳ, καθὼς σὺ ἐν ἀληθείᾳ περιπατεῖς. ⁴ μειζοτέραν τούτων οὐκ ἔχω χαράν, ἵνα ἀκούω τὰ ἐμὰ τέκνα ἐν τῇ ἀληθείᾳ περιπατοῦντα.

⁵ Ἀγαπητέ, πιστὸν ποιεῖς ὃ ἐὰν ἐργάσῃ εἰς τοὺς ἀδελφοὺς καὶ τοῦτο ξένους, ⁶ οἳ ἐμαρτύρησάν σου τῇ ἀγάπῃ ἐνώπιον ἐκκλησίας· οὓς καλῶς ποιήσεις προπέμψας ἀξίως τοῦ θεοῦ· ⁷ ὑπὲρ γὰρ τοῦ ὀνόματος ἐξῆλθαν μηδὲν λαμβάνοντες ἀπὸ τῶν ἐθνικῶν. ⁸ ἡμεῖς οὖν ὀφείλομεν ὑπολαμβάνειν τοὺς τοιούτους, ἵνα συνεργοὶ γινώμεθα τῇ ἀληθείᾳ.

⁹ Ἔγραψά τι τῇ ἐκκλησίᾳ· ἀλλ' ὁ φιλοπρωτεύων αὐτῶν Διοτρεφὴς οὐκ ἐπιδέχεται ἡμᾶς. ¹⁰ διὰ τοῦτο,

ἐὰν ἔλθω, ὑπομνήσω αὐτοῦ τὰ ἔργα ἃ ποιεῖ λόγοις πονηροῖς φλυαρῶν ἡμᾶς· καὶ μὴ ἀρκούμενος ἐπὶ τούτοις οὔτε αὐτὸς ἐπιδέχεται τοὺς ἀδελφούς, καὶ τοὺς βουλομένους κωλύει, καὶ ἐκ τῆς ἐκκλησίας ἐκβάλλει.

¹¹ Ἀγαπητέ, μὴ μιμοῦ τὸ κακόν, ἀλλὰ τὸ ἀγαθόν. ὁ ἀγαθοποιῶν ἐκ τοῦ θεοῦ ἐστίν· ὁ κακοποιῶν οὐχ ἑώρακεν τὸν θεόν. ¹² Δημητρίῳ μεμαρτύρηται ὑπὸ πάντων, καὶ ὑπ᾽ αὐτῆς τῆς ἀληθείας· καὶ ἡμεῖς δὲ μαρτυροῦμεν, καὶ οἶδας ὅτι ἡ μαρτυρία ἡμῶν ἀληθής ἐστιν.

¹³ Πολλὰ εἶχον γράψαι σοι, ἀλλ᾽ οὐ θέλω διὰ μέλανος καὶ καλάμου σοι γράφειν· ¹⁴ ἐλπίζω δὲ εὐθέως σε ἰδεῖν, καὶ στόμα πρὸς στόμα λαλήσομεν. Εἰρήνη σοι. ἀσπάζονταί σε οἱ φίλοι. ἀσπάζου τοὺς φίλους κατ᾽ ὄνομα.

NOTES

In the remarks on the results of textual revision prefixed to the Notes on each Chapter, it is not intended to enter minutely into each point, but to indicate generally the principal errors and corrections, and occasionally to state the grounds on which a reading is preferred.

CHAPTER I.

Ἰωάνου is preferred by the best recent editors to Ἰωάννου (W. & H. II. 159). The title of the Epistle is found in very different forms in ancient authorities, the earliest being the simplest. Ἰωάννου or Ἰωάνου ᾱ (AB). Ἰωάννου ἐπιστολὴ ᾱ (ℵ). Ἐπιστολὴ καθολικὴ τοῦ ἁγίου ἀποστόλου Ἰωάννου (L). A MS. of the thirteenth century has the singular title Βροντῆς υἱὸς Ἰωάννης τάδε χριστιανοῖσιν. In C the title has disappeared.

καθολική appears in most titles. It means 'general' in the sense of 'universal.' The Epistle is not addressed to any particular Church or individual, but to the whole Church throughout all ages. It is as suitable to the Church of England or of Rome in the nineteenth century as to that of Ephesus in the first. Origen was perhaps the first to call this Epistle καθολική, an epithet which he also gives to 1 Peter and Jude. Others used it of James and 2 Peter, and even of 2 and 3 John, of which one is certainly addressed to an individual and the other either to an individual or (less probably) to a particular Church. In the English versions 'general' does not appear in the title either in Wiclif, or Coverdale, or the Bishops' Bible, or the Rhemish.

3. Before ὑμῖν insert καί (ℵABC).

4. ἡμεῖς (ℵAB) for ὑμῖν (CKL). ἡμῶν (ℵBL) for ὑμῶν (AC).

5. ἔστιν αὕτη (ℵBC) for αὕτη ἐστίν (A). ἀγγελία (ℵAB) for ἐπαγγελία (C). φῶς ἐστίν. The enclitics ἐστίν, ἐσμέν, ἐστέ, εἰσίν are accented thus when the previous word cannot receive the accent: comp. ii. 5; iii. 3, 8, 23; iv. 2, 3, 4, 5, 6, 7, 17; v. 9, 11, 19; 3 John 11. ἐστὶν καί...Following the uncial MSS., the best editors add ν ἐφελκυστικόν before consonants and vowels alike : πᾶσι and δυσί being occasional exceptions, and perhaps γιγνώσκουσι (John x. 14). Winer, 44 note.

7. After 'Ιησοῦ omit Χριστοῦ with ℵBC against AKL with Syr. and Vulg.

In all these six cases ℵB have the right reading.

CH. I. 1—4. THE INTRODUCTION.

The first four verses are introductory. They are analogous to the first eighteen verses of the Gospel, and to the first three of the Revelation. Like the Prologue to the Gospel, this Introduction tells us that the Apostle's subject is **the Word who is the Life**. The similarity between the two Prefaces extends to details. "In each the main subject is described first (John i. 1, 2—5; 1 John i. 1): then the historical manifestation of it (John i. 6—13; 1 John i. 2): then its personal apprehension (John i. 14—18; 1 John i. 3 f.)."—Westcott.

Note that neither before nor after the Introduction is there any address or salutation, just as at the end there is neither valediction nor blessing. In form this Epistle is very unlike other Epistles in N. T.

1—4. A prolonged and somewhat involved construction. Such complicated sentences are not common in S. John: but comp. John vi. 22—24; xiii. 2—4. Some make ἐστίν understood to be the main verb: 'That which was from the beginning *is* that which we have heard, &c.' Others take ἐψηλάφησαν: 'That which was from the beginning, which..., which..., our hands also touched.' But almost certainly the main verb is ἀπαγγέλλομεν, and ὅ in each case introduces the thing declared. Verse 2 being parenthetical, part of *v.* 1 is repeated for clearness and emphasis (Winer, 709 note 4). The crowding of profound thoughts has proved almost too much for the Apostle's command of Greek. In the plurals, ἀκηκόαμεν, ἑωράκαμεν, &c., we have the testimony of the last survivor of those who had heard and seen the Lord, the sole representative of His disciples, speaking in their name.

1. The similarity to the opening of the Gospel is manifest: but the thought is not the same. There it is that the Λόγος existed before the *Creation*, here that the Λόγος existed before the *Incarnation*. With the neuter ὅ comp. John iv. 22; vi. 37; xvii. 2; Acts xvii. 23 (R.V.). The verbs ἑωράκαμεν, ἐθεασάμεθα, and ἐψηλάφησαν are fatal to the Socinian interpretation, that ὅ means the *doctrine* of Jesus. S. John employs the neuter as the most comprehensive expression to cover the attributes, words, and works of the Word and the Life manifested in the flesh.

ἦν. Not 'came into existence,' but 'was in existence' already. The difference between εἶναι (i. 1, 2) and γίνεσθαι (ii. 18) must be carefully noted. Christ the Word *was* from all eternity; antichrists *have arisen*, have come into existence in time. Comp. John i. 1 and 6. The clause is an instance of what is so characteristic of S. John—profound and almost unsearchable meaning expressed in very simple and apparently transparent language. ἀπ' ἀρχῆς. The meaning of ἀρχή always depends upon the context. Here ἦν πρὸς τὸν πατέρα (v. 2) determines the meaning, shewing that it points to a beginning prior even to Creation, and is therefore a stronger expression than ἀπὸ καταβολῆς κόσμου (Rev. xiii. 8, xvii. 8; and even than πρὸ καταβολῆς κόσ. (John xvii. 24). It contains a denial of the Arian position (ἦν ὅτε οὐκ ἦν), that there was a time when the Word was not. Comp. οὐχὶ σὺ ἀπ' ἀρχῆς, Κύριε ὁ Θεός μου, ὁ ἅγιός μου; (Hab. i. 12). Of idols it is said οὔτε γὰρ ἦν ἀπ' ἀρχῆς (Wisd. xiv. 13). The Gospel is no new-fangled mystery: its subject is as old as eternity. 'Απ' ἀρχῆς without the article is idiomatic (Hes., Pind., Hdt., Trag.): so also ἐξ ἀρχῆς (John vi. 64; xvi. 4; Hom., Soph., Plat., Xen.).

ὃ ἀκηκόαμεν. As in vv. 3, 5 and iv. 3, the perfect indicates permanent result of past action. We here pass from eternity into time. The first clause tells of the Word prior to Creation: the second of all that the Prophets and the Christ have said respecting Him. No need to make ὃ in each clause refer to different things; the words, miracles, glory, and body of Christ. Each ὃ indicates that collective whole of Divine and human attributes which is the Incarnate Word of Life.

ἑωράκ. τ. ὀφθ. ἡμῶν. A climax: seeing is more than hearing, and beholding (which requires time) is more than seeing (which may be momentary); while handling is more than all. 'With our eyes' is added for emphasis. The Apostle would have us know that 'see' is no figure of speech, but the expression of a literal fact. With all the language at his command he insists on the reality of the Incarnation, of which he can speak from personal knowledge based on the combined evidence of all the senses. The Docetic heresy of supposing that the Lord's body was unreal, and the Cerinthian heresy of supposing that He who 'was from the beginning' was different from Him whom they heard and saw and handled, is authoritatively condemned by implication at the outset. In the Introduction to the Gospel there is a similar assertion; 'The Word became flesh and dwelt among us—and we beheld His glory' (John i. 14). Comp. 2 Pet. i. 16. Of ὁρᾶν S. John uses no tense but the perfect (vv. 2, 3; iii. 6; iv. 20; 3 John 11). *Maxime illi qui eum in monte clarificatum viderunt, e quibus unus erat ipse Johannes* (Bede).

ὃ ἐθεασάμεθα...ἐψηλάφησαν. That *which we beheld and our hands handled.* After the imperfect ἦν we had a pair of perfects, and now a pair of aorists. Θεᾶσθαι implies deliberate and perhaps pleasurable sight (John i. 14, 34; Acts i. 11). We can hear and see without intending to do so; but we can scarcely behold and handle unintentionally. The aorists probably refer to definite occasions on which the beholding and handling took place. 'Εψηλάφησαν seems to be a direct reference to the test demanded by S. Thomas (John xx. 27) and offered to the other disciples (Luke xxiv. 39, where the same verb is used as here). "The clear reference to the Risen Christ in '*handled*' makes it probable that the special manifestation indicated by the two aorists is that given to the Apostles by the Lord after the Resurrection, which is in fact the revelation of Himself as He remains

with His Church...The tacit reference is the more worthy of notice
because S. John does not mention the fact of the Resurrection in his
Epistle" (Westcott). Tertullian is very fond of insisting on the fact
that the Lord was 'handled': *Adv. Prax.* xv. twice; *De Animâ* xvii.;
De Pat. iii.; comp. *Ad Uxorem* iv. So also Ignatius (*Smyr.* iii.); "I
know and believe that He was in the flesh even after the resurrection:
and when He came to Peter and his company, He said to them, Take,
handle Me, and see that I am not a bodiless demon." Bede points
out that the argument has special force as coming from the disciple
who had lain on the Lord's breast. No greater proof of the reality
of His Body before and after the Resurrection could be given.

περὶ τοῦ λόγου τῆς ζωῆς. Concerning *the Word of Life.* The interpretation of both λόγος and ζωή in this clause is disputed. Is
either of them personal? Does ὁ λόγος mean *the Revelation, the
Gospel;* or Him who revealed the Father by being revealed in the
Gospel, viz. *the Word?* Does ἡ ζωή mean *life;* or Him who is 'the
Way and the Truth and *the Life'?* In favour of the impersonal rendering of τοῦ λόγου is ὁ λόγος τοῦ Θεοῦ (John x. 35; comp. Matt. xiii.
19; Acts vi. 7; xiii. 26; xx. 32; 1 Cor. i. 18; Col. i. 5; 2 Tim. ii. 15).
Against this is ὁ Λόγος τοῦ Θεοῦ (Rev. xix. 13) and the probability that
λόγος in this Introduction has the same meaning as in the Introduction to the Gospel. Περὶ confirms this: comp. v. 9, 10; John i. 15,
22, 30, 48; ii. 25; v. 31, 32, 36, 37, 39, 46, &c. &c., where περί is used
of testimony concerning *persons.* Out of about twenty instances in
the Fourth Gospel all but two (xviii. 23 and xxi. 24) are of witness
about persons. And in xxi. 24 the τούτων may very likely be masculine: to take it so avoids tautology. Τοῦ λόγου, therefore, probably
means the Son of God, in whom had been hidden from eternity all
that God had to say to man, and who was the living expression of
the Nature and Will of God. See on John i. 1 for the history of the
term, which is peculiar to the phraseology of S. John. But of the two
terms, Word and Life, the latter is here the emphatic one as is shewn
by *v.* 2 and by the fact that 'the Life' is one of the main topics of the
Epistle (ii. 25, iii. 14, v. 11, 12, 20), whereas 'the Word' is not mentioned again. As to τῆς ζωῆς, the expression may be analogous to ὁ
ἄρτος τ. ζ. (John vi. 35), τὸ φῶς τ. ζ. (viii. 12), τὸ ξύλον τ. ζ. (Rev. ii.
7), τὸ ὕδωρ τ. ζ. (xxi. 6) where 'of life' seems to mean 'life-giving.'
More probably the genitive is one of apposition, as in περὶ τοῦ ναοῦ τοῦ
σώματος αὐτοῦ (John ii. 21); περὶ τῆς κοιμήσεως τοῦ ὕπνου (xi. 13); πρὸ
τῆς ἑορτῆς τοῦ πάσχα (xiii. 1). Winer, 666. 'The Word which is the
Life' is the meaning. Christ is at once the Word of God and the Life
of man. This is confirmed by *v.* 2, where ἡ ζωή is certainly personal.
But the transition from an impersonal to a personal signification is
easily made, as in the use of κόσμος in John i. 10. Tertullian (*De
An.* xvii.) quotes the verse as *Joannis testationem* thus: *Quod vidimus
quod audivimus, oculis nostris vidimus, et manus nostrae contrectave-
runt, de sermone vitae:* and again (*Adv. Prax.* xv.), adding *Sermo
enim vitae caro factus et auditus et visus et contrectatus,* shewing that
he took *Sermo* personally. He renders ὁ Λόγος by *Sermo, Verbum,*

and *Oratio.* Clement of Alexandria and Didymus considered ὁ λόγος here to be the personal Word. See p. 53.

2. καὶ ἡ ζωὴ ἐφανερώθη. Trebly characteristic of S. John. 1. The connexion by means of the simple conjunction. 2. The repetition of ζωή from *v.* 1, carrying on part of one sentence into the next for further elucidation and development, without the use of relatives. 3. The verb φανεροῦν, frequent in Gospel and Epistle and occurring twice in Revelation. Points which connect the Epistle with the Gospel, or either of these with the Apocalypse, should be carefully noted. The verbs are in logical order : the manifestation must precede the seeing, which must precede witness and announcement. Ἡ ζωὴ ἐφανερώθη is a less definite expression than ὁ λόγος σὰρξ ἐγένετο (John i. 14), but refers to the same fact. For 'the Life' as a name for the Christ comp. John xi. 25 and xiv. 6. **Μαρτυρεῖν** is another word which, by its frequency in all three, connects together Gospel, Epistle, and Revelation. Witness to the truth, to produce faith in the Truth, on which eternal life depends, is a favourite thought with S. John. But the frequency of μαρτυρεῖν in his writings is obscured in A.V. by rendering it, 'bear record' (v. 7), 'give record' (v. 10), and 'testify' (iv. 14, v. 9), as well as 'bear witness'; and so also in Gospel and Revelation. Similarly μαρτυρία is translated 'record' (v. 10, 11) and 'testimony' (Rev. i. 2, 9, vi. 9, &c.), as well as 'witness.' The R.V. has made great improvements in this respect. Comp. Acts i. 22 and ii. 32.

ἀπαγγέλλομεν. *We* declare, as in *v.* 3. The verb is frequent in S. Luke, but rare in S. John (xvi. 25, but not iv. 51 or xx. 18). As in *vv.* 1 and 3 the Apostle emphatically states that what he has to declare is guaranteed by full personal experience. Comp. John xix. 35 ; xx. 30, 31 ; xxi. 24. "Let us firmly hold that which we see not ; because those tell us who have seen" (Augustine). Note the sequence here and in *v.* 3 : 1. the *evidence* which produced conviction in them, ἑωράκαμεν ; 2. their declaration of their conviction as *Apostles,* μαρτυροῦμεν ; 3. their declaration of it as *Evangelists,* ἀπαγγέλλομεν. **τὴν ζωὴν τὴν αἰώνιον.** The *life,* the *eternal life.* The repetition of the article in this phrase occurs only here and ii. 25. Its effect is to present life and eternity as two distinct ideas : comp. ii. 7, 8. The more general expression, ζωὴ αἰώνιος, is the common form. It is another of S. John's phrases ; but its frequency is blurred in A.V., which rings the changes on 'eternal life,' 'life eternal,' 'everlasting life,' and 'life everlasting.' 'Eternal' is preferable to 'everlasting,' although in popular usage the words are nearly synonymous. And it is worth remembering that 'eternal' is etymologically identical with αἰώνιος. *Aeternus* through *aeviternus* comes from *aevum,* which is the same word as αἰών with the digamma. The phrase ζωὴ αἰώνιος occurs first Dan. xii. 2. S. John's ζωὴ αἰώνιος has nothing to do with time, but depends on our relation to Jesus Christ. He tells us repeatedly that eternal life can be possessed in this world (v. 11, 13, 20 ; iii. 15 : see on John iii. 36 ; v. 24 ; vi. 47). Excepting in Rev. xiv. 6, where he speaks of a εὐαγγέλιον αἰώνιον, he never applies αἰώνιος to anything but ζωή. With the subject of eternal life this Epistle begins

and ends (v. 20). It is remarkable that S. Paul in the same sentence
(Rom. xvi. 25, 26) applies the epithet αἰώνιος to two such different
subjects as χρόνοι and Θεός. In N. T. αἰώνιος is generally of two termi-
nations; but αἰωνίαν occurs 2 Thess. ii. 16; Heb. ix. 12. In Plato
(*Timaeus* 37) we have αἰώνιος φύσις, and this is perhaps the earliest
appearance of the word. For a full discussion of it see Plumptre's
Spirits in Prison 356—371.

ἥτις ἦν πρὸς τ. πατέρα. The compound qualitative relative denotes
that what follows is a special attribute: 'which was *such as to be* with
the Father.' Comp. ἅτινά ἐστιν ἀλληγορούμενα, 'which *class of things*
contain an allegory; ἥτις ἐστὶν "Αγαρ, '*inasmuch as she* is Hagar' (Gal.
iv. 24); ἥτις ἐστὶν εἰδωλολατρεία, 'inasmuch as it is idolatry' (Col. iii. 5).
In N. T. ὅστις occurs only in nom., neut. acc., and contracted gen.
(ἕως ὅτου). For the ἦν see on *v.* 1. Πρὸς τ. πατέρα is exactly parallel to πρὸς τ. Θεόν (John i. 1, 2). It indicates the distinct Personality
of ἡ ζωή. Had S. John written ἥτις ἦν ἐν τῷ π., we might have taken
'the Life' to mean a mere attribute of God. Πρὸς τ. π. is *apud Patrem*,
'face to face' or 'at home with the Father.' Comp. 1 Cor. xvi. 7;
Gal. i. 18; 1 Thess. iii. 4; Philem. 13. "The simple title ὁ πατήρ
occurs rarely in the Synoptic Gospels, and always with reference to
'the Son'....In the Acts only i. 4, 7; ii. 33. In S. Paul only Rom. vi.
4; 1 Cor. viii. 6; Eph. ii. 18; and not at all in the Epistles of S. Peter,
S. James or S. Jude, or in the Apocalypse. In S. John's Gospel on
the contrary, and in his Epistles, the term is very frequent" (Westcott).
In ἐφαν. ἡμῖν the statement with which the parenthesis began is repeated. But S. John's repetitions generally carry us a stage further.
The manifestation was not only made, but made *to us.* Note the contrast between the imperfect of the continuous pre-existence of Christ
and the aorist of the temporary manifestation. He who was from
everlasting with the Father has been made known, and made known
to men, as the source of all life, physical, intellectual, moral, and
spiritual.

3. In returning to his main sentence he repeats part of it, but
from a different point of view and with a change of thought. In *v.*
1 he is leading up to the Incarnation and thinking mainly of *what* he
has to declare, viz. One existing from all eternity and intimately
known to himself. In *v.* 3 he is starting from the Incarnation and
thinking mainly of *why* he declares this, viz. to promote mutual fellowship.

ἀπαγγ. καὶ ὑμῖν. *Declare we* to *you* also. It may seem a trifle, but
it is worth while to distinguish between πρὸς ὑμᾶς κ.τ.λ. after verbs of
speaking, '*unto* you' and ὑμῖν, '*to* you'; all the more so as the former
construction is a characteristic of S. Luke's writings. The 'also' may
mean either 'the declaration is made by us to you as well as by
others to us,' or (more simply) 'to you as well as to others
whom we have already told.' Comp. "We cannot but speak the things
which we saw and heard" (Acts iv. 20). *Where* does S. John declare
Him who was from the beginning and was so well known to him and
to others? Not in this Epistle, for no such declaration is found in it;

but in the Gospel, which consists of such a declaration. Some persons, however, make these opening verses the declaration. We shall miss the purport of the Epistle if we do not bear constantly in mind that it was written as a companion to the Gospel. "See whether his Epistle does not bear witness to his Gospel" (Augustine). Parallels between the two abound: in what follows we have a striking one. 'That ye also may have fellowship with us' is the counterpart of 'that they may be one, even as We are' (John xvii. 11). The Apostle's purpose is identical with his Master's prayer. See on *v.* 4. 'Ye also, who have *not* seen, or heard, or handled, may have a blessing at least equal to ours, who *have*' (John xx. 29). Just as it is possible for every Christian to share the blessedness of Christ's mother by obedience (Matt. xii. 49, 50), so it is possible for them to share the blessedness of His Apostles by faith. In N.T. κοινωνία is rare, excepting in this chapter and in S. Paul's writings. It is almost always used of fellowship with persons (1 Cor. i. 9; xiii. 13; Gal. ii. 9; Phil. ii. 1) or with things personified (2 Cor. vi. 14). It "generally denotes the fellowship of persons with persons in one and the same object, always common to all and sometimes whole to each" (T. S. Evans in *Speaker's Comm.* on 1 Cor. x. 16). In 2 Cor. ix. 13 and Rom. xv. 26 it has the special sense of almsgiving as an expression of fellowship. In S. John's idea of the Church each member of it possesses the Son, and through Him the Father: and in this common possession each has communion with all other members. Κοινωνίαν ἔχειν (*vv.* 3, 6, 7) is stronger than κοινωνεῖν (2 John 11), and is still further strengthened by the μετά instead of the simple genitive (Phil. iii. 10; Philem. 6).

καὶ ἡ κοιν. δὲ ἡ ἡμετέρα. **Yea and** *our fellowship.* For καὶ...δὲ... comp. John vi. 51; viii. 16, 17; xv. 27. Grammarians are not agreed as to which of the two conjunctions connects the clauses and which adds emphasis to the substantive: Winer, 553; Ellicott on 1 Tim. iii. 10. Anyhow we have here a double emphasis, first through the double conjunctions and secondly through the double article: see on τὴν ζωὴν τὴν αἰών. (*v.* 2). 'Yea and the fellowship which I mean, the fellowship which is ours' is the full force. S. John in the intense earnestness of his style is very fond of the double article: ἡ ἐντολὴ ἡ παλαιά, τὸ φῶς τὸ ἀληθινόν, ὁ υἱὸς ὁ μονογενής (ii. 7, 8; iv. 9), τοῖς ἔργοις αὐτοῦ τοῖς πονηροῖς, τῆς ἀδελφῆς σου τῆς ἐκλεκτῆς (2 John 11, 13): comp. John iv. 9; v. 30; vi. 38, 42, 44, 50, 51, 58, &c., &c. This is specially the case with ἐμός in Christ's discourses; ὁ λογὸς ὁ ἐμός (viii. 31, 43, 51), ἡ χαρὰ ἡ ἐμή (xv. 11; xvii. 13): comp. v. 30; vi. 38; vii. 6, 8; xiv. 15, 27, &c. The Vulgate rendering, *et societas nostra* sit *cum Patre,* accepted by Beza, is excluded by the δέ which shews that καὶ ἡ κοιν. κ.τ.λ. cannot be dependent upon ἵνα, but is a separate statement. In N. T. the indicative ἐστί is frequently omitted, the subjunctive ᾖ *very* rarely—even in S. Paul, who at times leaves so much to be understood: 2 Cor. viii. 11, 13; Rom. iv. 16.

μετὰ τοῦ π. καὶ μετὰ τ. υἱ. He shews what the fellowship that is ours really means: not merely communion with us, but with

the Father and the Son.   The title of the Son is given with solemn
fulness, as in iii. 23 and 2 John 3; perhaps to indicate that the
Christian Church is a family in which all in their relation to God
share in the Sonship of Christ.   S. Paul uses a similar fulness of
expression in stating the same fact: πιστὸς ὁ Θεὸς δι' οὗ ἐκλήθητε εἰς
κοινωνίαν τοῦ υἱοῦ αὐτοῦ 'Ι. Χρ. τοῦ κυρίου ἡμῶν (1 Cor. i. 9: comp.
2 Cor. i. 19).   S. Paul also teaches our fellowship with the Father
through the Son (Rom. viii. 17).   The repetition of the μετά and of the
τοῦ marks emphatically the distinction and equality between the Son and
the Father.   Thus two fundamental truths, which the philosophical
heresies of the age were apt to obscure or deny, are here clearly
laid down at the outset; (1) the distinctness of personality and
equality of dignity between the Father and the Son; (2) the identity
of the eternal Son of God with the historical person Jesus Christ.
The verse forms another parallel with the Gospel: comp. John xvii.
20—23, esp. *v.* 21, to the two halves of which the two halves of this
verse fit, each to each.

ἵνα πάντες ἓν ὦσιν,	ἵνα καὶ ὑμεῖς κοινωνίαν
καθὼς σύ, πάτερ, ἐν ἐμοὶ	ἔχητε μεθ' ἡμῶν·
κἀγὼ ἐν σοί,	
ἵνα καὶ αὐτοὶ ἐν ἡμῖν	καὶ ἡ κ. δὲ ἡ ἡμετ.
ὦσιν.	μετὰ τ. π. κ. μ. τ. υἱ.

4. καὶ ταῦτα γράφ. ἡμεῖς.   He here refers to the Epistle as a
whole in contrast to the Gospel, which is referred to in ἀπαγγέλλομεν
(*vv.* 2, 3).   The purpose of his writing is stated in the Epistle at
the outset, in the Gospel at the close (xx. 31).   Both **γράφομεν** and
ἡμεῖς are emphatic: it is a permanent message that is sent, and it
is sent by Apostolic authority.   *Scriptio valde confirmat* (Bengel).
Only in this solemn Introduction does the Apostle use the first
person plural: in the body of the Epistle he uses the singular,
γράφω or ἔγραψα.   The frequent use of this verb shews that in spite
of its unusual form the document is rightly called an Epistle.   The
'to you' of the A.V. and earlier Versions and *vobis* of the Vulgate
must be omitted.

ἵνα ἡ χαρὰ ἡμῶν ᾖ πεπλ.   *That our joy may be* **fulfilled.**   Tyndale
in his first edition (1525) has 'your'; in his second (1534) and third
(1535) 'our.'   "The confusion of ἡμ. and ὑμ. in the best authorities is
so constant that a positive decision on the reading here is impossible"
(Westcott).   The Latin varies between *nostrum* and *vestrum.*   Some
copies insert *gaudeatis et*, and are followed doubtfully by Cranmer
(who prints '*ye may rejoyce, and that*' in italics within brackets), and
without any marks of doubt by Wiclif and the Rhemish Version.
Bede evidently read *nostrum*.   He remarks, doubtless as the result
of his own experience, that the joy of *teachers* is made full when
by their preaching many are brought to the communion of the Church
and of Him through whom the Church is strengthened and increased.
Πεπληρωμένη must not be rendered as if it were πλήρης, all the less
so as 'joy fulfilled' or 'made full' is one of S. John's characteristic
phrases.   The active, πληρώσατέ μου τὴν χαράν occurs Phil. i. 11, but

the passive with χαρά is peculiar to S. John (John iii. 29; xv. 11; xvi. 24; xvii. 13; 2 John 12). Comp. especially ταῦτα λελάληκα ὑμῖν ἵνα...ἡ χαρὰ ὑμῶν πληρωθῇ, and ταῦτα λαλῶ ἐν τῷ κόσμῳ ἵνα ἔχωσιν τὴν χαρὰν τὴν ἐμὴν πεπληρωμένην ἐν ἑαυτοῖς (John xv. 11; xvii. 13). Once more, as in *v.* 3, the Master's prayer and the Apostle's purpose are one and the same. '*Our* joy' may mean either the *Apostolic* joy at the good results of Apostolic teaching; or the joy in which the *recipients* of the teaching share—'yours as well as ours.' In either case the joy is that serene happiness, which is the result of conscious union with God and good men, of conscious possession of eternal life (see on v. 13), and which raises us above pain and sorrow and remorse. The concluding words of the Introduction to the Epistle of Barnabas are striking both in their resemblance and difference: "Now I, not as a teacher, but as one of you, will set forth a few things, by means of which in your present case ye may be gladdened."

The following profound thoughts struggle for expression in these four opening verses. 'There is a Being who has existed with God the Father from all eternity: He is the Father's Son: He is also the expression of the Father's Nature and Will. He has been manifested in space and time; and of that manifestation I and others have had personal knowledge: by the united evidence of our senses we have been convinced of its reality. In revealing to us the Divine Nature He becomes to us life, eternal life. With the declaration of all this in our hands as the Gospel, we come to you in this Epistle, that you may unite with us in our great possession, and that our joy in the Lord may be made complete.'

We now enter upon the first main division of the Epistle, which extends to ii. 28 ; the chief subject of which (with much digression) is the theme GOD IS LIGHT, and that in two parts: i. the Positive Side— WHAT WALKING IN THE LIGHT INVOLVES; THE CONDITION AND CONDUCT OF THE BELIEVER (i. 5—ii. 11): ii. the Negative Side—WHAT WALKING IN THE LIGHT EXCLUDES; THE THINGS AND PERSONS TO BE AVOIDED (ii. 12—28). These parts will be subdivided as we reach them.

I. 5—II. 28.　GOD IS LIGHT.

I. 5—II. 11.　WHAT WALKING IN THE LIGHT INVOLVES.

This section is largely directed against the Gnostic doctrine that to the man of enlightenment all conduct is morally indifferent. Against every form of this doctrine, which sapped the very foundations of Christian Ethics, the Apostle never wearies of inveighing. So far from its being true that all conduct is alike to the enlightened man, it is the character of his conduct that will shew whether he is enlightened or not. If he is walking in the light his condition and conduct will exhibit these things; 1. *Fellowship with God and with the Brethren* (5—7); 2. *Consciousness and Confession of Sin* (8—10); 3. *Obedience to God by Imitation of Christ* (ii. 1—6); 4. *Love of the Brethren* (ii. 7—11).

5—7. FELLOWSHIP WITH GOD AND WITH THE BRETHREN.

5. καὶ ἔστιν αὕτη ἡ ἀγγ. And *the message which we have heard
from Him is this*: αὕτη is the predicate, as so often in S. John, and
means 'This is the sum and substance of it, This is what it consists
in.' Usually αὕτη precedes ἐστίν, as in iii. 11, 23; v. 3, 11, 14;
2 John 6; and hence some texts place αὕτη first here. Comp. αὕτη δέ
ἐστιν ἡ κρίσις (John iii. 19), αὕτη ἐστὶν ἡ ἐντολή (xv. 12), αὕτη δέ ἐστιν ἡ
αἰών. ζωή (xvii. 3). As in the Gospel (i. 19), the main portion of the
writing is connected with the Introduction by a simple καί. It does
not introduce an inference, and the 'And' of Tyndale, Cranmer, and
the Rhemish is rightly restored in R. V. The 'then' of A. V. comes,
like so many errors, from Geneva, probably under the influence of
Beza's *igitur*. The connexion of thought, as so often in S. John, is
not plain, but seems to be this. He desires that we should have
fellowship with God (*v.* 3): and in order to have this we must know
a. what God is (*v.* 5), and *β.* what we are consequently bound to be
(6—10). 'Αγγελία (frequent in LXX., 2 Sam. iv. 4; Prov. xii. 26;
xxv. 26; xxvi. 16; &c.) occurs nowhere else in N. T. but here and
iii. 11; in each case with ἐπαγγελία, as v. l. 'Αγγέλλειν occurs only
John xx. 18; with v. l. ἀπαγγέλλειν. Neither in his Gospel nor in his
Epistles does S. John ever use εὐαγγέλιον, εὐαγγελίζειν, or εὐαγγελί-
ζεσθαι. The Gospel with him is ὁ λόγος or ἡ ἀλήθεια.

Once more we have a striking parallel between Gospel and Epistle.
Each opens with the same kind of statement.

καὶ αὕτη ἐστὶν	καὶ ἔστιν αὕτη
ἡ μαρτυρία...	ἡ ἀγγελία...

All these similarities strengthen the belief that the two were written
about the same time, and were intended to accompany one another.

ἀπ' αὐτοῦ means from Christ, as the context shews: comp. ii. 12.
Christ was the last mentioned (*v.* 3) and has been the main subject of
the Introduction. It was from Christ, and not immediately from the
Father, that the Apostles received their mission. 'Ακούειν ἀπό is not
common in N.T. S. John generally writes ἀκούειν παρά (vi. 45; vii.
51; viii. 26, 38, 40; xv. 15).

ἀναγγέλλομεν ὑμῖν. We announce to you. The amount of difference between ἀπαγγέλλειν (*vv.* 2, 3) and ἀναγγέλλειν is not great, yet
for the sake of distinction one may be rendered 'declare' and the other
'announce'. The Vulgate renders both by *adnuntiare*; but ἀναγγ. is
rather *renuntiare*. Both have the meanings 'report, announce, proclaim.' Both also may have the meaning of making known *again to
others* what has been received elsewhere: yet this is more commonly
the force of ἀναγγ. And this is the meaning here. The Apostles hand
on to all men what they have received from Christ. It is no invention
for their own benefit. It is a message and not a discovery. So also
the Spirit reveals to us truths which proceed from the Father and the
Son (John xvi. 13, 14, 15): and the Messiah ἀναγγελεῖ ἡμῖν πάντα
(John iv. 25 based on Deut. xviii. 18). Of the Evangelists S. John
alone uses ἀναγγ. Comp. 2 Cor. vii. 7; 1 Pet. i. 2. The ἀπό in ἀπαγγ.

is 'from' rather than 'back': ἀπαγγ.=ἀγγ. ἀπό τινος. Hence, while the *destination* of the message (ἀνά) is prominent in ἀναγγ., the *origin* of it (ἀπό) is prominent in ἀπαγγ. The latter word is rare in S. John (only *vv.* 2, 3 and John iv. 51), but very frequent in S. Luke's writings. Although ἀγγέλλειν occurs only once in N.T. (John xx. 18), its compounds abound : διαγγέλλειν, ἐπαγγέλλεσθαι, ἐξαγγέλλειν, καταγγέλλειν, παραγγέλλειν, προεπαγγ., προκαταγγ.

ὁ Θεὸς φῶς ἐστίν. *God is Light.* This is on the whole the main theme of the first great division of the Epistle, as *God is Love* of the second. This verse stands in much the same relation to the first main division as *vv.* 1—4 to the whole Epistle.

No one tells us so much about the Nature of God as S. John. The name given to him by the Greek Church, ὁ θεολόγος, 'the Theologian,' is amply justified. It is from him that we learn most of the Divinity of the Word and of the meaning of 'Divine.' Other writers tell us what God *does*, and what attributes He *possesses;* S. John tells us what He *is.* There are three statements in the Bible which stand alone as revelations of the Nature of God, and they are all in the writings of S. John: 'God is spirit' (John iv. 24); 'God is light,' and 'God is love' (1 John iv. 8). In all these momentous statements the predicate has no article, either definite or indefinite : πνεῦμα ὁ Θεός : ὁ Θεὸς φῶς ἐστίν : ὁ Θεὸς ἀγάπη ἐστίν. We are not told that God is *the* Spirit, or *the* Light, or *the* Love : nor that He is *a* Spirit, or *a* light. Luther is certainly wrong in translating, "dass Gott *ein* Licht ist." But 'God is spirit, is light, is love': spirit, light, love are His very Nature. They are not mere attributes, like mercy and justice : they are Himself. They are probably the nearest approach to a definition of God that the human mind could frame or comprehend : and in the history of thought and religion they are unique. The more we consider them, the more they satisfy us. The simplest intellect can understand their meaning; the subtlest cannot exhaust it. No philosophy, no religion, not even the Jewish, had risen to the truth that God is light. 'The Lord shall be *to thee* an everlasting light' (Is. lx. 19, 20) is far short of it. But S. John knows it: and lest the great message which he conveys to us in his Gospel, 'God is spirit,' should seem somewhat bare and empty in its indefiniteness, he adds this other message in his Epistle, 'God is light, God is love.' No figure borrowed from the material world could give the idea of perfection so clearly and fully as *light.* It suggests ubiquity, brightness, happiness, intelligence, truth, purity, holiness. It suggests excellence without limit and without taint; an excellence whose nature it is to communicate itself and to pervade everything from which it is not of set purpose shut out. 'Let there be light' was the first fiat of the Creator; and on it all the rest depends. Light is the condition of beauty, and life, and growth, and activity: and this is as true in the intellectual, moral, and spiritual spheres as in the material universe.

Yet we must not suppose that S. John means this as a *mere* figure borrowed from the material world, as if sunlight were the reality and the Godhead something like it. Rather, the similarity exists, because light and its properties are reflexions of attributes which are Divine. In Platonic language, God is the ἰδέα or archetype of which light is the noblest earthly expression. Thus Philo says, ὁ Θεὸς φῶς ἐστί,...καὶ οὐ μόνον φῶς ἀλλὰ καὶ παντὸς ἑτέρου φωτὸς ἀρχέτυπον. S. James seems to have a similar thought in calling God ὁ πατὴρ τῶν φώτων (i. 17) : comp. Rev. xxii. 5.

Of the many beautiful and true ideas which the utterance 'God is light' suggests to us, three are specially prominent in this Epistle; *intelligence, holiness,* and *communicativeness.* The Christian, anointed with the Holy Spirit, and in communion with God in Christ, possesses (1) knowledge, (2) righteousness, and (3) necessarily communicates to others the truth which he knows and the righteousness which he practises. (1) 'Ye know Him which is from the beginning' (ii. 13,14); 'I have not written unto you because ye know not the truth, but because ye know it' (ii. 21); 'Ye need not that any one teach you' (ii. 27); &c. &c. (2) 'Every one that hath this hope on Him purifieth himself, even as He is pure' (iii. 3); 'Whosoever is begotten of God doeth no sin, because His seed abideth in him: and he cannot sin, because he is begotten of God'; &c. &c. (3) 'We have fellowship one with another' (i. 7); 'We love the brethren' (iii. 14); and the whole tone of the Epistle.

καὶ σκοτία οὐκ ἔστιν ἐν αὐτῷ οὐδεμία. This is the order of the words in B, Thebaic, and Memphitic, and it is very forcible: *and darkness there is not in Him, no, not any at all.* Gnostic systems which taught, that a series of Aeons ending in an evil one could emanate from the Supreme Being, are here condemned by anticipation. Out of Light no darkness can come. This 'antithetic parallelism' is a mark of S. John's style. He frequently emphasizes a statement by following it up with a denial of its opposite. Thus, in the very next verse, 'We lie and do not the truth': comp. *v.* 8, ii. 4, 10, 27 ; v. 12. So also in the Gospel : i. 3, 20; iii. 15 ; x. 5, 18; xviii. 20 ; xx. 27. And in Revelation ii. 13; iii. 9. It is one of many instances of the Hebrew cast of S. John's language. Parallelism is the very form of Hebrew poetry and is frequent in the Psalms (lxxxix. 30, 31, 38).

Another point of similarity between the Gospel and the Epistle must here be noticed. In the Prologue to the Gospel we have these four ideas in succession ; ὁ λόγος (*vv.* 1, 2), ἡ ζωή (*v.* 4), τὸ φῶς (*vv.* 4, 5), ἡ σκοτία (*v.* 5). The same four follow in the same order here : περὶ τοῦ λόγου τῆς ζωῆς, ἡ ζωὴ ἐφανερώθη, ὁ Θεὸς φῶς ἐστίν, καὶ σκοτία ἐν αὐτῷ οὐκ ἔστιν οὐδεμία. Has not the sequence of thought in the one case been influenced by the sequence of thought in the other? Such close correspondence between the ideas with which each writing opens cannot be accidental.

The figurative use of σκοτία for moral darkness, i.e. error and sin (*peccata, haereses, et odia nominat,* says Bede), is very frequent in S. John (ii. 8, 9, 11; John i. 5; viii. 12; xii. 35, 46): he only twice uses the form σκότος (*v.* 6; John iii. 9), which (excepting Matt. x. 27; Luke xii. 3) is the invariable form elsewhere in N.T. The passages just quoted shew that S. John's meaning here cannot be, 'God has

now been revealed, and is no longer a God that hideth Himself'
(Is. xlv. 15). The point is not that God can be known, but what kind
of God He is. The Apostle is laying the foundation of Christian
Ethics, of which the very first principle is that there is a God who
intellectually, morally, and spiritually is *light*.
"In speaking of 'light' and 'darkness' it is probable that S. John
had before him the Zoroastrian speculations on the two opposing
spiritual powers which influenced Christian thought at a very early
date" (Westcott).

6. An inference from the first principle just laid down. God is
light, utterly removed from all darkness: therefore to be in darkness
is to be cut off from Him. If God is light, then those who have communion with Him must (1) walk in light, (2) be conscious of sin, (3)
confess their sin (*vv.* 6—10).

ἐὰν εἴπωμεν. With great gentleness he states the case hypotheti-
cally, and with great delicacy he includes himself in the hypothesis.
As in his Gospel, he has in view only professing Christians, and he
warns them against three false professions, each introduced in the
same way (*vv.* 6, 8, 10). In between these three possible forms of false
doctrine is stated by way of antithesis the right course of action and
profession (7, 9). The symmetrical arrangement of clauses is very
marked throughout. Further on in the Epistle S. John varies the
form of expression from ἐὰν εἴπωμεν to ὁ λέγων (ii. 4, 6, 9) and ἐάν τις
εἴπῃ (iv. 20). The conditional particles ἐὰν and εἰ, especially the
former, are very frequent in this Epistle.

ἐν τῷ σκότει περιπατῶμεν. Comp. ὁ λαὸς ὁ πορευόμενος ἐν σκότει (Is.
ix. 1). Darkness is the sphere of the κόσμος, and the κόσμος is in antagonism to God. Περιπατεῖν is the Latin *versari* and signifies the
ordinary course of life. The word in this sense is frequent only
in S. Paul and in S. John. Comp. ii. 6, 11; 2 John 4, 6; 3 John
3, 4; Rev. xxi. 24; John viii. 12; Eph. v. 1, 9—15, &c. It
expresses not merely action, but habitual action. A life in moral
darkness can no more have communion with God, than a life in
a coal-pit can have communion with the sun. For 'what communion hath light with darkness?' (2 Cor. vi. 4). Light can be
shut out, but it cannot be shut in. Some Gnostics taught, not merely
that to the illuminated all conduct was alike, but that to reach the
highest form of illumination men must experience every kind of action,
however abominable, in order to work themselves free from the powers
that rule the world (Eus. *H. E.* IV. vii. 9). Ἐν τῷ σκότει should probably be rendered *in the darkness*: in *vv.* 6, 7, as in ii. 8, 9, 11, both
'light' and 'darkness' have the article, which is not merely generic but
emphatic; that which is light indeed is opposed to that which is darkness indeed. In 'What communion hath light with darkness?',
neither word has the article: τίς κοινωνία φωτὶ πρὸς σκότος; (2 Cor.
vi. 14).

ψευδόμεθα καὶ οὐ ποιοῦμεν τὴν ἀλ. As in *v.* 5, the affirmation is
enforced by denying its opposite. But here the negative clause carries

us further than the positive one: it includes conduct as well as speech. In John iii. 21 ποιεῖν τ. ἀλήθειαν is opposed to φαῦλα πράσσειν, to do what has true moral worth as opposed to practising what is morally good-for-nothing. Ethical rather than intellectual truth is here meant by ἀλήθεια. With ποιεῖν τὴν ἀλ. should be contrasted ποιεῖν ψεῦδος (Rev. xxi. 27; xxii. 15). In LXX. ποιεῖν ἐλεημοσύνην (or ἔλεος) καὶ ἀλήθ. occurs (Gen. xlvii. 29; 2 Sam. ii. 6; &c.); but there the ἔλεος renders ποιεῖν less startling. In Neh. ix. 33 the very phrase occurs; ἀλήθειαν ἐποίησας. S. Paul comes near to it when he opposes ἀλήθεια to ἀδικία (1 Cor. xiii. 6); shewing that with him also truth is not confined to speech. In this Epistle we find many striking harmonies in thought and language between S. John and S. Paul, quite fatal to the view that there is a fundamental difference in teaching between the two. See on ii. 16.

Note the exact correspondence between the two halves of the verse: ψευδόμεθα balances εἴπωμεν (speech); ποιοῦμεν balances περιπατῶμεν (action). Profession without conduct is a lie: *Nequaquam ergo sola fidei confessio sufficit ad salutem, cui bonorum operum attestatio deest* (Bede).

7. A further inference from the first principle laid down in *v.* 5: walking in the light involves not only fellowship with God but fellowship with the brethren. This verse takes the opposite hypothesis to that just considered and expands it. We often find (comp. *v.* 9) that S. John while seeming to go back or repeat, really progresses and gives us something fresh. It would have enforced *v.* 6, but it would have told us nothing fresh, to say 'if we walk in the light, and say that we have fellowship with Him, we speak the truth, and do not lie.' And it is interesting to find that the craving to make this verse the exact antithesis of the preceding one has generated another reading, 'we have fellowship with *Him*,' instead of 'with *one another*.' This reading is as old as the second century, for Tertullian (*De Pud.* xix.) quotes, '*si vero*,' *inquit,* '*in lumine incedamus,* communionem cum eo habebimus, et sanguis &c.*' Clement of Alexandria also seems to have known of this reading. Another ancient corruption is 'with *God*' (Harl.). This is evidence of the early date of our Epistle; for by the end of the second century important differences of reading had already arisen and become widely diffused.

περιπατῶμεν, ὡς αὐτὸς ἔστιν. We *walk;* God *is.* We move through space and time; He is in eternity. We progress from grace to grace, becoming sons of light by believing on the Light (John xii. 36; Eph. v. 8, 9). Of Him who is absolute Perfection, and knows no progress or change, we can only say 'He is.' That which *is* light must ever be *in* the light: comp. ἀναβαλλόμενος φῶς ὡς ἱμάτιον (Ps. civ. 2), and φῶς οἰκῶν ἀπρόσιτον (1 Tim. vi. 16), which embodies the same thought. Αὐτός, as commonly, but not invariably (see on *v.* 5 and ii. 12), in this Epistle, means God, not Christ. *Imitatio Dei, criterium communionis cum illo* (Bengel).

It is very possibly from this antithesis of walking in light and walking in darkness that the figure of "The Two Ways," called in the

Διδαχὴ τῶν δώδεκα ᾿Αποστόλων (i.—vi.) ὁδὸς τῆς ζωῆς and ὁδὸς τοῦ θανάτου, and in the Epistle of Barnabas (xviii.—xxi.) ὁδὸς τοῦ φωτός and
ὁδὸς τοῦ σκότους, took its rise.

κοινωνίαν ἔχ. μετ᾽ ἀλλήλων. It is quite clear from iii. 23; iv. 7, 12;
2 John 5 that this refers to the mutual fellowship of Christians *among
themselves*, and not to fellowship *between God and man*, as S. Augustine, Calvin, and others (desiring to make this verse parallel to *v.* 6),
have interpreted. But such barren repetitions are not in S. John's
manner: he repeats in order to progress. Moreover he would scarcely
have expressed the relation between God and man by a phrase which
seems to imply *equality* between those united in fellowship. Contrast
'I ascend to My Father and your Father, and My God and your God'
(John xx. 17). He would rather have said 'We have fellowship with
Him, and He with us.' The communion of Christians with one
another is a consequence of their walking in the light. In that 'thick
darkness' which prevailed 'in all the land of Egypt three days, *they
saw not one another, neither rose any from his place* for three days (Ex.
xi. 22, 23): i.e. there was an absolute cessation of fellowship. Society
could not continue in the dark: but when the light returned, society
was restored. So also in the spiritual world; when the light comes,
individuals have that communion one with another which in darkness
is impossible. In a similar spirit Cicero declares that real friendship
is impossible without virtue (*De Amic.* vi. 20).

καὶ τὸ αἷμα ᾿Ιησοῦ. Comp. Rev. v. 9; vii. 14; xii. 11. The καί
indicates that this is a further consequence of walking in the light.
One who is walking in spiritual darkness cannot appropriate that
cleansing from sin, which is wrought by the blood of Jesus, shed on
the Cross and offered to God as a propitiation for sin. It is by His
death that we participate in His life, and the sphere in which life is
found is light. The addition of τοῦ υἱοῦ αὐτοῦ is not at all redundant:
(1) it is a passing contradiction of Cerinthus, who taught that Jesus
was a mere man when His blood was shed, for the Divine element in
His nature left Him when He was arrested in the garden; and of the
Ebionites, who taught that He was a mere man from His birth to His
death; (2) it explains how this blood can have such virtue: it is the
blood of One who is the Son of God. Early Christian writers used
very extreme language in expressing this truth. Clement of Rome (ii)
speaks of the παθήματα of God; Ignatius (*Eph.* 1) of αἷμα Θεοῦ, (*Rom.*
vi.) of τὸ πάθος τοῦ Θεοῦ. Tatian (*ad Graec.* xiii.) has τοῦ πεπονθότος
Θεοῦ, Tertullian (*de Carn. Christi*, v.) *passiones Dei*, and (*ad Uxor.* ii.
iii) *sanguine Dei*. See Lightfoot, Appendix to Clement, p. 402.

καθαρίζει. Note the present tense of what goes on continually, that
constant cleansing which even the holiest Christians need (see on John
xiii. 10). One who lives in the light knows his own frailty and is
continually availing himself of the purifying power of Christ's sacri-
ficial death. 'This passage shews that the gratuitous pardon of sins is
given us not once only, but that it is a benefit perpetually residing in
the Church, and daily offered to the faithful' (Calvin). Note also the
'all'; there is no limit to its cleansing power: even grievous sinners

can be restored to the likeness of God, in whom is no darkness at all.
This refutes by anticipation the error of the Novatians, who denied
pardon to mortal sins after baptism.   Comp. 'How much more shall
the blood of Christ...cleanse your conscience' (Heb. ix. 14), and
' These are they which come out of the great tribulation, and *they washed
their robes and made them white in the blood of the Lamb*' (Rev. vii.
14).   And 'apart from shedding of blood there is no remission' (Heb.
ix. 25).   For ἁμαρτία in the singular, sin regarded as one great plague,
comp. iii. 4; John viii. 21; xvi. 8; and especially i. 29.   But the
addition of πάσης without the article shews us that this plague has
many forms: 'from every (kind of) sin.'   Winer, 137.   Comp. Matt.
xii. 31.   Clement of Alexandria (*Strom.* III. iv.) quotes *vv.* 6, 7 (with
the formula φησὶν ὁ Ἰωάννης ἐν τῇ ἐπιστολῇ) and omits πάσης.

8—10.   CONSCIOUSNESS AND CONFESSION OF SIN.

8—10.   Walking in the light involves the great blessings just stated,
—fellowship with God and with our brethren, and a share in the purifying blood of Jesus.   But it also involves something on our part.   It
intensifies our consciousness of sin, and therefore our desire to get rid
of it by confessing it.   No one can live in the light without being
abundantly convinced that he himself is not light.

8.   ἐὰν εἴπωμεν.   The second of the false professions : see on *v.*
6.   Some probably did say so, and others thought so: εἴπωμεν need
not mean more than 'say in our hearts.'   Portions of S. John's own
teaching (iii. 9, 10) might easily be misunderstood as countenancing
this error, if taken without his qualifications.   Ἁμαρτίαν ἔχειν is a
phrase peculiar to S. John in N. T.   It differs from ἁμαρτάνειν much
as ἁμαρτία or ἡ ἁμαρτία, sin as a whole, from ἁμαρτίαι or αἱ ἁμαρτίαι,
the separate sinful acts.   Comp. John ix. 41; xv. 22, 24; xix. 11.   We
need not enquire whether original or actual sin is meant: the expression covers sin of every kind.   Only one human being has been able
to say 'The things pleasing to God I always do'; 'Which of you con-
victeth Me of sin?'; 'The ruler of the world hath nothing in Me'
(John viii. 29, 46; xiv. 30).   The more a man knows of the meaning
of 'God is light', i.e. the more he realises the absolute purity and
holiness of God, the more conscious he will become of his own impurity and sinfulness: comp. Job ix. 2; xiv. 4; xv. 14; xxv. 4; Prov.
xx. 9; Eccles. vii. 20.

ἑαυτοὺς πλανῶμεν.   Not the middle, nor the passive, but a form of
expression which makes it quite clear that the erring is all our own
doing.   Not 'we err,' or 'we are deceived,' but **we lead ourselves
astray**, with an emphasis on 'ourselves.'   *Ipsi nos seducimus.*   We do
for ourselves what the archdeceiver Satan (Rev. xii. 9; xx. 10) en-
deavours to do for us.   Πλανᾶν in the active is frequent in S. John (ii.
26, iii. 7; John vii. 12; Rev. ii. 20; xii. 9; xiii. 14; xix. 20; xx. 3, 8,
10).   These passages indicate that the verb is a strong one and implies
serious departure from the truth.   For ἑαυτούς with the first person
comp. ἀνεθεματίσαμεν ἑαυτούς (Acts xxiii. 14), ἑαυτοὺς διεκρίνομεν (1 Cor.
xi. 31).   It occurs with the second person v. 21; 2 John 8 (see note);

John v. 42; and frequently in S. Paul's writings. Winer 178, 179, 321, 322. 'To deceive' would be rather ἀπατᾶν (James i. 26), ἐξαπατᾶν (1 Cor. iii. 18), φρεναπατᾶν (Gal. vi. 3), ἡ ἀλήθ. ἐν ἡμῖν οὐκ ἔστιν. Once more the positive statement is enforced by a negative one (*vv.* 5, 6). We are in an atmosphere of self-made darkness which shuts the truth out. It may be all round us, as sunlight round a closed house; but it does not enter into us, still less has a permanent place in us. All words about *truth* are characteristic of S. John's writings; ἀλήθεια, Gospel and all three Epistles; ἀληθής, Gospel, and 1 and 3 John; ἀληθινός, Gospel, 1 John, and Revelation; ἀληθῶς, Gospel and 1 John. 'The truth' is the correlative of 'witness', which, as shewn above (*v.* 2), is also characteristic of the Apostle.

9. ἐὰν ὁμολ. τὰς ἁμαρτ. ἡμῶν. The opposite case is now taken and developed, as in *v.* 7: see note there. But here we have no δέ, and the asyndeton is telling. Greek has such a wealth of connecting particles, that in that language asyndeton is specially remarkable. Here there is expansion and progress, not only in the second half of the verse where '*He* is faithful and righteous' takes the place of '*we* are true'; but in the first half also; where 'confess *our sins*' takes the place of 'say *we have sin.*' The latter admission costs us little: the confession of the particular sins which we have committed costs a good deal, and is a guarantee of sincerity. He who refuses to confess, may perhaps desire, but certainly does not *seek* forgiveness. 'He that covereth his transgressions shall not prosper: but whoso confesseth and forsaketh them shall obtain mercy' (Prov. xxviii. 13). Obviously confession to Him who is 'faithful and righteous,' and to those 'selves' whom we should otherwise 'lead astray,' is all that is meant. The passage has nothing to do with the question of confession to our fellow-men. Elsewhere S. John uses ὁμολογεῖν only of confessing *Christ* (ii. 23; iv. 2, 3, 15; 2 John 7; John i. 20; ix. 22; xii. 42; Rev. iii. 5).

πιστός ἐστιν κ. δίκαιος. *He is faithful and* **righteous,** to bring out the contrast with πάσης ἀδικίας here and the connexion with 'Ιησ. Χρ. δίκαιον (ii. 1). God is πιστός because He *keeps His word,* and δίκαιος because in doing so He *gives to each his due.* Comp. πιστὸς γὰρ ὁ ἐπαγγειλάμενος (Heb. x. 23); πιστὸν ἡγήσατο τὸν ἐπαγγειλάμενον (xi. 11). Δίκαιος εἶ ὁ ὤν...ὅτι ταῦτα ἔκρινας...ἀληθιναὶ καὶ δίκαιαι αἱ κρίσεις σου (Rev. xvi. 5—7). Beware of watering down δίκαιος into a vague expression for 'kind, gentle, merciful.' 'The Lord be a true and faithful witness between us' (Jer. xlii. 5) in LXX. is Ἔστω κύριος ἐν ἡμῖν εἰς μάρτυρα δίκαιον καὶ πιστόν.

ἵνα ἀφῇ. In spite of what some eminent scholars have said to the contrary, it is perhaps true that the Greek for these words includes to some extent the idea of *intention* and *aim.* Comp. iii. 1; John iv. 34; vi. 29, 40; xii. 23; xiii. 1. Thus the Vulgate and Beza, *fidelis est et justus, ut remittat nobis peccata nostra;* and Wiclif, 'He is feithful and just *that* He forgeve to us oure synnes'; and the Rhemish, 'He is faithful and just, *for to* forgive us our sinnes.' In S. John we find the conviction deeply rooted that all things happen in accordance with the decrees of God: events are the results of His purposes. And this conviction influences his language: so that constructions (ἴνα) which originally indicated a *purpose*, and which even in late Greek do not lose this meaning entirely, are specially frequent in his writings: see on John v. 36. It is God's decree and aim that His faithfulness and righteousness should appear in His forgiving us and cleansing us from sin. "Forgiveness and cleansing are ends to which God, being what He is, has regard" (Westcott). See Haupt's note and Winer, 577. Those particular acts of which we are conscious and which we have confessed are indicated by τὰς ἁμαρτίας: ἁμαρτία in the singular may be either sin in the abstract (John xvi. 9) or a single act of sin (v. 16); ἁμαρτίαι in the plural must mean particular sinful acts (ii. 2, 12; iii. 5; v. 10). Comp. Ps. xxxii. 5; Prov. xxviii. 13, where the doctrine, that confession of sins (not admission of sinfulness) leads to forgiveness, is plainly stated.

καθαρίσῃ ἡμ. ἀπὸ π. ἀδικίας. Not a repetition in other words of ἀφῇ τὰς ἁμ. It is a second and distinct result of our confession: 1. We are absolved from sin's punishment; 2. We are freed from sin's pollution. The reference to the phraseology of the Temple is obvious (Heb. ix. 23; John ii. 6; iii. 25). The one affects our peace, the other our character. The forgiveness is the averting of God's wrath; the cleansing is the beginning of holiness. "He takes from thee an evil security, and puts in a useful fear" (Augustine). Possibly, as in *v.* 6, there is exact correspondence between the two clauses. There, ψευδόμεθα evidently refers to εἴπωμεν, ποιοῦμεν to περιπατῶμεν. Here, ἀφῇ may look back to πιστός, καθαρίσῃ to δίκαιος. God is 'faithful' in forgiving our sins, because He has promised to do so, 'righteous' in cleansing us from *un*righteousness, because reunion with Him banishes what is contrary to Him. Light must expel darkness.

10. οὐχ ἡμαρτήκαμεν. This is the third false profession. It is not equivalent to ἁμαρτίαν οὐκ ἔχομεν (*v.* 8), which refers to the sinful state, the inward principle: whereas this indicates the *result* of that state, viz. the commission of sinful acts. 1. We may ignore the difference between right and wrong and thereby deny that sin exists (*v.* 6). 2. We may deny that our own nature is sinful (*v.* 8). 3. Or, admitting the reality of sin and the sinful tendency of our nature, we may deny that we, as a matter of fact, have sinned. Of course sins committed before baptism are not meant: no Christian would have denied these. Both in Gospel and in Epistles S. John has in mind adult Christians, not catechumens. The Greek perfect here again (*vv.* 1, 3) has its full force; present result of past action: 'We are in the condition of having avoided sin.'

ψεύστην ποιοῦμεν αὐτόν. At first sight this third false profession seems less serious than the others: but to avoid the other two and yet adopt this is more conspicuously a sin against light. There is a marked gradation of guilt. 'To lead ourselves astray' (*v.* 8) is worse than 'to lie' (*v.* 6): but 'to make God a liar' is worst of all. This use of ποιεῖν for 'to assert that one is' is another of S. John's characteristics: τίνα σεαυτὸν ποιεῖς; (John viii. 53); ποιεῖς σεαυτὸν θεόν (x. 33).

Comp. v. 18, xix. 7, 12. The O. T. proclaims the universality of sin. Moreover, God's whole scheme of salvation assumes that every human being sins and has need of redemption, the Redeemer only excepted. Therefore those who profess that they have never sinned, and have no need of a Redeemer, charge God with having deliberately framed a libel against themselves, and having misstated the possibilities of human nature. It has been acutely remarked of Renan's *Life of Jesus* that "sin does not appear in it at all. Now if there is anything which explains the success of the Good News among men, it is that it offered deliverance from sin—salvation" (Amiel).

ὁ λόγος αὐτοῦ οὐκ ἔστιν ἐν ἡμῖν. God's revelation of Himself has no home in our hearts: it remains outside us, as the light remains outside and separate from those who shut themselves up in darkness. Obviously ὁ λόγος here is not personal: nothing has been said about the indwelling of Christ. 'His word' means the whole of God's Revelation in both O. and N.T., especially in the Gospel (John x. 35; xvii. 6, 14, 17). Ὁ λόγος is more definite than ἡ ἀλήθεια (v. 8), and also more personal: it implies that the truth has been *uttered.* Utterance there must be in word or deed to make truth of any worth to mankind. The expressions εἶναι ἐν and μένειν ἐν, to express intimate relationship, are very characteristic of S. John: and either of the things related can be said to be in the other. Thus, either 'His word is not in us' (comp. ii. 14) or 'If ye abide in My Word' (John viii. 31): either 'The truth is not in us' (v. 8) or 'He standeth not in the truth' (John xiii. 44). Sometimes the two modes of expression are combined; 'Abide in Me, and I in you' (John xv. 4).

Note that the contrary hypothesis to the first and second false professions is given (*vv.* 7 and 9) but not to the third. That to the second (*v.* 9) covers the third also. The mere confession of sinfulness, which would be the exact contrary to the second false profession, is omitted as being of no moral value.

CHAPTER II.

4. Before ἔγνωκα insert ὅτι with אAB against CKL. א omits ἐν τούτῳ before ἡ ἀλήθεια and inserts τοῦ θεοῦ after it.

6. Before περιπατεῖν omit οὕτως with AB against אCK.

7. For ἀδελφοί (KL) read ἀγαπητοί (אABCP), and after ἠκούσατε omit ἀπ' ἀρχῆς with אABCP and Versions against KL.

8. For σκοτία (BC and Versions) A has σκία.

13. For γράφω with παιδία (K) read ἔγραψα (אABCP).

14. B has τὸ ἀπ' ἀρχῆς. B and the Thebaic omit τοῦ θεοῦ. Comp. v. 20.

15. AC read ἡ ἀγάπη τοῦ Θεοῦ. Some later authorities have the conflate reading ἡ ἀγάπη τοῦ Θεοῦ καὶ τοῦ πατρός.

18. Before ἀντίχριστος omit ὁ with א¹BC against AKL.

20. For καὶ οἴδατε πάντα (ACKL, Memphitic, Vulgate) we should perhaps read καὶ οἴδατε πάντες (ℵP) or οἴδατε πάντες (B, Thebaic). Comp. *v.* 14.   The reading remains uncertain.

23. After ἔχει add ὁ ὁμολογῶν τὸν υἱὸν καὶ τὸν πατέρα ἔχει with ℵABC and Versions against KL.   Omission through *homoeoteleuton.*

24. After the first ὑμεῖς omit οὖν with ℵABC and Versions against KL.

27. For ἐν ὑμῖν μένει (KL) read μένει ἐν ὑμῖν (ℵBC); for τὸ αὐτὸ (AKL) read τὸ αὐτοῦ (ℵBC); and for μενεῖτε (KL) read μένετε (ℵABC and Versions).   B has χάρισμα for the first χρῖσμα and ℵ¹ has πνεῦμα for the second.

28. For ὅταν (KL) read ἐάν (ℵABC), and for ἔχωμεν (ℵ¹KL) read σχῶμεν (ℵ³ABC).   ℵ omits καὶ νῦν...ἐν αὐτῷ through *homoeoteleuton.*

29. For εἰδῆτε (ℵBC, Vulgate) AKL and some Versions read ἴδητε. Before πᾶς insert καὶ with ℵAC, Peschito, Thebaic, and Vulgate against BKL.   B and some Versions omit both καὶ and πᾶς.

In nearly all these cases B preserves the original text.   The combination ℵB in no instance yields a doubtful reading.

Ch. II. 1—6.   OBEDIENCE TO GOD BY IMITATION OF CHRIST.

1—6. The Apostle is still treating of the condition and conduct of the believer as determined by his walking in the light; there is no break between the two chapters.   Having shewn us that even Christians constantly sin, he goes on (1) to point out the remedy for sin, (2) to exhort us not to sin.   The paragraph begins and ends with the latter point, but the former constitutes the chief link with the preceding paragraph: comp. i. 7.   He who craves to grow in sanctification, and yet is conscious of his own frailty must constantly have recourse to the Advocate and His cleansing blood: thus he will be enabled to obey God more and more perfectly.   The consideration of what it has cost to provide a remedy for sin will inspire him with a horror of sin.

1. τεκνία μου.   The diminutive does not imply that the Apostle is addressing persons of tender age: it is a term of endearment. Wiclif has 'litil sones' as a rendering of the *filioli* of the Vulgate; Tyndale, Cranmer, and the Genevan Version all waver between 'babes' (which is far too strong) and 'little children.'   Setting aside Gal. iv. 19, where the reading is uncertain, the word occurs only in this Epistle (*vv.* 12, 28; iii. 7, 18; iv. 4; v. 21) and once in the Gospel (xiii. 33).   Possibly it is a reminiscence of Christ's farewell address in John xiii.   S. John's conception of the Church is that of a family, in which all are children of God and brethren one of another, but in which also some who are elders stand in a parental relation to the younger brethren.   Thus there were families within the family, each with its own father.   And who had a better right to consider himself a father than the last surviving Apostle?   "The Apostles loved and cherished that name, and all that it implied, and all that illustrated it. They much preferred it to any title which merely indicated an office. It was more spiritual: it was more personal; it asserted better the divine order; it did more to preserve the dignity and sacredness of all domestic relations" (Maurice). Comp. the story of 'S. John and the Robber' (p. xxxii).

ταῦτα γράφω. Probably refers to what precedes rather than to what follows. They must not think that because he insists on the reality of sin and the sinfulness of all (i. 6—10), therefore he would have them acquiesce in sin as inevitable. Henceforward he drops the Apostolic first person plural and uses the more personal singular in harmony with τεκνία μου.

ἵνα μὴ ἁμάρτητε. *In order* **that ye may not sin.** The aorist is conclusive against the rendering 'that ye may not *continue* in sin.' He would help them to avoid every *act* of sin. Comp. ἵνα τις ἐξ αὐτοῦ φάγῃ καὶ μὴ ἀποθάνῃ (John vi. 50); and contrast i. 3; iii. 11; iv. 21; v. 3, where the present subjunctive is used. This is the moral effect of the death of Christ;—to unite men to the God who is Light, and to enable them to hate and avoid the darkness of sin. His aim throughout is ὁμοίωσις τῷ Θεῷ (iii. 2).

καὶ ἐάν τις ἁμάρτῃ. *Et si quis peccaverit. And if any one have sinned.* The aorist again shews that it is an act, and not a state of sin, that is contemplated. Not merely the habitual offender, but he who falls into a single sin, needs and has an Advocate. Sin and its remedy are placed in close proximity, just as they are found in the Church. Note the changes of construction: 'that *ye* sin not. And if *any one...we* have.' S. John's habit of writing in the Hebrew form by co-ordinating rather than by subordinating his clauses comes out here. A Greek would more probably have written: ταῦτα γράφω ἵνα μὴ ἁμάρ. καὶ ἵνα εἰδῆτε ὅτι, ἐάν τις ἁμ., π. ἔχομεν.

παράκλητον ἔχομεν. Just as we always have sin (i. 8) so we always have One ready to plead for pardon. S. John does not say '*he* hath an Advocate,' but '*we* have' one: he breaks the logical flow of the sentence rather than seem not to include himself in the need and possession of an Advocate, comp. v. 28. On Advocate or Paraclete (παράκλητος) see on John xiv. 16. It means one who is *summoned to the side of* another, especially to serve as his helper, spokesman (*causae patronus*), or intercessor. The word occurs in N.T. only in S. John; here in the Epistle and four times in the Gospel (xiv. 16, 26; xv. 26; xvi. 7). It is unlikely that S. John would use the word in totally different senses in the two writings, especially if the Epistle was written to accompany the Gospel. We must therefore find some meaning which will suit all five passages. Two renderings compete for acceptation, 'Comforter' and 'Advocate.' Both make good sense in the Gospel, and (though there is by no means agreement on the point) 'Advocate' makes the best sense. 'Advocate' is the only rendering which is at all probable here: it exactly suits the context. 'We have a *Comforter* with the Father' would be intolerable. Moreover, the passive form of the word is decisive, as well as the use of it in the Greek Orators; although some

of the Greek Fathers give it an active meaning, as if it were
παρακλήτωρ. The older English Versions (excepting Taverner, who
has 'spokesman') all have 'Advocate' here; and (excepting the
Rhemish, which has 'Paraclete') all have 'Comforter' in the Gospel:
and of course this unanimity influenced the translators of 1611. But
'Advocate' as the one rendering which suits all five passages should be
adopted throughout. Then we see the full meaning of Christ's promise
(John xiv. 16), 'I will pray the Father, and He shall give you *another*
Advocate.' Jesus Christ is one Advocate; the Holy Spirit is another.
As S. Paul says, 'the Spirit Himself *maketh intercession for* us with
groanings which cannot be uttered': and it is worthy of remark that
he uses precisely the same language (ἐντυγχάνειν) to express the intercession of the Spirit and the intercession of Christ (Rom. viii. 26, 27,
34). Comp. Heb. vii. 25; ix. 24; 1 Tim. ii. 5. Philo's use of the word
'Paraclete' throws considerable light upon its meaning. He often uses
it of the high-priest with his breastplate of judgment (Ex. xxviii. 29)
interceding on earth for Israel, and also of the Divine Word or Logos
giving efficacy in heaven to the intercession of the priest upon earth:
'It was necessary that the priest who is consecrated to the Father of
the world should employ as an *Advocate* most perfect in efficacy the
Son, for the blotting out of sins and the obtaining a supply of abundant
blessings' (*De Vita Mosis*, III. xiv. 155). It is evident that the whole
passage—'the blood of Jesus cleanseth us,' 'to cleanse us from all unrighteousness,' 'Advocate,' 'propitiation'—points back to the Mosaic
purifications by the blood of victims, and especially to the intercession
of the high-priest with the blood of the bullock and the goat on the
Day of Atonement. That great type, S. John affirms, has been
fulfilled in Jesus Christ. Comp. Heb. ix. 24; and an Easter Collect
in the Gelasian Sacramentary: "Be propitious to our supplications,
that our supreme High Priest interceding for us may reconcile us, in
that He is like unto us, and absolve us, in that He is equal to Thee."

πρὸς τὸν πατέρα. The πρός expresses either turning *towards* in
order to *plead*, or (as in i. 2; John i. 1) ever *before* His face. Cyprian
has *apud Patrem*, Augustine sometimes *ad* and sometimes *apud*,
Jerome *apud*. Πατέρα rather than Θεόν, because our Advocate is His
Son, through whom we also become sons. It is not a stern Judge
but a loving Father before whom He has to plead.

δίκαιον. Much more forcible placed here as a predicate than if it
had been added as an epithet to παράκλητον. It is not merely that we
have a righteous advocate, but that we have as our advocate One who
is in His own nature righteous. Thus He can so well plead with the
'righteous Father' (John xvii. 25; 1 John i. 9) for those who are
unrighteous: *justus namque advocatus injustas causas non suscipit*
(Bede). 'For such a high-priest became us, holy, guileless, undefiled,
separated from sinners' (Heb. vii. 26). It is the Sinless Man, the
perfected and glorified Jesus, who pleads for sinners before the Throne
of God. Note that neither in the body of the Epistle, any more than
in the body of the Gospel, does S. John speak of Christ as 'the Word.'
In both cases that title is used in the Introduction only. When he

speaks of the historic person Jesus Christ, S. John uses the name by which He is known in history. Of the perfect righteousness of this Man S. John has personal knowledge, and he alludes to it repeatedly in this Epistle.

2. καὶ αὐτὸς ἱλασμός ἐστιν. *And He* Himself *is* a *propitiation.* "Ἔχομεν...ἐστιν, present tense of what is continual. In His glorified Body the Son is ever acting thus. Contrast the aorist (ἔθηκεν) of what took place once for all (iii. 16), His death. Beware of the unsatisfactory explanation that 'propitiation' is the abstract for the concrete, 'propitiation' (ἱλασμός) for 'propitiator' (ἱλαστήρ). Had S. John written 'propitiator' we should have lost half the truth; viz. that our Advocate propitiates by offering *Himself.* He is both High Priest and Victim, both Propitiator and Propitiation. It is quite obvious that He is the former; the office of Advocate includes it. It is not at all obvious that He is the latter: very rarely does an advocate offer himself as a propitiation. 'Ἱλασμός occurs nowhere in N. T. but here and in iv. 10; in both places without the article and followed by περὶ τῶν ἁμ. ἡμῶν. It is one of the few great words in this Epistle which are not found in the Gospel. It signifies any action which has *expiation* as its object, whether prayer, compensation, or sacrifice. Thus 'the ram of the atonement' (Num. v. 8) is ὁ κριὸς τοῦ ἱλασμοῦ. Comp. Ezek. xliv. 27; Num. xxix. 11; Lev. xxv. 9. 'There is forgiveness with Thee' (Ps. cxxx. 4) is in LXX. παρὰ σοὶ ὁ ἱλασμός ἐστιν, 'Before Thee is the propitiation,' *Apud Te propitiatio est.* The full meaning of this is given here: Jesus Christ, as being righteous, is ever present before the Lord as the propitiation. Comp. the use of ἱλάσκεσθαι (Heb. ii. 17) and of ἱλαστήριον (Rom. iii. 25; Heb. ix. 5). These passages shew that in N. T. the word is closely connected with that form of expiation which takes place by means of *sacrifice* or *offering,* although this idea is not of necessity included in the radical signification of the word itself. See notes in all three places. Latin writers use *deprecatio, exoratio,* and *placatio* as translations, as well as *propitiatio.* Thus Tertullian (*De Pud.* xix.): *et ipse placatio est pro delictis nostris;* and again *Horum ergo erit venia per exoratorem patris Christum.* Augustine uses both *propitiatio* and *exoratio,* and also *propitiator.* See Appendix G. Comp. S. Paul's words καταλλαγή (Rom. v. 11; xi. 15; 2 Cor. v. 18, 19) and καταλλάσσειν (Rom. v. 10; 1 Cor. vii. 11; 2 Cor. v. 18—20). By the *advocacy* of Christ (παράκλητος) God is *propitiated* (ἱλασμός) and we are *reconciled* to Him (καταλλαγή).

περὶ τῶν ἁμαρτ. ἡμ. Literally, *concerning our sins:* our sins are matter respecting which propitiation goes on. So commonly in LXX. χίμαρον ἐξ αἰγῶν ἔνα περὶ ἁμαρτίας, ἐξιλάσασθαι περὶ ὑμῶν (Num. xxix. 5, 11; comp. Exod. xxx. 15, 16; xxxii. 30; Lev. iv. 20, 26, 31, 35, &c.). Comp. also John viii. 46; x. 33; xvi. 8. Note the plural: not merely the sinfulness of human nature, but the sins which we are daily committing, is the subject of the propitiation.

οὐ περὶ τῶν ἡμετέρων δὲ μόνον, ἀλλὰ καὶ π. ὅλου τ. κ. "The particle δέ marks the clause as guarding against error, not merely adding a new

thought" (Westcott). Once more we have a parallel with the Gospel,
and especially with chap. xvii. 'Neither for these only do I pray,
but for them also that shall believe on Me through their word...that
the world may believe that Thou didst send Me...that *the world* may
know that Thou didst send Me, and lovedst them, even as Thou
lovedst Me' (xvii. 20—23): 'Behold, the Lamb of God, which *taketh
away the sin of the world*' (John i. 29): 'We know that this is indeed
the Saviour of the world' (iv. 24). Comp. 1 John iv. 14. S. John's
writings are so full of the fundamental opposition between Christ or
believers and the world, that there was danger lest he should seem to
give his sanction to a Christian exclusiveness as fatal as the Jewish
exclusiveness out of which he and other converts from Judaism had
been delivered. Therefore by this (note especially 'the *whole* world')
and other plain statements both in Gospel (see xi. 51 in particular)
and Epistle he insists that believers have no exclusive right to the
merits of Christ. The expiatory offering was made for the whole world
without limitation. All who will may profit by it: *quam late peccatum,
tam late propitiatio* (Bengel). The disabilities under which the whole
human race had laboured were removed. It remained to be seen who
would avail themselves of the restored privileges. It is from the
Latin, *pro totius mundi* (understanding *peccatis*, which Beza inserts)
that the A.V. rendering, 'but also for *the sins of* the whole world,'
comes. So Luther: 'sondern auch *für der ganzen Welt.*' The supposed ellipse is neither necessary nor very probable: rather, as R.V., *but
also* **for the whole world.** Comp. John v. 36; Heb. ix. 7. The latter
passage shews that the ellipse is not necessary; and if it be said that
ἱλασμός *implies* τῶν ἁμαρτιῶν (which may be doubted), then let 'propitiation' *imply* 'sins' in the English. We are not justified in
inserting the word.

'Ο κόσμος is another of S. John's characteristic expressions. In
his writings it generally means those who are *alienated from God*,
outside the pale of the Church. " The world is a living tradition of
disloyalty and dislike to God and His kingdom, just as the Church is
or was meant to be a living tradition of faith, hope, and charity "
(Liddon's *Easter Sermons* xxii, perhaps the best existing commentary
on S. John's use of 'the world'). But we should fall into grievous error
if we assigned this meaning to the word indiscriminately. Thus, in
'the world was made by Him' (John i. 10) it means 'the universe'; in
'This is of a truth the Prophet that cometh into the world' (John vi.
14) it means 'the earth'; in 'God so loved the world' (John iii. 16) it
means, as here, 'the inhabitants of the earth, the human race.' But
still the prevalent meaning in both Gospel and Epistle is a *bad* one;
'those who have not accepted the Christ, unbelievers, especially the
great heathen organization of Rome.' The natural *order* has become
an unnatural *disorder*. S. Paul uses the word in the same sense (1 Cor.
ii. 12; vii. 33; 2 Cor. vii. 10; Col. ii. 8; Gal. iv. 3; vi. 14). In the
Apocalypse it occurs only thrice, once in the usual sense, 'The
kingdom of the world is become the kingdom of our Lord' (xi. 15), and
twice in the sense of 'the universe' (xiii. 8 ; xvii. 8).

3. ἐν τούτῳ γινώσκομεν ὅτι ἐγνώκαμεν αὐτόν. Herein *we* **come to know** *that we know Him;* or, *we perceive that we have come to know Him.* The difference between ἔγνωκα ('I have come to know' ='I know') and other tenses of γινώσκω ('I get to know, perceive, recognise') should be marked. Comp. the collect for First Sunday after Epiphany; 'that they may both *perceive* and *know* what things they ought to do.' Progressive knowledge gained by experience is implied in γινώσκειν (*vv.* 5, 18, 29; iii. 1, 19, 24, &c.). 'Εν τούτῳ followed by ἐάν (John xiii. 35), or ὅτι (1 John iii. 16; iv. 9, 10, 13) or ὅταν (v. 2), or ἵνα (John xv. 8 and perhaps 1 John iv. 17), is common in S. John's writings. The meaning of ἐν τούτῳ must in each case be determined by the context. Sometimes, as here, it refers to what follows: sometimes, as probably in iv. 17, to what precedes: generally to both; i.e. what has been already stated is elucidated by what follows. Comp. ἐκ τούτου (iv. 6) and διὰ τοῦτο (John v. 16, 18; vi. 65; vii. 22; viii. 47; ix. 23; x. 17; xii. 18, 27, 39, &c.), which also commonly looks both backwards and forwards: see on John xii. 39. Excepting Luke x. 20, ἐν τούτῳ is peculiar to S. John. Αὐτόν, as commonly in this Epistle, probably means God rather than Christ: αἱ ἐντολαὶ αὐτοῦ everywhere else means *God's* commandments (iii. 22, 24; v. 2, 3), and probably here also.

ἐὰν τ. ἐντ. αὐτοῦ τηρῶμεν. This = ἐν τῷ φωτὶ περιπατεῖν (i. 7) and μὴ ἁμαρτάνειν (ii. 1). There is no real knowledge of God, no fellowship with Him, without practical conformity to His will. *Nam quisquis eum non amat, profecto ostendit, quia quam sit amabilis, non novit* (Bede). S. John is again condemning that Gnostic doctrine which made excellence to consist in mere intellectual enlightenment. Divorced from holiness of life, says S. John, no enlightenment can be a knowledge of God. In his system of Christian Ethics the Apostle insists no less than Aristotle, that in morals knowledge without practice is worthless: 'not speculation but conduct' (οὐ γνῶσις ἀλλὰ πρᾶξις, *Nic. Eth.* I. iii. 6) is the aim of both the Christian and the heathen philosopher. Mere knowledge will not do: nor will knowledge 'touched by emotion' do. It is possible to know, and admire, and in a sort of way love, and yet act as if we had not known. But S. John gives no encouragement to devotion without a moral *life* (comp. i. 6). There is only one way of proving to ourselves that we know God, and that is by loving obedience to His will. Compare the very high standard of virtue set by Aristotle: he only is a virtuous man who does virtuous acts, πρῶτον μὲν ἐὰν εἰδώς, ἔπειτ' ἐὰν προαιρούμενος, καὶ προαιρούμενος δι' αὐτά, τὸ δὲ τρίτον καὶ ἐὰν βεβαίως καὶ ἀμετακινήτως ἔχων πράττῃ (*Nic. Eth.* II. iv. 3).

Τὰς ἐντολὰς τηρεῖν and τὸν λόγον τηρεῖν are phrases of frequent occurrence in S. John's writings, Gospel (xiv. 15, 21; xv. 10; viii. 51, 52, 55; xiv. 23; xv. 20; xvii. 6), Epistle (ii. 4; iii. 22, 24; v. [2,] 3; ii. 5) and Revelation (xii. 17; xiv. 12; iii. 8, 10). Comp. John xiv. 24; Rev. xxii. 7, 9. Τηρεῖν means to be on the watch to obey and fulfil; it covers both outward and inward observance.

These verses (3—5) exhibit the Vulgate as for once as capricious in its renderings as the A.V. In three consecutive sentences we have τηρεῖν translated in three different ways; *observemus, custodit, servat.*

4. The previous statement is again enforced by denying the opposite of it (i. 5, 6, 8). The construction ὁ λέγων, ὁ ἀγαπῶν, &c. now takes the place of ἐὰν εἴπωμεν, ἐὰν περιπατῶμεν, &c., but without change of meaning : after *v.* 11 both constructions cease and a new division begins. Comp. i. 6 which is exactly parallel to this.

ἐὰν εἴπωμεν ὅτι	ὁ λέγων ὅτι
κοινωνίαν ἔχομεν μετ᾽ αὐτοῦ,	Ἔγνωκα αὐτόν,
καὶ ἐν τῷ σκότει περιπατῶμεν,	καὶ τὰς ἐντ. αὐτοῦ μὴ τηρῶν,
ψευδόμεθα κ. οὐ π. τὴν ἀλήθ.	ψεύσ. ἐστ., κ. ἐν τ. ἡ ἀλ. οὐκ ἔστ.

By writing μὴ τηρῶν rather than οὐ τ. S. John states the case as generally and gently as possible, without asserting that any such person exists : comp. iii. 10, 14; iv. 8, 20; v. 10, 12; Matt. xii. 30, &c. Winer, 606.

5. The statement in *v.* 3 is still further emphasized by taking the opposite of *v.* 4, which is the opposite of *v.* 3. But this does not bring us back to *v.* 3, but to an expansion of it. S. John's apparent retrogressions are real advances.

τὸν λόγον is a wider expression than τὰς ἐντολάς, covering the sum total of the revelation of God's will : comp. *v.* 14. It is certainly wrong to interpret this of the 'continued indwelling' of 'the Personal Word.' Here the emphasis is on τηρῇ; in *v.* 4 on ἐντολάς. **ἀληθῶς**, should be **truly**, or *of a truth*, to distinguish it from ἀμήν, *verily*, in our Lord's discourses. Here it stands first for emphasis, as in John viii. 31 : *truly in him.* Like i. 7, this verse insists on the necessity for *reality* in holiness.

ἡ ἀγάπη τ. Θεοῦ τετελείωται. The full force of the perfect is found here as in i. 1, 2, 10 : 'hath been made perfect and remains so'; *perfecta est* or *consummata est :* Beza has *adimpleta est.* Obedience, not feeling, is the test of perfect love. This declaration shews that it is quite wrong to make 'we know Him' in *v.* 3 and 'I know Him' in *v.* 4 a Hebraism for '*love* Him'. Even if 'know' is ever used in the sense of 'love,' which may be doubted, S. John would hardly in the same sentence use 'know' in two totally different senses (*v.* 3). S. John's mention of love here shews that when he means 'love' he writes 'love' and not 'know.' He declares that true knowledge involves love, but they are not identical, any more than convex and concave. Ἡ ἀγάπη τ. Θεοῦ here means 'the love of man to God' : this is the common usage in this Epistle (ii. 15; iii. 17; iv. 12; v. 3) Winer, 232. Only once is the genitive subjective and means 'the love of God for man'; and there the context makes this quite clear (iv. 9). Ἀγάπη and ἀγαπᾶν are among S. John's favourite words. His Gospel is the Gospel of Love and his Epistle the Epistle of Love. **Τελειοῦν** is also much more common in his writings than elsewhere in N.T., excepting the Epistle to the Hebrews, especially in the passive voice (iv. 12, 17, 18 ; John xvii. 23; xix. 28). S. John is here speaking, as often in this Epistle, of an *ideal* state of things. No

Christian's love to God is perfect: but the more perfect his knowledge, the more perfect his obedience and his love. For the parallel
in the Διδαχὴ τῶν ιβ' Ἀποστόλων see Appendix F.

ἐν αὐτῷ ἐσμέν. Comp. ἐν αὐτῷ ζῶμεν καὶ κινούμεθα καὶ ἐσμέν (Acts
xvii. 28).

6. ὁ λέγων. He who declares his position is morally bound to act
up to the declaration which he has made. To profess to abide in God
involves an obligation to imitate the Son, who is the concrete expression
of God's will. **Μένειν** is another of the Apostle's very favourite expressions, a fact greatly obscured in A.V. by capricious changes of
rendering: see on v. 24. ' To abide in ' implies *habitual* fellowship.
Note the climax; to know Him (v. 3), to be in Him (v. 5), to abide in
Him (v. 6): *cognitio, communio, constantia* (Bengel). Profession of
such close intimacy involves a debt (ὀφείλει, *debet*). S. John does not
say 'must' (δεῖ, *oportet*) which might seem to imply constraint. The
obligation is internal and personal. ' Must ' (δεῖ), frequent in the
Gospel and Revelation, does not occur in these Epistles. See on iii. 16.

καθὼς ἐκεῖνος π. Not simply ὡς, *as*, but καθώς, *even as :* the imitation must be exact. It is always well in translation to mark the
difference between ὡς and καθώς. For καθώς comp. vv. 18, 27; iii. 2,
12, 23, and for καθὼς ἐκεῖνος, iii. 3, 7; iv. 17. Ἐκεῖνος in this Epistle
is always Christ: iii. 3, 5, 7, 16; iv. 17. *Nomen facile supplent cre-
dentes, plenum pectus habentes memoria Domini* (Bengel). S. Peter says
of Christ, ὑμῖν ὑπολιμπάνων ὑπογραμμὸν ἵνα ἐπακολουθήσητε τοῖς ἴχνεσιν
αὐτοῦ (1 Pet. ii. 21); and (still more closely to S. John) S. Paul says
περιπατεῖτε ἐν ἀγάπῃ, καθὼς καὶ ὁ Χριστὸς ἠγάπησεν ὑμᾶς (Eph. v. 1).
Comp. Rom. xv. 5; Heb. xii. 2; and the Collect for the Second Sunday
after Easter. In all cases it is His loving self-sacrifice that is to be
imitated. Hence the next section.

7—11. LOVE OF THE BRETHREN.

7—11. Walking in the light involves not only fellowship with God
and with the brethren (i. 5—7), consciousness and confession of sin
(i. 8—10), obedience by imitation of Christ (ii. 1—6), but also *love of
the brethren*. In nothing did Christ more express the Father's Nature
and Will than by His love: therefore in obeying the Father by imitating Christ we also must love. "This whole Epistle which we have
undertaken to expound to you, see whether it commendeth aught else
than this one thing, charity. Nor need we fear lest by much speaking
thereof it come to be hateful. For what is there to love, if charity
come to be hateful?" (S. Augustine). Comp. iii. 10; iv. 7.

7. ἀγαπητοί. This, the true reading, is specially suitable as the
opening to this section (7—11), in which the subject of ἀγάπη comes to
the front. In the second part of the Epistle, in which ἀγάπη is the
main subject, ἀγαπητοί becomes the prevailing form of address (iii. 2,
21; iv. 1, 7, 11). Augustine always in this Epistle renders ἀγαπητοί
dilectissimi, the Vulgate always *carissimi;* but *Contra Pelag.* 13
Jerome has *dilectissimi* in 1 John ii. 3. **οὐκ ἐντολὴν καινὴν γράφω.**

The order of the Greek is worth preserving: **not a new commandment do I write.** What commandment is here meant? To imitate
Christ (*v.* 6)? Or, to practise brotherly love (*vv.* 9—11)? Practically
it makes little matter which answer we give, for at bottom these are
one and the same. They are different aspects of *walking in the
light.* But a definite command of some kind is meant, not vaguely
the whole Gospel: had he meant the latter, S. John would rather
have said 'the word' or 'the truth.' See on *v.* 11. Καινός, as
distinct from νέος, is 'fresh, novel,' as opposed to 'worn out' and
'familiar.' It may imply either praise, as being a reformation (κ.
διαθήκη, κ. κτίσις, οὐρανὸς κ. καὶ γῆ κ.), or blame, as being an innovation (διδαχὴ κ., κ. θεοί). Νέος is 'new, young,' as opposed to 'old,
aged.' In Mark ii. 22 we have both words: '*new* wine into *fresh* wine-
skins.' Trench, *Synonyms of N. T.*, 209; Cremer, 321. In its better
sense καινός is a favourite word with S. John.

εἴχετε ἀπ᾽ ἀρχῆς. As already noticed (i. 1) the meaning of 'beginning' must always depend upon the context. Several interpretations
have been suggested here, and all make good sense. (1) From the
beginning *of the human race:* brotherly love is an original human
instinct. Christian Ethics are here as old as humanity. S. Athanasius takes it in this sense. (2) From the beginning *of the Law:* 'Thou
shalt love thy neighbour as thyself' (Lev. xix. 18) was commanded
by Moses. Christian Ethics are in this only a repetition of Judaism.
(3) From the beginning *of your life as Christians.* This was one of
the first things ye were taught. On the whole this seems best, especially as we have the aorist, *which ye heard,* not the perfect, as A. V.,
ye have heard (see on *v.* 18): comp. *v.* 24 and especially iii. 11;
2 John 5, 6. The second ἀπ᾽ ἀρχῆς is not genuine: see critical notes.
Note that both ἐντολή and λόγος, being convertible terms, have the
article. See on iii. 4.

8. πάλιν ἐντ. καινὴν γρ. ὑμ., ὃ ἐστιν ἀληθές. Either, *Again, a new
commandment I write unto you, which thing is true:* Or, *Again, as a
new commandment I write unto you* a **thing which** *is true:* Or, *Again,
a new commandment write I unto you,* namely that which *is true.* It
is difficult to decide between these three renderings; but the third is
simpler than the first. Both Tyndale and the Genevan Version have
'a thing that is true': Beza; *id quod verum est in ipso:* Luther; *das
da wahrhaftig ist.* If we adopt the rendering of A. V. and R. V.,
the meaning seems to be, that *the newness of the commandment is*
true, both in the case of Christ, who promulgated it afresh, and in
the case of you, who received it afresh. If we prefer the simpler rendering, the meaning will be, that what has already been shewn to be
true by the pattern life of Christ and by the efforts of Christians to
imitate it, is now given by S. John as a new commandment. The
πάλιν introduces a new view: that which from one point of view was
an old commandment, from another was a new one. It was old, but
not obsolete, ancient, but not antiquated: it had been renewed in a
fuller sense; it had received a fresh sanction. Thus both those who

feared innovations and those who disliked what was stale might feel satisfied.

ἐν αὐτῷ καὶ ἐν ὑμῖν. Note the double preposition, implying that it is true in the case of Christ in a different sense from that in which it is true in the case of Christians. He reissued the commandment and was the living embodiment and example of it; they accepted it and endeavoured to follow it: both illustrated its truth and soundness. See on i. 3, where μετά is repeated, and on John xx. 2. where πρός is repeated. The reading ἐν ἡμῖν is certainly to be rejected.

ὅτι ἡ σκ. παράγεται. *Because the darkness is passing away*: present tense of a process still going on (*v.* 17). All earlier English Versions are wrong here, from Wiclif onwards, misled by *transierunt tenebrae* in the Vulgate. So also Luther: *denn die Finsterniss ist vergangen* On σκοτία see on i. 5. The ὅτι introduces the reason why he writes as a new commandment what has been proved true by the example of Christ and their own experience. The ideal state of things, to which the perfect fulfilment of this commandment belongs, has already begun: 'The darkness is on the wane, the true light is shewing its power; *therefore* I bid you to walk as children of light.' Comp. 1 Cor. vii. 31, where παράγει used intransitively is rightly rendered 'passeth away,' *praeterit, vergehet*. Παράγεται here is middle rather than passive, of a cloud withdrawing rather than of a veil being withdrawn. Comp. Rom. xiii. 12; 1 Thes. v. 5.

The difference between the Vulgate (*Cod. Am.*) and Jerome (*Adv. Jovin.* i. 40) is here remarkable. In his own treatise he has *Mandatum novum scripsi vobis, quod est verissimum, et in Christo, et in nobis: quia tenebrae praeterierunt et lux jam lucet.* In the Vulgate he has *Iterum mandatum novum scribo vobis, quod est verum et in ipso et in vobis; quoniam tenebrae transierunt et lumen verum jam lucet.*

τὸ φῶς τὸ ἀλ. ἤδη φαίνει. The light, the true light, is already shining. For the repetition of the article comp. *v.* 7; i. 2. 'Is shining' rather than 'shineth,' to correspond with 'is passing away.' It is the nature of light not merely to appear (φαίνεσθαι) but to *lighten* (φαίνειν): comp. John i. 5. We might render here, as in Gen. i. 17, 'is already *giving light*.' Ἀληθινόν is 'true' as opposed to 'spurious,' while ἀληθές in the previous clause is 'true' as opposed to 'lying': the one is *verum*, the other *verax*. Ἀληθινός is 'genuine,' and hence 'perfect,' as realising the idea formed of it. It is represented by the old English 'very,' the word which both Wiclif and Purvey here employ, although they translate *verum* in the first part of the verse by 'true.' 'Very God of Very God' in the Nicene Creed is Θεὸν ἀληθινὸν ἐκ Θεοῦ ἀληθινοῦ. Christ and the Gospel are 'the perfect Light' in opposition to the imperfect light of the Law and the Prophets. They are realities; the others were types and figures. They are 'the genuine Light' in opposition to the false light of Gnostic philosophy. Ἀληθινός is almost peculiar to S. John; four times in this Epistle, nine times in the Gospel, ten times in Revelation: elsewhere in N. T. only five times. Christ is ὁ ἄρτος ὁ ἀληθινός (John vi. 32) and ἡ ἄμπελος ἡ ἀληθινή (xv. 1) as well as τὸ φῶς τὸ ἀληθινόν (i. 9).

This last passage combined with John i. 5 renders it probable that Christ is intended here, rather than the light of the truth or the kingdom of heaven: although the difference between the three interpretations is not important. The contrast with the impersonal darkness does not disprove this here any more than in John i. 5. Darkness is never personal; it is not an effluence from Satan as light is from God or from Christ. It is the result, not of the presence of the evil one, but of the absence of God. Comp. 'Ye were once darkness, but now light in the Lord: walk as children of light' (Eph. v. 8).

9—11. The form of these three verses is similar to that of *vv.* 3—5, and still more so to i. 8—10. In each of these three triplets a case is placed between two statements of the opposite to it; confession of sin, obedience, and love, between two statements of denial of sin, disobedience, and hate. But in none of the triplets do we go from one opposite to the other and back again: in each case the side from which we start is restated in such a way as to constitute a distinct advance upon the original position. There is no weak tautology or barren see-saw. The emphasis grows and is marked by the increase in the predicates. In *v.* 9 we have *one* predicate: ἐν τῇ σκοτίᾳ ἐστὶν ἕως ἄρτι: in *v.* 10 we have *two*; ἐν τῷ φωτὶ μένει, καὶ σκάνδαλον οὐκ ἔστιν ἐν αὐτῷ: in *v.* 11, *three; ἐν τῇ σκ. ἐστίν, καὶ ἐν τῇ σκ. π., καὶ οὐκ οἶδεν ποῦ ὑπάγει. The *Sinaiticus* spoils this climax by making the predicate in *v.* 9 to be twofold; ψεύστης ἐστὶν καὶ ἐν σκ. κ.τ.λ. This reading is wrongly ascribed to Cyprian (*Test. adv. Jud.* iii. 3).

9. For the fifth time the Apostle indicates a possible inconsistency of a very gross kind between profession and conduct (i. 6, 8, 10; ii. 4). We shall have a sixth in iv. 20. In most of these passages he is aiming at some of the Gnostic teaching already prevalent. And this introduces a fresh pair of contrasts. We have had light and darkness, truth and falsehood; we now have love and hate.

τὸν ἀδελφὸν αὐτοῦ. *Ipsa appellatio amoris causam continet* (Bengel). Does this mean 'his fellow-Christian' or 'his fellow-man,' whether Christian or not? The common meaning in N. T. is the former; and though there are passages where ἀδελφός seems to have the wider signification, e.g. Matt. v. 22; Luke vi. 41; Jas. iv. 11, yet even here the spiritual bond of brotherhood is perhaps in the background. In S. John's writings, where it does not mean actual relationship, it seems generally if not universally to mean 'Christians': not that other members of the human race are excluded, but they are not under consideration. Just as in the allegories of the Fold and of the Good Shepherd, nothing is said about goats, and in that of the Vine nothing is said about the branches of other trees; so here in the great family of the Father nothing is said about those who do not know Him. They are not shut out, but they are not definitely included. In *this Epistle* this passage, iii. 10, 14—17, and iv. 20, 21 are somewhat open to doubt: but v. 1, 2 seems very distinctly in favour of the more limited meaning; and in v. 16 the sinning 'brother' is certainly a fellow-Christian. In 2 John the word does not occur: 3 John 3, 5,

10 confirm the view here taken.   In the *Gospel* the word is generally
used of actual relationship : but in the two passages where it is used
otherwise it means Christians : in xx. 17 Christ speaks of the disciples
as τοὺς ἀδελφούς μου, and in xxi. 23 Christians are called τοὺς ἀδελφούς
(see note).   In the *Apocalypse*, omitting xxii. 9 as doubtful, all the
passages where the word occurs require the meaning 'Christian' (i. 9;
vi. 11; xii. 10; xix. 10).   Note that throughout this Epistle the singular is used; τὸν ἀδελφὸν αὐτοῦ, not τοὺς ἀδελφοὺς αὐτοῦ.

ἐν τῇ σκοτίᾳ ἐστὶν ἕως ἄρτι.   *Is in the darkness*, to bring out the
full contrast with the light, as in i. 6: *even until now,* i. e. in spite of
the light which 'is *already* shining,' and of which he has so little real
experience that he believes light and hatred to be compatible.   Years
before this S. Paul had declared (1 Cor. xiii. 2), 'If I have the gift of
prophecy, and know all mysteries and all knowledge...but have not
love, I am nothing.'   "Fictitious sanctity dazzles the eyes of almost
all men, while love is neglected, or at least driven into the farthest
corner" (Calvin).   The light in a man is darkness until it is warmed
by love.   The convert from heathendom who professes Christianity
and hates his brother, says S. Augustine, is in darkness even until
now.   "There is no need to expound; but to rejoice, if it be not so, to
bewail, if it be."   Ἄρτι is specially frequent in S. John's Gospel: it
indicates the present moment not absolutely, but in relation to the
past or the future.   The peculiar combination ἕως ἄρτι occurs John ii.
10; v. 17; xvi. 24; Matt. xi. 12; 1 Cor. iv. 13; viii. 7; xv. 6; a fact
much obscured in A.V. by the variety of renderings; 'until now,'
'hitherto,' 'unto this day,' 'unto this hour,' 'unto this present.'

10.   ὁ ἀγαπῶν.   Nothing is said about what he *professes;* it is what
he *does* that is of consequence.   **μένει** means not only has entered
into the light, but has it for his *abode :* see on *v.* 24.

σκάνδαλον οὐκ ἔστιν ἐν αὐτῷ.   There are four ways of taking this;
three taking αὐτῷ as masculine, and one taking it as neuter, referring
to τῷ φωτί.   1. He has *in him* nothing likely to ensnare *him* or cause
him to stumble.   2. He has *in him* nothing likely to cause *others* to
stumble.   3. There is *in his case* nothing likely to cause stumbling.
4. *In the light* there is nothing likely to cause stumbling.   All make
good sense, and the last makes a good antithesis to 'knoweth not
whither he goeth' in *v.* 11: but the first is to be preferred on account
of *v.* 11.   Yet in favour of the second it is worth noting that σκάνδαλον is commonly, if not always, used of offence caused to *others.*   The
parallel expressions 'the truth is not in him' (*v.* 4), 'His word is not
in us' (i. 10; comp. i. 8), make 'in him' more probable than 'in his
case.'   And nothing here suggests the notion that the brother-hater
leads *others* astray: it is his own dark condition that is contemplated:
ipse sibi offendiculum est.   Moreover, there is the very close parallel
in John xi. 9, 10; 'If a man walk in the day, he stumbleth not, because he seeth the light of this world.   But if a man walk in the
night, he stumbleth, because the light is not in him.'   Comp. Ps. cxix.
165, 'Great peace have they which love Thy law: and nothing shall
offend them'; i. e. there is no stumbling-block before them: οὐκ ἔστιν

αὐτοῖς σκάνδαλον. It is not impossible that this passage was in the Apostle's mind: his ἐν may represent the 'to' in the Hebrew original. Comp. 1 Sam. xxv. 31 where σκάνδαλον represents the Hebrew *mikshol*, 'a stumbling.' Elsewhere it represents *moqesh* 'a snare' (Judg. ii. 3; viii. 27). It combines the notions of tripping up and ensnaring. The word is a late form of σκανδάληθρον (Aristoph. *Ach.* 687) the 'bait-stick' in a trap.

11. ἐν τῇ σκ. ἐστίν, κ. ἐν τῇ σκ. π. The *darkness* is his home and the sphere of his activity. The contrast between the godly and the wicked is similarly indicated in Prov. iv. 18, 19: αἱ δὲ ὁδοὶ τῶν δικαίων ὁμοίως φωτὶ λάμπουσιν· προπορεύονται καὶ φωτίζουσιν, ἕως κατορθώσῃ ἡ ἡμέρα. αἱ δὲ ὁδοὶ τῶν ἀσεβῶν σκοτειναί· οὐκ οἴδασιν πῶς προσκόπτουσιν. Here ποῦ ὑπάγει is literally, *where he is departing: ὑπάγειν is 'to go away.'* S. John frequently joins ποῦ with ὑπάγειν: John iii. 8; viii. 14; xii. 35, 36; xiv. 5; xvi. 5; vii. 35. Elsewhere in N. T. this construction occurs only Heb. xi. 8. In late Greek ποῦ and ὅπου are frequently used for ποῖ and ὅποι, ἐκεῖ for ἐκεῖσε (John xviii. 3; Matt. ii. 22; Rom. xv. 24), ὧδε for ἐνθάδε (John xx. 27; comp. Rev. iv. 1; xi. 12). Neither ποῖ nor ὅποι occurs in N.T. Winer, 591. The effect of joining an adverb of rest to a verb of motion may sometimes be to express *both* rest and motion. But this is commonly done by the converse process of joining an adverb or preposition of motion to a verb of rest: εὑρέθη εἰς Ἄζωτον, '*was carried to* Azotus and *found there*' (Acts viii. 40): comp. John viii. 26; xx. 7.—Another close parallel between Gospel and Epistle exists here: part of John xii. 35 is almost verbatim the same.

ὅτι ἡ σκ. ἐτύφλωσεν. *Because the darkness hath blinded.* This is just one of those cases where it is the Greek idiom to use the aorist, but the English idiom to use the perfect; and therefore the Greek aorist should be rendered by the English perfect. Comp. John xiii. 13, 34; xv. 9, 12. But the A.V. frequently turns aorists into perfects without justification (see on i. 1; ii. 18, 24, 25, 27; 2 John 6), and occasionally turns perfects into aorists (iv. 9; 2 John 4). 'Blinded' must not be weakened into 'dimmed': the verb means definitely 'to make blind' (John xii. 40; 2 Cor. iv. 4). Animals kept in the dark, e.g. ponies in coal-mines, become blind: the organ that is never exercised loses its power. So also the conscience that is constantly ignored at last ceases to act. The source of the metaphor is perhaps Is. vi. 10: comp. Rom. xi. 10.

Before proceeding further let us briefly sum up the Apostle's line of argument thus far. 'God is light. Christ is that light revealed. The life of Christ was a life of obedience and a life of love. In order, therefore, to have fellowship through Him with God believers must obey and love. The state of things in which this is possible has already begun. Therefore I write to you a command which is both old and new; walk in the light by imitating the love of Christ.' In this manner he lays the foundations of Christian Ethics. The last three verses (9—11) shew that the special aspect of walking in light which is referred to in the commandment which is at once old and new is *love:* and if this be so, we can hardly doubt that in calling it 'a new commandment' he has in his mind Christ's farewell words, John xiii. 34; 'A new commandment I give unto you, that ye love one another; even as I have loved you, that ye also love one another.' The latter half of the verse is, therefore, the special interpretation of 'ought himself also to walk even as He walked.'

It is not easy to determine whether the division which follows (*vv.* 12—28) is best regarded as a subdivision of the first main portion of the Epistle, or as a co-ordinate portion. In favour of the latter view are these facts: 1. The idea of *light* which runs through the whole of the division just concluded (i. 5—ii. 11), and which is mentioned six times in it, now disappears altogether. 2. The Epistle now takes a distinctly hortatory turn. The first part lays down principles: this part gives warnings and exhortations. 3. The Apostle seems to make a fresh start: *vv.* 12—14 read like a new Introduction. In favour of making this part a sub-division of the first main division it may be urged: 1. Though the idea of light is no longer mentioned, yet other ideas to which it directly led, love, the truth, abiding in God, still continue: the parts evidently overlap. 2. The hortatory turn is but a partial change of form occurring only in *vv.* 15 and 28. In the intermediate verses the aphoristic mode of expression continues. 3. The quasi-Introduction in *vv.* 1 and 7.

On the whole it seems best to consider what follows as a subordinate part of the first main division of the Epistle. Thus far we have had THE CONDITION AND CONDUCT OF THE BELIEVER considered on its *positive side*. We now have the *negative side*—WHAT WALKING IN THE LIGHT EXCLUDES.

12—28. THE THINGS AND PERSONS TO BE AVOIDED.

These are summed up under two heads: i. *The World and the Things in the World* (15—17); ii. *Antichrists* (18—26). The section begins with a *threefold statement* of the happy experiences which those addressed have had in the Gospel, and gives these as a reason for their being addressed (12—14), and ends with an *exhortation to abide in Christ* as the best safe-guard from the dangers against which the Apostle has been warning them (27, 28).

12—14. THREEFOLD STATEMENT OF REASONS FOR WRITING.

"Hitherto St John has stated briefly the main scope of his Epistle. He has shewn what is the great problem of life, and how the Gospel meets it with an answer and a law complete and progressive, old and new. He now pauses, as it were to contemplate those whom he is addressing more distinctly and directly, and to gather up in a more definite form the charge which is at once the foundation and the end of all he writes" (Westcott).

These verses have given rise to much discussion (1) as to the different classes addressed, (2) as to the meaning of the change of tense, from γράφω, *I write*, to ἔγραψα, *I wrote* or *have written*. In the true text each of these forms occurs thrice. We have to deal with a change from a triplet with γράφω to a triplet with ἔγραψα. This arrangement is of importance in discussing the two difficulties. (1) The question as to the classes addressed is much the easier of the two. It will be observed that in each triplet we have 'little children' followed by 'fathers' and 'young men'; the sole difference being the use of τεκνία in the first case and παιδία in the second. But this need not make us give a different interpretation in each case. 'Little children' throughout the Epistle, whether expressed as in *vv.* 14 and 18 (παιδία), or as in *vv.* 1, 12, 28; iii. 7, 18; iv. 4; v. 21 (τεκνία), probably means the Apostle's readers generally, and has nothing to do with age or with standing in the Christian community. It indicates neither those who are of tender years, nor those who are young in the faith. It is a term of affection for all the Apostle's 'dear children.' But this is not the case with either 'fathers' or 'young men.' These terms are probably in each triplet to be understood of the older and younger men among the Christians addressed. This fully accounts for the order in each triplet; first the whole community, then the old, then the young. If 'little children' had reference to age, we should have had either 'children, youths, fathers,' or 'fathers, youths, children.' There is, however, something to be said for the view that *all* S. John's readers are addressed *in all three cases*, the Christian life of all having analogies with youth, manhood, and age; with the innocence of childhood, the strength of prime, and the experience of full maturity. Thus S. Augustine says that Christians are *filioli, quia baptismo neonati sunt; patres, quia Christum patrem et antiquum dierum agnoscunt; adolescentes, quia fortes sunt et validi.* But the other interpretation is better. To make τεκνία refer to the whole body of readers, and παιδία to a subdivision coordinate with πατέρες and νεανίσκοι, violently dislocates the grouping : so strange an arrangement may safely be rejected.

(2) The question as to the change from γράφω to ἔγραψα is much more difficult and cannot be decided with confidence. It is much easier to shew that other explanations are unsatisfactory than to produce an explanation that is free from serious objection. The following interpretations of the change from the present to the aorist have been suggested. 1. 'I write' refers to the Epistle, 'I wrote' to the Gospel which it accompanies. The Apostle first gives reasons why he *is writing* this letter to the Church and to particular portions of it; and then gives reasons, partly the same and partly not, why *he wrote* the Gospel to which it makes such frequent allusions. On the whole this seems least unsatisfactory. It gives an intelligible meaning to each tense and accounts for the abrupt change. But it must be admitted that ἔγραψα in v. 21 cannot easily be referred to the Gospel : v. 26 is not parallel. 2. 'I write' refers to this Epistle; 'I wrote' to a former Epistle. But of any former Epistle we have no evidence whatever. 3. 'I write' refers to the whole Epistle; 'I wrote' to the first part down to ii. 11. But would S. John have *first* said that he wrote the *whole* letter for certain reasons, and *then* said that he wrote a *portion* of it for much the same reasons? Had 'I wrote' preceded 'I write,' and had the reasons in each triplet been more different,

this explanation would have been more satisfactory. 4. 'I write' refers to what follows, 'I wrote' to what precedes. This is a *construction louche* indeed! The objection urged against the preceding explanation applies still more strongly. 5. 'I write' is written from the writer's point of view, 'I wrote' from the reader's point of view: the latter is the epistolary aorist, like *scripsi* or *scribebam* in Latin (comp. Phil. ii. 25, 28; Philem. 12, and especially 19 and 21). But is it likely that S. John would make three statements from his own stand-point, and then repeat them from his readers' stand-point? And if so, why make any change in them? 6. The repetition is made for emphasis. This explains the repetition, but not the change of tense. Hence ὁ γέγραφα γέγραφα (John xix. 22) and χαίρετε ἐν κυρίῳ πάντοτε· πάλιν ἐρῶ, χαίρετε (Phil. iv. 4) are not analogous; for there the same *tense* is repeated. 7. S. John may have left off writing at the end of *v.* 13, and then on resuming may have partly repeated himself from the new point of time, saying 'I wrote' where he had previously said 'I write.' This is conceivable, but is a little fine-drawn.—Without, therefore, confidently affirming that it is the right explanation, we fall back upon the one first stated, as intelligible in itself and more satisfactory than the others. Commentators on the Vulgate are not confronted by the difficulty, both γράφω and ἔγραψα being rendered alike *scribo*, excepting by Jerome (*Cod. Amiatinus*) who omits one ἔγραψα and translates the last *scripsi*. Latin translators probably regarded ἔγραψα as an epistolary aorist.

A parallel arrangement will help the reader to consider the two questions for himself.

γράφω ὑμῖν, τεκνία, ὅτι ἀφέωνται ὑμῖν αἱ ἁμαρτίαι διὰ τὸ ὄνομα αὐτοῦ.	ἔγραψα ὑμῖν, παιδία, ὅτι ἐγνώκατε τὸν πατέρα.
γράφω ὑμῖν, πατέρες, ὅτι ἐγνώκατε τὸν ἀπ᾽ ἀρχῆς.	ἔγραψα ὑμῖν, πατέρες, ὅτι ἐγνώκατε τὸν ἀπ᾽ ἀρχῆς.
γράφω ὑμῖν, νεανίσκοι, ὅτι νενικήκατε τὸν πονηρόν.	ἔγραψα ὑμῖν, νεανίσκοι, ὅτι ἰσχυροί ἐστε, καὶ ὁ λόγος τοῦ Θεοῦ ἐν ὑμῖν μένει, καὶ νενικήκατε τὸν πονηρόν.

τεκνία. As in *v.* 1 (τεκνία **μου**), *v.* 28; iii. 18; iv. 4; v. 21, this address includes all his readers (in iii. 7 the reading is disputable). *Omnes suos auditores, quos ipse in Christo praecesserat, filiorum nomine glorificat* (Bede). Some would render **ὅτι ἀφέωνται ὑμ. αἱ ἁμαρτ.** '*that* your sins are forgiven you'; and so in each of these six sentences substituting 'that' for 'because.' Of course this is possible grammatically, but otherwise is highly improbable. See on *v.* 21. The Vulgate has *quoniam*, Augustine *quia*, Luther *denn*. The verses are not quoted by Tertullian or Cyprian. S. John is evidently not telling his children *what* he is writing, but *why* he writes it. The very first condition of Christian morals is the forgiveness of sins (i. 7); therefore he reminds all of them of this first. Ἀφέωνται (Luke v. 20, 23; vii. 47; and perhaps John xx. 23) is now commonly admitted to be a perfect indicative (=ἀφεῖνται) of Doric origin but used sometimes by Attic writers: Winer, 96, 97; Veitch, 104. The *remittuntur* of the Vulgate is therefore inadequate: not 'are being forgiven,' but 'have been forgiven and remain so.'

διὰ τὸ ὄν. αὐτοῦ. Here, as in i. 5, it is obvious that αὐτοῦ refers to Jesus Christ and not to the Father. It was by believing on *His Name* that they acquired the right to become children of God (John i. 12). 'The Name of Jesus Christ' is not a mere periphrasis for Jesus Christ. Names in Scripture are constantly given as marks of character possessed or of functions to be performed. This is the case with all the Divine Names. The Name of Jesus Christ indicates His attributes and His relations to man and to God. It is through these that the sins of S. John's dear children have been forgiven. Comp. iii. 23; v. 13; 3 John 7. For διὰ τὸ ὄνομα comp. Matt. x. 22; xxiv. 9; Mark xiii. 13; Luke xxi. 17; John xv. 21; Rev. ii. 3.

13. πατέρες. The older men among his readers: comp. Jud. xvii. 10; xviii. 19; 2 Kings ii. 12; vi. 21; xiii. 14. The address stands alone in N. T. The nearest approaches to it are Eph. vi. 4 and Col. iii. 21, where the actual fathers of children are addressed. Comp. Tit. ii. 1—8, where S. Paul in like manner gives directions as to the exhortations suitable for Christians of different ages. ἐγνώκατε. **Ye know:** 'ye have come to know' and therefore 'ye know,' as in *v.* 3. The knowledge possessed by the old is fitly expressed by a word which signifies the result of progressive experience. τὸν ἀπ' ἀρχῆς means Christ, not the Father, as is plain from the opening words of the Epistle. By the knowledge of Christ which these older Christians had gradually acquired is certainly not meant the having seen Him in the flesh. Very few, if any, of S. John's readers could have done that. And if they had, the Apostle would not have attached any moral or spiritual value to the fact (2 Cor. v. 16, 17). Besides which, in order to express this we should require 'ye have seen Jesus our Lord' (1 Cor. ix. 1) rather than 'ye have come to know Him that was from the beginning.' On ἀπ' ἀρχῆς see on i. 1.

νεανίσκοι. The younger half of his readers; men in the prime, or not yet in the prime of life: *adolescentes, juvenes.* For νενικήκατε comp. John xvi. 33. Throughout both Epistle and Gospel S. John regards eternal life as a prize already won by the believer (John iii. 36; v. 24; vi. 47, 54; xvii. 3): the contest is not to gain, but to retain. These three perfects, ἀφέωνται, ἐγνώκατε, νενικήκατε, once more express the abiding result of past action (i. 1, 2, 5, 10). He bases his appeals to the young on the victory which their strength has won, just as he bases his appeals to the aged on the knowledge which their experience has gained, and his appeals to all on the forgiveness which they have all received. There is the confidence of victory in all S. John's writings.

τὸν πονηρόν. It is important to have a uniform rendering for πονηρός, respecting which there has been so much controversy with regard to the last petition in the Lord's Prayer. The A. V., following earlier Versions, wavers between 'wicked' and 'evil,' even in the same verse (iii. 12). 'Evil' is to be preferred throughout. Almost

all are agreed that *the* evil *one* here means the devil, although the
Genevan Version has 'the evil *man*,' as in Matt. xii. 35. Wiclif,
Tyndale, and Cranmer supply neither 'man' nor 'one,' but write 'the
wicked' or 'that wicked.' 'The wicked' in English would inevitably
be understood as plural. For this name for Satan comp. v. 18; Matt.
xiii. 19 and also 1 John iii. 12; v. 19; John xvii. 15; Eph. vi. 16. In
these last four passages the gender, though probably masculine, may,
as in Matt. vi. 13, possibly be neuter. S. John elsewhere speaks of
the evil one as ὁ διάβολος (iii. 8, 10; John viii. 44; xiii. 2), ὁ Σατανᾶς
(John xiii. 27), ὁ ἄρχων τοῦ κόσμου τούτου (John xii. 31; xvi. 11), ὁ
τοῦ κόσμου ἄρχων (John xiv. 30), ὁ κατήγωρ τῶν ἀδελφῶν ἡμῶν (Rev. xii.
10), ὁ ὄφις ὁ ἀρχαῖος, ὁ καλούμενος Διάβολος καὶ ὁ Σατανᾶς (Rev. xii. 9 :
comp. xx. 2), ὁ δράκων (Rev. xii. 7, 8; xiii. 2; xvi. 13; xx. 2).

ἔγραψα ὑμῖν, παιδία. All the chief MSS., confirmed by the Versions, give ἔγραψα and not γράφω here. The latter reading probably
arose from interpreting παιδία as a subdivision of τεκνία, co-ordinate with πατέρες and νεανίσκοι. Beyond reasonable doubt παιδία
is coextensive with τεκνία and includes *all* his readers. The two
words should, however, be distinguished in translation. Keeping
'little children' for τεκνία, we may render παιδία little ones. The
Vulgate has *filioli* for τεκνία and here has *infantes* for παιδία, but
inconsistently has *filioli* in *v.* 18. Augustine has *pueri* for παιδία.
Τεκνία implies both juniority and relationship; παιδία implies the
former only. Both are terms of affection. 'Εγνώκατε, as in *vv.* 3 and
13, *ye* know. In *v.* 12 the Apostle attributes to them the possession
of spiritual *peace* through the remission of sins: here he attributes to
them the possession of spiritual *truth* through knowledge of the
Father. This knowledge they had acquired specially through S.
John's Gospel, in which the Fatherhood of God is a most prominent
doctrine. In the fourth Gospel God is called the Father twice as
frequently as in all three Synoptics: the numbers are about as follows;
S. Matthew 40 times, S. Mark 5, S. Luke 17, S. John 126. While the
addresses to his children as a whole and to the younger section of
them vary, the two addresses to the fathers are the same, excepting the
change of tense. Their spiritual experience is practically complete
and cannot be better summed up than by the knowledge of the
Incarnate Word. The Vulgate both Old and New omits the second
address to the 'fathers': but Augustine and Bede have it.

14. 'Ισχυρός is frequent in the Apocalypse ; elsewhere in S. John's
writings here only. Comp. Eph. vi. 10—20.

ὁ λόγος τοῦ Θεοῦ. B and the Thebaic or Sahidic Version (2nd or
3rd cent.) omit τοῦ Θεοῦ. In *v.* 20 we again find B and the
Thebaic alone in a reading which is very likely original : comp.
Acts xxvii. 37; Rom. xiii. 13; Col. iii. 6; Heb. iii. 2; 2 John 8.
The clause is an echo of John xv. 7. This possession is the secret of
their strength and the source of their victory. They conquer because
they are strong, and they are strong because God's word is ever
in their hearts. They have God's will, especially as revealed in
Scripture, and in particular in the Gospel, as a *permanent* power

within them : hence the permanence of their victory. So long as they
trust in this and not in themselves, and remember that their victory
is not yet final, they may rejoice in the confidence which the consciousness of strength and of victory gives them. *Humiles estote, ne
in pugna cadatis* (Bede).

It is plain from the context and from John v. 38; x. 35; xvii. 6, 14;
Rev. i. 9; vi. 9, that ὁ λόγος τοῦ Θεοῦ here does not mean the Word, the
Son of God. See on *v.* 5 and i. 10. S. John never uses the term
ὁ λόγος in this sense in the body either of his Gospel or of his Epistle,
but only in the theological Introductions to each.

15—17. THE THINGS TO BE AVOIDED ;—THE WORLD AND ITS WAYS.

Having reminded them solemnly of the blessedness of their condition
as members of the Christian family, whether old or young, and having
declared that this blessedness of peace, knowledge, and strength is his
reason for writing to them, he goes on to exhort them to live in
a manner that shall be worthy of this high estate, and to avoid all that
is inconsistent with it. In chap. i. walking in darkness was shewn to
be incompatible with fellowship with God. Here love of God is shewn
to be incompatible with affection for the world.

15. μὴ ἀγαπᾶτε τὸν κόσμον. The asyndeton is remarkable. S.
John has just stated his premises, his readers' happiness as Christians.
He now abruptly states the practical conclusion, without any introductory οὖν or διὰ τοῦτο. Our equally abrupt 'Love not the world' comes
from the Rhemish. Tyndale and others weaken it by expansion ; ' So
that ye love not the worlde.' And obviously S. John is once more addressing *all* his readers, not the νεανίσκοι only. *Omnibus his pariter man-
dat* (Bede). As was said above on *v.* 2, we must distinguish between the
various meanings of the Apostle's favourite word, κόσμος. In John iii.
16 he tells us that 'God loved the world', and here he tells us that *we*
must *not* do so. " S. John is never afraid of an apparent contradiction when it saves his readers from a real contradiction......The
opposition which is on the surface of his language may be the best way
of leading us to the harmony which lies below it" (Maurice). The world
which the Father loves is the whole human race. The world which we
are not to love is all that is alienated from Him, all that prevents men
from loving Him in return. The world which God loves is His creature
and His child : the world which we are not to love is His rival. The
best safeguard against the selfish love of what is sinful in the world is
to remember God's unselfish love of the world. Ὁ κόσμος here is that
from which S. James says the truly religious man keeps himself
ἄσπιλον, friendship with which is ἔχθρα τοῦ Θεοῦ (Jas. i. 27; iv. 4).
It is not enough to say that 'the world' here means 'earthly things,
so far as they tempt to sin, ' or 'sinful lusts,' or 'worldly and impious
men.' It means all of these together: all that acts as a rival to God ;
all that is alienated from God and opposed to Him, especially sinful
men with their sinful lusts. Ὁ κόσμος and ἡ σκοτία are almost
synonymous. To love the one is to love the other (John iii. 19). To

be ἐν τῇ σκοτίᾳ (*vv.* 9, 11) is to be ἐκ τοῦ κόσμου (*v.* 16; iv. 5). Nor is μὴ ἀγαπᾶτε to be weakened into 'love not *too much*': it means quite literally, 'love not at all.' The world 'lies in the evil one' (*v.* 19); and those who 'have overcome the evil one' cannot love the world.

μηδὲ τὰ ἐν τῷ κ. *Nor yet the things &c.* 'Love not the world; no, nor anything in that sphere.' Comp. Matt. vi. 25; xxiii. 9, 10; and μὴ συναναμίγνυσθαι......τῷ τοιούτῳ μηδὲ συνεσθίειν (1 Cor. v. 11). Τὰ ἐν τῷ κόσμῳ, as is plain from *v.* 16, are not material objects, which can be desired and possessed quite innocently, although they may also be occasions of sin. Rather, they are those elements in the world which are necessarily evil, its lusts and ambitions and jealousies, which stamp it as the kingdom of 'the ruler of this world' (John xii. 31) and not the kingdom of God.

ἐάν τις ἀγαπᾷ. Once more, as in *v.* 1, the statement is made quite general by the hypothetical form: everyone who does so is in this case. The Lord had proclaimed the same principle; 'No man *can* serve two masters......Ye *cannot* serve God and mammon' (Matt. vi. 24). So also S. James; 'Whosoever would be a friend of the world maketh himself an enemy of God' (iv. 4). Comp. Gal. i. 10. Thus we arrive at another pair of those opposites of which S. John is so fond. We have had light and darkness, truth and falsehood, love and hate; we now have love of the Father and love of the world. The world which is coextensive with darkness must exclude the God who is light.

ἡ ἀγάπη τοῦ πατρός occurs nowhere else: hence the reading of AC, ἡ ἀγ. τ. Θεοῦ. It means man's love to the Father, not His to man (see on *v.* 5); and it points to the duty of Christians as *children* of God. They must not love their Father's enemies. The order of the Greek is perhaps to be preserved. *There is not the love of the Father in him.* Whatever profession there may be of Christianity, the guiding principle of his life is something quite different from devotion to God.

16. Proof of the preceding statement by shewing the fundamental opposition in detail.

πᾶν τὸ ἐν τῷ κ. Neuter singular: in *v.* 15 we had the neuter plural. The *material* contents of the universe cannot be meant. To say that these did not originate from God would be to contradict the Apostle himself (John i. 3, 10) and to affirm those Gnostic doctrines against which he is contending. The Gnostics, believing everything material to be radically evil, maintained that the universe was created, not by God, but by the evil one, or at least by an inferior deity. By 'all that is in the world' is meant the spirit which animates it, its tendencies and tone. These, which are utterly opposed to God, did not originate in Him, but in the free and rebellious wills of His creatures, seduced by 'the ruler of this world.'

The Latin writers, almost without exception, translate (with some differences of wording); "All that is in the world *is* the lust of the flesh.' The *est* appears in Cyprian four times, in Ambrose, in Augustine frequently, in Jerome twice, in Ambrosiaster, Zeno of Verona, Gelasius, &c.   See Appendix G.

ἡ ἐπιθυμία τῆς σαρκός.   Not 'the lust *for* the flesh,' any more than ἡ ἐπ. τῶν ὀφθαλμῶν means 'the lust *for* the eyes.'   In both instances the genitive is subjective, as is generally the case with genitives after ἐπιθυμία in N.T.   Comp. ἐν ταῖς ἐπ. τῶν καρδιῶν (Rom. i. 24) ; ἀνθρώπων ἐπιθυμίαις (1 Pet. iv. 2) ; τῆς ἐπ. τῆς ψυχῆς σου (Rev. xviii. 14).   See also Gal. v. 16; Eph. ii. 3.   The meaning is the lusts which have their seats in the flesh and in the eyes respectively.

"Tell me where is fancy bred.

*   *   *   *   *

It is *engendered in the eyes.*"

Merchant of Venice, III. ii.

The former, therefore, will mean the desire for *unlawful pleasures of sense;* for enjoyments which are sinful either in themselves or as being excessive.

Note that S. John does not say ἡ ἐπιθ. τοῦ σώματος.   Σῶμα in N. T. is perhaps never used to denote the innately corrupt portion of man's nature : for that the common term is ἡ σάρξ.   S. John and S. Paul are here also in harmony : see on i. 3, 6; ii. 1, 6, 19.   Τὸ σῶμα is the neutral portion which may become either good or bad.   It may be sanctified as the abode and instrument of the Spirit, or degraded under the tyranny of the flesh.   See Introduction Chap. II. § vii.

ἡ ἐπιθ. τῶν ὀφθαλμῶν.   The eyes are the chief channel between the flesh and the outside world ; and 'the lust of the eyes' is the desire of seeing unlawful sights for the sake of the sinful pleasure to be derived from the sight; idle and prurient curiosity.   Familiar as S. John's readers must have been with the foul and cruel exhibition of the circus and amphitheatre, this statement would at once meet with their assent.   Tertullian, though he does not quote this passage in his treatise *De Spectaculis*, is full of its spirit : "The source from which all circus games are taken pollutes them......What is tainted taints us" (VII., VIII.).   Similarly S. Augustine on this passage; "This it is that works in spectacles, in theatres, in sacraments of the devil, in magical arts, in witchcraft; none other than curiosity."   See also *Confessions* VI. vii., viii., x. xxxv. 55.   In the *Testament of the Twelve Patriarchs* the second of the seven spirits of seduction is πνεῦμα ὁράσεως, μεθ᾽ ἧς γίνεται ἐπιθυμία (Lücke).

ἡ ἀλαζονεία τοῦ βίου.   Or, as Tischendorf, Westcott and Hort prefer, ἡ ἀλαζονία τ. β.: the vainglory *of life.*   Latin writers vary much in their renderings : *superbia vitae* (Vulgate Old and New); *ambitio saeculi* (Cyprian, Augustine, Zeno Veron., Gelasius); *jactantia vitae* (Ambrose); *superbia hujus vitae* (Jerome).   Ἀλαζονεία occurs elsewhere only Jas. iv. 16, and there in the plural ; where A. V. has 'boastings' and R. V. 'vauntings.'   The cognate adjective (ἀλαζών) occurs Rom. i. 30 and 2 Tim. iii. 2, where A. V. has 'boasters' and R. V. 'boastful.'   Pretentious ostentation, as of a wandering mountebank, is the radical signification of the word.   In Classical Greek the pretentiousness is the predominant notion; in Hellenistic Greek, the ostentation. Compare the account of this vice in Aristotle (*Nic. Eth.* IV. vii.) with Wisd. v. 8; 2 Macc. ix. 8; xv. 6. Ostentatious pride in the things which one possesses is the signification of the term here; 'life' meaning 'means of life, goods, possessions.' Βίος must be carefully distinguished from ζωή. Βίος occurs again iii. 17, and elsewhere in N. T. only 8 times. Ζωή occurs 13 times in this Epistle, and elsewhere in N. T. over 100 times. This is what we might expect from the meaning of the two words. Βίος means (1) *period of human life*, as 1 Tim. ii. 2; 2 Tim. ii. 4; (2) *means of life*, as here, iii. 17; Mark xii. 44; Luke viii. 14, 43; xv. 12, 30; xxi. 4. In 1 Pet. iv. 3 the word is not genuine. Ζωή means that *vital principle* which through Christ man shares with God (i. 2; John i. 4). With the duration of mortal life and the means of prolonging it the Gospel has comparatively little to do. It is concerned rather with that spiritual life which is not measured by time (see on i. 2), and which is independent of material wealth and food. For this kind of life ζωή is invariably used. By ἡ ἀλ. τ. βίου, therefore, is meant *ostentatious pride in the possession of worldly resources*. See Trench, *Synonyms of N. T.*, 87, 95; Cremer, 272.

These three evil elements or tendencies 'in the world' are co-ordinate: no one of them includes the other two. The first two are wrongful desires of what is not possessed; the third is a wrongful behaviour with regard to what is possessed. The first two may be the vices of a solitary; the third requires society. We can have sinful desires when we are alone, but we cannot be ostentatious without company. See Appendix A.

οὐκ ἔστιν ἐκ τ. πατρός. Does not derive its origin from (ἐκ) Him, and therefore has no natural likeness to Him or connexion with Him. S. John says 'the Father' rather than 'God' to emphasize the idea of parentage. Its origin is from the world and its ruler, the devil. Comp. 'Ye are of (ἐκ) your father the devil, and the lusts of your father ye will to do' (John viii. 44). The phrase εἶναι ἐκ is highly characteristic of S. John.

ἀλλὰ ἐκ τοῦ κόσμου ἐστίν. Cyprian twice renders *sed ex* concupiscentia *saeculi*, and twice *sed ex* concupiscentia *mundi*. Zeno of Verona makes the same insertion. An instance of Western interpolation.

17. παράγεται. Is passing away; as in *v.* 8: the process is now going on. We owe the verb '*pass* away' here to Coverdale: it is a great improvement on Tyndale's '*vanisheth* away'. Comp. 'The fashion of this world *is passing away*' (1 Cor. vii. 31), where the same verb is used, and where the active in a neuter sense (παράγει) is equivalent to the middle here and in *v.* 8.

ἡ ἐπιθ. αὐτοῦ. Not the lust *for* the world, but the lust which it exhibits, the sinful tendencies mentioned in *v.* 16. The world is passing away with all its evil ways. How foolish, therefore, to fix one's affections on what not only cannot endure but is already in process of dissolution! 'The lust thereof' = 'all that is in the world.' Codex A omits αὐτοῦ, and is supported in this by some other authorities.

τὸ θέλημα τ. Θεοῦ. This is the exact opposite of πᾶν τὸ ἐν τῷ κόσμῳ. The one sums up all the tendencies to good in the universe, the other all the tendencies to evil. We see once more how S. John in giving us the antithesis of a previous idea expands it and makes it fructify. He says that the world and all its will and ways are on the wane: but as the opposite of this he says, not merely that God and His will and ways abide, but that 'he that doeth the will of God abideth for ever.' This implies that he who follows the ways of the world will not abide for ever. Again he speaks of the love of the world and the love of the Father; but as the opposite of the man who loves the world he says not 'he that loveth the Father,' but 'he that doeth the will of the Father.' This implies that true love involves obedience. Thus we have a double antithesis. On the one hand we have the world and the man who loves it and follows its ways: they both pass away. On the other hand we have God and the man who loves Him and does His will: they both abide for ever. Instead of the goods of this life (βίος) in which the world would allow him to vaunt for a moment, he who doeth the will of God has that eternal life (ζωή) in which the true Christian has fellowship with God. In this far higher sense what was ignorantly said of S. John himself becomes literally true of every believer: 'That disciple shall not die.' Heracleon, the earliest commentator on S. John that is known to us (c. A.D. 170), says of the devil μὴ ἔχειν θέλημα, ἀλλ' ἐπιθυμίας. Εἰς τὸν αἰῶνα is literally 'unto the age', i. e. 'unto the age to come', the kingdom of heaven. He who does God's will shall abide until the kingdom of God comes *and be a member of it.* The latter fact, though not stated, is obviously implied. It would be a punishment and not a blessing to be allowed, like Moses, to see the kingdom but not enter it. The followers of the world share the death of the world: the children of God share His eternal life. Augustine adds at the close of this verse *sicut et ipse manet in aeternum.* Other Latin authorities have *quomodo et Deus manet* (or *manebit*) *in aeternum.* Another case of Western interpolation. Cyprian quotes the passage four times, always with this addition in some form or other. See Appendix G.

Here probably we should make a pause in reading the Epistle. What follows is closely connected with what precedes and is suggested by it: but there is, nevertheless, a new departure which is made with much solemnity.

18—26. THE PERSONS TO BE AVOIDED ;—ANTICHRISTS.

18. παιδία. *Little ones.* See on *v.* 14. It is difficult to see anything in this section specially suitable to children: indeed the very reverse is rather the case. S. John's readers in general are addressed, irrespective of age. Both his Epistle and Gospel are written for adults and for well-instructed Christians.

ἐσχάτη ὥρα ἐστίν. *It is the last* hour; possibly, but not probably, *it is a last hour.* The omission of the definite article is quite intelligible and not unusual: the idea is sufficiently definite without it, for there can be only one last hour. Similarly (Jude 18) we have ἐπ' ἐσχάτου χρόνου: and (Acts i. 8; xiii. 47) ἕως ἐσχάτου τ. γῆς. A great deal has been written upon this text in order to avoid a very plain but unwelcome conclusion, that by the 'last hour' S. John means the time immediately preceding the return of Christ to judge the world. Hundreds of years have passed away since S. John wrote these words, and the Lord is not yet come. Rather, therefore, than admit an interpretation which seemed to charge the Apostle with a serious error, commentators have suggested all kinds of explanations as substitutes for the obvious one. The following considerations place S. John's meaning beyond all reasonable doubt.

1. He has just been stating that the world is on the wane and that its dissolution has already begun. 2. He has just declared that the obedient Christian shall abide 'unto the age' of Christ's kingdom of glory. 3. He goes on to give as a proof that it is the 'last hour', that many Antichrists have already arisen ; it being the common belief of Christians that Antichrist would immediately precede the return of Christ (Matt. xxiv. 23, 24). 4. Ἡ ἐσχάτη ἡμέρα is a phrase peculiar to S. John (John vi. 39, 40, 44, 54; xi. 24; xii. 48), and invariably means the end of the world, not the Christian dispensation. 5. S. John's Gospel contains the prophecy, 'There cometh an hour (ἔρχεται ὥρα), in which all that are in the tombs shall hear His voice, and shall come forth, &c.' (v. 28). 6. Analogous phrases in other parts of N. T. point in the same direction: 'In the last days grievous times shall come' (2 Tim. iii. 1); 'Ye are guarded through faith unto a salvation ready to be revealed in the last time' (1 Pet. i. 5); 'In the last days mockers shall come with mockery' (2 Pet. iii. 3). These and other passages shew that by 'the last days', 'last time', 'last hour', and the like, Christian writers did not mean the whole time between the first and second coming of Christ, but only the concluding portion of it. 7. We find similar language with similar meaning in the sub-apostolic age. Thus Ignatius (*Eph.* XI.) writes ; "These are the last times (ἔσχατοι καιροί). Henceforth let us be reverent; let us fear the longsuffering of God, lest it turn into a judgment against us. For either let us fear the wrath which is to come, or let us love the grace which now is."

Of other interpretations of 'the last hour' the most noteworthy are these. (1) *The Christian dispensation,* which we have every reason to believe is the last. Comp. Acts ii. 17. This is the sense in which S. John's words are *true;* but this is plainly not his *meaning.* The appearance of Christ, not of Antichrist, proves that the Christian dispensation is come. (2) *A very grievous time; tempora periculosa pessima et abjectissima.* This is quite against usage whether in classical or N.T. Greek: comp. 2 Tim. iii. 1. The classical phrase, 'to suffer the last things', i.e. 'to suffer extremities' (τὰ ἔσχατα παθεῖν), supplies no analogy: there the notion of 'grievous' comes from the verb. (3) *The eve of the destruction of Jerusalem.* How could the appearance of Antichrist prove that this had arrived? And Jerusalem had perished at least a dozen years before the probable date of this Epistle. (4) *The eve of S. John's own death.* Antichrists could be no sign of that.

It is admitted, even by some of those who reject the obvious inter-

pretation, that "the Apostles expected a speedy appearing or manifestation of Jesus as the Judge of their nation and of all nations "
(Maurice): which is to admit the whole difficulty of the rejected explanation. Only gradually was the vision of the Apostles cleared to
see the true nature of the spiritual kingdom which Christ had founded
on earth and left in their charge. Even Pentecost did not at once
give them perfect insight. Being under the guidance of the Holy
Spirit they could not teach what was untrue: but, like the Prophets
before them, they sometimes uttered words which were true in a sense
far higher than that which was present to their own minds. In this
higher sense S. John's words here are true. Like others, he was
wrong in supposing 'that the kingdom of God was immediately to
appear' (Luke xix. 11), for 'it was not for them to know times or
seasons which the Father hath set within His own authority' (Acts i.
7). He was right in declaring that, the Messiah having come, it was
the 'last hour.' No event in the world's history can ever equal the
coming of Christ until He comes again. The epoch of Christianity,
therefore, is rightly called the 'last hour,' although it has lasted nearly
two thousand years. What is that compared with the many thousands
of years since the creation of man, and the limitless geological periods
which preceded the creation of man? What again in the eyes of Him
in whose sight 'a thousand years are but yesterday'?

"It may be remarked that the only point on which we can certainly
say that the Apostles were in error, and led others into error, is in
their expectation of the immediate coming of Christ; and this is the
very point which our Saviour says (Mark xiii. 32) is known only to the
Father" (Jelf).

καὶ καθὼς ἠκούσατε ὅτι ἀντίχριστος ἔρχ. *And* even as *ye* heard
that Antichrist cometh. For ὅτι ἀντίχρ. A reads ὁ ἀντίχρ. For καθώς see
on *v.* 6. This seems to be a case in which the aorist should be retained
in English. As in *v.* 7, the reference is probably to a definite point
in their instruction in the faith. See on *v.* 11. 'Cometh' points to
the analogy between the Christ and the Antichrist. The one was
hoped for, and the other dreaded, with equal certainty; and hence
each might be spoken of as 'He that cometh' (ὁ ἐρχόμενος). 'Art
Thou *He that cometh?*' (Matt. xi. 3; Luke xix. 20). Comp. Mark viii.
38; xi. 9; John iv. 25; vi. 14; xi. 27, &c. &c. And as to the coming of
Antichrists the N.T. seems to be as explicit as the O.T. with regard to
the coming of Christ. 'Many shall come in My name, saying I am
the Christ; and shall lead many astray... There shall arise false
Christs, and false prophets, and shall shew great signs and wonders;
so as to lead astray, if possible, even the elect' (Matt. xxiv. 5, 24).
Comp. Mark xiii. 22, 23; Acts xx. 29; 2 Tim. iii. 1; 2 Pet. ii. 1; and
especially 2 Thess. ii. 3, which like the passage before us seems to
point to one distinct person or power as the one Antichrist, whose
spirit animates all antichristian teachers.

The term 'Antichrist' in Scripture occurs only in the First and
Second Epistles of S. John (ii. 18, 22; iv. 3; 2 John 7). The earliest
instance of its use outside Scripture is in S. Polycarp (*Ep. ad Phil.*

VII.), in a passage which shews that this disciple of S. John (A.D.112—
118) knew our Epistle: see on iv. 3. The term does not mean merely
a *mock Christ* or *false Christ*, for which the N.T. term is ψευδόχριστος
(Matt. xxiv. 24; Mark xiii. 22). Nor does it mean simply *an opponent
of Christ*, for which we should probably have ἐχθρὸς τοῦ Χριστοῦ, like
τοὺς ἐχθροὺς τ. σταυροῦ τ. Χρ. (Phil. iii. 18) and ἐχθρὸς τοῦ Θεοῦ (Jas. iv.
4). But it includes *both* these ideas of counterfeiting and opposing;
it means an *opposition Christ* or *rival Christ;* just as we call a rival
Pope an 'antipope'. The Antichrist is, therefore, a *usurper*, who
under false pretences assumes a position which does not belong to
him, and who *opposes* the rightful owner. The idea of opposition is
the predominant one.

It is not easy to determine whether the Antichrist of S. John is
personal or not. But the discussion of this question is too long for a
note: see Appendix B.

ἀντίχρ. πολλοὶ γεγόνασιν. **Have there arisen** *many Antichrists.*
The Christ *was* from all eternity (i. 1); the Antichrist and his company *arose* in time: they *are come into being.* We have a similar
contrast in the Gospel. 'Εν ἀρχῇ ἦν ὁ λόγος (i. 1). ἐγένετο ἄνθρωπος
ἀπεσταλμένος παρὰ Θεοῦ (i. 6). Note the difference of tense between
ἐγένετο and γεγόνασιν: the perfect indicates that these antichrists are
for the most part still alive. The word occurs nowhere else in this
Epistle. For καθὼς...καὶ...instead of καθὼς...οὕτως...comp. *v.* 6; iv.
17; John xvii. 18; xx. 21. These 'many antichrists' are probably to
be regarded as at once forerunners of the Antichrist and evidence that
his spirit is already at work in the world: the one fact shews that he
is not far distant, the other that in a sense he is already here. In
either case we have proof that the return of Christ, which is to be
heralded by the appearance of Antichrist, is near.

ὅθεν γινώσκομεν ὅτι ἐσχ. ὥρα ἐστίν. **Whence we come to know**
that it is the last **hour.** "Οθεν in the sense of 'from which data, from
which premises' hardly occurs elsewhere in N.T., excepting perhaps
in Hebrews (ii. 17; vii. 25; viii. 3), where it is uniformly rendered
'wherefore' in both A.V. and R.V. It is similar in meaning to ἐκ
τούτου (iv. 6).

It is difficult to see what S. John could have meant by this, if by
the 'last hour' he understood the Christian dispensation as a whole
and not the concluding portion of it (comp. 2 Tim. iii. 1). The multitude of false teachers who were spreading the great lie (*v.* 22) that
Jesus is not the Christ, were evidence, not of the existence of Christianity, but of antichristianity. Nor could evidence of the former be
needed by S. John's readers. They did not need to be convinced
either that the Gospel dispensation had begun, or that it was the last
in the history of the Divine Revelation. The Montanist theory that a
further dispensation of the Spirit, distinct from that of the Son, was
to follow and supersede the Gospel, as the Gospel had superseded
Judaism, the dispensation of the Father, was a belief of later growth.
(For an account of this theory as elaborated by Joachim of Flora [fl.
A.D. 1180—90] see Döllinger's *Prophecies and the Prophetic Spirit in the*

Christian Era, pp. 114—119.) In the Apostolic age the tendency was
all the other way;—to believe that the period since the coming of
Christ was not only the last in the world's history, but would be very
brief. It was thought that some of the generation then existing might
live to see the end (1 Thess. iv. 15, 16; 1 Cor. xv. 51, 52).

19. The relation of these antichristian teachers to the Church
of Christ. They were formerly nominal members, but never real
members of it. They are now not members in any sense. Note the
repetition, so characteristic of S. John, of the key-word ἡμῶν, which
means the Christian Church. It occurs five times in this one verse.

ἐξ ἡμῶν ἐξῆλθαν. Tenses, which in other respects are second
aorists in form, frequently in LXX. and N.T. have the α of the first
aorist. Comp. 2 John 5, 7; 3 John 7. Winer, 86, 87. Note the
chiasmus: ἐξ ἡμῶν stands first in the one clause and last in the other
for emphasis. 'Out from us they went; it was their own doing,—a
distinct separation from our communion: but that very fact proves
that their origin is not from us'. We can hardly express in English
the simple and forcible antithesis of ἐξ ἡμῶν. It is incredible that the
first clause means 'they proceeded from us *Jews*.' What point is
there in that? Moreover, S. John never writes as a Jew, but always
as a Christian to Christians. Ἡμῶν includes all true Christians, whether Jews or Gentiles in origin. Comp. καὶ ἐξ ὑμῶν αὐτῶν ἀναστήσονται
ἄνδρες λαλοῦντες διεστραμμένα (Acts xx. 30), which may refer to these
very antichrists (the words are addressed to the Ephesian presbyters):
and ἐξῆλθον ἄνδρες παράνομοι ἐξ ὑμῶν καὶ ἀπέστησαν τοὺς κατοικοῦντας
τὴν πόλιν αὐτῶν (Deut. xiii. 14). In the second clause ἐξ ἡμῶν is exactly
analogous to ἐκ τοῦ πατρός and ἐκ τοῦ κόσμου in *v.* 16. The contrast
between the single act of departure (ἐξῆλθαν) and the lasting condition
of origin (ἦσαν) is clearly marked by the tenses. Comp. John iv. 27,
47, 50; v. 9; vi. 1, 2, 16, 17, 66; vii. 14, 30, 31, 44.

μεμεν. ἂν μεθ' ἡμῶν. *They* **would have abided** *with us*. See on
v. 24. The 'no doubt' of A. V. corresponds to nothing in the Greek,
and the intrusion is interesting. Almost all the earlier English Versions go wrong as to 'no doubt.' Tyndale and Cranmer have 'no
dout,' the Genevan has 'douteles,' and the Rhemish 'surely.' Probably these are attempts to translate the *utique* of the Vulgate, *permansissent utique nobiscum:* and the *utique*, which is as old as Tertullian (*De Praescr. Haer.* III.), is a mistaken endeavour to give a separate
word to represent the Greek particle ἄν. Wiclif (not Purvey) has
'sotheli' to represent *utique;* 'sotheli they hadden dwelte with
us'. Luther inserts 'ja'; 'so wären sie *ja* bei uns geblieben';
which looks as if he also were under the influence of the *utique.*
There is a similar instance John viii. 42, where Wiclif has '*sotheli*
ye schulden love Me', Cranmer, '*truly* ye wolde love Me', and the
Rhemish, '*verely* ye would love Me', because the Vulgate (not
Tertullian) gives *diligeretis utique Me* for ἠγαπᾶτε ἂν ἐμέ. Comp.
3 John 9, where the Vulgate has *scripsissem forsitan* to represent the
reading ἔγραψα ἄν. The meaning here is that secession proves a
want of fundamental union from the first. As Tertullian says: *Nemo*

Christianus, nisi qui ad finem perseveraverit. Note that S. John does not say 'they would have abided *among* us (ἐν ἡμῖν)', but '*with* us (μεθ᾽ ἡμῶν)'. This brings out more clearly the idea of *fellowship:* 'these antichrists had no real sympathy with us'.

ἀλλ᾽ ἵνα φανερωθῶσιν. ᾽Αλλ᾽ ἵνα is an elliptical expression very frequent in S. John's Gospel (i. 8; ix. 3; xiii. 18; xiv. 31; xv. 25). The ellipse may be filled up thus ; ἀλλὰ τοῦτο γέγονεν ἵνα, or by supplying a verb from the previous sentence; ἀλλ᾽ ἐξῆλθαν ἵνα. Winer, 398, 774. The Apostle's favourite construction with ἵνα (see on i. 9) again points to the Divine government of events. It was God's will that these spurious members should be made known as such. The κρίσις, which all through the Gospel is given as the necessary result of the manifestation of the Son, still continues after His return to the Father —the separation of light from darkness, of the Church from the world, of real from unreal Christians (see introductory note to John v.). S. John assures his readers that the appearance of error and unbelief in the Church need not shake their faith in it: it is all in accordance with the Divine plan. Revelation of the truth necessarily causes a separation between those who accept and those who reject it, and is designed to do so. God does not will that any should reject the truth; but He wills that those who reject should be made manifest. S. Paul states this truth the other way ; that the *faithful* need to be distinguished from the rest: δεῖ γὰρ καὶ αἱρέσεις ἐν ὑμῖν εἶναι, ἵνα οἱ δόκιμοι φανεροὶ γένωνται ἐν ὑμῖν (1 Cor. xi. 19).

ὅτι οὐκ εἰσὶν πάντες ἐξ ἡμῶν. Does this mean 'that *not all* are of us', as in the margin of R. V., or 'that they are *not, any of them*, of us'? Certainly the latter. 'That they *were* not all of us', as A. V. is doubly wrong. Where the negative immediately precedes πᾶς, it negatives the πᾶς, and the meaning is *non omnis*, 'not every one' or 'not all'. Where the verb intervenes, the οὐ negatives the verb and not the πᾶς: 'not any one' or 'all...not'. This idiom appears to be a Hebraism, far more common in LXX. than in N. T.; comp. Ex. xii. 16, 44 ; xx. 40 ; &c. &c. Contrast οὐ πᾶσα σὰρξ ἡ αὐτὴ σάρξ (1 Cor. xv. 39) with οὐκ ἂν ἐσώθη πᾶσα σάρξ (Matt. xxiv. 22). Wiclif, Tyndale, and Cranmer rather avoid the difficulty by omitting 'all'; but the omission gives the right sense in a weakened form. The erroneous 'were' comes from Tyndale and Cranmer: Wiclif, the Genevan and the Rhemish are right. For οὐ......πᾶς comp. Rev. xxi. 27 ; Luke i. 37; Rom. iii. 20. Winer, 214.

In this verse S. John does not teach that the Christian cannot fall away; his exhortations to his readers not to love the world, but to abide in Christ, is proof of that. He is only putting in another form the declaration of Christ, 'I give unto them eternal life; and they shall never perish, and no one shall snatch them out of My hand' (John x. 28). Apostasy is possible, but only for those who have never really made Christ their own, never fully given themselves to Him.

20. καὶ ὑμεῖς χρῖσμα ἔχετε. And *ye have an* anointing (as in *v.* 27) *from the Holy One.* S. John, in his manner, puts two contrasted parties side by side, the Antichrist with his antichrists, and the Christ with His christs; but the fact of there being a contrast does not warrant us in turning S. John's simple 'and' (καί) into 'but.' Tyndale holds fast to 'and', in spite of Wiclif's 'but' and the Vulgate's *sed.* Just as the Antichrist has his representatives, so the Anointed One, the Christ, has His. All Christians in a secondary sense are what Christ is in a unique and primary sense, the Lord's anointed. 'These anointed', says the Apostle to his readers, '*ye* are'. The 'ye' is not only expressed in the Greek, but stands first after the conjunction for emphasis: 'ye' in contrast to these apostates. The word for 'anointing' or 'unction' (χρῖσμα) strictly means the 'completed act of anointing': but in LXX. it is used of the unguent or anointing oil (Deut. xxx. 25); and Tyndale, Cranmer and the Genevan have 'oyntment' here. In N. T. it occurs only here and v. 27. Kings, priests, and sometimes prophets were anointed, in token of their receiving Divine grace. Hence oil both in O. and N. T. is a figure of the Holy Spirit (Ps. xlv. 6, 7; cv. 15; Is. lxi. 1; Acts x. 38; Heb. i. 9; 2 Cor. i. 21). It is confusing cause and effect to suppose that this passage was influenced by the custom of anointing candidates at baptism: the custom though ancient (for it is mentioned by Tertullian, c. A.D. 195, *De Bapt.* VII., and by S. Cyril of Jerusalem, c. A.D. 350, *Catech. Lect.* XXI. 3, 4), is later than this Epistle. More probably the custom was suggested by this passage. The opening of S. Cyril's 21st Lecture throws much light on this passage. "Having been baptized into Christ and...being made partakers of Christ, *ye are properly called christs,* and of you God said, Touch not My christs, or anointed. Now ye were made christs *by receiving the emblems of the Holy Spirit;* and all things were in a figure wrought in you, because ye are figures of Christ. He also bathed Himself in the river Jordan, and...came up from the waters; and the Holy Spirit in substance lighted on Him, like resting upon like. In the same manner to you also, after you had come up from the pool of the sacred streams, was given the unction, the emblem of that wherewith Christ was anointed; and this is the Holy Spirit". Similarly S. Augustine; "In the unction we have a sacramental sign (*sacramentum*); the virtue itself is invisible. The invisible unction is the Holy Spirit" (*Hom.* III. 12). Comp. Eph. i. 13.

It may be doubted whether S. John in this verse makes any allusion to the anointing which was a feature in some Gnostic systems.

ἀπὸ τοῦ ἁγίου. This almost certainly means *Christ,* in accordance with other passages both in S. John and elsewhere (John vi. 69; Rev. iii. 7; Mark i. 24; Acts iii. 14; Ps. xx. 10), and in harmony with Christ being called δίκαιος in vv. 1, 29, and ἁγνός in iii. 3. Moreover in John xiv. 26; xv. 26; xvi. 7, 14 Christ promises to give the Holy Spirit. It may possibly mean God the Father (Hab. iii. 3; Hos. xi. 9; 1 Cor. vi. 19). It cannot well mean the Holy Spirit, unless some other meaning be found for χρῖσμα. The meaning then is "a chrism from the Christ."

καὶ οἴδατε πάντα. The reading is profoundly uncertain: see critical notes. Here, as in v. 14, it is possible that B and the Thebaic Version preserve the original reading: οἴδατε πάντες with a colon after τοῦ ἁγίου. In which case the meaning may be either 'Ye all know this'; or 'Ye all know—I have not written to you because ye know not the truth, but because ye know it', with a very intelligible anacoluthon. "The harmony between B and the Thebaic in characteristic readings, for which they stand almost or quite alone, is well worth notice : e.g. Acts xxvii. 37; Rom. xiii. 13; Col. iii. 6; Heb. iii. 2; 1 John ii. 14, 20" (Scrivener). If A.V. and R.V. are right with καὶ οἴδατε πάντα, the meaning will be, 'It is you (and not these antichristian Gnostics who claim it) that are in possession of the true knowledge, in virtue of the anointing of the Spirit of truth. Christians possess *the truth* in a far higher sense than any unchristian philosopher. The unbeliever's knowledge is all out of balance and proportion. The material side is exaggerated, the spiritual is distorted or ignored. Whichever reading we adopt, the meaning is strictly in harmony with the promise of Christ ; ὅταν δὲ ἔλθῃ ἐκεῖνος, τὸ Πνεῦμα τῆς ἀληθείας, ὁδηγήσει ὑμᾶς εἰς πᾶσαν τὴν ἀλήθειαν—*into all the truth* (John xvi. 13). Similarly S. Ignatius writes; ὧν οὐδὲν λανθάνει ὑμᾶς, ἐὰν τελείως εἰς Ἰησοῦν Χρ. ἔχητε τὴν πίστιν καὶ τὴν ἀγάπην (*Eph.* xiv. 1): and S. Polycarp; οὐδὲν ὑμᾶς λέληθεν (xii.). Comp. οἱ δὲ ζητοῦντες τὸν Κύριον συνήσουσιν ἐν παντί (Prov. xxviii. 5), and see 1 Tim. iv. 9.

The whole verse is very remarkable as being addressed by the Apostle to the Christian *laity*, and is in marked contrast to the clerical exclusiveness of some later teachers.

21. οὐκ ἔγραψα. Whatever may be the explanation of the tense in *v.* 14, here we probably have the *epistolary aorist,* which may be represented by either the present or the perfect in English. But some would refer this also to the Gospel; and the absence of ταῦτα renders this not impossible. More probably, however, as appears from *v.* 26, ἔγραψα both here and there refers to this section about antichrists. 'Do not think from my warning you against lying teachers that I suspect you of being ignorant of the truth: you who have been anointed with the Spirit of truth cannot be ignorant of the truth. I write as unto men who will appreciate what I say. I write, not to teach, but to confirm.' "S. John does not treat Christianity as a religion containing elements of truth, or even more truth than any religion which had preceded it. S. John presents Christianity to the soul as a religion which must be everything to it, if it is not really to be worse than nothing " (Liddon).

ὅτι οὐκ οἴδατε τ. ἀλ., ἀλλ' ὅτι οἴδ. αὐτήν, καὶ ὅτι. There are no less than three ways of taking this, depending upon the meaning given to the thrice repeated conjunction (ὅτι), which in each place may mean either 'because' or 'that'. 1. As A.V.; *because,*...but *because* ...and *that.* The A.V. follows the earlier Versions in putting 'that' in the last clause: so Tyndale, Cranmer, &c. 2. As R.V.; 'because' in each clause. 3. 'That' in each clause: 'I have not written *that* ye know not the truth, but *that* ye know it, and *that* &c.' This last is almost certainly wrong. As in *vv.* 13, 14 the verb 'write' introduces the reason for writing and not the subject-matter or contents of the Epistle. And if the first conjunction is 'because', it is the sim-

62   1 *S. JOHN.*   [II. 21—

plest and most natural to take the second and third in the same way.
The Apostle warns them against antichristian lies, not because they are
ignorant, but (1) because they possess the truth, and (2) because every
kind of lie is utterly alien to the truth they possess. "There is the
modesty and the sound philosophy of an Apostle! Many of us think
that we can put the truth *into* people, by screaming it into their ears.
We do not suppose that they have any truth *in* them to which we can
make appeal. S. John had no notion that he could be of use to his
dear children at Ephesus unless there was a truth in them, a capacity
of distinguishing truth from lies, a sense that one must be the eternal
opposition of the other" (Maurice). Comp. ὑπομνῆσαι δὲ ὑμᾶς βούλομαι,
εἰδότας ἅπαξ πάντα (Jude 5).

πᾶν ψεῦδος ἐκ τ. ἀλ. οὐκ ἔστιν. As in iii. 15, the negative belongs
to the verb and not to the πᾶν; "all...not, not any, none': *No lie is
of the truth.* There is nothing Hebraistic in this form of expression,
as in *v.* 19: comp. Eph. v. 5; John iii. 16. 'Εκ expresses origin, as in
vv. 16, 19; ἐκ τοῦ πατρός, ἐκ τοῦ κόσμου, ἐξ ἡμῶν. Comp. τὸ βάπτισμα
'Ιωάννου ἐξ οὐρανοῦ ἦν, ἢ ἐξ ἀνθρώπων; (Luke xx. 5). Every lie is from its
very source utterly removed from the truth. The truth springs from
ὁ ἀψευδὴς Θεός (Tit. i. 2); lying from the devil, ὅτι ψεύστης ἐστὶ καὶ ὁ
πατὴρ αὐτοῦ (John viii. 44): ἀλήθεια γὰρ ὁπαδὸς Θεοῦ (Philo *Vita Mosis*
III): πάντη ἄρα ἀψευδὲς τὸ θεῖον (Plato *Rep.* II. 208 E).

22. τίς ἐστιν ὁ ψεύστης. *Who is* the *liar?* R.V. is here again
superior to previous English Versions. But we must beware of
exaggerating the article in *interpretation*, although it is right to
translate it. It merely marks the passage from the abstract to the
concrete: 'Every lie is absolutely alien from the truth. Who then is
the one who speaks lies? There are no liars if he who denies that
Jesus is the Christ is not one.' The exactly parallel construction in
v. 4, 5 shews that 'the liar' here does not mean 'the greatest liar
possible'. Moreover, this would not be true. Is denying that Jesus is
the Christ a greater lie than denying the existence of the Son, or of
God? Nor does this lie include all falsehood. A Jew or Mahometan
possesses a large portion of the truth along with this falsehood. It is,
however, an instance of what Plato calls τὸ ὡς ἀληθῶς ψεῦδος, a lie περὶ
τὰ κυριώτατα, i.e. a veritable falsehood on the most momentous subjects. Cerinthus and his Gnostic hearers, who profess to be in possession of the higher truth, are really possessed by one of the worst of
lies (see Introduction).

The abruptness of the Apostle's question is startling. Throughout
these verses (22—24) "clause stands by clause in stern solemnity
without any connecting particles" (Westcott).

οὗτός ἐστιν ὁ ἀντ. This *is* the *antichrist*, as R. V. The article,
almost certainly spurious in *v.* 18, is certainly genuine here, iv. 3, and
2 John 7. But here ὁ ἀντίχριστος does not seem to mean the great
personal rival of the Christ, but the antichristian teacher who exhibits
his spirit and acts as his mouthpiece.

ὁ ἀρνούμενος τ. πατέρα κ. τ. υἱόν. This clause takes the place of ὁ
ἀρν. ὅτι 'Ιησοῦς οὐκ ἔστιν ὁ Χριστός. The change, which is quite in S.

John's manner, implies that to deny the one truth is to deny the other. Jesus is the Christ, and the Christ is the Son of God; therefore to deny that Jesus is the Christ is to deny the Son. And to deny the Son is to deny the Father; not merely because Son and Father are correlatives and mutually imply one another, but because the Son is the revelation of the Father, without whom the Father cannot be known. 'Neither doth any know the Father, save the Son, and *he to whomsoever the Son willeth to reveal Him*' (Matt. **xi**. 27). 'No one cometh unto the Father *but by Me*' (John xiv. 6). Comp. John v. 23, xv. 23. Some would put a full stop at 'antichrist,' and connect what follows with *v.* 23, thus; *This is the antichrist. He that denieth the Father (denieth) the Son also: every one that denieth the Son hath not the Father either.*

23. The previous statement is emphasized by an expansion of it stated both negatively and positively. The expansion consists in declaring that to deny the Son is not merely to do that, and indeed not merely to deny the Father, but also (οὐδέ) to debar oneself from communion with the Father. So that we now have a third consequence of denying that Jesus is the Christ. To deny this is (1) to deny the Son, which is (2) to deny the Father, which is (3) to be cut off from the Father. 'To have the Father' must not be weakened to mean 'to hold as an article of faith that He is the Father'; still less, 'to know the Father's will'. It means, quite literally, 'to have Him as his own Father'. Those who deny the Son cancel their own right to be called τέκνα Θεοῦ: they *ipso facto* excommunicate themselves from the great Christian family in which Christ is the Brother, and God is the Father, of all believers. 'To as many as received Him, to them gave He the *right to become children of God*' (John i. 12). The verse is a condemnation of those who insist on the Fatherhood of God and yet deny the Divinity of Jesus Christ. And the condemnation is made with special comprehensiveness: not merely ὁ ἀρνούμενος but πᾶς ὁ ἀρν. As if the Apostle would say, 'Some may think that there are exceptions to this principle; but it holds good of *every one*'. Comp. *v.* 29; iii. 4, 6, 9, 10, 15; iv. 7; v. 1, 4, 18; 2 John 9.

ὁ ὁμολογῶν. **He that confesseth**, as R. V. The translation of ὁμολογεῖν should be uniform in i. 9; iv. 2, 3, 15; 2 John 7. It is surprising that A. V., while admitting the passage about the three Heavenly Witnesses (v. 7) without any mark of doubtfulness, prints the second half of this verse in italics, as if there were nothing to represent it in the Greek. Excepting the 'but', the sentence is undoubtedly genuine, being found in all the best MSS. (אABC) and many other authorities. A few authorities omit it accidentally, owing to the two halves of the verse ending in the Greek with the same three words (τὸν πατέρα ἔχει). Tyndale, Luther, and the Genevan omit the sentence: Cranmer and the Rhemish retain it; Cranmer marking it as wanting authority, and both omitting 'but', which Purvey inserts, although there is no conjunction in the Vulgate. Other Versions insert different conjunctions. The asyndeton is impressive and continues through three verses, 22, 23, 24. "The sentences fall on the reader's soul like notes of a trumpet. Without cement, and therefore all the more ruggedly clasping each other, they are like a Cyclopean wall" (Haupt). It would be possible to translate, 'He that confesseth, hath the Son and the Father' (comp. 2 John 9): but this is not probable.

24. ὑμεῖς ὃ ἠκούσατε. The οὖν is an erroneous insertion in many of the inferior MSS. which omit the second half of *v.* 23: it weakens the force of the charge. As for you (with great emphasis, in contrast to these antichristian liars), *let that abide in you which* ye heard *from the beginning.* For the *nominativus pendens* comp. John vi. 39; vii. 38; xiv. 12; xv. 2; xvii. 2; Rev. ii. 26; iii. 12, 21: Winer, 718. Ἠκούσατε should be rendered as an aorist: as in *v.* 7 and iii. 11, it points to the definite time when they were instructed in the faith. 'Hold fast what ye first heard, and reject these lying innovations'.

In this passage the arbitrary distinctions introduced by the translators of 1611 reach a climax. The same Greek word (μένειν) is translated in three different ways in one verse; 'abide...remain...continue'. Elsewhere it is rendered in four other ways, making seven English words to one Greek; 'dwell' (John i. 39; vi. 56; xiv. 10, 17), 'tarry' (iv. 40; xxi. 22, 23), 'endure' (vi. 27), 'be present' (xiv. 25). The translators in their *Address to the Reader* tell us that these changes were often made knowingly and sometimes of set purpose. See Trench *On the A. V. of N. T.* pp. 85—87. They are generally regretable, and here are doubly so: (1) an expression highly characteristic of S. John (Gospel, 1 and 2 Epp., Rev.) and of deep meaning is blurred, (2) the emphasis gained by iteration, which is also characteristic of S. John, is entirely lost. 'Let the truths which were first taught you have a home in your hearts: if these have a home in you, ye also shall have a home in the Son and in the Father'. The Son is mentioned first because it is by abiding in Him that we abide in the Father. Bede quaintly suggests another reason: *ne dicant Ariani, Filium minorem Patre propterea credendum, quia nunquam ante Patrem nominatus inveniatur.* But there was 'The grace of our Lord Jesus Christ &c.' (2 Cor. xiii. 14) to forbid so weak an argument.

25. καὶ αὕτη ἐστὶν ἡ ἐπ. ἣν αὐτὸς ἐπ. ἡμῖν. And the promise which He Himself promised us is this. As in i. 5; iii. 23; v. 11, 14, αὕτη is the predicate and refers to what follows, not to what precedes: comp. *v.* 22. 'This is what His promise amounted to—no less than eternal life'. But the connexion with what precedes is close; for eternal life is only another name for abiding in the Son and the Father. Ἐπαγγελία, frequent in the Acts, S. Paul, and Hebrews, occurs here only in S. John: ἐπαγγέλλεσθαι also is used nowhere else by him. For the promise itself see John iii. 15; iv. 14; vi. 40, 51, 54, 58, &c. Αὐτός, as commonly in the nominative, is emphatic: *et haec est repromissio quam ipse pollicitus est nobis* (New Vulgate). Augustine has *pollicitatio*; the Old Vulgate *promissio* and *vobis.* Comp. *v.* 2. Of course αὐτός means Christ, "who in this passage forms the centre round which the statements of the Apostle move" (Huther). B reads ὑμῖν for ἡμῖν, but the other Uncials and almost all Versions are unanimous for ἡμῖν, which has internal evidence strongly on its side. Note the double article, τὴν ʕ. τὴν αἰών., as in i. 2 and nowhere else *in this phrase:* but see on i. 3. Note also that the substantive placed after a relative clause is attracted to the case of the relative: comp. Acts xxi. 16 ; Phil. iii. 18; Philem. 10.

26. ταῦτα ἔγραψα. This is not parallel to ἔγραψα in *vv.* 14, 21 where there is no ταῦτα. Here the reference must be to the Epistle, or rather to the section about the antichrists (18—25) : *v.* 14 probably refers in all three sentences to the Gospel: *v.* 21 is doubtful, but is best taken in conjunction with this as referring to the paragraph in which it occurs.

τῶν πλανώντων. **That lead you astray,** i.e. that are endeavouring to do so : see on i. 8. Thus Satan is called ὁ πλανῶν τὴν οἰκουμένην ὅλην. In both cases the present participle expresses habitual effort, not success. In such cases the participle with the article is almost a substantive, and as such loses all notion of time. Winer, 444.

27, 28. THE PLACE OF SAFETY ;—CHRIST.

27. καὶ ὑμεῖς τὸ χρ. ὃ ἐλάβετε. As in *v.* 2, we have the false and the true Christians put side by side in contrast; but this does not justify us in turning S. John's simple 'and' (καί) into 'but'. As in *v.* 24, we have the pronoun put first with great emphasis, and as a *nominativus pendens.* Moreover, the reception of the chrism refers to the definite occasion when Christ poured out His Spirit upon them, viz. their baptism; and therefore the aorist should be retained. Wherefore, as R.V., **And as for you,** *the anointing which* **ye received.**

μένει ἐν ὑμῖν. In order to convey a command or a rebuke gently, we often state as a fact what ought to be a fact. This may be the meaning here; and hence the Vulgate reads *maneat in vobis.* If not, it is an expression of the Apostle's great confidence in the spiritual condition of his children. For λαμβάνειν ἀπό comp. iii. 22; 3 John 7. S. John more often writes λαμβάνειν παρά, 'to receive at the hands of'; v. 41, 44; x. 18; 2 John 4; Rev. ii. 27.

οὐ χρείαν ἔχετε ἵνα. *Ye have no such need that any one teach you.* The construction is peculiar to S. John (Gospel ii. 25; xvi. 30): elsewhere either the infinitive or a genitive. For the meaning comp. *v.* 20. He who has once been anointed with the Spirit of truth has no need even of an Apostle's teaching, This seems to be quite conclusive against 'little children' anywhere in this Epistle meaning children in years or children in knowledge of the Gospel. S. John writes throughout for adult and well-instructed Christians, to whom he writes not to give information, but to confirm and enforce and perhaps develope what they have all along known. Of course S. John does not mean that the anointing with the Spirit supersedes all necessity for instruction. The whole Epistle, and in this chapter *vv.* 6, 7, 24, are conclusive against such a view. S. John assumes that his readers have been thoroughly instructed in 'the word' and 'the truth', before receiving the outpouring of the Spirit which shows them the full meaning of 'the word' and confirms them in 'the truth'. If S. John has no sympathy with a knowledge which professed to rise higher than Christian teaching, still less has he sympathy with a fanaticism which would dispense with Christian teaching. While he condemns the Gnosticism of his own age, he gives no encouragement to the Montanism of a century later. But he does testify to the high position of the Christian laity who make good use of their privileges.

There are several various readings of importance in the second half of this verse: see critical notes. The A.V. deserts Wiclif, Purvey, Tyndale, Cranmer, and the Rhemish to follow the Genevan in preferring μενεῖτε to μένετε (אABC and Versions). The possible constructions are almost as numerous as the readings and are less easily determined, but they do not seriously affect the general sense. We may render (1) *But as His anointing teacheth you concerning all things, and is* true, *and is no lie, and even as* it taught *you,—do ye abide in Him;* making only one sentence with a long protasis. Or (2) we may break it into two sentences, each with a protasis and apodosis; *But as His anointing teacheth you concerning all things, it is* true *and is no lie ; and even as* it taught *you, do ye abide in Him.* The majority of English Versions, including R.V., are for the former: so also the Vulgate. Commentators are much divided; but Huther claims to have most on his side for the latter. He has against him Alford, Braune, De Wette, Düsterdieck, Ewald, Lücke, Neander, Westcott. The sentence seems to be a recapitulation of the sentence :—ὡς τὸ αὐτοῦ χρίσμα διδάσκει ὑμᾶς περὶ πάντων recalls *v.* 20 ; ἀληθές ἐστιν καὶ οὐκ ἔστιν ψεῦδος recalls *vv.* 21—23; μένετε ἐν αὐτῷ recalls *vv.* 24, 25. The καθώς emphasizes the exactness of the conformity, *even as:* comp. *vv.* 6, 8 ; iii. 2, 3, 7, 23; iv. 17; 2 John 4, 6. What is the nominative to ἐδίδαξεν? Probably 'He' implied in αὐτῷ. This explains the change of tense : ἐδίδαξεν refers to the gift of the Spirit made once for all by Christ; διδάσκει to the continual illumination which is the result of that gift. Winer, 764. Whether μένετε is indicative, like the μένει just before, or imperative, like the μένετε just following, is uncertain and unimportant. Therefore we adopt (3) *But as His anointing teacheth you concerning all things, and is* true, *and is no lie, and even as* He taught *you,—ye abide in Him,* or *abide in Him.* The number of passages in S. John's writings in which verbs occur which may be either imperative or indicative, is remarkable : comp. *v.* 29; John v. 39; xii. 19; xiv. 1; xv. 18, 27. As in *v.* 10, ἐν αὐτῷ is ambiguous : it may be neuter and mean ἐν τῷ χρίσματι, as some Latin Versions seem to have taken it; *permanete in ipsa* (*unctione*). But the next verse is decisive: ἐν αὐτῷ in both cases must mean in Christ. And this confirms the rendering '*He* taught' as preferable to 'it taught'. Luther makes ἐν αὐτῷ refer to καθὼς ἐδίδαξεν: *und wie sie euch gelehret hat, so bleibet bei demselbigen.*

28.　καὶ νῦν introduces the practical conclusion: see on 2 John 5 and comp. John xvii. 5, where Jesus, 'having accomplished the work given Him to do', prays καὶ νῦν δόξασόν με σύ, πάτερ. So also in Acts iii. 17; vii. 34; x. 5. Haupt thinks that καὶ νῦν introduces the new division of the Epistle, which (almost all agree) begins near this point. The truth seems to be that *vv.* 28 and 29 are at once the conclusion of one division and the beginning of another: τεκνία recalls the beginning of this section (*v.* 18), and no doubt means all S. John's readers.

ἐὰν φανερωθῇ. If *He shall* be manifested, as R.V. In inferior authorities the more difficult ἐάν has been softened into ὅταν. 'If' *seems* to imply a doubt as to Christ's return, and the change to 'when' has probably been made to avoid this. But 'if' implies no doubt as to the *fact*, it merely implies indifference as to the *time:* 'if He should return in our day' (see on John vi. 62; xii. 32; xiv. 3). **Be manifested** is greatly superior to 'appear' (as Augustine's *manifestatus fuerit* is superior to the Vulgate's *apparuerit*) because (1) φανερωθῇ is passive; (2) φανεροῦν is a favourite word with S. John and should be translated uniformly in order to mark this fact (i. 2; ii. 19; iii. 2, 5, 8; iv. 9; Rev. iii. 18; xv. 4; John i. 31; iii. 21, &c. &c.). Beza has *conspicuus factus fuerit*. As applied to Christ it is used of His being manifested in His Incarnation (i. 2; iii. 5, 8), in His words and works (John ii. 11; xvii. 6), in His appearances after the Resurrection (John xxi. 1, 14), in His return to judgment (here and iii. 2). S. John alone uses the word in this last sense, for which other N.T. writers have 'to be revealed' (ἀποκαλύπτεσθαι), a verb never used by S. John excepting once (John xii. 38) in a quotation from O.T. (Is. liii. 1), where he is under the influence of the LXX.

Note the correspondence between the clauses: ἐὰν φανερωθῇ = ἐν τῇ παρουσίᾳ αὐτοῦ, and σχῶμεν παρρησίαν = μὴ αἰσχυνθῶμεν ἀπ' αὐτοῦ.

σχῶμεν παρρησίαν. The R.V. has *we may have* **boldness.** At first sight this looks like one of those small changes which have been somewhat hastily condemned as 'vexatious, teasing, and irritating.' The A.V. wavers between 'boldness' (iv. 17; Acts iv. 13, 29, 31, &c.) and 'confidence,' with occasionally 'boldly' (Heb. iv. 16) instead of 'with boldness.' The R.V. consistently has 'boldness' in all these places. Παρρησία means literally 'freedom in *speaking*, readiness to *say anything*, frankness, intrepidity.' In this Epistle and that to the Hebrews it means especially the fearless trust with which the faithful soul meets God: iii. 21; iv. 17; v. 14. Comp. 1 Thess. ii. 19. In σχῶμεν S. John once more breaks the logic of his sentence rather than seem to exempt himself from what he tells others : μένετε, ἵνα σχῶμεν is parallel to ἐάν τις ἁμάρτῃ, ἔχομεν (*v.* 2).

μὴ αἰσχυνθῶμεν ἀπ' αὐτοῦ. The graphic terseness can scarcely be reproduced in English. We see the averted face and shrinking form, which are the results of the shame, clearly indicated in the Greek. 'Turn with shame *from* Him' and 'Shrink with shame *from* Him' have been suggested as renderings. Comp. μὴ φοβηθῆτε ἀπὸ τῶν ἀποκτεινόντων τὸ σῶμα (Matt. x. 28), 'Shrink not away in fear from them.' 'Receive shame from Him' is almost certainly not the meaning, although the Vulgate has *confundamur ab eo:* ἀπὸ means 'away from' not 'proceeding from.' Comp. προσέχετε ἀπὸ (Matt. vii. 15; x. 17; xvi. 11; Luke xii. 1; xx. 46) and φυλάσσεσθε ἀπὸ (Luke xii. 15) and the LXX. of Is. i. 29; Jer. ii. 36; xii. 13; and the speechless confusion of him who had no wedding-garment (Matt. xxii. 13).

ἐν τῇ παρουσίᾳ. The word occurs nowhere else in S. John's writings. In N. T. it is almost a technical term to express Christ's return to judgment (Matt. xxiv. 3, 27, 37, 39; 1 Cor. xv. 23; 1 Thess. ii. 19; iii. 13; iv. 15; v. 23; Jas. v. 7, 8; 2 Pet. i. 16, &c.). S. John uses it, as he uses ὁ Λόγος and ὁ πονηρός, without explanation, confident that his readers understand it. This is one of many small indications that he writes to well-instructed believers, not to children or the recently converted. The single occurrence of the word here, "where it might easily have been omitted, in exactly the same sense as it bears in all the other groups of apostolic writings, is a signal example of the danger of drawing conclusions from the negative phenomena of the books of N.T. The fact is the more worthy of notice as the subject of eschatology falls into the background in the Gospel and Epistles of S. John. Comp. John xxi. 22" (Westcott).

S. John's divisions are seldom made with a broad line across the text (see on iii. 10 and 24). The parts dovetail into one another and intermingle in a way that at times looks like confusion. Wherever we may place the dividing line we find similar thoughts on each side of it. Such is the case here. If we place the line between *vv.* 27, 28 we have the idea of *abiding in Christ* (*vv.* 24, 27, 28) on both sides of it. If we place it between *vv.* 28, 29, we have the idea of Divine *righteousness and holiness* (i. 9; ii. 1, 12, 20, 29) prominent in both divisions. If we make the division coincide with the chapters, we have the leading ideas of *boldness towards Christ and God* (*v.* 28; iii. 2, 21; iv. 17; v. 14), of *Christ's return to judgment* (*v.* 28; iii. 2; iv. 17), of *doing righteousness* (*v.* 29, iii. 7—10), and of *Divine sonship* (*v.* 29; iii. 1, 2, &c.), on both sides of the division. It seems quite clear therefore that both these verses (28, 29) belong to both portions of the Epistle, and that *v.* 29 at any rate is more closely connected with what follows than with what precedes.

The close connexion between the parts must not lead us to suppose that there is no division here at all. The transition is gentle and gradual, but when it is over we find ourselves on new ground. The antithesis between light and darkness is replaced by that between love and hate. The opposition between the world and God becomes the opposition between the world and God's children. The idea of having fellowship with God is transformed into that of being sons of God. Walking in the light is spoken of as doing righteousness. And not only do previous thoughts, if they reappear, assume a new form, but new thoughts also are introduced: the Second Advent, the boldness of the faithful Christian, the filial relation between believers and God. Although there may be uncertainty as to where the new division should begin, there is none as to the fact of there being one.

II. 29—V. 12.   God is Love.

There seems to be no serious break in the Epistle from this point onwards until we reach the concluding verses which form a sort of summary (v. 13—21). The key-word 'love' is distributed, and not very unevenly, over the whole, from iii. 1 to v. 3. Subdivisions, however, exist and will be pointed out as they occur. The next two subdivisions may be marked thus; *The Children of God and the Children of the Devil* (ii. 29—iii. 12); *Love and Hate* (iii. 13—24). The two, as we shall find, are closely linked together, and might be placed under one heading, thus ; *The Righteousness of the Children of God in their relation to the Hate of the World* (ii. 29—iii. 24).

II. 29—III. 12. THE CHILDREN OF GOD AND THE CHILDREN OF THE DEVIL.

29. ἐὰν εἰδῆτε ὅτι δίκαιός ἐστιν. This probably does not mean Christ, although the preceding verse refers entirely to Him. 'To be born of Christ,' though containing "nothing abhorrent from our Christian ideas," is not a Scriptural expression; whereas 'to be born of God' is not only a common thought in Scripture, but is specially common in this Epistle and occurs in the very next verse. And clearly 'He' and 'Him' must be interpreted alike: it destroys the argument (ὁ δίκαιος δικαίους γεννᾷ, *justus justum gignit*, as Oecumenius and Bengel put it) to interpret 'He is righteous' of Christ and 'born of Him' of God. Moreover, this explanation gets rid of one abrupt change by substituting another still more abrupt. That 'He, Him, His' in *v.* 28 means Christ, and 'He, Him' in *v.* 29 means God, is some confirmation of the view that a new division of the letter begins with *v.* 29. That 'God is righteous' see i. 9 and John xvii. 25. But S. John is so full of the truth that Christ and the Father are one, and that Christ is God revealed to man, that he makes the transition from one to the other almost imperceptibly. Bede interprets both δίκαιός ἐστιν and ἐξ αὐτοῦ of Christ.

γινώσκετε. Once more we are in doubt as to indicative or imperative: see on *v.* 27. The Vulgate has *scitote*, and hence Wiclif and the Rhemish, as also Tyndale and Cranmer, have the imperative. But the indicative is more in harmony with *vv.* 20, 21: *Ye know that everyone also*, i. e. not only Christ, but every righteous believer, **is a** son of God. Beza has *nostis*, which the Genevan mistranslates 'ye *have* known'. Note the change from εἰδῆτε to γινώσκετε, the one expressing the knowledge that is intuitive or simply possessed, the other that which is acquired by experience: 'If ye *are aware* that God is righteous, ye must *recognise*, &c.' Contrast *vv.* 11, 20, 21 with 3, 4, 5, 13, 14, 18. Comp. ὃ ἐγὼ ποιῶ σὺ οὐκ οἶδας ἄρτι, γνώσῃ δὲ μετὰ ταῦτα (John xiii. 7): πάντα σὺ οἶδας σὺ γινώσκεις ὅτι φιλῶ σε (xxi. 17): and conversely, εἰ ἐγνώκειτέ με, καὶ τὸν πατέρα μου ἂν ᾔδειτε (xiv. 7).

ὁ ποιῶν. 'That *habitually* doeth:' not the fact of having done a righteous act here and there, but the habit of righteousness, proves sonship. Morality in the highest sense can come of no lower source than God. **τὴν δικαιοσύνην.** The article possibly means **His** *righteousness*, or *the righteousness* that is rightly known as such; but it is safer to omit it in translation. The omission of the article before abstract nouns is the rule; but the exceptions are very numerous,

and among the exceptions are the many cases in which the article is
used for a possessive pronoun. Winer, 148. Again, "the Article is
rightly prefixed to words by which a system of action, familiar to the
mind as such, is intended to be signified" (Green, *Grammar of the N. T.*
p. 17). It is difficult to decide between these two explanations, but
the latter seems better. Comp. ποιεῖν τὴν ἀλήθειαν.

ἐξ αὐτοῦ γεγέννηται. *Of Him* hath *he been* begotten and His child
he remains: ἐξ αὐτοῦ first for emphasis. Just as only he who habitually walks in the light has true fellowship with the God who is light
(i. 6, 7), so only he who habitually does righteousness is a true son of
the God who is righteous. Thus the writer to *Diognetus* says that
the Christian is Λόγῳ προσφιλεῖ γεννηθείς, while the Son is πάντοτε
νέος ἐν ἁγίων καρδίαις γεννώμενος (xi.). Other signs of the Divine birth
are *love* of the brethren (iv. 7) and *faith* in Jesus as the Christ (v. 1).
Righteousness begins in faith and ends in love.

CHAPTER III.

1. After κληθῶμεν insert καὶ ἐσμέν with ℵABCP, Justin Martyr
and Versions against KL. ℵKL have ὑμᾶς for ἡμᾶς.

2. After οἴδαμεν omit δέ with ℵABC against KL.

5. After ἁμαρτίας omit ἡμῶν with AB and most Versions against
ℵCKL and the Thebaic. ℵ and the Thebaic have οἴδαμεν for οἴδατε.

7. AC have παιδία for τεκνία (ℵBKL).

11. ℵC have ἐπαγγελία for ἀγγελία (ABKL).

13. After ἀδελφοί omit μου with ℵABC against KL.

14. After ἀγαπῶν omit τὸν ἀδελφόν with ℵAB against CKL.

15. ℵAC have ἑαυτῷ for αὐτῷ or αὑτῷ (BKL). The reading remains
doubtful.

16. For τιθέναι (KL) read θεῖναι (ℵABC).

18. After τεκνία omit μου with ℵABC against KL. Before γλώσσῃ
insert τῇ with ABCKL against ℵ, and before ἔργῳ insert ἐν with ℵABCL
against K.

19. For γινώσκομεν (KL) read γνωσόμεθα (ℵABC). AB, Syriac,
and Vulgate omit καί before ἐν τούτῳ. A¹B, Peschito, and Thebaic
read τὴν καρδίαν for τὰς κ. (ℵA²CKL).

21. With AB omit ἡμῶν after καρδία. BC omit ἡμῶν after καταγινώσκῃ.

22. For παρ' αὐτοῦ (KL) read ἀπ' αὐτοῦ (ℵABC).

23. For πιστεύσωμεν (BKL) we should perhaps read πιστεύωμεν
(ℵAC).

Once more B almost invariably has the true text: in no case has it
a reading which is certainly wrong.

In *vv.* 1—3 the Apostle states the present and future condition of the children of God. For the present they have both in name and fact a parentage that is Divine: but the world, which has not recognised their Parent, does not recognise them. Their future is not yet fully revealed: but they are to be like Him; and this thought inspires their strivings after holiness.

1. ποταπήν. The same word occurs Matt. viii. 27; Mark xiii. 1; Luke i. 29; vii. 39; 2 Pet. iii. 11: it always implies astonishment, and generally admiration. The radical signification is 'of what country,' the Latin *cujas;* which, however, is never used as its equivalent in the Vulgate, because in N. T. the word has entirely lost the notion of place. It has become *qualis* rather than *cujas:* 'what *amazing* love'. In LXX. the word does not occur.

ἀγάπην. This is the key-word of this whole division of the Epistle (ii. 29—v. 12), in which it occurs 16 times as a substantive, 25 as a verb, and 5 times in the verbal adjective ἀγαπητοί. Here it is represented almost as something concrete, a gift which could be actually seen. S. John does not use his favourite interjection (ἴδε ὁ ἀμνὸς τ. Θεοῦ, ἴδε ὁ ἄνθρωπος, κ.τ.λ.), but the plural of the imperative, ἴδετε. ᾽Αγάπην δίδοναι occurs nowhere else in N. T.

ἡμῖν ὁ πατήρ. The words are in emphatic proximity: *on us* sinners *the Father* hath bestowed this boon. *Quid majus quam Deus? quae propior necessitudo quam filialis?* (Bengel.) Comp. ἔσομαι αὐτῷ Θεός, καὶ αὐτὸς ἔσται μοι υἱός (Rev. xxi. 7). ᾽Ο Πατήρ rather than ὁ Θεός because of what follows. B reads ὑμῖν for ἡμῖν and has some support in inferior authorities, but it can hardly be right. The confusion between ὑμ. and ἡμ. is easily made and is very frequent even in the best MSS.

ἵνα τ. Θεοῦ κληθ. S. John's characteristic construction, as in i. 9. " The final particle has its full force" (Westcott). This was the purpose of His love, its tendency and direction. Winer, 575. Comp. *vv.* 11, 23; iv. 21; John xiii. 34; xv. 12, 17. Καλεῖσθαι "is especially used of titles of honour, which indicate the possession of a certain dignity: see Matt. v. 9; Luke i. 76; 1 John iii. 1" (Winer, 769). With R.V. we must render τέκνα Θεοῦ children *of God*, not with A.V. and earlier Versions, '*the sons* of God'. There is no article; and we must not confuse S. Paul's υἱοὶ Θεοῦ with S. John's τέκνα Θεοῦ. Both Apostles tell us that the fundamental relation of Christians to God is a *filial* one: but while S. Paul gives us the legal side (adoption), S. John gives us the natural side (generation). To us the latter is the closer relationship of the two. But we must remember that in the Roman Law, under which S. Paul lived, adoption was considered as absolutely equivalent to actual parentage. In this 'unique apostrophe' in the centre of the Epistle two of its central leading ideas meet, Divine love and Divine sonship; a love which has as its end and aim that men should be called children of God. Note that Θεοῦ, as Θεόν in iv. 12, has no article. This shews that it is the idea of Divinity that is prominent rather than the relation to ourselves. The meaning is that we are children of One who is not human but Divine, rather that we are related to One who is our God.   See on iv. 12.

After 'children of God' we must insert on overwhelming authority (אABC and Versions), and we are: God has allowed us to be *called* children, and we *are* children.   The *simus* of the Vulgate and S. Augustine and the 'and *be*' of the Rhemish are probably wrong.   Tyndale, Beza, and the Genevan omit.   The present indicative after ἵνα is not impossible (John xvii. 3; 1 Cor. iv. 6; Gal. iv. 17: Winer, 362): but would S. John have put κληθῶμεν in the subjunctive and ἐσμέν in the indicative, if both were dependent upon ἵνα?   With καὶ ἐσμέν here comp. καὶ ἔσται in 2 John 2.   It is in this passage with the true reading that we have something like proof that Justin Martyr knew this Epistle.   In the *Dial. c. Try.* (cxxiii.) he has καὶ Θεοῦ τέκνα ἀληθινὰ καλούμεθα καὶ ἐσμέν.

διὰ τοῦτο.   **For this cause,** as R.V., reserving 'therefore' as the rendering of οὖν, a particle which is very frequent in the narrative portions of the Gospel, but which does not occur anywhere in this Epistle.   In ii. 24 and iv. 19 οὖν is a false reading.   Tyndale, Cranmer, the Genevan and the Rhemish all have 'for this cause': the A.V., as not unfrequently, has altered for the worse.   It may be doubted whether the R.V. has not here altered the punctuation for the worse, in putting a full stop at 'we are.'   Διὰ τοῦτο in S. John does not merely anticipate the ὅτι which follows; it refers to what precedes. 'We are children of God; and for this cause the world knows us not: because the world knew Him not.'   The third sentence explains how the second sentence follows from the first.   In logical phraseology we might say that the conclusion is placed between the two premises. Comp. John v. 16, 18; vii. 22; viii. 47; x. 17; xii. 18, 27, 39.   For 'the world' see on ii. 2.   S. Augustine compares the attitude of the world towards God to that of sick men in delirium who would do violence to their physician.   After the experiences of the persecutions under Nero and Domitian this statement of the Apostle would come home with full force to his readers.   The persecution under Domitian was possibly just beginning at the very time that this First Epistle was written.   Comp. John xv. 19.   All spiritual forces are unintelligible and offensive to 'the world.'   For οὐκ ἔγνω see on iv. 8.

2.   ἀγαπητοί.   Vulgate *carissimi*, as usual : Jerome (*Con. Pelag.* 13) *dilectissimi*.   In the first part of the Epistle this form of address occurs only once (ii. 7), just where the subject of love appears for a few verses.   In this second part it becomes the more common form of address (*vv.* 2, 21; iv. 1, 7, 11), for here the main subject is love. Similarly, in *v.* 13, where *brotherly* love is the special subject, ἀδελφοί is the form of address.   Νῦν and οὔπω each stand first in their respective clauses in emphatic contrast, and καί, as so often in S. John, introduces an antithesis.   Our privileges in this world are certain ; and yet our glories in the world to come are still veiled.   But they will be connected with our blessings here (καί), not something quite different (ἀλλά).   With this τέκνα Θεοῦ agrees: 'child' implies a future development; 'son' does not.   **Φανεροῦσθαι** in both places should be rendered, as in R.V., **be made manifest** or **be manifested**, in order to preserve the passive voice and uniformity of rendering with i. 2; ii. 19, 28. It is one of S. John's characteristic expressions. 'Appear' comes from the Vulgate: Augustine uses both *apparere* and *manifestari*, Tertullian *revelari*.

ἐὰν φανερωθῇ. **If it** *shall* **be manifested**, or **if He** *shall* **be manifested**. Here there is no difference of reading, as there is in ii. 28, between ὅταν and ἐάν; but earlier English Versions, under the influence of the Vulgate (*cum apparuerit*) have 'when' in both passages. Ambrose and Augustine have *cum* also; Tertullian has *si*. In both cases 'if' is right; but it has been either changed in the Greek, or shirked in translation, as appearing to imply a doubt respecting the manifestation. It implies no doubt as to the fact, but shews that the *results* of the fact are more important than the *time:* comp. '*If* I be lifted up from the earth,' and '*If* I go and prepare a place for you' (John xii. 32; xiv. 3).

It is less easy to determine between 'if *it* shall be manifested' and 'if *He* shall be manifested;' 'it' meaning what we shall be hereafter, and 'He' meaning Christ. No nominative is expressed in the Greek, and it is rather violent to supply a new nominative, differing from that of the very same verb in the previous sentence: therefore 'it' seems preferable. 'We know that if our future state is made manifest we, who are children of God, shall be found like our Father.' On the other hand, ii. 28 favours 'if *He* shall be manifested.' Note the οἴδαμεν and comp. ii. 20, 21. No *progress* in knowledge is implied; no additional *experience*. Our future resemblance to our Father is a fact of which as Christians we *are aware*. Contrast γινώσκομεν (ii. 3, 18; iii. 24; iv. 6, 13; v. 2). The 'but' of A.V. from δέ of T. R. introduces a false antithesis. But yet another way is possible. We may read here, as R. V. in *v.* 20, ὃ τι ἐάν, and translate, *We know—* **whatever may be manifested**—that we shall be like Him. But this does not seem probable: it is unlike S. John, and (perhaps we may say) unlike Scripture generally.

ὅμοιοι αὐτῷ. We are once more in doubt as to the meaning of αὐτῷ. If ἐὰν φαν. be rendered 'if He shall be manifested,' this will naturally mean that we shall be like *Christ;* which, however true in itself, is not the point. The point is that children are found to be like their Father. This is an additional reason for preferring 'it' with Tyndale and Cranmer to 'He' with Wiclif, Purvey, Genevan, and Rhemish. The precise nature of the ὁμοιότης (not ἰσότης) is left undetermined. *Similes, quia beati*, says Bede. Man was created κατ' εἰκόνα καὶ καθ' ὁμοίωσιν τοῦ Θεοῦ (Gen. i. 26, 27), and this likeness, marred at the Fall, is renewed here by Christ's Blood and perfected hereafter. ὅτι ὀψόμεθα αὐτὸν καθώς ἐστιν. **Because** *we shall see Him even as* **He** *is:* 'because' as in *vv.* 9, 20, 22; ii. 13, 14, &c., and 'even as' as in *vv.* 3, 7, 23; ii. 6, 27, &c. 'Because' or 'for' may give the cause either (1) of our *knowing* that we shall be like Him, or (2) of our *being* like Him. Both make good sense; but, in spite of 'we know' being the principal sentence *grammatically*, the statement which most needs explanation is the subordinate one, that we shall be like God. 'We shall be like Him,' says the Apostle, 'because, as you know, we shall see Him.' Comp. 'But we all, with unveiled face *reflecting* as a mirror *the glory of the Lord, are transformed into the same image* from glory to glory' (2 Cor. iii. 18); the sight of God will glorify us. This also is in harmony with the prayer of the great High Priest; 'And the glory which Thou hast given Me, I have given unto them' (John xvii. 22). Comp. 'And they shall see His face' (Rev. xxii. 4). The '*even* as' emphasizes the reality of the sight: no longer 'in a mirror, darkly,' but 'face to face.'

3. πᾶς ὁ ἔχων. Once more, as in ii. 23, 29, the Apostle explicitly states that there is *no* exception to the principle laid down. It is not only a general rule that he who has this hope of becoming like God purifies himself, but it is a rule without any exceptions; πᾶς ὁ ἔχων. There is absolutely no room for the Gnostic belief that to the enlightened man sin brings no pollution. 'Επ' αὐτῷ of course does not mean '*in* Him,' but '*on* Him': *in eo sitam*, as Beza. Every man who has the hope, *based upon God*, of one day being like Him, purifies himself. Comp. ἐπ' αὐτῷ ἔθνη ἐλπιοῦσιν (Rom. xv. 12): ἠλπίκαμεν ἐπὶ Θεῷ ζῶντι (1 Tim. iv. 10).

ἀγνίζει. In LXX. this verb (ἀγνίζειν) is used chiefly in a technical sense of ceremonial purifications, e.g. of the priests for divine service: and so also even in N. T. (John xi. 55; Acts xxi. 24, 26; xxiv. 18). But we need not infer that, because the outward cleansing is the dominant idea in these passages, it is therefore the only one. Here, Jas. iv. 8, and 1 Pet. ii. 22, the inward purification and dedication become the dominant idea, though perhaps not to the entire exclusion of the other.

ἀγν. ἑαυτόν. See on i. 8 and v. 21. S. John once more boldly gives us an apparent contradiction, in order to bring out a real truth. In i. 7 it is 'the blood of Jesus' which 'cleanseth us from all sin:' here the Christian 'purifieth himself.' Both are true, and neither cleansing will avail to salvation without the other. Christ cannot save us if we withhold our efforts: we cannot save ourselves without His merits and grace.

καθὼς ἐκεῖνος ἁγνός ἐστιν. As in *v.* 2, the '*even* as' brings out the reality of the comparison: similarly in John xvii. 11, 22 we have 'that they may be one, *even* as we are.' It is not easy to determine with certainty whether 'He' means the Father or Christ. The change of pronoun in the Greek from 'on Him' (ἐπ' αὐτῷ) to 'He' (ἐκεῖνος) favours, though it does not prove, a change of meaning. Probably throughout this Epistle ἐκεῖνος means Christ (*vv.* 5, 7, 16; ii. 6; iv. 17). He who, relying on God, hopes to be like God hereafter, purifies himself now after the example of Christ. Christ conformed Himself to the Father; we do the like by conforming ourselves to Christ. This interpretation brings us once more in contact with Christ's great prayer. 'For their sakes I consecrate Myself, that they themselves may be consecrated in truth' (John xvii. 19). Moreover, would S.

John speak of God as 'pure'? God is 'holy' (ἅγιος); Christ in His perfect sinlessness as man is 'pure' (ἀγνός). The Vulgate here renders
ἀγνός *sanctus*, as the Corbey MS. in James iii. 17, where the Vulgate
has *pudicus*. The usual Vulgate rendering is *castus*. Note that
S. John does not say 'even as He purified Himself:' that grace which
the Christian has to seek diligently is the inherent attribute of Christ.
The consecration of Christ for the work of redemption is very different from the purification of the Christian in order to be like Him
and the Father. Comp. Heb. xii. 14.

4. As so often, the Apostle emphasizes his statement by giving the
opposite case, and not the simple opposite, but an expansion of it.
Instead of saying 'every one that hath not this hope' he says **every
one that doeth** *sin*. The A. V. not only obscures this antithesis by
changing 'every man' to 'whosoever,' but also the contrast between
'doing righteousness' (ii. 29) and 'doing sin' by changing from 'do'
to 'commit.' This contrast is all the more marked in the Greek
because both words have the article; 'doeth the righteousness,' 'doeth
the sin.' Equally unfortunate is the A. V. rendering of καὶ τὴν
ἀνομίαν ποιεῖ, 'transgresseth also the law:' which destroys the parallel between ποιῶν τ. ἁμαρτ. and τ. ἀνομ. ποιεῖ. Note the *chiasmus*, and
render with R. V.; *Every one that* doeth *sin*, doeth *also* lawlessness.
To bring out the contrast and parallel it is imperative to have the
same verb in both clauses and also in ii. 29: to do sin is to do lawlessness, and this is the opposite of to do righteousness. The one marks
the children of God, the other the children of the devil. 'Lawlessness' both in English and Greek (ἀνομία) means not the *privation* of
law, but the *disregard* of it: not the having no law, but the acting as if one had none. (Comp. the Hebrew *pesha* and the LXX.
rendering of it, Is. xlii. 27; Amos iv. 4: it implies faithless disregard
of a covenant. This was precisely the case with some of the Gnostic
teachers: they declared that their superior enlightenment placed them
above the moral law; they were neither the better for keeping it nor
the worse for breaking it. Sin and lawlessness, says the Apostle, are
convertible terms: they are merely different aspects of the same state.
(Hence the predicate as well as the subject has the article: see below.)
And it is in its aspect of disregard of God's law that sin is seen to be
quite irreconcilable with being a child of God and having fellowship
with God. See on v. 17.

The 'for' of A. V. is sanctioned by no reading or ancient Version: it comes from Tyndale, Beza, and the Genevan. The Vulgate
preserves the *chiasmus* as well as the καί: *Omnis qui facit peccatum, et iniquitatem facit; et peccatum est iniquitas.* So also
Tertullian, but with the African rendering *delictum* in each case
for *peccatum*. So also, quite naturally, Luther: *Wer Sünde thut,
der thut auch Unrecht, und die Sünde ist das Unrecht.* For instances in which *both* terms in a proposition that can be converted simply have the article comp. ἡ ἐντολὴ ἡ παλαιά ἐστιν ὁ λόγος
ὅν ἠκούσατε (ii. 7): ἡ ζωὴ ἦν τὸ φῶς τῶν ἀνθρώπων (John i. 4): ἡ πέτρα
ἦν ὁ Χριστός (1 Cor. x. 4; comp. xi. 3; xv. 56). Winer, 142, note.
Green, 35, 36.

5. That sin is incompatible with Divine birth is further enforced by two facts respecting the highest instance of Divine birth. The Son of God (1) entered the world of sense in order to put away sin; and therefore those who sin thwart His work: (2) was Himself absolutely free from sin; and therefore those who sin disregard His example.

οἴδατε. ℵ and the Thebaic read οἴδαμεν. As in *v.* 2 and ii. 21, the Apostle appeals to that knowledge which as Christians they must possess. The translation of ἐφανερώθη here must govern the translation in *v.* 2 and ii. 28, where see note. Here, as in *v.* 8 and i. 2, the manifestation of the Λόγος in becoming visible to human eyes is meant,—the Incarnation. The expression necessarily implies that He existed previous to being made manifest.

ἵνα τὰς ἁμαρτ. ἄρῃ. Literally, *that He might take away the sins,* i.e. all the sins that there are. If 'our sins' means 'the sins of us men' and not 'the sins of us Christians,' the rendering is admissible, even if the addition ἡμῶν (ℵC Thebaic) is not genuine. As already stated, the article is often used in Greek where in English we use a possessive pronoun. 'To take away' is the safest rendering; for this is all that the Greek word necessarily means (see on John i. 29). Vulgate, *tolleret;* Augustine, *auferat.* Yet it is not improbable that the meaning of 'to bear' is included: He took the sins away *by bearing them Himself* (1 Pet. ii. 24). This, however, is not S. John's point. His argument is that the Son's having become incarnate in order to abolish sin shews that sin is inconsistent with sonship: the *way* in which He abolished it is not in question.

καὶ ἁμ....οὐκ ἔστιν. This is an independent proposition and must not be connected with οἴδατε ὅτι. The order of the Greek is impressive; *sin in Him does not exist.* And the tense is significant. Christ not merely was on earth, but *is* in heaven, the eternally sinless One. He is the perfect pattern of what a son of God should be. This, therefore, is yet another proof that sin and sonship are incompatible. Comp. John vii. 18. *Nemo tollit peccata, quae nec lex quamvis sancta et justa et bona potuit auferre, nisi ille in quo peccatum non est* (Bede).

6. πᾶς ὁ μένων. **Every one that** *abideth.* Here, as in ii. 23, 29; iii. 3, 4, 9, 10, 15; iv. 7; v. 1, 4, 18, it is well to bring out in translation the full sweep of the Apostle's declaration. He insists that there are no exceptions to these principles.

οὐχ ἁμαρτάνει. The Christian sometimes sins (i. 8—10). The Christian abides in Christ (ii. 27). He who abides in Christ does not sin (iii. 6). By these apparently contradictory statements put forth one after another S. John expresses that internal contradiction of which every one who is endeavouring to do right is conscious. What S. John delivers as a series of aphorisms, which mutually qualify and explain one another, S. Paul puts forth dialectically as an argument. 'If what I would not, that I do, it is no more I that do it, but sin which dwelleth in me' (Rom. vii. 20). And on the other hand, 'I live; yet not I, but Christ liveth in me' (Gal. ii. 20).

πᾶς ὁ ἁμαρτ....αὐτον. **Every one that** *sinneth, hath not seen Him,* *neither* **knoweth** *Him.* For ἑώρακεν see on i. 1, for ἔγνωκεν on ii. 3. It is possible that S. John alludes to some who had claimed authority because they had seen Christ in the flesh. No one who sins, has seen Christ or attained to a knowledge of Him. What does S. John mean by this strong statement? It will be observed that it is the antithesis of the preceding statement; but, as usual, instead of giving us the simple antithesis, 'Every one that sinneth abideth *not* in Him,' he expands and strengthens it into 'Every one that sinneth hath not seen Him, neither come to know Him.' S. John does not say this of every one who commits a sin (ὁ ἁμαρτήσας), but of the habitual sinner (ὁ ἁμαρτάνων). Although the believer sometimes sins, yet not sin, but opposition to sin, is the ruling principle of his life; for whenever he sins he confesses it, and wins forgiveness, and perseveres with his self-purification.

But the habitual sinner does none of these things: sin is his ruling principle. And this could not be the case if he had ever really known Christ. Just as apostates by leaving the Church prove that they have never really belonged to it (ii. 19), so the sinner by continuing in sin proves that he has never really known Christ.—Seeing and knowing are not two names for the same fact: to see Christ is to be spiritually conscious of His presence; to know Him is to recognise His character and His relation to ourselves. For a collection of varying interpretations of this passage see Farrar's *Early Days of Christianity* ii. p. 434, note.

7. τεκνία. The renewed address adds solemnity and tenderness to the warning. From the point of view of the present subject, viz. the Divine parentage, he again warns them against the ruinous doctrine that religion and conduct are separable; that to the spiritual man no action is defiling, but all conduct is alike. The language implies that the error set before them is of a very grave kind: *let no man lead you astray*: see on i. 8.

ὁ ποιῶν. Not ὁ ποιήσας, any more than ὁ ἁμαρτήσας (*v.* 6). It is he who *habitually* does righteousness, not he who simply does a righteous act. If faith without works is dead (Jas. ii. 17, 20), much more is knowledge without works dead. There is only one way of proving our enlightenment, of proving our parentage from Him who is Light; and that is by *doing* the righteousness which is characteristic of Him and His Son. This is the sure test, the test which Gnostic self-exaltation pretended to despise. Anyone can say that he possesses a superior knowledge of Divine truth; but does he act accordingly? Does he do divine things, after the example of the Divine Son? S. John speaks of both the Father (i. 9) and the Son (ii. 2) as δίκαιος; but here as elsewhere in this Epistle, it is best to take ἐκεῖνος as meaning Christ: see on ii. 6 and iii. 3.

8. ὁ ποιῶν τ. ἁμαρτ. *He that* **doeth** *sin,* as in *v.* 4, to bring out the contrast with 'he that *doeth* righteousness.' *Qui facit peccatum.* The first half of this verse is closely parallel to the second half of *v.* 7.

The habitual doer of sin has the devil as the source (ἐκ), not of his existence, but of the evil which rules his existence and is the main element in it. "The devil made no man, begat no man, created no man: but whoso imitates the devil, becomes a child of the devil, as if begotten of him. In what sense art thou a child of Abraham? Not that Abraham begat thee. In the same sense as that in which the Jews, the children of Abraham, by not imitating the faith of Abraham, are become children of the devil" (S. Augustine). Jerome (*Hom. in Jerem. vi.*) quotes this passage thus ; *Omnis qui facit peccatum, ex zabulo natus est.* Neither the *omnis* nor the *natus* is in the Vulgate or in the Greek. The form *zabulus* occurs in MSS. of Cyprian and Lactantius, and also in Hilary and Ambrose: it is not found in the Vulgate. (With *zabulus* for διάβολος comp. ζάχολος, ζαπληθής, ζάπυρος, ζάπλουτος, ζάχρυσος: and *zeta* for δίαιτα.) Jerome continues; *Toties ex zabulo nascimur, quoties peccamus. Infelix iste qui semper generatur a zabulo. Rursumque multum beatus qui semper ex Deo nascitur.* It is one of the characteristics of these closing words of N. T. that they mark with singular precision the personality of Satan, and his relation to sin, sinners, and redemption from sin.

ὅτι ἀπ᾽ ἀρχῆς ὁ δ. ἁμ. **Because from the beginning the devil sinneth.** *Ab initio diabolus peccat* (Vulgate): *a primordio delinquit* (Tertullian). 'From the beginning' stands first for emphasis. What does it mean? Various explanations have been suggested. (1) From the beginning of *sin*. The devil was the first to sin and has never ceased to sin. (2) From the beginning of the *devil*. This comes very near to asserting the Gnostic and Manichaean error of two co-eternal principles or Creators, one good and one evil. The very notion of sin involves departure from what is good. The good therefore must have existed first. To avoid this, (3) from the beginning of the devil *as such*, i.e. from the time of his becoming the devil, or (4) from the beginning of his *activity;* which is not very different from (3) if one believes that he is a fallen angel, or from (2) if one does not. (5) From the beginning of the *world*. (6) From the beginning of the *human race*. The first or last seems best. "The phrase 'From the beginning' intimates that there has been no period of the existence of human beings in which they have not been liable to the assaults of this Tempter; that accusations against God, reasons for doubting and distrusting Him, have been offered to one man after another, to one generation after another. This is just what the Scripture affirms; just the assumption which goes through the book from Genesis to the Apocalypse." (Maurice.) Note the present tense: not he has sinned, but he is sinning; his whole existence is sin.

ὁ υἱὸς τοῦ Θεοῦ. In special contrast to those habitual sinners who are morally the children of the devil. Origen here gives the reading γεγέννηται, which is probably a mere slip of memory. There seems to be no trace of it elsewhere. The metaphor in ἵνα λύσῃ has probably nothing to do with loosening bonds or snares. All destruction is dissolution. The word in a figurative sense is a favourite one with the Apostle: comp. John ii. 19; v. 18; vii. 23; x. 35, where either notion, loosening or dissolving, is appropriate. Comp. χρῄζω οὖν πραότητος, ἐν ᾗ καταλύεται ὁ ἄρχων τοῦ αἰῶνος τούτου (Ign. *Trall.* iv). The ἔργα of the devil are the sins which he causes men to commit. Christ came to *undo* these sins, to 'take away' both them and their consequences. They are the opposite of τὰ ἔργα τοῦ Θεοῦ (John ix. 3), the same as τὰ ἔργα τοῦ σκότους (Rom. xiii. 12).

The recognition of the personality of the devil in this passage is express and clear, as in John viii. 44, where we have Christ's declaration on the subject. It is there implied that he is a fallen being; for he 'did not stand firm in the truth' (οὐκ ἔστηκεν). He is here the great opponent of the Son of God manifest in the flesh and the author of men's sins. In both passages he appears as morally the parent of those who deliberately prefer evil to good. Nothing is said either as to his origin, or the origin of moral evil.

9. This is the opposite of *v.* 8, as *v.* 8 of *v.* 7; but, as usual, not the plain opposite, but something deduced from it, is stated.

πᾶς ὁ γεγεννημένος ἐκ τ. Θ. *Every one that* (see on *v.* 6) *is* begotten *of God.* Note the perfect tense; 'every one that has been made and that remains a child of God.' The expression is very frequent throughout the Epistle (ii. 29; iv. 7; v. 1, 4, 18) and the rendering should be uniform; all the more so, because the phrase is characteristic. The A. V. wavers between 'born' and 'begotten,' even in the same verse (v. 1, 18). The R. V. rightly prefers 'begotten' throughout: 'born' throughout is impossible, for in v. 1 we have the active, 'begat.' The expression 'to be begotten of God' is found only in S. John; once in the Gospel (i. 13) and eight or nine times in the Epistle: comp. John iii. 3, 5, 6, 7, 8.

ἁμαρτίαν οὐ ποιεῖ. As R. V., doeth no sin (see on *v.* 4): the opposition between 'doing sin' and 'doing righteousness' must be carefully marked. The strong statement is exactly parallel to *v.* 6 and is to be understood in a similar sense. It is literally true of the Divine nature imparted to the believer. That does not sin and cannot sin. A child of the God who is Light can have nothing to do with sin which is darkness: the two are morally incompatible.

ὅτι σπέρμα αὐτοῦ ἐν αὐ. μ. As R. V., because *his seed* abideth *in him:* see on ii. 24. This may mean either (1) 'His seed,' the new birth *given by God*, 'abideth in him;' or (2) 'his seed,' the new birth *received by him*, 'abideth in him;' or (3) 'His seed,' *God's child*, 'abideth in *Him*.' The first is probably right. The third is possible, but improbable. σπέρμα is sometimes used for 'child' or 'descendant;' but would not S. John have written τέκνον as in *vv.* 1, 2, 10, v. 2? To resort to the parable of the sower for an explanation, and to interpret 'seed' as 'the word of God' is scarcely legitimate. The whole analogy refers to human generation, not to the germination of plants; but comp. 1 Pet. i. 23. John iii. 5—8 would lead us to interpret seed as meaning the Holy Spirit. Justin Martyr may have had this verse in his mind when he wrote οἱ πιστεύοντες αὐτῷ εἰσιν ἄνθρωποι ἐν οἷς οἰκεῖ τὸ παρὰ τοῦ Θεοῦ σπέρμα ὁ λόγος (*Apol.* i. xxxii).

80   1 *S. JOHN.*   [III. 9—

οὐ δύναται ἁμαρτ. It is a moral impossibility for a child of God to
sin. It is because of the imperfection of our sonship that sin is possible, an imperfection to be remedied and gradually reduced by the
blood of Jesus (i. 7) and self-purification (iii. 3). *In quantum in
eo manet, in tantum non peccat* (Bede). Οὐ δύναται of what is morally
impossible is frequent in S. John's Gospel (v. 30; vi. 44, 65; vii. 7;
viii. 43; xii. 39; xiv. 17). Comp. iv. 20. Augustine, followed by
Bede, limits the impossibility in this case to the violation of the
principle of love. That is *the* sin which is impossible to the true child
of God.

10. ἐν τούτῳ. This phrase, like διὰ τοῦτο (*v.* 1) commonly looks
back at what has just been stated. In doing or not doing sin lies the
test. A man's principles are invisible, but their results are visible:
'By their fruits ye shall know them' (Matt. vii. 16—20).

τὰ τέκνα τ. διαβόλου. The expression occurs nowhere else in N. T.
Acts xiii. 10 we have υἱὲ διαβόλου, and Matt. xiii. 38 οἱ υἱοὶ τοῦ πονηροῦ.
Comp. ὑμεῖς ἐκ τοῦ πατρὸς τοῦ διαβόλου ἐστέ (John viii. 44). All mankind are God's children by creation: as regards this a creature can
have no choice. But a creature endowed with free will can choose his
own parent in the moral world. The Father offers him the 'right
to become a child of God' (John i. 12); but he can refuse this and
become a child of the devil instead. There is no third alternative.

It was for pressing the doctrine that a tree is known by its fruits to
an extreme, and maintaining that a world in which evil exists cannot
be the work of a good God, that the heretic Marcion was rebuked
by S. John's disciple Polycarp, in words which read like an adaptation
of this passage, Ἐπιγιγνώσκω τὸν πρωτότοκον τοῦ Σατανᾶ (Iren.
Haer. iii. iii. 4). And Polycarp in his Epistle (vii. 1) writes, ὃς ἂν μὴ
ὁμολογῇ τὸ μαρτύριον τοῦ σταυροῦ, ἐκ τοῦ διαβόλου ἐστίν.

καὶ ὁ μὴ ἀγαπῶν. The καί is almost epexegetic: 'not to love' is
only a special form of 'not to do righteousness.' As in ii. 4 (ὁ λέγων
καὶ μὴ τηρῶν), S. John does not say that there is any such person (ὁ
οὐκ ἀγαπῶν); but if there be such, this is his condition. Comp. iv. 8,
20; v. 12; 2 John 7, 9. Here also we may again note the manner in
which S. John's divisions shade off into one another (see on ii. 28,
29). Doing righteousness, the mark of God's children, suggests the
thought of brotherly love, for love is *righteousness in relation to others;*
'For the whole law is fulfilled in one word, even in this; Thou shalt
love thy neighbour as thyself' (Gal. v. 14). Love suggests its opposite,
hate; and these two form the subject of the next paragraph. Some
editors would make the new section begin here in the middle of *v.* 10.
It is perhaps better to draw the line between *vv.* 12 and 13, considering *vv.* 11 and 12 as transitional.

'He that loveth not his brother is not of God,' for a child of God
will love all whom God loves. This prepares us for the statements in
iv. 7, 20, 21.

11. ὅτι αὕτη ἐστίν. Because *the message is this;* this is what it
consists in (see on i. 5). For ἵνα see on i. 9. "Here the notion of

purpose is still perceptible" (Winer, 425). The first ἀγγελία told us the nature of God (i. 5); the second tells us our duty towards one another. 'Απ' ἀρχῆς as in ii. 7: it was one of the very first things conveyed to them in their instruction in Christianity and had been ceaselessly repeated, notably by the Apostle himself. Jerome tells us that during S. John's last years 'Little children, love one another' was the one exhortation which, after he had become too infirm to preach, he still insisted upon as sufficient and never obsolete. "It is the Lord's command," he said; "and if this is done, it is enough." 'Love one another' addressed to Christians must primarily mean the love of Christians to fellow-Christians; and this shews what 'loving his brother' must mean. But the love of Christians to non-Christians must certainly not be excluded: the arguments for enforcing brotherly love cover the case of love to all mankind.

12. A brother's love suggests its opposite, a brother's hate, and that in the typical instance of it, the fratricide Cain.

οὐ καθὼς Κάϊν. As R.V., *Not as* **Cain was** *of the evil one.* In A. V. the definite article has been exaggerated into a demonstrative pronoun, '*that* wicked one.' The same fault occurs John i. 21, 25; vi. 14, 48, 69; vii. 40. For ὁ πονηρός see on ii. 13. In ἀπ' ἀρχῆς ἁμαρτάνει (*v.* 8) S. John took us back to the earliest point in the history of sin. The instance of Cain shewed how very soon sin took the form of hate, and fratricidal hate. It is better not to supply any verb with 'not'; although the sentence is grammatically incomplete, it is quite intelligible. 'We are not, and ought not to be, of the evil one, as Cain was.' Commentators quote the "strange Rabbinical view" that while Abel was the son of Adam, Cain was the son of the tempter. Of course S. John is not thinking of such wild imaginations: Cain is only *morally* 'of the evil one.' Here, as elsewhere in the Epistle (ii. 13, 14; v. 18, 19), S. John uses 'the evil one' as a term with which his readers are quite familiar. He gives no explanation. To render τοῦ πονηροῦ 'that *wicked* one' while πονηρά is translated 'evil,' mars the Apostle's point. Cain's πονηρὰ ἔργα prove that he is ἐκ τοῦ πονηροῦ.

καὶ ἔσφαξεν τ. ἀδελφόν. This is special proof of his devilish nature. The devil ἀνθρωποκτόνος ἦν ἀπ' ἀρχῆς (John viii. 44). Σφάζειν is a link between this Epistle and the Apocalypse: it occurs nowhere else in N. T. Its original meaning was 'to cut the throat' (σφαγή), especially of a victim for sacrifice. In later Greek it means simply to slay, especially with violence. But perhaps something of the notion of slaying a victim clings to it here, as in most passages in Revelation (v. 6, 9, 12; vi. 9; xiii. 3, 8; xviii. 24).

καὶ χάριν τίνος. S. John puts this question to bring out still more strongly the diabolical nature of the act and the agent. Was Abel at all to blame? On the contrary, it was his *righteousness* which excited the murderous hate of Cain. Cain was jealous of the acceptance which Abel's righteous offering found, and which his own evil offering did not find: and 'who is able to stand before envy?' (Prov. xxvii. 4). Cain's offering was evil, (1) because it 'cost him nothing' (2 Sam.

xxiv. 24); (2) because of the spirit in which it was offered. The καί
emphasizes the question. Comp. καὶ τίς ἐστιν, κύριε; (John ix. 36): καὶ
τίς ἐστί μου πλησίον; (Luke x. 29): καὶ τίς δύναται σωθῆναι; (Luke xviii.
26). Winer, 545. Elsewhere in N. T. χάριν follows its case, as commonly in classical Greek. The exceptional arrangement seems to
emphasize the χάριν: 'And *because* of what?'

δίκαια. This is the last mention of the subject of δικαιοσύνη, with
which the section opened in ii. 29: comp. iii. 7, 10. Neither δικαιοσύνη
nor δίκαιος occurs again in the Epistle, righteousness being merged in
the warmer and more definite aspect of it, love. This is a reason for
including from ii. 29 to iii. 12 in one section, treating of the righteousness of the children of God. Comp. 'By faith Abel offered unto
God a more excellent sacrifice than Cain, through which he had witness borne to him *that he was righteous*' (Heb. xi. 4).

13—24. LOVE AND HATE: LIFE AND DEATH.

μὴ θαυμάζετε. Comp. John v. 28, and contrast iii. 7. The antagonism between the light and the darkness, between God and the evil
one, between righteousness and unrighteousness, has never ceased
from the time of the first sin (*v.* 8) and of the first murder (*v.* 12).
The moral descendants of Cain and of Abel are still in the world, and
the wicked still hate the righteous. Therefore Christians need not be
perplexed, if the world (as it does) hates *them.*

Both in Jewish (Philo, *De sacr. Abelis et Caini*) and in early Christian (*Clem. Hom.* III. xxv., xxvi.) literature Abel is taken as the
prototype of the good and Cain as the prototype of the wicked. For
the wild sect of the Cainites, who took *exactly the opposite view*, see
Appendix C. It is possible that some germs of this monstrous heresy
are aimed at in *v.* 12.

ἀδελφοί. The form of address is in harmony with the subject of
brotherly love. It occurs nowhere else in the Epistle. In ii. 7 ἀδελφοί
is a false reading. **εἰ μισεῖ ὑμᾶς ὁ κ.** As R. V., *if the world* **hateth**
you: the fact is stated gently, but without uncertainty. The construction θαυμάζειν εἰ is the more common in Attic. The hypothetical εἰ is gentler and more considerate than the blunt matter-of-fact
ὅτι. Both constructions occur in N. T.: with εἰ Mark xv. 44; with ὅτι
Luke xi. 38; John iii. 7; Gal. i. 6. In Gal. i. 6 the bluntness is quite
in keeping with the passage. This verse is another echo of Christ's
last discourses as recorded in the Gospel: εἰ ὁ κόσμος ὑμᾶς μισεῖ (pres.
indicative with εἰ, as here), γινώσκετε ὅτι ἐμὲ πρῶτον ὑμῶν μεμίσηκεν.
Comp. μεγέθους ἐστὶν ὁ Χριστιανισμός, ὅταν μισῆται ὑπὸ τοῦ κόσμου (Ign.
Rom. iii.).

14. Love means life and hate means death.

ἡμεῖς οἴδαμεν. The pronoun is very emphatic : 'the dark world
which is full of devilish hate may think and do what it pleases about
us; *we know* that we have left the atmosphere of death for one of life.'
This knowledge is part of our consciousness (οἴδαμεν) as Christians :
comp. ii. 20, 21; iii. 2, 5. Cain hated and slew his brother: the world

hates and would slay us. But for all that, it was Cain who passed from life into death, while his brother passed to eternal life, and through his sacrifice 'he being dead yet speaketh' (Heb. xi. 4). The same is the case between the world and Christians. Philo in a similar spirit points out that Cain really slew, not his brother, but himself.

μεταβεβ. ἐκ τ. θ. εἰς τ. ζ. *Have passed* over out of *death* into *life*, have left *an abode in* the one region for *an abode in* the other : another reminiscence of the Gospel (John v. 24). The Greek perfect here has the common meaning of permanent result of past action: 'we have passed into a new home *and abide there.*' The metaphor is perhaps taken from the Passage of the Red Sea (Exod. xv. 16), or of the Jordan.

ὅτι ἀγαπῶμεν. This depends upon οἴδαμεν; our love is the infallible sign that we have made the passage. The natural state of man is selfishness, which involves enmity to others, whose claims clash with those of self: to love others is proof that this natural state has been abandoned. Life and love in the moral world correspond to life and growth in the physical: in each case the two are but different aspects of the same fact. The one marks the state, the other the activity. Comp. συνέφερεν δὲ αὐτοῖς ἀγαπᾶν, ἵνα καὶ ἀναστῶσιν (Ign. *Smyr.* vii.).

μένει ἐν τῷ θανάτῳ. The μένει shews that death is the original condition of all, out of which we pass by becoming children of God. But each child of God loves God's children. Therefore he who does not love is still in the old state of death. Comp. ὁ δὲ ἀπειθῶν τῷ υἱῷ οὐκ ὄψεται ζωήν, ἀλλ᾽ ἡ ὀργὴ τοῦ Θεοῦ μένει ἐπ᾽ αὐτόν (John iii. 36). Note that both θάνατος and ζωή, like σκοτία and φῶς in the earlier part of the Epistle, have the article. That which in the fullest sense is death, life, darkness, and light, is meant in each case.

15. πᾶς ὁ μισῶν. Every one that *hateth.* There is no exception. A man may call himself an enlightened believer, but if he has no love, οὐθέν ἐστι. See on *v.* 4. Quite as a matter of course S. John passes from not loving to hating. The crisis caused in the world by the coming of the light leaves no neutral ground: all is either light or darkness, of God or of the evil one, of the Church or of the world, in love or in hate. A Christian cannot be neither loving nor hating, any more than a plant can be neither growing nor dying.

ἀνθρωποκτόνος ἐστίν. Most of the earlier Versions render *is a manslayer.* The word occurs only here and John viii. 44. The mention of Cain just before renders it certain that 'murderer' is not to be understood figuratively as '*soul*-destroyer.' Human law considers overt acts; God considers motives. The motives of the hater and of the murderer are the same: the fact that one is, and the other is not, deterred by laziness or fear from carrying out his hatred into homicidal action, makes no difference in the moral character of the men, though it makes all the difference in the eyes of the law. This is only applying to the sixth commandment the principle which the Lord Himself applies to the seventh (Matt. v. 28).

οἴδατε. Once more (*v.* 14) the Apostle appeals to their consciousness as Christians: it is not a matter of experience gradually acquired (γινώσκετε), but of knowledge once for all possessed. He who is a murderer at heart cannot along with the deadly spirit which he cherishes have eternal life as a sure possession. Comp. 'Ye *have not* His word *abiding in* you,' John v. 38. S. John of course does not mean that hatred or murder is a sin for which there is no forgiveness. But 'the soul that sinneth, it shall *die*'; and the sin of which the special tendency is destruction of life is absolutely incompatible with the possession of eternal life. 'But for...murderers...their part shall be in the lake that burneth with fire and brimstone; which is the second death' (Rev. xxi. 8). Here, as elsewhere, S. John speaks of eternal life as something which the Christian already *has*, not which he hopes to *win:* comp. v. 13; John iii. 36; v. 24; vi. 47, 54, &c. Eternal life has nothing to do with time, and is neither lost nor gained by physical death: see on John xi. 25.—The form of expression in this verse is similar to ii. 19, being literally, *every murderer hath not*, instead of 'no murderer hath.' *Omnis homicida non habet.*

16. ἐν τούτῳ ἐγνώκαμεν τ. ἀγ. The A. V. here collects the errors of previous Versions. Tyndale and Cranmer have 'perceave we.' Wiclif, Purvey, and the Rhemish insert 'of God' from the Vulgate without any support from Gk. MSS. The Genevan is right on both points; 'Hereby have we perceaved love.' Better, as R. V., *Hereby* know we love. Why not 'Here*in*'? In the concrete example of Christ's vicarious death we have obtained the knowledge of what love is. Christ is the archetype of self-sacrificing love, as Cain is of brother-sacrificing hate. Love and hate are known by their works. The article has its full force; τὴν ἀγάπην, love in its very essence: comp. iv. 10. The Vulgate here, as in iv. 16, inserts *Dei* after *caritas:* Western interpolation.

ὅτι...ἔθηκεν. For ἐν τούτῳ followed by ὅτι see on ii. 3. Τιθέναι may mean 'to *pay* down' in the way of ransom or propitiation, or simply 'to lay *aside.*' Classical usage sanctions the former interpretation: Demosthenes uses the verb of paying interest, tribute, taxes. And this is supported by 'for us' (ὑπὲρ ἡμῶν), i.e. 'on our behalf.' But 'I lay down My life that I may *take it again*' (John x. 17, 18), and 'layeth *aside* His garments' (xiii. 4; comp. xiii. 12), are in favour of the latter: they are quite against the rendering 'He *pledged* His life.' The phrase τιθέναι τὴν ψυχὴν αὐτοῦ is peculiar to S. John (x. 11, 15, 17; xiii. 37, 38; xv. 13). In Greek the pronoun (ἐκεῖνος as in ii. 6 and iii. 7) marks more plainly than in English who laid down His life: but S. John's readers had no need to be told. Ἐκεῖνος and ὑπὲρ ἡμῶν are in emphatic juxtaposition: '*He for us* His life laid down.'

καὶ ἡμεῖς ὀφείλομεν. The ἡμεῖς is emphatic: this on *our* side is a Christian's duty; he 'ought himself also to walk *even as* He walked' (ii. 6). The argument seems to shew that though 'the brethren' specially means believers, yet heathen are not to be excluded. Christ laid down His life not for Christians only, 'but also *for the whole world*' (ii. 2). Christians must imitate Him in this: their love must be (1) practical, (2) absolutely self-sacrificing, (3) all-embracing. 'God commendeth His own love toward us, in that, *while we were yet sinners*, Christ died for us' (Rom. v. 8). Tertullian quotes this dictum of the Apostle in urging the duty of martyrdom : "If he teaches that we must die for the brethren, how much more for the Lord" (*Scorp.* xii.). Comp. Prov. xxiv. 11. See on iv. 18. 'Οφείλειν occurs four times in these Epistles (ii. 6; iv. 11; 3 John 8), twice in the Gospel (xiii. 14; xix. 7), and not at all in Revelation. In the Gospel and Revelation we commonly have δεῖ. Bengel on 1 Cor. xi. 10 thus distinguishes the two: "*ὀφείλει notat obligationem, δεῖ necessitatem; illud morale est, hoc quasi physicum; ut in vernaculâ,* wir sollen und müssen."

17. ὃς δ' ἂν ἔχη. The phrase is as wide in its sweep as πᾶς ὁ ἔχων: comp. ii. 5. The δέ is full of meaning. 'Not many of us are ever called upon to die for others: but smaller sacrifices are often demanded of us; and what if we fail to respond?' *Si nondum es idoneus mori pro fratre, jam idoneus esto dare de tuis facultatibus fratri* (Bede). **τὸν βίον τ. κόσμου** is to be rendered, as in R. V., **the world's goods**: βίος, as in ii. 16 (see note), signifies 'means of life, subsistence,' including all resources of wealth and ability. Τὸν βίον τ. κ., therefore, means all that supports and enriches the life of this world (ii. 15) in contrast to ζωὴ αἰώνιος (*v.* 15).

θεωρῇ τ. ἀδ. αὐτ. χρείαν ἔχοντα. Beholdeth *his brother* having *need.* He not only sees him (ἰδεῖν), but looks at him and considers him (θεωρεῖν). It is a word of which the contemplative Apostle is very fond (John ii. 23; vii. 3; xii. 45; xiv. 19; xvi. 16; &c.), and outside the Gospels and Acts it is found only in S. John's writings and Heb. vii. 4. It is a pity to spoil the simple irony of the original by weakening χρείαν ἔχοντα into '*in* need' (R. V.). So also Luther; *siehet seinen Bruder darben.* This misses the contrast between ἔχη τ. βίον and χρείαν ἔχοντα. The one *has* as his possession *wealth*, the other *has* as his possession—*need.* The New Vulgate has *necessitatem habere*, which is far better than *necesse habere*, as in ii. 27: the Old Vulgate has *necesse habere* in both places. Cyprian has *desiderantem* here twice.

κλείσῃ τ. σπλάγχνα αὐτ. ἀπ' αὐτ. The ancients believed the bowels to be the seat of the affections (Gen. xliii. 30; 1 Kings iii. 26; Jer. xxxi. 20; Phil. i. 8; ii. 1; Philem. 7, 12, 20) as well as the heart, whereas we take the latter only. Coverdale (here, as often, following Luther) alters Tyndale's 'shutteth up his compassion' into 'shutteth up his heart.' And in fact, 'shutteth up his bowels from him' is the same as 'closeth his heart against him.' The phrase occurs nowhere else in N. T., but comp. 2 Cor. vi. 12. The '*from* him' is picturesque, as in ii. 28: it expresses the moving away and turning his back on his brother. Comp. οὐκ ἀποστρέψεις τὴν καρδίαν σου οὐδὲ μὴ συσφίγξεις τὴν χεῖρά σου ἀπὸ τοῦ ἀδελφοῦ σου (Deut. xv. 7).

πῶς. For the abrupt argumentative interrogation comp. πῶς τοῖς ἐμοῖς ῥήμασιν πιστεύσετε; (John v. 47). See also 1 Cor. xiv. 7, 9, 16; xv. 12. The order of the Greek is worth keeping, as in R. V., *how* *doth the love of God* **abide** *in him?* For μένειν ἐν, 'to have a *home* in,' see on ii. 24. For ἡ ἀγάπη τ. Θ., which again means man's love to God, see on ii. 5. The idea that God is the source of that love which man feels towards Him may be included here. The question here (πῶς) is equivalent to the statement in iv. 20 (οὐ), that to love God and hate one's brother is morally impossible.

18. τεκνία, μὴ ἀγ. λόγῳ. The Apostle, as in ii. 28; iii. 13; iv. 1, 7, hastens on to a practical application of what he has been stating as the principles of Christian Ethics; and in each case he prefaces his gentle exhortation with a word of tender address. 'Dear children, do not think that I am giving you a series of philosophical truisms; I am telling of the principles which must govern your conduct and mine, if we are children of the God who is Light and Love.' Note the present subjunctive after μή, indicating a continuous feeling, somewhere in existence, which is to be discontinued or avoided: 'Do not let us go on loving in word, as some people do.' In N. T. when μή prohibitive is joined with the *third* person, the verb is always in the *imperative* (Matt. vi. 3; xxiv. 17, 18; Rom. vi. 12; xiv. 16; &c.): when it is joined with the *first* person, as here, the verb is in the *subjunctive* (John xix. 24; 1 Cor. x. 8; Gal. v. 26; vi. 9; &c.). Winer, 629. The above examples shew that both present and aorist are used frequently in both moods.

μηδὲ τῇ γλώσσῃ. As R. V. (emended reading), *neither* **with the** *tongue;* "*the* tongue as the particular member for the expression of the word" (Huther). Perhaps '*with* word' would be better than '*in* word,' if 'in word' were not the usual idiom. The simple datives, λόγῳ and τῇ γλώσσῃ, seem to indicate the instruments *with* which the false love is shewn, the preposition, ἐν. λ. καὶ ἀλ., the sphere *in* which it is shewn. For the contrast between λόγος and ἔργον, so common in Thucydides, comp. Luke xxiv. 19; Acts vii. 22; Rom. xv. 18; 2 Cor. x. 11; Col. iii. 17. Is there any difference between loving in word and loving with the tongue? And is there any difference between loving in deed and loving in truth? The answer must be the same to both questions. The oppositions between 'word' and 'deed' and between 'tongue' and 'truth' are so exact as to lead us to believe that there *is* a difference. To love in word is to have that affection which is genuine as far as it goes, but which is so weak that it never gets further than affectionate words: such love is opposed, not to truth, but to loving *acts*. To love with the tongue is to profess an affection which one does not feel, which is sheer hypocrisy: it is opposed, not to deeds, but to *truth*. It may shew itself also in hypocritical acts, done (as Bede points out) not with the wish to do good, but to win praise, or to injure others. Tyndale and the Rhemish Version have no second 'in' before 'truth': it should of course be omitted, as in R. V. Comp. James ii. 15; Rom. xii. 9.

What follows, though intimately connected with the first part of the section (see next note), almost amounts to a fresh departure. The subject of love and its opposite is transformed into *the security and serenity of conscience which genuine and active love is able to produce.*

19. ἐν τούτῳ γνωσ. Herein we shall know. The omission of καί by AB, Syriac, and Vulgate, is probably right. Ἐν τούτῳ sometimes refers to what follows (v. 16; iv. 2, 9), sometimes to what precedes (ii. 5). Here to what precedes: by loving in deed and truth we shall attain to the knowledge that we are morally the children of the Truth. Ἡ ἀλήθεια here is almost equivalent to ὁ Θεός. Ἐκ τῆς ἀληθ. εἶναι is to have the Truth as the source whence the guiding and formative influences of thought and conduct flow. Comp. ii. 21; John iii. 31; viii. 47; and especially xviii. 37.

The construction and punctuation of what follows is doubtful; also the reading in the first and second clauses of *v.* 20. Certainty is not attainable, and to give all possible variations of reading and rendering would take up too much space. The conclusions adopted here are given as good and tenable, but not as demonstrably right.

ἔμπρ. αὐτοῦ. First for emphasis. It is in His presence that the truth is realised. The self-deceiver, who walks in darkness, hating his brother (ii. 11), can quiet his heart, 'because the darkness has blinded his eyes': but this is not done ἔμπροσθεν τοῦ Θεοῦ.

πείσομεν τὰς καρδίας ἡμ. As the Rhemish, *shall* **persuade** *our hearts.* This clause is probably coordinate with γνωσόμεθα, not dependent on it. The meaning is not 'we shall know that we shall persuade,' but 'we shall know and we shall persuade.' The powerful combination of B, Peschito, and Thebaic, coupled with the fact that everywhere else in both Gospel and Epistle S. John uses the singular and not the plural, inclines one to prefer τὴν καρδίαν to τὰς καρδίας. "The singular fixes the thought upon the personal trial in each case" (Westcott). Obviously it means, not the *affections* (2 Cor. vii. 3; Phil. i. 7), but the *conscience* (Acts ii. 37; vii. 54). S. Paul's word, συνείδησις, emphasizes the *knowledge* of what the man recognizes in himself. S. John's word, καρδία, emphasizes the *feeling* with which what is recognized is regarded. 'Shall persuade our heart' of *what?* *That it need not condemn us:* and hence the rendering in A. V. and R. V., 'assure.' But this is interpretation rather than translation; for πείθειν in itself does not mean 'assure.' Tyndale and the Genevan have 'quiet'; Beza *secura reddemus.* And if the context in the Greek shews that πείθειν means this here, then let the context speak for itself in the English. Comp. ἡμεῖς πείσομεν αὐτὸν καὶ ὑμᾶς ἀμερίμνους ποιήσομεν (Matt. xxviii. 14): and πείσαντες Βλάστον (Acts xii. 20).

20. ὅτι ἐὰν καταγινώσκῃ ἡμῶν. The Revisers follow Lachmann in reading ὅ τι ἐάν, a construction found Acts iii. 23 and Gal. v. 10, and possibly Col. iii. 17. The clause is then attached to what precedes: *shall persuade our heart before Him,* **whereinsoever** *our heart condemn us.* But this is not probable (see next note). "A Christian's heart burdened with a sense of its own unworthiness forms an unfavourable opinion of the state of the soul, pronounces against its salvation. If we are conscious of practically loving the brethren, we

can adduce this as evidence of the contrary, and give the heart ground
to change its opinion, and to reassure itself. Anyone who has had
experience of the doubts and fears which spring up in a believer's
heart from time to time, of whether he is or is not in a state of condemnation, will feel the need and the efficacy of this test of faith and
means of assurance" (Jelf).

ὅτι μείζων ἐστὶν ὁ Θεός. Either, because *God is greater*, or that
God is greater. *If* the R. V. is right as regards what precedes, '*because* God is greater' will make good sense. Because God is superior
to our consciences in being omniscient, we may (when our love is
sincere and fruitful) persuade our consciences before Him to acquit
us. Our consciences through imperfect knowledge may be either too
strict or too easy with us: God cannot be either, for He knows and
weighs all.

But it seems almost certain that 'if our heart condemn us' must be
right, as the natural correlative of 'if our heart condemn us not,' which
is indisputably right. This progress by means of opposites stated side
by side has been S. John's method all through: 'if we confess our sins'
and 'if we say that we have not sinned' (i. 9, 10); 'he that loveth his
brother' and 'he that hateth his brother' (ii. 10, 11); 'he that doeth
righteousness' and 'he that doeth sin' (iii. 7, 8); 'every spirit that
confesseth' and 'every spirit that confesseth not' (iv. 2, 3). But, if
this is accepted, what is to be done with the apparently redundant ὅτι?
Two plans are suggested: 1. to supply 'it is' before ὅτι='because';
2. to supply 'it is plain' (δῆλον) before ὅτι='that.' The latter
seems preferable: for what can be the meaning of 'if our heart condemn us, (it is) *because* God is greater than our heart'? Whereas,
'if our heart condemn us, (it is plain) that God is greater than our
heart' makes excellent sense. There is perhaps a similar ellipse of
'it is plain' (ὅτι=δῆλον ὅτι) 1 Tim. vi. 7; 'We brought nothing into
the world, and (it is plain) that we can carry nothing out'; where
א³D³KL insert δῆλον before ὅτι οὐδὲ ἐξενεγκεῖν τι δυνάμεθα. Field
(*Otium Norvicense* III. 127) quotes other instances from S. Chrysostom
of the ellipse of δῆλον.

We must not give 'God is greater' a one-sided interpretation, either
'God is more merciful' or 'God is more strict.' It means that He is
a more perfect judge than our heart can be. It is the difference between conscience and Omniscience.

καὶ γινώσκει πάντα. The καί is epexegetic; it explains the special
character of God's superiority when the soul stands before the judg-
ment-seat of conscience. He knows all things; on the one hand the
light and grace against which we have sinned, on the other the reality
of our repentance and our *love*. It was to this infallible omniscience
that S. Peter appealed, in humble distrust of his own feeling and
judgment; 'Lord, Thou knowest all things; Thou knowest that I love
Thee' (John xxi. 17). It is the reality and activity of our love (*vv.*
18, 19) which gives us assurance under the accusations of conscience.
Comp. 'If ye forgive men their trespasses,' having genuine love for

them, 'your heavenly Father will also forgive you,' and ye will be able to persuade your hearts before Him (Matt. vi. 14).

The force of *vv.* 19, 20 may be thus summed up: 'By loving our brethren in deed and truth we come to know that we are God's children and have His presence within us, and are enabled to meet the disquieting charges of conscience. For, if conscience condemns us, its verdict is not infallible nor final. We may still appeal to the omniscient God, whose love implanted within us is a sign that we are not condemned and rejected by Him.

21. ἀγαπητοί. See on *v.* 2.

ἐὰν ἡ καρδία μὴ καταγ. An argument *à fortiori:* if before God we can persuade conscience to acquit us, when it upbraids us, much more may we have assurance before Him, when it does *not* do so. It is not quite evident whether 'condemn us not' means '*ceases* to condemn us,' because we have persuaded it, or 'does not condemn us *from the first*,' because it had no misgivings about us. Either makes good sense. Καταγινώσκειν occurs elsewhere in N. T. Gal. ii. 11 only, ὅτι κατεγνωσμένος ἦν. Comp. Ecclus. xiv. 2, 'Blessed is he whose conscience hath not condemned him' (οὐ κατέγνω).

παρρ. ἔχομεν. *We have* **boldness**: see on ii. 28. The 'then' of A. V. is not needed. With πρὸς τὸν Θεόν here comp. ἀπρόσκοπον συνείδησιν ἔχειν πρὸς τὸν Θεὸν καὶ τοὺς ἀνθρώπους (Acts xxiv. 16). We approach Him boldly as children, not fearfully as criminals. Comp. v. 14. This is not the same as 'persuading our heart before Him,' but is a natural result of it. Comp. Rom. v. 1.

22. This verse is so closely connected with the preceding one, that not more than a comma or semicolon should be placed between them. When a good conscience gives us boldness towards God our prayers are granted, for children in such relations to their heavenly Father cannot ask anything which He will refuse.

καὶ ὃ ἐὰν αἰτῶμεν. The καί is probably epexegetic, as in *v.* 20, and explains the special character of our boldness. See on v. 15.

λαμβάνομεν. The present is to be taken quite literally; not as the present for the future. It may be a long time before we see the results of our prayer; but it is granted at once. As S. Augustine says, "He who gave us love cannot close His ears against the groans and prayers of love." For λαμβάνειν ἀπό see on ii. 27.

τὰς ἐντολὰς αὐτ. τ. This should certainly be plural, *commandments:* previous English Versions have the plural, and there seems to be no trace of a various reading, so that one suspects a misprint in the edition of 1611. Ὅτι depends upon λαμβάνομεν, not upon παρρησίαν ἔχομεν: we receive because we are loyal. This is in harmony with the Gospel and with Scripture generally: 'We know that God heareth not sinners: but if any man be a worshipper of God, and *do His will, him He heareth*' (John ix. 31); 'The Lord is far from the wicked, but He heareth the prayer of the righteous' (Prov. xv. 29; comp. Ps. lxvi. 18, 19; Job xxvii. 8, 9; Isai. i. 11—15). For τὰς ἐντολὰς τηρεῖν see on ii. 3.

τὰ ἀρεστά...ποιοῦμεν. Not the same as τὰς ἐντολὰς τηρεῖν: the one is *obedience*, and may be slavish; the other is *love*, and is free. We seem to have here another reminiscence of the Gospel: ὅτι ἐγὼ τὰ ἀρεστὰ αὐτῷ ποιῶ πάντοτε (viii. 29). Excepting Acts vi. 2, xii. 3, ἀρεστός occurs nowhere else in N. T. The different phrases ἔμπροσθεν αὐτοῦ (*v.* 19) and ἐνώπιον αὐτοῦ suit their respective contexts. Both indicate the Divine Presence: but ἔμπροσθεν brings out the man's regard to God, ἐνώπιον God's regard to him.

23. καὶ αὕτη...αὐτοῦ. *And His commandment is this :* see on i. 5. For ἵνα after ἐντολή comp. John xiii. 34; xv. 12: after ἐντέλλομαι, John xv. 17. In such cases ἵνα perhaps merely "gives the nature and contents of the commandment, not the aim" (Jelf): but see on i. 9. This verse is the answer to those who would argue from the preceding verses that all that is required of us is to *do* what is right; it does not much matter what we *believe*. Not so says the Apostle. In order to do what is right it is necessary to believe: this is the first step in our obedience to God's commands.

πιστεύωμεν τῷ ὀνόματι. **Believe the Name.** Beza rightly substitutes *credamus nomini* for the Vulgate's *credamus in nomine*. A.V. has 'believe *on*': R.V. has 'believe *in*'; which would be πιστ. εἰς or ἐπί or ἐν. 'To believe the Name' means to believe all that His Name implies; His Divinity, His Sonship, and His office as Mediator, Advocate, and Saviour. Hence the solemn fulness with which the Name is given, *His Son Jesus Christ.* The reading τῷ υἱῷ αὐτοῦ Ἰ. Χριστῷ is an obvious correction of an unusual phrase. A copyist would argue, 'One can believe a person (John iv. 21; v. 24, 38, 46), and one can believe a statement (John iv. 50; v. 47), but how can one believe a name?' The phrase πιστεύειν εἰς τὸ ὄνομα is frequent in S. John's writings (v. 13; John i. 12; ii. 23; iii. 18).

καὶ ἀγαπῶμεν ἀλλ. Here καί is not epexegetic: it adds something fresh, giving active love as the necessary effect of living faith. 'Faith if it have not works is dead' (James ii. 17). καθώς. **Even as** Christ (just mentioned) *gave us commandment ;* in reference to the ἐντολὴ καινή (John xiii. 34; xv. 12, 17). There must be exact correspondence (καθώς) between His command and our love: i.e. we must love one another 'in deed and truth.' In N.T. the phrase ἐντολὴν διδόναι is peculiar to S. John (xi. 57; xii. 49; xiii. 34): it occurs in Demosthenes (250, 14).

24. καὶ ὁ τηρῶν τ. ἐντ. This looks back to the same phrase in *v.* 22, not to καθὼς ἔδωκεν ἐντ. in *v.* 23, which is parenthetical. Therefore αὐτοῦ means God's, not Christ's. A.V. again spoils S. John's telling repetition of a favourite word by translating μένει first 'dwelleth' and then 'abideth': see on ii. 24. "Let God be a home to thee, and be thou a home of God" (Bede). Comp. 'Lord, Thou hast been our *dwelling-place* in all generations' (Ps. xc. 1). This mutual abiding expresses union of the strongest and closest kind: comp. iv. 13, 16; John vi. 56; xv. 4, 5. S. John once more insists on what may be regarded as the main theme of this exposition of Christian Ethics;

that *conduct* is not only not a matter of indifference, but is all-important. We may possess many kinds of enlightenment, intellectual and spiritual; but there is no union with God, and indeed no true knowledge of Him, without *obedience:* comp. i. 6, ii. 4, 6, 29; iii. 6, 7, 9. 'He that *willeth to do His will* shall know' (John vii. 17).

καὶ ἐν τούτῳ. *And herein*, as in *vv.* 16, 19; ii. 3, 5; iv. 9, 10, 13, 17; v. 2. This probably refers to what follows; but the change of preposition in the Greek, a change obliterated in both A.V. and R.V., renders this not quite certain. S. John writes, not ἐν τούτῳ γιν....ἐν τῷ πνεύματι, nor ἐκ τούτου γιν...ἐκ τοῦ πνεύματος, either of which would have made the connexion certain, but ἐν...ἐκ, which leaves us in doubt: comp. iv. 12, 13. The Vulgate preserves the change of preposition : *in hoc...de Spiritu.* The indwelling of God is a matter of Christian experience (γινώσκομεν not οἴδαμεν), and the source (ἐκ) whence the knowledge of it springs is the Spirit. This is the first express mention of the Spirit in the Epistle; but in ii. 20 He is plainly indicated. It was at Ephesus that S. Paul found disciples who had not so much as heard whether the Holy Spirit was given (Acts xix. 2). There was perhaps still need of explicit teaching on this point.

οὗ ἡμῖν ἔδωκεν. *Which He* **gave** *us.* Although this is a case where the English perfect might represent the Greek aorist, yet as the Apostle probably refers to the definite occasion when the Spirit was given, the aorist seems better. This occasion in S. John's case would be Pentecost, in that of his readers, their baptism. Thus in our Baptismal Service we are exhorted to pray that the child " may be baptized with water and the Holy Ghost"; and in what follows we pray, "wash him and sanctify him with the Holy Ghost"; and again, "give Thy Holy Spirit to this infant, that he may be born again": after which follows the baptism.

It would be possible to translate 'by the Spirit *of* which He has given us,' a partitive genitive, meaning '*some* of which' as in *Macbeth*, **i.** iii. 80,

"The earth hath bubbles as the water has,
And these are *of them.*"

And in Bacon's Essays, *Of Atheisme*, "You shall have *of them*, that will suffer for Atheisme, and not recant." But the Greek genitive here is probably not partitive but the result of attraction. S. John commonly inserts a preposition (ἐκ) with the partitive genitive (2 John 4; John i. 24; vii. 40; xvi. 17; Rev. ii. 10; xi. 9; comp. John xxi. 10). Tyndale here translates 'Therby we knowe that ther abydeth in us *of* the sprete which He gave us,' making 'of the Spirit' (=a portion of the Spirit) the nominative to 'abideth'; which is grammatically possible, but scarcely in harmony with what precedes. The change from Tyndale's rendering to the one adopted in A.V., and (with change of 'hath given' to 'gave') in R.V. also, is due to Coverdale.

Once more (see notes between ii. 28 and 29 and on iii. 10) we are
led to a fresh section almost without knowing it. In the last six
verses of this chapter (19—24) the transition from verse to verse
is perfectly smooth and natural; so also in the previous six verses
(13—18). Nor is the transition from *v.* 18 to *v.* 19 at all violent or
abrupt. By a very gradual movement we have been brought from
the contrast between love and hate to the gift of the Spirit. And
this prepares the way for a new subject; or rather for an old subject
treated from a new point of view. Like the doublings of the Maeander near which he lived, the progress of the Apostle at times looks
more like retrogression than advance: but the progress is unmistak-
able when the whole field is surveyed. Here we seem to be simply
going back to the subject of the antichrists (ii. 18—28); but whereas
there the opposition between the Holy Spirit in true believers and
the lying spirit in the antichrists is only suggested (ii. 20, 22, 27), here
it is the dominant idea.

"The Apostle speaks first of the Spirit by which we know that
God dwells in us; then of other spirits that were in the world which
might or might not be of God......They require to be tried. And he
intimates very distinctly that there were men in his day who were
turning the faith in spiritual influence to an immoral account"
(Maurice).

CHAPTER IV.

2. For γινώσκετε (א³ABCL) א¹ has γινώσκομεν: K, Peschito, and
Vulgate have γινώσκεται. For ἐληλυθότα (אAC) B has ἐληλυθέναι: see
also possibly the Vulgate (*venisse*).

3. For ὃ μὴ ὁμολογεῖ (all Greek MSS. and all Versions except
the Latin) some 'old copies' mentioned by Socrates read ὃ λύει, which
is supported by nearly all Latin authorities with *solvit* or *destruit.*
After Ἰησοῦν omit Χριστὸν ἐν σαρκὶ ἐληλυθότα with AB, Vulgate, and
Thebaic against אKL. For Χριστόν א has Κύριον. See Appendix G.

6. For ἐκ τούτου (אBKL, Peschito) A, Vulgate, and Thebaic have
ἐν τούτῳ.

10. For ἠγαπήσαμεν (א³A) we should perhaps read ἠγαπήκαμεν
(B): א¹ has the impossible ἠγάπησεν.

15. After Ἰησοῦς B inserts Χριστός.

16. After ἐν αὐτῷ we should perhaps insert μένει with אBKL and
Thebaic against A and Vulgate.

19. After ἡμεῖς A, Peschito, and Vulgate insert οὖν. After ἀγαπῶμεν omit αὐτόν with AB against KL. For αὐτόν א has τὸν Θεόν. For
αὐτός (אBKL, Thebaic) A and Vulgate have ὁ Θεός.

20. For πῶς δύναται (AKL, Peschito, Vulgate) read οὐ δύναται (אB,
Thebaic).

21. For ἀπ' αὐτοῦ (BKL) A and Vulgate have ἀπὸ τοῦ Θεοῦ. B omits from τόν to τόν : *homoeoteleuton.*

Once more note that B very rarely supports a doubtful reading, and never an impossible one, excepting the accidental omission in *v.* 21.

The main subject still continues, that **God is Love** ; and that from this truth flows the moral obligation on Christians not only to love God but one another. But, as in chap. iii., there are subdivisions, each of which has a unity in itself as well as intimate and subtle relations to the whole. These subdivisions are mainly two: *The Spirit of Truth and the Spirit of Error* (1—6); *Love as the Mark of the Children of the God who is Love* (7—21). If we are asked as to the relation which this chapter bears to the preceding one, the answer would seem to be something of this kind. Chap. iii. insists upon the necessity of *deeds* in order to prove our relationship to God (iii. 3, 7, 10, 16—18, 22) ; chap. iv. points out the *certainty* of our relationship to God as attested by our deeds (iv. 4, 6, 7, 12, 13, 15—17). The one gives us the *evidence* of our sonship, viz. deeds of righteousness towards God (iii. 1—10) and deeds of love towards men (iii. 11—21): the other shews us the *source* of our sonship, viz. possession of the Spirit as proved by confession of the Incarnation (iv. 1—6) and by love of the brethren (iv. 7—21).

1—6. The Spirit of Truth and the Spirit of Error.

1—6. This section is an amplification of the sentence with which the preceding chapter ends. We certainly have the Holy Spirit as an abiding gift from God, for otherwise we could not believe and confess the truth of the Incarnation. As usual, S. John thinks and teaches in antitheses. The test which proves that we have the Spirit of God proves that the antichrists have not this gift but its very opposite. In chap. ii. the antichrists were introduced as evidence of the transitoriness of the world (ii. 18): here they are introduced as the crucial negative instance which proves that every true believer has the Spirit of God.

1. ἀγαπητοί. See on iii. 2. The tender address once more introduces a matter of deep practical importance: comp. iii. 21.

μὴ παντὶ πνεύματι πιστεύετε. This exhortation does not give us the main subject of the section, any more than ' Marvel not, brethren, if the world hate you' (iii. 12) gave us the main subject of the last section (iii. 12—24). In both cases the exhortation is introductory and momentary. Having spoken of the Spirit by which we know that God abides in us, the Apostle goes on to speak of other spiritual influences which indubitably exist, and of which every one has experience, but which are not necessarily of God because they are spiritual. '' He does not discredit the fact that spiritual influences were widely diffused; he does not monopolize such influences for the Christian Church. How could he discredit this fact? How can we? Are there

not myriads of influences about us continually, which do not act upon
our senses but upon our spirits, which do not proceed from things
which may be seen and handled, but from the spirits of men?"
(Maurice). But besides ordinary spiritual influences, S. John probably
has in his mind those extraordinary and supernatural powers which
at various periods of the Church's history persons have claimed to
possess. Such claims exhibit themselves in professed revelations,
prophecies, miracles, and the like. About all such things there are
two possibilities which must put us on our guard: (1) they may be
unreal ; either the delusions of fanatical enthusiasts, or the lies of deliberate impostors: (2) even if real, they need not be of God. Miraculous powers are no absolute guarantee of the possession of truth. The
present imperative has the same force as in iii. 13 : 'do not continue
to believe, as I fear some do, whenever occasion arises'.

δοκιμάζετε. **Prove** *the spirits*. There are two words in N. T. meaning 'to try, test, prove' ; δοκιμάζειν and πειράζειν. The latter is used
of the Jews trying or tempting Christ (Mark viii. 11; x. 2 ; &c.) and
of the temptations of Satan (Matt. iv. 1, 3, &c.). Neither are common
in S. John's writings. He nowhere else uses δοκιμάζειν, which occurs
about 20 times in N. T., and only 4 times uses πειράζειν (John vi. 6;
Rev. ii. 2, 10, iii. 10), which occurs about 40 times in N. T. The
A. V. is very capricious in its renderings of the former; 'allow'
(Rom. xiv. 22), 'approve' (Rom. ii. 18), 'discern' (Luke xii. 56),
'examine' (1 Cor. xi. 28), 'like' (Rom. i. 28), 'prove' (Luke xiv. 19),
'try' (1 Cor. iii. 13); while the latter is rendered 'examine' (2 Cor.
xiii. 5), 'prove' (John vi. 6), 'tempt' (Matt. xxii. 18), 'try' (Rev. ii. 2).
The Revisers have somewhat reduced this variety. In the one case
'allow' has been changed to 'approve'; 'examine' and 'try' to
'prove': in the other case 'examine' has been changed to 'try.' The
difference between the two words (which are found together 2 Cor.
xiii. 5 and Ps. xxvi. 2) is on the whole this, that δοκιμάζειν commonly implies a good, if not a friendly object ; to prove or test in the
hope that what is tried will stand the test; whereas πειράζειν often
implies a sinister object ; to try in the hope that what is tried will be
found wanting. The metaphor here is from testing metals. Comp.
'*Prove* all things; hold fast that which is good' (1 Thess. v. 21).

εἰ ἐκ τοῦ Θεοῦ. Whether their origin (ἐκ) is from God: comp.
iii. 2, 12. With δοκιμάζειν εἰ comp. πειράζειν εἰ (2 Cor. xiii. 5).

A verse such as this cuts at the root of such pretensions as the
Infallibility of the Pope. What room is left for Christians to 'prove
the spirits,' if all they have to do is to ask the opinion of an official?
The Apostle's charge, 'prove *ye* the spirits,' may be addressed to
Christians singly or to the Church collectively: it cannot be addressed
to one individual exclusively. Comp. Rom. xii. 2; Eph. v. 10 ; 1 Cor.
x. 15; xi. 13. The verse also shews us in what spirit to judge of such
things as the reported miracles at Lourdes and the so-called 'mani-
festations' of Spiritualism. When they have been proved to be real,
they must still further be proved to see 'whether they are of God.'
We are not to judge of doctrine by miracles, but of miracles by doc-

trine. A miracle enforcing what contradicts the teaching of Christ
and His Apostles is not ' of God' and is no authority for Christians.
Comp. Gal. i. 8; Deut. xiii. 1—3.

ὅτι πολλοὶ ψευδοπρ. The caution is against no imaginary or merely
possible danger; it already exists. Warnings respecting the coming
of such had been given by Christ, S. Paul, S. Peter, and S. Jude; and
now S. John, writing long afterwards, tells the Church that these
prophecies have been fulfilled. The πολλοὶ ψευδοπροφῆται include the
antichrists of ii. 18; and what is here said of them seems to indicate
that like Mahomet, Swedenborg, the Irvingites, and others, they put
forth their new doctrine as a *revelation.*

ἐξεληλύθασιν εἰς τ. κ. This probably has no reference to what is
said in ii. 19 about their ' going out from us'. It need mean no more
than that they have appeared in public; but it perhaps includes the
notion of their having a *mission* from the power that sent them: comp.
John iii. 17; vi. 14; x. 36; xi. 27; xii. 47, 49; and especially xvi. 28.
We need not confine these 'many false prophets' to the antichrists
who had left the Christian communion. There would be others who,
like Apollonius of Tyana, had never been Christians at all: and others
even more dangerous who still professed to be members of the Church.
The difficulties in the Church of Corinth caused by the unrestrained
' speaking with tongues' point to dangers of this kind.

2. ἐν τούτῳ γινώσκετε. Once more we have a verb which may be
either indicative or imperative (ii. 27, 29). The indicative is to be
preferred in spite of the imperative in *v.* 1. The passage is closely
analogous to iii. 16, 19, 24, which must be indicative. In all four
cases the Apostle appeals to the progressive experience of Christians.
'Εν τούτῳ refers to what follows: see on iii. 19. Nowhere else in the
Epistle is ἐν τούτῳ joined to an imperative.

πᾶν πν. ὃ ὁμολογεῖ. This idea of 'confessing' one's belief is
specially frequent in S. John: ii. 23; iv. 15; 2 John 7; John ix. 22;
xii. 42; comp. Rom. x. 9.

'Ιησ. Χρ. ἐν σαρκὶ ἐληλύθοτα. See on 2 John 7. This is the
crucial test, and one which would at once expose 'the spirits' of
Cerinthian and Docetic teachers. We are not to suppose that all other
articles of faith are unimportant; or that to deny this truth is the
worst of all denials (see on ii. 22); or that such denial involves every
kind of doctrinal error. But against the errors prevalent in that age
this was the great safeguard. The confession must of course be not
with the tongue only but in truth, and in deed as well as in word (iii.
18): *non lingua sed factis, non sonando sed amando* (Bede).

The sentence may be taken in more ways than one: (1) as both A.V.
and R.V.; (2) more accurately and with some difference of meaning,
confesseth Jesus Christ as come *in the flesh;* (3) *confesseth* that Jesus
is the Christ *come in the flesh.* Remark that S. John does not say
'come *into* the flesh,' but '*in* the flesh': Christ did not descend (as
Cerinthus said) into an already existing man, but He came in human
nature; He '*became* flesh.' Moreover he does not say that the con-

fession is to be of a Christ who *came* (ἐλθόντα), but of a Christ who *is come* (ἐληλυθότα). This 'coming' is not an exhausted fact: He is come and abides in the flesh. Some Latin writers have *in carnem venisse* for *in carne venisse;* but this is bad Latin rather than bad doctrine. The translator has not been able to mark the difference between εἰς σάρκα and ἐν σαρκί.

S. Paul gives almost exactly the same test: 'I give you to understand that no man speaking in the Spirit of God saith, Jesus is anathema; and no man can say, Jesus is Lord, but in the Holy Spirit' (1 Cor. xii. 3).

ἐκ τοῦ Θεοῦ ἐστίν. Proceeds from Him as its source. Comp. *vv.* 3, 6, 7; ii. 16; iii. 10; 3 John 11; John vii. 17; viii. 47. Outside S. John's writings the expression is not common: comp. Acts v. 38; 1 Cor. xi. 12. It is closely akin to the idea of Divine birth (ii. 29; iii. 9) and being children of God (iii. 1, 2, 10). "To confess that Jesus the anointed is come in the flesh, is to confess that there is a medium of spiritual communications between the visible and the invisible world, between earth and heaven. It is to confess that there is one Mediator for all men" (Maurice).

3. ὃ μὴ ὁμολογεῖ τὸν Ἰ. The words inserted in ℵ and some other authorities are an obvious interpolation by some early transcriber who wished to make the two sides of the antithesis exactly equal. But, as we have repeatedly seen (i. 5, 6, 7, 8, 10, ii. 10, 22, 23, &c.), this is rarely the case in S. John's oppositions.

There is yet another very ancient and very interesting difference of reading here: *every spirit which severeth Jesus*, or *unmaketh Jesus*, or *destroyeth Jesus*, or, as the margin of R.V., which *annulleth Jesus* (ὁ λύει, *qui solvit*), the verb which in iii. 8 is used for 'to destroy.' This reading appears to have been known to Tertullian (A. D. 210), who quotes S. John, *qui jam antichristos dicit processisse in mundum praecursores antichristi spiritus, negantes Christum in carne venisse, et solventes Jesum, scilicet in Deo creatore* (*Adv. Marcion.* v. xvi.), and to Irenaeus (A.D. 180), who quotes the whole passage, and in this place has *omnis spiritus qui* solvit Jesum (*Haer.* III. xvi. 8). But it can scarcely be genuine, for it is *not found in a single Greek MS.*, *nor in any version* except the Vulgate. And we have no certain knowledge that any Greek Father had this reading. 'Qui solvit' in the Latin translators of Irenaeus and of Origen may be interpretation rather than literal translation. Socrates the historian (A.D. 440) charges the Nestorians with tampering with the text and ignoring the reading ὃ λύει τὸν Ἰ.; just as Tertullian accuses the Valentinians of falsifying the text of John i. 13, and S. Ambrose the Arians of inserting οὐδὲ ὁ υἱός into Mark xiii. 32 and of mutilating John i. 6. In all these cases the supposed heretical reading is the right one. In this very verse Nestorius was blamed for a reading which his opponent Cyril has also. See Appendix G.

The passage in S. Polycarp's Epistle already alluded to (see on ii. 18) is against the reading advocated by Socrates: 'For every one who confesseth not that Jesus Christ has come in the flesh is an Antichrist;

and whosoever confesseth not the witness of the Cross is of the devil'
(*Phil.* VII.). The expressions 'confess', 'come in the flesh', 'Antichrist', 'is of the devil', place S. Polycarp's knowledge of his master's
First Epistle beyond all reasonable doubt. This is very early testimony (A.D. 112—118) to the existence of the First Epistle.
The variations as regards reading are testimony to the same effect.
Such things take time to arise and spread. If a corrupt reading is
known to Tertullian in Africa, and (apparently) adopted by Irenaeus
in Gaul, before the end of the second century, then the original document written in Asia Minor cannot be much later than the end of the
first century, at which time S. John was still living.
Note the μή after the relative; 'every spirit who *is of such a kind as
not* to confess'. Comp. ᾧ μὴ πάρεστι ταῦτα, τυφλός ἐστιν (2 Pet. ii. 9).
The μή in Col. ii. 18 is of very doubtful authority. Winer, 603.

ἐκ τ. Θεοῦ οὐκ ἔστιν. S. John gives two tests: one for trying
human conduct, the other for trying spiritual claims. 'Everyone that
doeth not righteousness *is not of God*, neither he that loveth not his
brother' (iii. 10). And 'Every spirit which confesseth not Jesus *is not
of God*'.

τὸ τοῦ ἀντιχρίστου. The (*spirit*) *of antichrist*. Nothing better than
'spirit' can well be inserted in English, and some insertion is necessary. But we need not suppose that πνεῦμα is to be understood. Τὸ
τοῦ ἀντ. is a comprehensive term covering all the principles and
powers, all the essential characteristics of Antichrist: what Aristotle
would call τὸ τί ἦν εἶναι (*Eth. Nic.* II. vi. 17), and we might call 'the
antichristian nature'. The nearest parallel is τὸ τῆς ἀληθοῦς παροιμίας
(2 Pet. ii. 22), 'the very thing which the true proverb says': Matt. xxi.
21; 1 Cor. x. 24; James iv. 14 are parallel only as regards the gram-
matical construction.

ὅτι ἔρχεται. As R.V., *that it* cometh. Wiclif, Purvey, and the
Rhemish have '*he* cometh'. Most English Versions before 1611 have
'he' for 'it'; as also has Luther. This is due to the Vulgate, which
has *antichristus* for *illud antichristi*. 'It' is certainly right. Not
Antichrist, but the antichristian nature, is affirmed to be *now in
the world already*. The spirit of antagonism to Christ has passed
from "the invisible world of spiritual wickedness" to the visible world
of human action. The addition of 'already' hints that something
more may be expected to follow. Comp. τὸ γὰρ μυστήριον ἤδη ἐνεργεῖται
τῆς ἀνομίας (2 Thess. ii. 7). Here ἤδη comes last for emphasis, as in
λευκαί εἰσιν πρὸς θερισμὸν ἤδη (John iv. 35); where, however, some
editors put a stop at θερισμόν and join ἤδη to the next verse. The
ἔρχεται points once more to the parallel and opposition between the
Christ and the Antichrist: each may be spoken of as ὁ ἐρχόμενος
(ii. 18).

4. ὑμεῖς. *Ye*, with emphasis and in marked contrast to the false
teachers, *are of God*. The emphasis is intensified by the asyndeton.

νενικήκατε αὐτούς. In the masculine S. John passes from the
antichristian spirits to the false prophets who are their mouthpieces.

By not listening to these seducers his 'little children' have overcome them. 'A stranger will they not follow, but will flee from him, for they know not the voice of strangers' (John x. 5). Thus the stranger is defeated.

ὅτι μείζων ἐστὶν ὁ ἐν ὑμῖν. *Qui audit ' Vicistis' erigit caput, erigit cervicem, laudari se vult. Noli te extollere. Vide quis in te vicit* (S. Augustine). 'Not by might, nor by power, but by My Spirit, saith the Lord of Hosts' (Zech. iv. 6). It is precisely for this reason that they may have confidence against all spiritual enemies: it is not confidence in themselves (1 Cor. xv. 57 and especially Ephes. vi. 10— 17). In ὁ ἐν ὑμῖν and ὁ ἐν τῷ κόσμῳ we have two *personal* powers opposed to one another: and therefore ὁ ἐν ὑμῖν must be understood of God or Christ rather than of ὁ λόγος τοῦ Θεοῦ.

ὁ ἐν τῷ κόσμῳ. The same as ὁ ἄρχων τοῦ κόσμου τούτου (John xii. 31), the devil, the father of these lying teachers (iii. 10; John viii. 44), whose works Christ came to destroy (iii. 8). By saying 'in the world' rather than 'in them', the Apostle indicates that they belong to 'the world'. "S. John constantly teaches that the Christian's work in this state of probation is to conquer 'the world'. It is, in other words, to fight successfully against that view of life which ignores God, against that complex system of attractive moral evil and specious intellectual falsehood which is organized and marshalled by the great enemy of God, and which permeates and inspires non-Christianized society" (Liddon).

5. αὐτοὶ ἐκ τ. κ. εἰσίν. The pronouns at the beginning of all three verses are in emphatic opposition; ὑμεῖς...αὐτοί...ἡμεῖς. That they, the antichristian teachers, are 'of the world' was implied in ii. 19, where it is stated that they are 'not of us': for there is no middle neutral position. The verse is another reminiscence of the Lord's farewell discourses: 'If ye were of the world, the world would love its own' (John xv. 19; comp. xvii. 14).

διὰ τοῦτο ἐκ τ. κ. λαλοῦσιν. *Therefore of the world they speak:* as in John iii. 31, the Greek order is impressive and worth preserving. (See on iii. 1; but here διὰ τοῦτο is not followed by ὅτι.) The impressive repetition of 'the world' is very characteristic of S. John's style; e.g. John i. 10; iii. 17; xv. 19; xvii. 14. Comp. 'He that is of the earth, of the earth he is, and of the earth he speaketh' (iii. 31): where, however, ἐκ τῆς γῆς λαλεῖν is to speak of God's work on earth; whereas ἐκ τ. κόσμου λ. is to speak what is alien from God's work and opposed to it. 'To speak *of* ' (λαλεῖν ἐκ) is not the same as 'to speak *concerning*' (λέγειν περί) v. 16; John i. 22, 47; ii. 21, &c. 'To speak of the world' is to have the world as the *source* of one's words, so that one's inspiration flows from it: and of course the world 'heareth,' i.e. loves to hear, the wisdom derived from itself. It expects to secure everything, the honour of the Christian name and the credit of lofty spiritual γνῶσις, without any humiliation or crucifixion of the flesh.

6. ἡμεῖς. Once more we have no barren seesaw, but an advance. Αὐτοί is opposed to ὑμεῖς, and ἡμεῖς is opposed to αὐτοί: but ἡμεῖς is

not a return to ὑμεῖς. The contrast between ὑμεῖς and αὐτοί is that between true and false *Christians*. The contrast between αὐτοί and ἡμεῖς is that between false and true *teachers*. As in *v.* 14 and i. 4, ἡμεῖς probably means the Apostles. Comp. 1 Cor. xiv. 37.

ὁ γινώσκων τὸν Θεόν. Both the verb itself and the present participle are very expressive; ' He that *is increasing in the knowledge* of God '. It is with a view to this increase that Christ has given us διάνοια (v. 20); and he who has it ἀκούει ἡμῶν, *listens to us.* Here again we have that magisterial tone of Apostolic authority which is so conspicuous in the Prologue (i. 1—4). It underlies the whole Epistle, as it does the whole of the Fourth Gospel, but here and there comes to the surface. It is the quiet confidence of conscious strength. Comp. 'He that is of God heareth the words of God; for this cause ye hear them not because ye are not of God '; and, 'Every one that is of the Truth heareth My voice' (John viii. 47; xviii. 37). For ordinary Christians to adopt this language is presumptuous sectarianism.

Note, that, as usual, the antithesis is not exact: 'he that *knoweth* God' is balanced by 'he that *is not of* God'; indicating that it is the child of God who comes by experience to know Him.

ἐκ τούτου. A fresh sentence should begin here. It is not certain whether 'from this' refers to the whole section (1—6), or to the latter half (4—6), or only to the first half of *v.* 6. In any case the meaning is, *not* that those who hear the Apostle have the Spirit of truth, while those who refuse to hear have the spirit of error; *but* that the Apostles have the Spirit of truth because God's children listen to them, while the false prophets have the spirit of error because the world listens to them. On the other hand the world does not listen to the Apostles, because it has no sympathy or affinity with what they have to teach (1 Cor. ii. 14).

τὸ πνεῦμα τῆς ἀληθείας. The Holy Spirit; John xiv. 17; xv. 26; xvi. 13: comp. 1 Cor. ii. 12. It is not easy to decide whether τῆς ἀληθείας expresses the *character* of the Spirit, as in τῷ πνεύματι τῆς ἐπαγγελίας τῷ ἁγίῳ (Eph. i. 13), and τὸ πνεῦμα τῆς χάριτος (Heb. x. 29), or the *source*, as τῷ πνεύματι τοῦ Θεοῦ (1 Cor. vi. 11). The Spirit is the Truth (v. 6), proceeds from Him who is the Truth (John xiv. 6, 26), communicates and interprets the Truth (John xvi. 13, 14).

τὸ πνεῦμα τῆς πλάνης. The expression occurs nowhere else in N.T. Comp. τὸ πνεῦμα τοῦ κόσμου (1 Cor. ii. 12). It is the spirit which emanates from him who 'is a liar and the father thereof' (John viii. 44).

7—21. LOVE IS THE MARK OF THE CHILDREN OF THE GOD WHO IS LOVE.

7. ἀγαπητοί, ἀγαπῶμεν ἀλλήλ. See on iii. 2 and iv. 11. The transition seems abrupt, as if the Apostle had summarily dismissed an unwelcome subject. But the connexions of thought in S. John's writings are often so subtle, that it is rash to assert anywhere that two consecutive verses or sections are entirely without connecting

links. Two such links may be found here. 1. The power to love one
another, no less than the power to confess the Incarnation, is the gift
of the Spirit (*vv.* 2, 12, 13). And faith and love mutually aid one
another. This is the case even between man and man. Faith and
trust soon pass into love. 2. The antichristian spirit is a selfish one;
it makes self, i. e. one's own intellect and one's own interest, the
measure of all things. Just as it severs the Divine from the human
in Christ, so it severs Divine love from human conduct in man.
'Beloved, let us do far otherwise. Let us love one another'.

For the third and last time in this Epistle the Apostle introduces
the subject of brotherly love. First it was introduced as a consequence and sign of walking in the light (ii. 7—11). Next it was
introduced as a special form of righteousness and mark of God's
children (iii. 10—18). Here it appears as a gift of the Spirit of God,
a contrast to the antichristian spirit, and above all as an effluence
from the very Being of God.

'Love one another' here, as in iii. 11, applies primarily to the
mutual love of *Christians*. The love of Christians to unbelievers is
not expressly excluded, but it is not definitely before the Apostle's
mind.

ἡ ἀγάπη ἐκ τ. Θεοῦ ἐστίν. And 'we are of God' (*v.* 6), and 'ye are
of God' (*v.* 4); therefore there should be the family bond of love
between us.

πᾶς ὁ ἀγαπῶν κ.τ.λ. This follows from the preceding statement.
If God is the source of all love, then whatever love a man has in him
comes from God; and this part of his moral nature is of Divine origin.
Of '*every one* that loveth' is this true, whether he be heathen or
Christian: there is no limitation. If a Socrates or a Marcus Aurelius
loves his fellow-men, it is by the grace of God that he does so. See
first note on iii. 3.

γεγέννηται. 'Hath been begotten of God and remains His child';
the full sense of the perfect. Translate with R.V. *is* begotten *of God.*
καὶ γινώσκει. *And groweth in the knowledge of God:* see on ὁ γινώσκων in *v.* 6. A loyal child must increase in knowledge of its father.

8. ὁ μὴ ἀγαπῶν. For the μή comp. iii. 10, 14; ii. 4. οὐκ ἔγνω.
Literally, *knew not God,* i.e. never attained to a knowledge of Him.
Comp. iii. 1; John xvi. 3. We have here a remarkable instance of
S. John's habit of not making the second part of an antithesis the
exact counterpart of the first, but an advance beyond. Instead of saying 'is not born of God' he says 'never knew God', which is much
stronger. Not to have known love is not to have known God.

ὁ Θεὸς ἀγάπη ἐστίν. This is the third of S. John's great statements
respecting the Nature of God: 'God is Spirit' (John iv. 24); 'God is
light' (1 John i. 5), and 'God is love'. See on i. 5. Here, as in the
other cases, the predicate has no article, and expresses not a quality
which He *possesses*, but one which embraces all He *is*. This is clear
from S. John's argument. It does not follow, because God is *full of*
love, that one who does not love cannot have known God: all that

follows from this is that his knowledge of God is very incomplete. Only if God *is* love, i.e. if love is Himself, is the statement true, that to have no personal knowledge of love is to have no personal knowledge of God. And here we may remark that to attain by experience to a knowledge of God (γινώσκειν τὸν Θεόν) is a very different thing from knowing something *about* Him (εἰδέναι τι περὶ αὐτοῦ). The Gnostics knew a good deal about God, but they did not know Him; for instead of loving those brethren who did not share their intellectual attainments, they had an arrogant contempt for them. They had recognized that 'God is spirit', and to some extent that 'God is light'; for they knew Him to be an immaterial Being and the highest Intelligence: but they had wholly failed to appreciate that 'God is love'. And yet of the three great truths this is the chief. The other two are incomplete without it. The first, 'God is spirit', is almost more negative than positive: God is not material; 'He dwelleth not in temples made with hands'. The second might seem in making our idea of Him more definite to remove Him further away from us: God is perfect intelligence, perfect purity, perfect holiness. The third not only makes His Nature far more clearly known, but brings Him very close to us. The spirit is shewn to be personal, the light to have warmth and life.

If no previous religion, not even the Jewish, had attained to the truth that 'God is light', still less had any attained to the truth that 'God is love'. To the heathen world God is a powerful, a terrible, and often a cruel being; one whose fierce wrath needs to be deprecated and whose ill-will needs to be propitiated, rather than one on whose love men may rely. To the Jews He is a just and a jealous, if also a merciful God, of whose inmost being all that was known was I AM THAT I AM. To the Christian alone He is known as LOVE.

As already stated, this truth, God is love, dominates the second main division of the Epistle. In no *Book* in N.T. does the substantive 'love' (ἀγάπη) occur so often as in these two and a half *chapters* (iii. 1—v. 12); and in no Book in N.T., excepting the Fourth Gospel, does the verb 'to love' (ἀγαπᾶν) occur *half* so many times as here. No wonder that the writer of this Epistle has been known in the Church as 'the Apostle of Love'. "If nothing were said in praise of love throughout the pages of this Epistle, if nothing whatever throughout the other pages of the Scriptures, and this one thing only were all we were told by the voice of the Spirit of God, *For God is Love;* nothing more ought we to require" (S. Augustine).

9. ἐν τούτῳ ἐφ. For the sake of uniformity with *vv.* 10, 13, 17, **Herein** *was manifested:* we have the same Greek in all four verses. 'Herein' plainly refers to what follows: comp. iii. 16 and see on iii. 19. For **ἐφανερώθη** see on i. 2. This is a second reason for our loving one another. We must do this (1) because love is the very Being of Him whose children we are; (2) because of the transcendent way in which His love was manifested. The context shews that 'the love of God', which usually in this Epistle means our love to God, here means His love to us: comp. iii. 16.

ἐν ἡμῖν. Rather **in** *us* than 'toward us': we are in the sphere in which God's love is exhibited: comp. *v.* 16 and John ix. 3, which is very parallel. The latter passage tends to shew that ἐν ἡμῖν is to be joined with ἐφανερώθη rather than with ἡ ἀγάπη τ. Θεοῦ: *Herein was the love of God manifested in us.* The rendering 'in our case' (R.V. margin) is improbable: comp. *v.* 12.

τὸν υἱὸν αὐτοῦ τὸν μον. *His Son, His only-begotten:* comp. John iii. 16. As in τὴν ζωὴν τὴν αἰώνιον (i. 2), ἡ κοινωνία ἡ ἡμετέρα (i. 3), ἡ ἐντολὴ ἡ παλαιά (ii. 7), and τὸ φῶς τὸ ἀληθινόν (ii. 8), the repetition of the article makes both ideas, 'son' and 'only-begotten', prominent and distinct. Comp. 2 John 11, 13. His Son was much to send, but it was also His only Son. Μονογενής as applied to Christ is peculiar to S. John: it occurs four times in the Gospel (i. 14, 18; iii. 16, 18) and here. 'Only-born' would be a more accurate rendering: Christ is the only *born* Son as distinct from the many who have *become* sons. The word occurs in LXX. to translate a Hebrew word (*yachid*), which is elsewhere rendered ἀγαπητός ('beloved' or 'darling'): and oddly enough where the Greek has μονογενής the A.V. has 'darling' and *vice versa.* Contrast Gen. xxii. 2, 12, 16 with Ps. xxii. 21; xxxv. 17: in the latter texts R.V. has 'my only one' in the margin. The Vulgate has *unigenitus* and *unicus.* Comp. Rom. v. 8; viii. 32.

ἀπέσταλκεν. **Hath** *sent;* the perfect indicates the permanent result of Christ's mission and should be distinguished from the aorists, ἠγάπησεν and ἀπέστειλεν, which express past acts without reference to their permanent effects (*v.* 10).

ἵνα ζήσωμεν δι' αὐτοῦ. These are the important words, setting forth that in which God's love is so conspicuous and so unique. The only Son has been sent *for this purpose* (ἵνα), that we may live, and not die, as we should otherwise have done; comp. iii. 14; v. 11; John iii. 16, 17, 36; x. 10; xi. 25, 26. Just as πάντα δι' αὐτοῦ ἐγένετο (John i. 3), so He was sent ἵνα σωθῇ ὁ κόσμος δι' αὐτοῦ (John iii. 17) and ἵνα ζήσωμεν δι' αὐτοῦ.

10. ἐν τούτῳ. This again refers to what follows: Love in its full perfection is seen, not in man's love to God, but in His to man, which reached a climax in His sending His Son to save us from our sins. The superiority of God's love does not lie merely in the fact of its being Divine. It is first in order of time and therefore necessarily spontaneous: ours is at best only love in return for love. His love is absolutely disinterested; ours cannot easily be so. Comp. Titus iii. 4. For ἱλασμός and περὶ τῶν ἁμ. see on ii. 2; ἱλασμὸς περὶ τ. ἁμ. is parallel to ἵνα ζήσωμεν δι' αὐτοῦ in the previous verse, but an advance on it. It is by being a propitiation for our sins that He wins life for us. Bede tells us that some MSS. had the reading '*Et misit Filium suum litatorem pro peccatis nostris,* adding *Litator autem sacrificator est.* But *litator* is more than *sacrificator,* it is 'one who sacrifices *with favourable results*'. Augustine has *litator,* Lucifer *expiator,* the Vulgate *propitiatio.*

11. ἀγαπητοί. For the sixth and last time the Apostle uses this appropriate address. Here also it affectionately emphasizes a de-

duction of practical importance.   See on iii. 2 and comp. iv. 7.   No
address of any kind occurs again until the last verse of the Epistle.

εἰ οὕτως ὁ Θ. ἠγ. ἡμᾶς.   'If, as is manifest, to *this* extent God loved
us'.   The fact is stated gently, but not doubtfully, just as in iii. 13;
v. 9.   Comp. εἰ οὖν ἐγὼ ἔνιψα ὑμῶν τοὺς πόδας,...καὶ ὑμεῖς ὀφείλετε ἀλλήλων νίπτειν τοὺς πόδας (John xiii. 14).   Οὕτως is emphatic, and refers
to *vv.* 9, 10.

καὶ ἡμεῖς ὀφείλομεν.   As R.V., *we also ought* : καί belongs to ἡμεῖς;
we as well as God.   In the spiritual family also *noblesse oblige*.   As
children of God we must exhibit His nature, and we must follow His
example, and we must love those whom He loves.   Nor is this the only
way in which the Atonement forms part of the foundation of Christian
Ethics.   It is only when we have learned something of the infinite
price paid to redeem us from sin, that we rightly estimate the moral
enormity of sin, and the strength of the obligation which lies upon us
to free ourselves from its pollution.   And it was precisely those false
teachers who denied the Atonement who taught that idolatry and
every abominable sin were matters of no moral significance.

12.   Θεὸν οὐδεὶς πώποτε τεθέαται.   As R.V., *No man hath* beheld
God at any time, to mark the shade of difference between this and
Θεὸν οὐδεὶς ἑώρακεν πώποτε (John i. 18).   Here gazing and contemplation are implied ; there not.   Each word suits its own context.   The
order here is striking : *God no man ever yet hath beheld*.   In both
cases Θεόν stands first with great emphasis and *without the article*.
Dr Westcott tabulates a number of instances and draws the following
conclusion from them : "In Θεός the general conception of divinity is
prominent, and in ὁ Θεός that of the One Being in personal relation
to others".   This distinction holds good with great precision in
the present passage.   Comp. ὃν εἶδεν οὐδεὶς ἀνθρώπων οὐδὲ ἰδεῖν δύναται
(1 Tim. vi. 16).

Once more (see on *v.* 7) the connecting lines of thought are not on
the surface, and cannot be affirmed with certainty.   What follows seems
to give the clue to what otherwise looks like an abrupt transition.
'I say we must love one another, for by so doing we have proof of the
presence of the invisible God.   No amount of contemplation ever yet
enabled any one to detect God's presence.   Let us love one another,
and then we may be sure that He is not only *with* us but *in* us, and
not merely *is*, but *abides*'.   For μένει see on ii. 24 : He is not a
momentary visitant but a permanent friend and guest.

ἡ ἀγάπη αὐτοῦ.   **The love of Him.**   'His love to us' can hardly be
meant: in what sense would our loving one another perfect that?
Moreover, as already noticed, 'the love of God' in this Epistle commonly means man's love to Him, not His to man (ii. 5, iii. 17, v. 3).
'His love' might possibly mean the love which characterizes Him, or
the love which He has implanted in us; but the other is simpler.   Our
love to God is developed and perfected by our loving one another.
We practise and strengthen our love of the Unseen by shewing love to
the seen.   See on ii. 5.

τετελειωμένη ἐν ἡμῖν ἐστίν. *In a perfected form is in us:* 'is perfected in us' hardly does justice to the Greek. Τελειοῦσθαι is frequent
in Hebrews (v. 9; vii. 28; xi. 40; xii. 23) and in this Epistle (ii. 5;
iv. 17, 18).

13. This should be compared with iii. 24, to which it is closely
parallel. There, as here, the gift of the Spirit is the proof of God's
abiding presence: but there this is connected with keeping His commandments; here it is connected with the special duty of brotherly
love.

ἐκ τοῦ πνεύματος αὐτοῦ δέδ. *We receive of* His Spirit. Of Christ
alone was it said in the fullest sense that οὐκ ἐκ μέτρου is the Spirit
given to Him (John iii. 34). Christians are said sometimes τὸ Πνεῦμα
λαβεῖν (Gal. iii. 2: comp. iv. 6), sometimes ἐκ τοῦ Πνεύματος λαβεῖν, as
here. Only the former is true of Christ. See on iii. 24 and 2 John 4.

14. τεθεάμεθα καὶ μαρτ. As R.V., *we have* beheld *and* bear witness: see on *v.* 12 and i. 2. ἡμεῖς is emphatic, and as in the
Prologue and in *v.* 6, means S. John and the other Apostles. See on
i. 4 and iv. 6. With their own eyes the Twelve saw the Son working
out His mission as the Saviour of the world. Τεθεάμεθα points back
to τεθέαται in *v.* 12 : ' God Himself no one hath ever yet beheld, but *we*
have beheld His Son '.

ἀπέσταλκεν. Hath *sent*, as in *v.* 9. τοῦ κόσμου is important.
The Son has been sent as Saviour, not of the Jews only, nor of the
'enlightened' Gnostics only, but of all. There is no limit to His
mission to save, and no limit to its success, excepting man's unwillingness to accept salvation by believing on the Saviour. See on ii. 2
and comp. John iii. 17. Only twice in his writings does S. John use
the word σωτήρ, here and in the Samaritans' confession (John iv. 42).
In both places it is followed by τοῦ κόσμου.

15. ὃς ἂν ὁμολ. *Quicunque confessus fuerit* (Vulgate): less well,
Si quis confessus fuerit (Jerome *Adv. Jovin.* II. 29). This explains
and confirms τοῦ κόσμου. Without any exception, *Whosoever shall
confess* (see on ii. 5) God abideth *in him :* but this was just what the
false prophets refused to do. See on *vv.* 2 and 3, and on *v.* 1. Comp.
Eph. iii. 17.

ὁ Θεός...τῷ Θεῷ. The communion is of the closest kind: comp.
iii. 24; John vi. 56; xiv. 20; xv. 5. Even Apostles, who have beheld
and borne witness, can have no more than this Divine fellowship,
which is open to every believer. For μένει see on ii. 24. *Vicissim in
se habitant qui continet et qui continetur. Habitas in Deo, sed ut con-
tinearis : habitat in te Deus, sed ut contineat ne cadas, quia sic de ipsa
caritate apostolus ait ;* Caritas nunquam cadit. *Quomodo cadit quem
continet Deus ?* (Bede).

16. καὶ ἡμεῖς. This is perhaps the Apostolic ' we' again, as in the
Prologue and *vv.* 6, 14.

ἐγνώκ. καὶ πεπιστ. τὴν ἀγάπην. The accusative shews that
ἐγνώκαμεν is the leading verb: *we have come to know the love and*

have believed it. The Vulgate has *cognovimus et credidimus cari-tati*, as if S. John had written τῇ ἀγάπῃ, and adds *Dei* as in iii. 16. Obviously knowledge, when it precedes, is the main thing. Faith then follows as a matter of course : and this is the natural order—progressive knowledge (γινώσκειν) leading up to faith. But sometimes faith precedes knowledge (John vi. 69). In either case each completes the other. Sound faith is intelligent ; sound know-ledge is believing. We must be ' ready always to give answer to every man that asketh a reason concerning the hope that is in us' (1 Pet. iii. 15). This verse is a fulfilment of the conclusion of Christ's High-Priestly prayer ; ' I made known unto them Thy name, and will make it known ; that the love wherewith Thou lovedst Me may be in them, and I in them' (John xvii. 26). With ἀγάπην ἔχειν (here and John xiii. 35) comp. ἐλπίδα ἔχειν (iii. 3).

ἐν ἡμῖν. In *us*, as in *v.* 9, not ' *to* us'. Note the characteristic repetition of the characteristic verb μένειν ; thrice in one verse, like ὁ κόσμος in *v.* 5 : comp. ii. 24. Cyprian (according to the best authori-ties) translates ; *Deus* agape *est, et qui manet in* agape *in Deo manet, et Deus in eo* (*Test.* iii. 2). So also in some MSS. *Quomodo* agape *Dei manet in illo* (1 John ii. 17 quoted *Test.* iii. 1). Was agape the original African rendering, afterwards altered to *caritas* or *dilectio*?

17. ἐν τούτῳ τ. ἡ ἀγ. μεθ᾽ ἡμῶν. Here R.V. *Herein is love* **made perfect with us,** or the margin of A.V. *Herein is* **love with us** *made perfect,* is to be preferred to A.V. Most earlier English Versions agree with R.V. ; and μεθ᾽ ἡμῶν probably belongs to τετελείωται, not to ἡ ἀγάπη. So also the Vulgate (*Cod. Am.*), *perfecta est nobiscum cari-tas:* while Augustine renders *perfecta est dilectio in nobis.* Ἡ ἀγάπη here must mean our love towards God: His love towards us cannot have any fear (*v.* 18) in it. This love takes up its abode, is developed, and perfected, *with us.* Ἐν τούτῳ may refer to either of the clauses which follow. Ἐν τούτῳ......ἵνα is a possible construction, and perhaps occurs John xv. 8; and ἐν τούτῳ ὅτι occurs 1 John iii. 16; iv. 9, 10. But it is perhaps best to make ἐν τούτῳ refer to what precedes; to our abiding in God and God in us. This avoids the awkwardness of making perfection of love in the *present* depend upon our attitude at the Judgment, which though near (ii. 18) according to S. John's view, is still *future.* In this way we can give its full meaning to ἵνα: by close union with God our love is made perfect, *in order that* we may have boldness at the Day of Judgment. For παρρησία see on ii. 28. *Quisquis fiduciam habet in die judicii, perfecta est in illo caritas* (Bede from Augustine).

τῇ ἡμέρᾳ τῆς κρίσεως. The full phrase occurs nowhere else: the usual form being ἡμέρα κρίσεως (Matt. x. 15; xi. 22, 24; xii. 36; 2 Pet. ii. 9; iii. 7). S. John elsewhere calls it ἡ ἐσχάτη ἡμέρα (John vi. 39, 40, 44, 54; xi. 24; xii. 48), or ἡ ἡμέρα ἡ μεγάλη (Rev. vi. 17) or ἡ ἡμ. ἐκείνη ἡ μεγάλη (xvi. 14). Other Scriptural phrases are ἡ ἡμ. ἐκείνη (Matt. xiii. 1; Mark xiii. 32; Luke x. 12), ἡ ἡμ. τοῦ Κυρίου (1 Cor. v. 5; 2 Cor. i. 14; 2 Thess. ii. 2), ἡ τοῦ Θεοῦ ἡμέρα (2 Pet. iii. 12), ἡ ἡμ. (Heb.

x. 25), ἡμ. αἰῶνος (2 Pet. iii. 18), κρίσις μεγάλης ἡμ. (Jude 6), ἡ κρίσις (Matt. xii. 41, 42; Luke x. 14).

καθὼς ἐκεῖνος......καὶ ἡμεῖς. For καθὼς...καὶ... see on ii. 18. 'Εκεῖνος, as elsewhere in this Epistle (ii. 6; iii. 3, 5, 7, 16), almost certainly means Christ. Our assurance with regard to the future Judgment is not presumption, because so far as is possible in this world we are in character like Christ. The resemblance is marked as close, 'even so are we' (καθώς); comp. ii. 6; iii. 3, 7. In what does this close resemblance specially consist? In love: the whole context points to this. He need not fear the judgment of Christ who by loving has become like Christ. ἐν τῷ κ. τούτῳ does not belong to both clauses; otherwise we should have had καθὼς ἐκεῖνος ἦν. The plural throughout is to be noted: μεθ' ἡμῶν...καὶ ἡμεῖς. "The Apostle does not write to any individuals as individuals, but to the members of the congregation as such. In the Church alone, but certainly there, is to be found such a consummation of love, such a perfection of fellowship with God" (Haupt).

Here again Jerome differs considerably from his own Vulgate. In the latter; *In hoc perfecta est nobiscum caritas, ut fiduciam habeamus in die judicii, quia sicut ille est et nos sumus in hoc mundo:* in his own works (*Adv. Jovin.* I. 40); *In hoc perfecta est nostra caritas, si fiduciam habeamus in diem judicii; ut quomodo ille est, sic et nos simus in hoc saeculo.*

18. Proof of the preceding statement that perfect love will give us boldness, by shewing the mutually exclusive nature of love and fear. Love moves towards others in the spirit of self-sacrifice: fear shrinks from others in the spirit of self-preservation. The two are to be understood quite generally; neither love of God nor fear of God is specially meant. In all relations whatever, perfect love excludes fear, and fear prevents love from being perfect. And the two vary inversely: the more perfect the love, the less possibility of fear; and the more the fear, the less perfect the love. But, though as certain as any physical law, the principle, that perfect love excludes all fear, is an ideal that has never been verified in fact. Like the first law of motion, it is verified by the approximations made to it. No believer's love has ever been so perfect as entirely to banish fear; but every believer experiences that as his love increases his fear diminishes. It is worthy of note that S. John here abandons his antithetic method. He does not go on to state anything about him that feareth *not*. And rightly, for the absence of fear proves nothing: it may be the result of ignorance, or presumption, or indifference, or unbelief, or inveterate wickedness.

Tertullian quotes this verse in insisting on the duty of suffering martyrdom, adding "What fear would it be better to understand than that which gives rise to denial (of Christ)? What love does he assert to be perfect, but that which puts fear to flight, and gives courage to confess (Christ)? What penalty will He appoint as the punishment of fear, but that which he who denies is to pay, who has to be slain, body and soul, in hell" (*Scorp.* xii.). Simon Magus is said to have "freed his disciples from the danger of death" by martyrdom, "by teaching them to regard idolatry as a matter of indifference" (Origen *c. Celsum* vi. xi.).

ὁ φόβος κόλασιν ἔχει. As R.V., *fear hath* punishment. 'Torment' would be βάσανος (Matt. iv. 24; Luke xvi. 23, 28). Wiclif has 'peyne' representing *poena* in the Vulgate. Other Versions have 'painfulness', Luther *Pein*. Κόλασις, common in classical Greek and not rare in LXX., occurs only here and Matt. xxv. 46 in N.T. Its primary meaning is 'pruning', and hence 'checking, correcting, punishing': whereas the primary meaning of βάσανος is 'testing', and hence 'trying by torture, tormenting'. Comp. ἵνα τὴν λείπουσαν ταῖς βασάνοις προσαναπληρώσωσι κόλασιν (Wisd. xix. 4).

ὁ δὲ φοβ. The δέ, omitted in A.V., connects this clause with the first one, ἀλλ'...ἔχει being parenthetical. Wiclif has 'forsothe' and Purvey 'but', the Genevan, Rhemish, and R.V. have 'and'. None are satisfactory, owing to the preceding ἀλλά. The passage is a good instance of the difference between ἀλλά and δέ (*sed* and *autem, sondern* and *aber*). The one introduces a sharp opposition, the other a qualification, objection, or contrast. Winer, 551, 552. The present participle indicates a constant condition: the habitual fearer is necessarily imperfect in his love.

S. Paul teaches the same doctrine; 'Ye received not the *spirit of bondage* again unto *fear;* but ye received the *spirit of adoption,* whereby we cry, *Abba, Father'* (Rom. viii. 15). The servile fear, which perfect love excludes, is therefore altogether different from the childlike awe, which is a necessary element in the creature's love for its Creator. Even servile fear is necessary as a *preparation* for perfect love. 'The fear of the Lord is the beginning of wisdom'; and it is also the beginning of love. The sinner must begin by fearing the God against whom he has sinned. Bengel gives the various stages thus: 'Neither love nor fear; fear without love; both fear and love; love without fear'. Fear is the child of bondage; love of freedom. In this case also the bondwoman and her son must be cast out (Gal. iv. 30).

19. ἡμεῖς ἀγαπῶμεν. The Old Vulgate here is trebly wrong: *nos ergo diligamus invicem,* the New has *Deum;* Augustine omits both,— *Nos diligamus.* (1) The οὖν inserted in A and some other authorities is a false reading. (2) There is no *invicem* either stated or implied by the Greek. (3) Ἀγαπῶμεν is indicative, not subjunctive, as is shewn in the ἡμεῖς: the hortative verb would hardly have the pronoun expressed; contrast *v.* 7. Some authorities insert τὸν Θεόν or αὐτόν after ἀγαπῶμεν: so A. V., 'we love *Him*'. Nothing is to be understood, Christian love of every kind being meant. The power of loving is a Divine gift.

ὅτι αὐτὸς πρῶτος. The πρῶτος is the important word and implies three things. 1. Our love owes its origin to God's love, from which it is an effluence (*v.* 7). 2. Love is checked by fear when it is doubtful whether it is returned; and our love has no such check, for God's love has been beforehand with it. 3. Gratitude easily blossoms into affection, especially gratitude for love. With God's priority in loving us

Bede compares Christ's priority in choosing His disciples (John xv. 16).

20. ἐάν τις εἴπῃ. We return to the form of statement which was so common at the beginning of the Epistle (i. 6, 8, 10). The case here contemplated is one form of the man that feareth *not*. His freedom from fear is caused, however, not by the perfection of love, but by presumption. He is either morally blind or a conscious hypocrite. Comp. ii. 4, 9.

ὁ γὰρ μὴ ἀγαπῶν. As we have seen already (iii. 14, 15), S. John treats not loving as equivalent to hating. For μή see on ii. 4; iii. 10, 14.

ὃν ἑώρακεν. S. John does not say 'whom he can see', but 'whom he has continually before his eyes'. The perfect tense, as so often, expresses a permanent state continuing from the past. His brother has been and remains in sight, God has been and remains out of sight. 'Out of sight, out of mind' is a saying which holds good in morals and religion as well as in society. And if a man fails in duties which are ever before his eyes and are easy, how can we credit him with performing duties which require an effort to bear in mind and are difficult? And in this case the seen would necessarily suggest the unseen: for the *brother* on earth implies the *Father* in heaven. If therefore even the seen is not loved, what must we infer as to the unseen? The seen brother and unseen God are put in striking juxtaposition in the Greek; 'He that loveth not his brother whom he hath seen, the God whom he hath not seen cannot love'. But in English this would be misunderstood.

οὐ δύναται. It is a moral impossibility: comp. iii. 9; John iii. 3, 5, 27; v. 19, 30; vii. 7, 34; viii. 21, 43; xii. 39; xiv. 17. The reading πῶς δύναται is perhaps a reminiscence of iii. 17 or John iii. 4, 9; v. 44; vi. 52; ix. 16. See critical notes.

21. καὶ τ. τ. ἐντ. ἔχ. ἀπ' αὐτοῦ. The Apostle drives home his arguments for the practice of brotherly love by the fact that God has commanded all who love Him to love their brethren. So also S. Paul, here again in harmony with S. John: 'The whole law is fulfilled in one word, even in this; Thou shalt love thy neighbour as thyself' (Gal. v. 14). Some take 'Him' to mean Christ. But this is unlikely, as Christ has not been mentioned for several verses: although it must be admitted that S. John is so full of the truth that 'I and My Father are one', that he makes the transition from the Father to the Son and from the Son to the Father almost unconsciously. Where has God given this commandment? In the whole Law, which is summed up in loving God with all one's heart and one's neighbour as oneself (Deut. vi. 5; Lev. xix. 18; Luke x. 27). The Apostle thus anticipates a possible objection. A man may say, 'I *can* love God without loving my brother, and I can prove my love by keeping His commandments' (John xiv. 15). 'Nay', says S. John, 'your own argument shews your error: you cannot keep His commandments without loving your brother'. Thus then we have two revelations of God: our brother, who is His image; and commandment, which is His will. Not to love our brother is a flagrant violation of both. As Pascal puts it, we must know men in order to love them, but we must love God in order to know Him.

ἵνα…ἀγαπᾷ. "The final particle (ἵνα) gives more than the simple contents of the commandment. It marks the injunction as directed to an aim" (Westcott). See on i. 9.

CHAPTER V.

1. After ἀγαπᾷ we should perhaps omit καί with B, Vulgate, and Thebaic against אAKL and Syriac.

2. For τηρῶμεν (אKL) read ποιῶμεν (B and Versions). A omits from αὐτοῦ in v. 2 to αὐτοῦ in v. 3: *homoeoteleuton.*

5. The δέ which B has after ἐστιν and after τίς is possibly genuine. It is represented in several Versions.

6. After αἵματος אA, Thebaic, and Memphitic insert καὶ πνεύματος: B, Peschito, and Vulgate omit. With אAB omit ὁ before Χριστός.

7. For the notorious interpolation here see Appendix D. The disputed words (ἐν τῷ οὐρανῷ ὁ πατὴρ ὁ λόγος καὶ τὸ ἅγιον πνεῦμα· καὶ οὗτοι οἱ τρεῖς ἕν εἰσι. καὶ τρεῖς εἰσιν οἱ μαρτυροῦντες ἐν τῇ γῇ) are absent from *every Greek MS.* earlier than the *fourteenth* century, from *every Greek Father* in discussing the doctrine of the Trinity, and from *every ancient Version.* The insertion is of Latin origin and even in Latin is not older than the fifth century. Another Western interpolation.

9. For ἦν (KL) read ὅτι with אAB and most Versions.

10. After τὴν μαρτυρίαν A, Vulgate, and Memphitic insert τοῦ Θεοῦ. For ἑαυτῷ (א) read αυτῷ (ABKL). But it remains doubtful whether αυτῷ represents αὐτῷ or αὑτῷ: the latter seems preferable. For τῷ Θεῷ (אBKL, Memphitic) A and Vulgate have τῷ υἱῷ to which others add τοῦ Θεοῦ or αὐτοῦ.

13. After ὑμῖν omit τοῖς πιστεύουσιν εἰς τὸ ὄνομα τοῦ υἱοῦ τοῦ Θεοῦ with אAB, Vulgate, Memphitic, Thebaic, and Syriac against KL. For καὶ ἵνα πιστεύητε (KL) read τοῖς πιστεύουσιν (א¹B, Syriac): but οἱ πιστεύοντες (א³A, Vulgate, Memphitic, Thebaic) is strongly supported.

15. For παρ᾽ αὐτοῦ (AKL) read ἀπ᾽ αὐτοῦ (אB). א¹A omit from ἡμῶν to ἡμῶν: *homoeoteleuton.*

18. For ἑαυτόν (אA²KLP) read αὐτόν (A¹B, Vulgate).

20. For γινώσκωμεν (B²K) read γινώσκομεν (אAB¹L). A and Vulgate add Θεόν after τ. ἀληθινόν. Before ζωὴ αἰώνιος omit ἡ with אAB against L: K inserts ἡ after ζωή.

21. Omit the final ἀμήν with אAB and most Versions against KL.

In all these cases B is almost certainly right; in not one is it certainly wrong. The combination אB proves to be always right.

The chapter falls into two parts. The first twelve verses form the last section of the second main division of the Epistle, GOD IS LOVE (ii. 29—v. 12): the last nine verses form the conclusion and summary of the whole. Some editors break up the first part of the chapter into two sections, 1—5 and 6—12, but texts and versions seem to be right in giving the whole as one paragraph. The second part does contain two smaller sections, 13—17 and 18—21. We may analyse the chapter therefore as follows: *Faith is the Source of Love, the Victory over the World, and the Possession of Life* (1—12). Conclusion and Summary: *Intercessory Love the Fruit of Faith and of the Possession of Life* (13—17); *The Sum of the Christian's Knowledge* (18—20); *Final practical Injunction* (21).

It will be observed that in the middle of the first section we have what looks at first sight a digression and yet is intimately connected with the main subject of the section. This main subject is *Faith*, a word which (strangely enough) occurs nowhere else in S. John's Epistles, nor in his Gospel. And faith necessarily implies *witness*. Only on the strength of testimony is faith possible. Therefore in this paragraph on Faith and its effects the Apostle gives in detail the various kinds of witness on which the Christian's faith is based (6—12). The paragraph shews plainly S. John's view of the relation of Faith to Love. The two are inseparable. Faith that does not lead to Love, Love that is not based on Faith, must come to nothing.

CH. V. 1—12. FAITH IS THE SOURCE OF LOVE, THE VICTORY OVER THE WORLD, AND THE POSSESSION OF LIFE.

1. πᾶς ὁ πιστεύων. *Every one that believeth:* the construction is identical with that in ii. 29; iii. 3, 4; iv. 2, 3, 7, and in the second half of this verse. See first note on iii. 3. The verb πιστεύω which occurs only three times in the rest of the Epistle, occurs six times in these first 13 verses. After the third verse the word 'love', which has been the keyword of the last two chapters, ceases to appear. With the first sentence comp. John i. 12.

The verse is a couple of syllogisms condensed into an irregular Sorites.

Every one who believes the Incarnation is a child of God.
Every child of God loves its Father.
∴ Every believer in the Incarnation loves God.

Every believer in the Incarnation loves God.
Every one who loves God loves the children of God.
∴ Every believer in the Incarnation loves the children of God.

To believe that Jesus is the Christ is to believe that One who was known as a man fulfilled a known and Divine commission; that He who was born and was crucified is the Anointed, the Messiah of Israel, the Saviour of the world. To believe this is to accept both the Old and the New Testaments; it is to believe that Jesus is what He claimed to be, One who is equal with the Father, and as such demands of every believer the absolute surrender of self to Him. Belief without love is, as S. Augustine remarks, the belief of a demon (James ii. 19).

γεγέννηται. As R. V., *is* begotten, for the sake of uniformity in this verse and elsewhere. A good deal is lost if γεγέννηται, γεννήσαντα and γεγεννημένον are not translated alike. See on *v.* 18.

τὸν γεγεννημένον. Not Christ, but any believer, as the next verse shews. "Since God regenerates us by faith, He must be loved by us as a Father: and this love embraces all His children" (Calvin). Here again the verb may be either the indicative or the hortative subjunctive; and, as in iv. 19, the indicative is preferable: 'loveth' rather than 'let him love'.

This verse shews that iv. 20 ought not to be interpreted to mean that through love of the invisible brother we ascend to the love of the invisible God. On the contrary the love of the Father is the source of love of His children. "That is the natural order; that, we may say it confidently, is the universal order" (Maurice).

2. The converse of the truth insisted upon in iv. 20, 21 is now stated. Their love and obedience to God were shewn to involve love of His children: here love of God's children is said to follow from our love and obedience to God. The two (or three) ideas mutually imply one another. Love to God implies obedience, and either of these implies love of His children, which again implies the other two. In short, love to God and love to the brethren confirm and prove each other. If either is found alone, it is not genuine. Fellowship with God and fellowship one with another (i. 3, 7) necessarily exist together. A man may be conscious of kindliness towards others and yet doubt whether he is fulfilling the law of brotherly love. For such the Apostle gives this test, 'Do you love God? Do you strive to obey Him? If so your love of others is of the right kind'. For the characteristic phrase 'keep His commandments' see on ii. 3: but here the true reading seems to be **do** *His commandments*, a phrase which occurs nowhere else. This reading is supported by B, all ancient Versions, and several Fathers. Note the 'when', or more literally, 'whenever' (ὅταν): whenever we love and obey we have fresh evidence that our philanthropy is Christian. Nowhere else in these Epistles does ὅταν occur.

3. αὕτη γάρ ἐστιν. '*This* is what it tends towards; *this* is its outcome': see on i. 5. Love implies obedience. Comp. John xiv. 15, 21, 23; xv. 10; 2 John 6. For ἵνα comp. John vi. 29; xvii. 3; 2 John 6.

βαρεῖαι οὐκ εἰσίν. For three reasons: 1. Because He gives us strength to bear them; *juvat qui jubet* (Phil. iv. 13); 2. Because of the greatness of the reward—πρὸς τὴν μέλλουσαν δόξαν (Rom. viii. 18); 3. Because love makes them light; *dilige et quod vis fac* (Augustine). They are not like the 'burdens grievous to be borne' which the legal rigour of the Pharisees laid on men's consciences. Here again we have an echo of the Master's words: 'My yoke is easy, and My burden is light' (Matt. xi. 30).

4. Reason why keeping even the difficult commandment of loving others rather than oneself is not a grievous burden. It is the world and its ways which makes the Divine commands grievous, and the new birth involved in faith gives us a new unworldly nature and a strength which conquers the world. Without this new nature and strength we should find God's commandments, in spite of their reasonableness, intolerable.

ὅτι πᾶν τὸ γεγ. ἐκ τ. Θ. **Because** *whatsoever is* **begotten** *of God:* see on *v.* 1. The collective neuter, '*whatsoever*', gives the principle a wide sweep by stating it in its most abstract form: comp. John vi. 37; xvii. 2. Moreover, whereas the masculine would make the victorious *person* prominent, the neuter emphasizes rather the victorious *power*. It is not the man, but his birth from God, which conquers. In *v.* 1 we had the masculine and in *v.* 18 return to the masculine again. In all three cases we have the perfect, not the aorist, participle. It is not the mere fact of having received the Divine birth that is insisted on, but the permanent results of the birth. Comp. John iii. 6, 8, where we have the same tense and a similar change from neuter to masculine.

ἡ νίκη ἡ νικήσασα τ. κ. *The victory that* **overcame** *the world:* aorist participle of a victory won once for all. Under the influence of the Vulgate (*quae vincit mundum*) Wiclif, Luther, Tyndale and others, all have the present tense here. Faith, which is 'the proof of things not seen' (Heb. xi. 1) which 'are eternal' (2 Cor. iv. 18), has won a decisive victory over the world which is visible and which 'is passing away' (ii. 17). Faith is both the victory and the victor. *Illa nimirum fides quae per dilectionem operatur. Illa fides, qua ejus humiliter auxilium flagitamus, qui ait…confidite, ego vici mundum* (Bede). Πίστις occurs nowhere else in these Epistles, nor in the Gospel; νίκη nowhere else in N.T. Note the characteristic repetition of τὸν κόσμον, thrice in two verses, and always in the sense of the great human tradition of indifference or antagonism to God. See on ii. 2.

5. τίς ἐστιν ὁ νικῶν. Here the present tense is right. The Apostle appeals to the daily experience of every victorious Christian. B inserts a δέ after ἐστιν, ℵ after τίς: so also Luther, *Wer ist aber.* The faith that conquers is no mere vague belief in the existence of God, but a definite belief in the Incarnation: comp. *v.* 1; ii. 22; iii. 23; iv. 2, 3. For the form of question comp. ii. 22: this verse shews that 'the liar' (ὁ ψεύστης) there does not mean 'the supreme liar', for 'he that overcometh' (ὁ νικῶν) cannot mean 'the supreme conqueror'. The one sole Victor, who is such in the highest and unique sense, is Christ. Comp. 'Thanks be to God, which giveth us the victory through our Lord Jesus Christ' (1 Cor. xv. 57). Belief in Christ is at once belief in God and in man. It lays a foundation for love and trust towards our fellow men. Thus the instinctive distrust and selfishness, which reign supreme in the world, are overcome. Comp. the Sarum Collect for Trinity Sunday, weakened by Cosin in 1661, *quaesumus ut ejusdem fidei firmitate ab omnibus semper muniamur adversis.* Our Creed is our spear and shield.

6. οὗτός ἐστιν ὁ ἐλθών. Closely connected with what precedes. 'This *Son of God* is He that came'. The identity of the historic person Jesus with the eternal Son of God is once more insisted upon as the central and indispensable truth of the Christian faith. Faith in this truth is the only faith that can overcome the world and give eternal life. And it is a truth attested by witness of the highest and most extraordinary kind.

δι' ὕδατος καὶ αἵματος. Literally, **by means of** or **through** *water and blood*. This is the most perplexing passage in the Epistle and one of the most perplexing in N.T. A very great variety of interpretations have been suggested. It would be simply confusing to discuss them all; but a few of the principal explanations, and the reasons for adopting the one preferred, may be stated with advantage. The water and the blood have been interpreted to mean :—

(1) The Baptism by means of water in the Jordan and the Death by means of blood upon the Cross.

(2) The water and blood which flowed from Christ's pierced side.

(3) Purification and Redemption (λουτρόν and λύτρον).

(4) The Sacraments of Baptism and of the Eucharist.

These are fairly representative interpretations; the first two making the water and blood refer to facts in the earthly career of the Messiah; the last two making them symbolical of mysteries. It will be observed that these explanations are not all exclusive one of another: either of the last two may be combined with either of the first two; and in fact the fourth is not unfrequently combined with the second. The second, which is S. Augustine's, has recently received the support of the *Speaker's Commentary* and of Canon F. W. Farrar in *The Early Days of Christianity* : but in spite of its attractiveness it appears to be scarcely tenable. The difficult passage in John xix. 34 and the difficult passage before us do not really explain one another. That *"in these two passages alone, of all Scripture, are blood and water placed together,"* would, if true, amount to nothing more than a presumption that one may be connected with the other. And such a presumption would be at once weakened by the change of order: instead of the 'blood and water' of the Gospel we have 'water and blood' here. But the statement is not true; e.g., *five* times in Exod. vii. 17—25; 'He took *water* and washed his hands before the multitude, saying, I am innocent of the *blood* of this righteous man' (Matt. xxvii. 24); 'He shall cleanse the house with the *blood* of the bird, and with the running *water*' (Lev. xiv. 52); 'He took the *blood* of the calves and the goats, with *water* and scarlet wool and hyssop,' &c. (Heb. ix. 19). And is it credible that S. John would speak of effusions from the dead body of Jesus as the Son of God "coming through water and blood"? Moreover, what, on this interpretation, can be the point of the emphatic addition, 'not in the water only, but in the water and in the blood'? At the piercing of the side it was the water, not the blood, that was so marvellous. So that, to make the reference clear, the whole ought to run somewhat in this manner: 'This is He that shed forth blood and water, even Jesus Christ; not the blood only, but the blood and the water'.

The first of the four explanations is far more tenable, and is adopted by Bede, but not to the entire exclusion of the second. So also Dr Westcott, who thinks the additional reference to John xix. 34 "beyond question". The Baptism in the water of Jordan and the Death by the shedding of blood sum up the work of redemption. Christ's Baptism, with the Divine proclamation of Him as the Son of God and the Divine outpouring of the Spirit upon Him, is not merely the opening but the explanation of the whole of His Ministry. The bloody death upon the Cross is not merely the close but the explanation of His Passion. 'Coming' when spoken of the Christ includes the notion of His *mission* (John i. 15, 27, 30; iii. 31; vi. 14; vii. 27, 31, 41, &c., &c.). Therefore, when we are told that the Son of God '*came* by means of *water* and *blood*', we may reasonably understand this as meaning that He fulfilled His mission by the Baptism with which His public work began and the bloody Death with which He finished it (John xix. 30). (1) This interpretation explains the *order;* 'water and blood', not 'blood and water'. (2) It explains the *first preposition;* 'through' or 'by means of' (διά with the genitive : comp. the remarkable parallel Heb. ix. 12). (3) It also explains the *second preposition;* 'in' (ἐν, of the element *in* which, without the notion of means: comp. the remarkable parallel Heb. ix. 25). Christ's Baptism and Death were in one sense the *means by which,* in another sense the *spheres in which* His work was accomplished. (4) Above all it explains the emphatic addition, 'not in water only, but in the water and in the blood'. The Gnostic teachers, against whom the Apostle is writing, admitted that the Christ came 'through' and 'in' *water:* it was precisely at the Baptism, they said, that the Divine Word united Himself with the man Jesus. But they denied that the Divine Person had any share in what was effected 'through' and 'in' *blood:* for according to them the Word departed from Jesus at Gethsemane. S. John emphatically assures us that there was no such separation. It was the Son of God who was baptized; and it was the Son of God who was crucified: and it is faith in this vital truth that produces brotherly love, that overcomes the world, and is eternal life.

It may reasonably be admitted, however, that there is this large amount of connexion between the 'water and blood' here and the 'blood and water' in the Gospel. Both in a symbolical manner point to the two great sacraments. Thus Tertullian says, " He had *come by means of water and blood,* just as John had written; that He might be baptized by the water, glorified by the blood; to make us in like manner *called* by water, *chosen* by blood. These two baptisms He sent out from the wound in His pierced side, in order that they who believed in His blood might be bathed in the water; they who had been bathed in the water might likewise drink the blood' (*De Bapt.* xvi.).

οὐκ ἐν τῷ ὕδ. μ., ἀλλ. ἐν τῷ ὕδ. κ. ἐν τῷ αἵμ. As R.V., *not* **with the** *water only, but* **with the** *water and* **the** *blood.* The ἐν marks the element or sphere in which the thing is done. The use of ἐν here and

Heb. ix. 25 may, however, come direct from LXX. Comp. εἰσελεύσεται
'Ααρὼν εἰς τὸ ἅγιον ἐν μόσχῳ ἐκ βοῶν περὶ ἁμαρτίας (Lev. xvi. 3), of the
ceremonies on the great Day of Atonement. The Hebrew may mean
' in ', ' with ', or ' by '. The article here in all three places means 'the
water' and ' the blood' already mentioned.

As applied to *us* these words will mean, ' Christ came not merely to
purify by His baptism, but to give new life by His blood; "for the
blood is the life".' In short, all that is said in the Gospel, especially
in chapters iii. and vi., respecting water and blood may be included
here. The Epistle is the companion treatise of the Gospel.

καὶ τὸ πν. ἐστιν τὸ μαρτ. Here again there are great diversities of
interpretation. S. Augustine, who makes the water and blood refer to
the effusions of Christ's side, takes 'the spirit' to mean the spirit
which He committed to His Father at His death (John xix. 30;
Luke xxiii. 46). But in what sense could Christ's human spirit be
said to be 'the Truth'? Far more probably it is the Holy Spirit that
is meant (iii. 24; iv. 13; John i. 32, 33; vii. 39; Rev. ii. 7, 11, 17, 29,
&c.). Bede takes this view and understands the witness of the Spirit
at Christ's baptism to be meant. The *form* of the sentence is exactly
parallel to τὸ πνεῦμά ἐστιν τὸ ζωοποιοῦν (John vi. 63). We might render
in each case, ' The spirit is the life-giver', ' And the Spirit is the
witness-bearer'. The Spirit bears witness in two ways: 1. in Scripture ; 2. by His action on the wills of men. " The evidence for the
Resurrection was not stronger on the Day of Pentecost than it was on
the day before. But the Descent of the Spirit made it morally possible for three thousand converts to do that evidence something like
justice" (Liddon).

τὸ μαρτυροῦν. We have seen already (note on i. 2) that witness to
the truth in order to produce faith is one of S. John's leading thoughts
in Gospel, Epistles, and Revelation. Here it becomes the dominant
thought : the word ' witness' (verb or substantive) occurs ten times in
five verses. In the Gospel we have seven witnesses to Christ; *Scripture* (v. 39—47), the *Baptist* (i. 7), *the Disciples* (xv. 27; xvi. 30),
Christ's works (v. 36; x. 25, 38), *Christ's words* (viii. 14, 18; xviii. 37),
the Father (v. 37; viii. 18), *the Spirit* (xv. 26). Of these seven three
are specially mentioned in the Epistle, *the Disciples* in i. 2, *the Father*
in vv. 9, 10, and *the Spirit* here; but to these are added two more, *the
water* and *the blood*.

ὅτι τὸ πν. κ.τ.λ. It would be possible to translate ' It is the Spirit
that beareth witness *that* the Spirit is the truth ': but this self-attes-
tation of the Spirit would have no relation to the context. (Comp.
ii. 12—14, where ὅτι is six times capable of either rendering.) It is
the witnesses to Christ, to the identity of Jesus with the Son of God,
that S. John is marshalling before us. It is **because** *the Spirit is the
Truth* that His testimony is irrefragable : He can neither deceive nor
be deceived. He is ' the Spirit of Truth' (John xiv. 16; xv. 26), and
He glorifies the Christ, taking of His and declaring it unto the Church
(John xvi. 14).

There is a remarkable Latin reading, *quoniam Christus est veritas,* 'It is the Spirit that beareth witness that *the Christ* is the Truth,' but it has no authority. Westcott suspects a confusion between XPC (Χριστός) and SPS (*Spiritus*).

7. For a discussion of the famous interpolation respecting the Three Heavenly Witnesses, see Appendix D. The Revisers have only performed an imperative duty in excluding it from both text and margin. Three facts ought never to be forgotten: and one of them singly would be decisive; combined they are irresistible. 1. *Not a single Greek Codex earlier than the fourteenth century* contains the passage. 2. *Not one of the Greek or Latin Fathers* ever quotes the passage *in conducting the controversies about the Trinity* in the first four and a half centuries. 3. *No Version earlier than the fifth century* contains the passage, and, excepting the Latin, none earlier than the fourteenth.

τρεῖς εἰσὶν οἱ μαρτ. *Those who bear witness are three.* For μαρτυρεῖν see on i. 2. S. John does not say merely οἱ μάρτυρες but οἱ μαρτυροῦντες. They are not merely witnesses who might be called: they are perpetually delivering their testimony. The masculine points to the personality of the Spirit. The Apostle is answering the misgivings of those who fancied that when he, the last of the Apostles, was taken from them, the Church would possess only second-hand evidence, and a tradition ever growing fainter, as to the Person and Mission of the Christ. 'Nay', says he, 'evidence at first-hand is ever present, and each believer has it in himself' (*v.* 10). Comp. John xv. 26.

It is very doubtful whether the Trinity is even remotely symbolized. Perhaps S. John wishes to give the full complement of evidence recognised by law (Matt. xviii. 16; 2 Cor. xiii. 1; Deut. xix. 15; comp. John viii. 17).

8. τὸ ὕδωρ καὶ τὸ αἷμα. These of course have the same meaning as before; Christ's Baptism and Death. "The real value of our Lord's baptism and His death may be estimated by supposing that neither had taken place, and that our Lord had appeared on His mission without openly confessing His mission from God in submitting to the baptism of John; or that He had died quietly, as other men die" (Jelf).

καὶ οἱ τρεῖς εἰς τὸ ἕν εἰσιν. Literally, *and the three are* (united) *into the one;* or, *are for the one* object of establishing this truth. This may mean either that they are joined so as to become one witness, or that they co-operate in producing one result. "The trinity of witnesses furnish one testimony". 'To be one' (ἓν εἶναι) occurs John x. 30; xvii. 11, 21, 22, and (εἶς ἐστε) Gal. iii. 28: 'into one' (εἰς ἕν) occurs John xi. 52; xvii. 23: but 'to be into one' or 'to be into the one' occurs nowhere else in N.T. Τὸ ἕν here has been made into an argument for the genuineness of *v.* 7. It is said that '*the* one' plainly implies that 'one' has preceded. But this lands us in absurdity by making 'one' in *v.* 8 mean the same as 'one' in *v.* 7. 'One' in *v.* 7 means 'one Substance', the 'Unity in Trinity'. But what sense can

'The spirit, the water, and the blood agree in the Unity in Trinity' yield?

9—11. S. John's characteristic repetition of the word 'witness' is greatly weakened in A.V. by the substitution of 'testify' in *v.* 9, and 'record' in *vv.* 10 and 11: see on i. 2; ii. 15, 24; iv. 5.

9. εἰ τ. μαρτ. τ. ἀνθρ. λαμβάνομεν. '*If* we receive such testimony— and it is quite notorious that we do so'. Comp. εἰ οὕτως ὁ Θεὸς ἠγά- πησεν ἡμᾶς (iv. 11). In neither case does εἰ imply any doubt about the fact. See on 2 John 10. The argument is *a fortiori* and reads like an echo of that of Christ to the Pharisees 'In your law it is written that the witness of two *men* is true' (John viii. 17); how much more there- fore the witness of the Father and the Son? For λαμβάνειν in the sense of 'accept as valid', comp. John iii. 11, 32, 33.

ὅτι αὕτη ἐστὶν ἡ μαρτ. Because the witness of God is this (see on i. 5). This first ὅτι is elliptical. 'I say the witness of God, *because...*', or, 'I use this argument, *because...*', Winer, 774. The second ὅτι (אAB and most Versions) is less easy, and hence the corruption to the simple ἥν. This ὅτι may be epexegetic of αὕτη, or epexegetic of μαρτυ- ρία, or parallel to the first ὅτι. The first of these possibilities seems best: that He hath borne witness. 'I appeal to the witness of God, *because* (ὅτι) the witness of God is this, that (ὅτι) He hath borne witness concerning His Son'. Μαρτυρεῖν περὶ is frequent in the Gospel (i. 8, 15; ii. 25; v. 31, 32, 36, 37, 39, &c.). The perfect, as so constantly in S. John, gives the permanent result of a past act: the testimony still abides. Comp. ὁ ἑωρακὼς μεμαρτύρηκεν...ἵνα καὶ ὑμεῖς πιστεύσητε (John xix. 35).

10. ὁ πιστεύων εἰς τ. υἱὸν τ. Θ. The present participle again indi- cates what is habitual: not a transitory conviction (ὁ πιστεύσας), but a permanent attitude of faith (ii. 10, 22, 23; iii. 3, 4, 6, 7, 8, &c.). For the first time in this Epistle we have the full phrase πιστεύειν εἰς, of which S. John is so fond in his Gospel, where it occurs nearly 40 times. Elsewhere in N.T. it occurs only about 10 times. It expresses the strongest confidence and trust; faith moves towards and reposes on its object. Whereas 'to believe a person' (πιστεύειν τινί) need mean no more than to believe what he says (iv. 1), 'to believe *on* or *in* a person' (πιστεύειν εἴς τινα) means to have full trust in his character.

ἔχει τὴν μαρτυρίαν. Some authorities add τοῦ Θεοῦ, which is right as an interpretation, though not as a part of the text. He has it as an abiding possession (John v. 38; Heb. x. 34): ἔχει does not mean merely 'he accepts it'. Comp. 'The Spirit Himself beareth witness with our spirit, that we are children of God' (Rom. viii. 16); 'God sent forth the Spirit of His Son into our hearts, crying, Abba, Father' (Gal. iv. 6).

ἐν αὐτῷ. The differences of reading here, ἐν αὐτῷ, ἐν αὑτῷ, ἐν ἑαυτῷ, are immaterial: 'in him' in this context cannot mean anything but 'in himself.' The external witness faithfully accepted becomes internal certitude. Our faith in the Divinity of Christ attests its own Divine origin, for we could not have obtained it otherwise than from God. "The human mind is made for truth, and so rests in truth, as it cannot rest in falsehood. When then it once becomes possessed of a truth, what is to dispossess it? But this is to be certain; therefore once certitude, always certitude. If certitude in any matter be the termination of all doubt or fear about its truth, and an unconditional conscious adherence to it, it carries with it an inward assurance, strong though implicit, that it shall never fail" (J. H. Newman).

ὁ μὴ πιστεύων τῷ Θεῷ. He that has not even enough faith to induce him to believe what God says (see first note on this verse). There are great diversities of reading here; 'God,' 'the Son', 'the Son of God', 'His Son', 'Jesus Christ': of these 'God' (אBKLP) is certainly to be preferred. The others have arisen from a wish to make 'he that believeth not' more exactly balance 'he that believeth'. But, as we have repeatedly seen, S. John's antitheses seldom balance exactly. Yet it is by no means impossible that all five are wrong, and that we ought simply to read '*He that believeth not* hath made Him a liar': comp. John iii. 18, of which this verse seems to be an echo. In 'he that believeth not', the case is stated quite generally and indefinitely (ὁ μὴ πιστεύων): the Apostle is not pointing at some one person who was known as not believing (ὁ οὐ πιστεύων); comp. iii. 10, 14; iv. 8, 20; v. 12. But in the second clause the point of view becomes one of fact and not of mere possibility; ὅτι οὐ πεπίστευκεν. Contrast ὅτι μὴ πεπίστευκεν (John iii. 18). Winer, 594. For the antithetic parallelism comp. *v.* 12; ii. 4, 27.

ψεύστην πεποίηκεν αὐτόν. See on i. 10. He has given God the lie as to His whole scheme of redemption. οὐ πεπίστευκεν...μεμαρτύρηκεν. As R.V., hath *not* believed in *the* witness *that* God hath *borne*. See on i. 2. The perfect in both cases indicates a permanent result. He has been and remains an unbeliever in the witness which God has given and continually supplies concerning His Son. Πιστεύειν εἰς τὴν μαρτυρίαν occurs nowhere else in N.T. Usually we have πιστ. τῇ μ. See on iii. 23.

11. καὶ αὕτη ἐστὶν ἡ μαρτ. As R.V., And the witness is this, as in *v.* 9: this is what the external witness of God, when it is internally appropriated by the believer, consists in; viz. the Divine gift of eternal life.

ζωὴν αἰώνιον. See on i. 2 and on John iii. 36; v. 24. Ἔδωκεν is literally gave; but perhaps this is a case in which the English perfect may represent the Greek aorist. But at any rate 'gave' must not be weakened into 'offered', still less into 'promised'. The believer already possesses eternal life.

καὶ αὕτη ἡ ζωὴ κ.τ.λ. This is a new independent statement, coordinate with the first clause: it is not, like the second clause, dependent upon the first. Eternal life has its seat and source in the Son, who is the 'Prince' or 'Author of life' (Acts iii. 15): see on John i. 4; v. 26.

12. A deduction from the preceding clause. If the Son has the life in Himself, then whoever has the Son has the life, and no man can have the one without the other. 'To have the Son' must be compared with 'to have the Father' in ii. 23. In both cases 'have' signifies possession in living union through faith.

ἔχει τὴν ζωήν. As R.V., *hath* the *life*; not merely 'the life just mentioned', or 'the life which God gave us', but the life which in the full sense of the word is such.

ὁ μὴ ἔχων. As in *v.* 10, the negative alternative is stated generally and indefinitely (μή not οὐ). The addition of τοῦ θεοῦ is neither fortuitous nor pleonastic. Those who possess Him know that He is the Son of God; those who do not, need to be reminded Whose Son it is that they reject.

The verse constitutes another close parallel with the Gospel: comp. the last words of the Baptist (John iii. 36).

13—21. CONCLUSION AND SUMMARY.

Some modern writers consider that *v.* 13 constitutes the conclusion of the Epistle, the remainder (14—21) being a postscript or appendix, analogous to chap. xxi. of the Gospel, and possibly by another hand. Some go so far as to conjecture that the same person added chap. xxi. to the Gospel and the last nine verses to the Epistle after the Apostle's death.

Not much can be urged in favour of these views. No MS. or version seems to exist in which these concluding verses are wanting. Tertullian quotes *vv.* 16, 17, 18 (*De Pudicitia* xix.) and *v.* 21 (*De Corona* x.): Clement of Alexandria quotes *vv.* 16, 17 (*Strom.* II. xv.); and both these writers in quoting mention S. John by name. This shews that at the end of the second century these verses were an integral part of the Epistle. Against such evidence as this, arbitrary statements that the division of sins into sins unto death and sins not unto death, the sternness of *v.* 19, and the warning against idolatry, are unlike S. John, will not have much weight. The diction is S. John's throughout, and some of the fundamental ideas of the Epistle reappear in these concluding verses. Moreover, the connexion with the first half of the chapter is so close, that there is no reason for supposing that, while unquestionably by S. John himself, yet it is, like chap. xxi. of the Gospel, a subsequent addition to the original work. Indeed so close is the connexion with what precedes that some commentators consider only the last four verses, or even only the last verse, to be the proper conclusion of the Epistle.

The Conclusion, as here arranged, falls into three parts. In the first, three main thoughts are retouched; faith in the Son of God, eternal life, and love of the brethren shewing itself in intercession (13—17). In the second, three great facts of which believers have certain knowledge are restated (18—20). In the third, a farewell practical warning is given (*v.* 21).

13—17. INTERCESSORY LOVE THE FRUIT OF FAITH AND OF THE
POSSESSION OF LIFE.

13—17. Eternal life, faith, and brotherly love shewing boldness in
intercession, are the leading ideas of this section. We have had most
of these topics before, and the section is more or less of a recapitulation. But S. John "cannot even recapitulate without the introduction of new and most important thoughts" (F. W. Farrar); and the
combination of the idea of boldness in prayer (iii. 21, 22) with that of
love of the brethren leads to very fruitful results.

13. ταῦτα ἔγραψα. 'These things' will cover the whole Epistle,
and such is probably the meaning, as in i. 4, where S. John states the
purpose of his Epistle in words which are explained by what he says
here: there is nothing there or here, as there is in ii. 26, to limit
'these things' to what immediately precedes. As in ii. 21, 26, ἔγραψα
is the epistolary aorist, which may be represented in English either by
the present or the perfect.

In the remainder of the verse the divergences of reading are very
considerable, and authorities are much divided. The original text
seems to be that represented by ℵ¹B, which has been adopted in R.V.
These things have I written unto you, **that ye may know that ye have
eternal life,—unto you that believe on the name of the Son of God.**
The awkwardness of the explanatory clause added at the end has led
to various expedients for making the whole run more smoothly. Comp.
the similarly added explanation in *v.* 16; τοῖς ἁμαρτάνουσιν μὴ πρὸς
θάνατον.

ἵνα εἰδῆτε ὅτι ζ. ἔχ. αἰ. At the opening of the Epistle S. John said
'These things we write that our joy may be fulfilled' (i. 4). The
context there shews what constitutes this joy. It is the consciousness
of fellowship with God and His Son and His saints; in other words it
is the conscious possession of eternal life (John xvii. 3). Thus the
Introduction and Conclusion of the Epistle mutually explain one
another. This verse should also be compared with its parallel in the
Gospel (xx. 31), a passage which has probably influenced some of the
various readings here. We see at once the similar yet not identical
purposes of Gospel and Epistle. S. John writes his Gospel, 'that ye
may *have life*'; he writes his Epistle 'that ye may *know* that ye have
life'. The one leads to the obtaining of the boon; the other to the
joy of knowing that the boon has been obtained. The one is to produce faith; the other is to make clear the fruits of faith. For πιστ.
εἰς τὸ ὄνομα see on *v.* 10 and on iii. 23.

14. καὶ αὕτη ἐστὶν ἡ παρ. *And the* **boldness** *that we have* **towards**
Him is this: see on i. 5 and ii. 28. For the fourth and last time in
the Epistle the Apostle touches on the subject of the Christian's
'boldness'. Twice he speaks of it in connexion with the Day of
Judgment (ii. 28; iv. 17); twice in connexion with approaching God
in prayer (iii. 21, 22 and here). In the present case it is with special
reference to intercessory prayer that the subject is retouched. Thus
two more leading ideas of the Epistle meet in this recapitulation,

boldness towards God and brotherly love; for it is love of the brethren
which induces us to pray for them. For the difference between αἰτεῖσθαι
and ἐρωτᾶν see on *v.* 16. The difference between αἰτεῖσθαι and αἰτεῖν
is not great, as is seen in *v.* 15: but the middle rather implies that
the request in some way is for the gratification of the petitioner.
κατὰ τὸ θέλημα αὐτοῦ. This is the only limitation, and it is an
exceedingly gracious limitation. His will is always for His children's
good, and therefore it is only when they ignorantly ask for what is not
for their good that their prayers are denied. Comp. S. Paul's case,
2 Cor. xii. 9. 'Ακούει of course means that He hears and *grants* what
we ask (John ix. 31; xi. 41, 42). Comp. 'The desire of the righteous
shall be granted' (Prov. x. 24).

15. ἐὰν οἴδαμεν ὅτι ἀκούει...οἴδ. ὅτι ἔχομεν. The one certitude
depends on the other: if we trust God's goodness, we are perfectly
certain that our trust is not misplaced. Comp. πάντα ὅσα προσεύχεσθε
καὶ αἰτεῖσθε, πιστεύετε ὅτι ἐλάβετε, καὶ ἔσται ὑμῖν (Mark xi. 24). Here
the present ἔχομεν states the fact (comp. Matt. vii. 8); in Mark xi. 24
the future ἔσται states the result of the fact. Our petitions are granted
at once: the results of the granting are perceived in the future. For
the exceptional construction **ἐὰν οἴδαμεν** comp. ἐὰν δὲ ἀπὸ τῶν πετεινῶν
ὁλοκάρπωμα **προσφέρει** δῶρον τῷ κυρίῳ (Lev. i. 14): **ἐὰν** ὑμεῖς **στήκετε ἐν**
κυρίῳ (1 Thess. iii. 8). In Rom. xiv. 8 ἀποθνήσκομεν seems to be a
false reading: so also ἐλευθερώσει in John viii. 36. But in Acts viii. 31
ὁδηγήσει is probably correct. Winer, 369.

ἃ ᾐτήκαμεν. *Which we have asked of Him,* as R.V. Note the
change from middle to active without change of meaning. 'Απ' αὐτου
is amphibolous: it may go either with ἔχομεν or ᾐτήκαμεν. The order
favours the latter connexion; but αἰτεῖν is more commonly followed
by παρά (John iv. 9; Acts iii. 2; ix. 2; James i. 5) than by ἀπό. Hence
the confusion of readings here and Matt. xx. 20.

16. 'The prayer of faith' is all-prevailing when it is in accordance
with God's will. This is the sole limit as regards prayer on our own
behalf. Is there any other limit in the case of prayer on behalf of
another? Yes, there is that other's own will: this constitutes a further
limitation. Man's will has been endowed by God with such royal
freedom, that not even His will coerces it. Still less, therefore, can a
brother's prayer coerce it. If a human will has deliberately and obstinately resisted God, and persists in doing so, we are debarred from
our usual certitude. Against a rebel will even the prayer of faith in
accordance with God's will (for of course God desires the submission of
the rebel) may be offered in vain.—For exhortations to intercession
elsewhere in N.T. see 1 Thess. v. 25; Heb. xiii. 18, 19; James v. 14—
20; comp. Phil. i. 4.

τὸν ἀδελφόν. Here 'brother' must mean 'fellow-*Christian*', not
any human being, whether Christian or not.

ἁμαρτάνοντα ἁμαρτίαν. As R.V., *sinning a sin.* The supposed case
is one in which the sinner is seen in the very act. No earlier English
Version marks the participle; neither does Luther, nor the Vulgate

(*peccare peccatum*). Ἀμαρτάνειν ἀμαρτίαν occurs nowhere else in N.T.; but περὶ τῆς ἁμαρτίας αὐτοῦ ἧς ἥμαρτε occurs repeatedly in LXX. (Lev. v. 6, 10, 13; Ezek. xviii. 24.)

αἰτήσει. Future equivalent to imperative; *he shall ask*, as A.V. and R.V.: or, *he will ask;* i.e. a Christian in such a case is sure to pray for his erring brother. The latter seems preferable. Comp. τότε νηστεύσουσιν ἐν ἐκείνῃ τῇ ἡμέρᾳ (Mark ii. 20); i.e. the children of the bridechamber not only can fast, but will fast, when the Bridegroom is taken away.

δώσει αὐτῷ ζωήν. Ambiguous. The nominative may be either God or the intercessor; and αὐτῷ may be either the intercessor or the sinner for whom he intercedes. If the latter alternatives be taken, we may compare 'he shall save a soul from death' (James v. 20). Commentators are much divided. On the one hand it is urged that throughout Scripture asking is man's part and giving God's: but, on the other hand, when two verbs are connected so closely as these, 'will ask and will give' (αἰτήσει καὶ δώσει), it seems rather violent to give them different nominatives; 'he will ask and God will give'. It seems better to translate, *he will ask and will give him life,—them that sin not unto death.* 'Them' is in apposition to 'him', the clause being an explanation rather awkwardly added, similar to that at the end of *v.* 13. If 'God' be inserted, 'them' is the *dativus commodi;* 'God will grant the intercessor life *for* those who sin'. The change to the plural makes the statement more general: 'sinning not unto death' is not likely to be an isolated case. The New Vulgate is here exceedingly free; *petat, et dabitur ei vita peccanti non ad mortem.* Tertullian also ignores the change of number; *postulabit, et dabit ei vitam dominus qui non ad mortem delinquit.* The Old Vulgate has *petit, et dabit ei vitam, peccantibus non ad mortem.*

ἔστιν ἁμαρτία πρὸς θάν. *There is sin unto death;* we have no τις or μία, a fact which is against the supposition that any *act* of sin is intended. In that case would not S. John have named it, that the faithful might avoid it, and also know when it had been committed? The following explanations of 'sin unto death' may be safely rejected. 1. Sin punished by the law with death. 2. Sin punished by Divine visitation with death or sickness. 3. Sin punished by the Church with excommunication. As a help to a right explanation we may get rid of the idea which some commentators assume, that 'sin unto death' is a sin which can be *recognised* by those among whom the one who commits it lives. S. John's very guarded language points the other way. He implies that *some* sins may be known to be '*not* unto death': he neither says nor implies that all 'sin unto death' can be known as such. As a further help we may remember that no sin, if repented of, can be too great for God's mercy. Hence S. John does not speak even of this sin as 'fatal' or 'mortal', but as '*unto* death' (πρὸς θάνατον). Death is its natural, but not its absolutely inevitable consequence. It is possible to close the heart against the influences of God's Spirit so obstinately and persistently that repentance becomes a moral impossibility. Just as the body may starve itself to such an extent

as to make the digestion, or even the reception, of food impossible ; so
the soul may go on refusing offers of grace until the very power to receive grace perishes. Such a condition is necessarily sin, and 'sin unto
death'. No passing over out of death into life (iii. 14) is any longer
(without a miracle of grace) possible. 'Sin unto death', therefore, is
not any *act* of sin, however heinous, but a *state* or *habit* of sin wilfully
chosen and persisted in: it is constant and consummate opposition to
God. In the phraseology of this Epistle we might say that it is the
deliberate and persistent preference of darkness to light, of falsehood
to truth, of sin to righteousness, of the world to the Father, of spiritual
death to eternal life.

οὐ περὶ ἐκείνης λέγω ἵνα ἐρωτήσῃ. **Not concerning that do I say that
he should make request.** This reproduces the telling order of the
Greek; it avoids the ambiguity which lurks in 'pray for it'; it preserves the emphatic ἐκείνης; and marks better the difference between
the verb (αἰτεῖν) previously rendered 'ask' (*vv.* 14, 15, 16) and the one
(ἐρωτᾶν) here rendered in A. V. 'pray'. Of the two verbs the latter is
the *less* suppliant (see on John xiv. 16), whereas 'pray' is *more* suppliant than 'ask'. Two explanations of the change of verb are suggested. 1. The Apostle does not advise request, much less does he
advise urgent supplication in such a case. 2. He uses the less humble
word to express a request which seems to savour of presumption.
See on 2 John 5. With ἐκείνης here, indicating something distinct,
alien, and horrible, comp. ἐκεῖνος of Judas (John xiii. 27, 30).

(1) Note carefully that S. John, even in this extreme case, *does not
forbid intercession:* all he says is that he does not command it. For
one who sins an ordinary sin we may intercede in faith with certainty
that a prayer so fully in harmony with God's will is heard. The sinner
will receive grace to repent. But where the sinner has made repentance impossible S. John does not encourage us to intercede. Comp.
Jer. vii. 16 ; xiv. 11. Yet, as S. Bernard says, *Fides aliquando recipit,
quod oratio non praesumit,* and he instances the sisters' faith in 'Lord,
if Thou hadst been here my brother had not died'.

(2) Note also that, whilst distinguishing between deadly and not
deadly sin, *he gives us no criterion by which we may distinguish the
one from the other.* He thus condemns rather than sanctions those
attempts which casuists have made to tabulate sins under the heads
of 'mortal' and 'venial'. Sins differ indefinitely in their intensity
and effect on the soul, ending at one end of the scale in 'sin unto
death'; and the gradations depend not merely or chiefly on the sinful
act, but on the *motive* which prompted it, and the *feeling* (whether of
sorrow or delight) which the recollection of it evokes. Further than
this it is not safe to define or dogmatize. This seems to be intimated
by what is told us in the next verse. Two facts are to be borne in
mind, and beyond them we need not pry.

17. πᾶσα ἀδικία ἁμαρτία ἐστίν. A warning against *carelessness*
about breaches of duty, whether in ourselves or in others. All such
things are sin and need the cleansing blood of Christ (i. 9; ii. 2).
Here, therefore, is a wide enough field for brotherly intercession. The

statement serves also as a farewell declaration against the Gnostic doctrine that to the enlightened Christian declensions from righteousness involve no sin.   Comp. the definition of sin as lawlessness in iii. 4.

ἔστιν ἁμαρτία οὐ πρὸς θάν.   As before, *there is sin not unto death*. Luther has *etliche Sünde* here, *eine Sünde* in v. 16: Wiclif, Purvey, Tyndale, Cranmer and the Genevan omit the indefinite article here, although they insert it in v. 16.   While the preceding statement is a warning against carelessness, this is a warning against *despair*, whether about ourselves or about others.   Not all sin is mortal:—an answer by anticipation to the heathen rigour of Stoicism and to the unchristian rigour of Montanism and Novatianism.

Note the change in vv. 16, 17 from ἁμαρτ. μὴ πρὸς θάν. (in a supposed case) to ἁμαρτ. οὐ π. θ. (in a statement of fact).   Tertullian, the Vulgate, Harcleian Syriac, and Thebaic omit the negative and read *et est peccatum* (or *delictum*) *ad mortem*.

18—20.   THE SUM OF THE CHRISTIAN'S KNOWLEDGE.

18—20.   The Epistle now draws rapidly to a close.   Having briefly, yet with much new material, retouched some of the leading ideas of the Epistle, eternal life, faith in Christ, and boldness in prayer united with brotherly love (13—17), the Apostle now goes on to emphasize once more three great facts about which Christians have sure knowledge, facts respecting themselves, their relations to the evil one and his kingdom, and their relations to the Son of God.   Each verse is a condensation of what has been said elsewhere.   Ver. 18 is a combination of iii. 9 with ii. 13; *v.* 19 a combination of the substance of i. 6; ii. 8, 15 and iii. 10, 13: *v.* 20 condenses the substance of iv. 9—11 and v. 1— 12.   "Hence we have in these last verses a final emphasis laid on the fundamental principles on which the Epistle rests; that *through the mission of the Lord Jesus Christ we have fellowship with God; that this fellowship protects us from sin; and that it establishes us in a relation of utter opposition to the world*" (Haupt).   Fellowship with one another is not mentioned again, but it is included in the threefold 'we know'.

18.   οἴδαμεν.   This confident expression of the certitude of Christian faith stands at the beginning of each of these three verses, and is the link which binds them together.   We have had it twice before (iii. 2, 14; comp. ii. 20, 21; iii. 5, 15): and perhaps in all cases it is meant to mark the contrast between the real knowledge of the believer, which is based upon Divine revelation in Christ, and the spurious knowledge of the Gnostic, which is based upon human intelligence.

The triple οἴδαμεν at the close of the Epistle confirms the view that John xxi. 24 is by the Apostle's own hand, and not added by the Ephesian elders.

πᾶς ὁ γεγενν. ἐκ τ. Θεοῦ.   As R.V., *whosoever is* **begotten** *of God*. A.V. changes the verb ('born', 'begotten'), which does not change in the Greek, and does not change the tense, which does change in a very remarkable way (γεγεννημένος, γεννηθείς).

οὐχ ἁμαρτάνει. To the *non peccat* of the Vulgate Bede adds *peccatum videlicet ad mortem;* which is clearly not S. John's meaning. The condition of Divine sonship is incompatible, not merely with sin unto death, but with sin of any description. The sentence is a return to the statement made in iii. 9, where see notes. Once more the Apostle is not afraid of an apparent contradiction (see on ii. 15). He has just been saying that if a Christian sins his brother will intercede for him; and now he says that the child of God does not sin. The one statement refers to possible but exceptional facts; the other to the habitual state. A child of God may sin; but his normal condition is one of resistance to sin. " Two things a genuine Christian never does. He never makes light of any known sin, and he never admits it to be invincible " (Liddon).

ὁ γεννηθεὶς ἐκ τ. Θεοῦ τηρεῖ αὐτόν. **The Begotten** *of God keepeth* **him.** The interpretation of ὁ γεννηθεὶς and the reading as to the pronoun cannot either of them be determined with certainty. The latter is the easier question and it throws light on the former. 'Him' (αὐτόν), on the high authority of A¹B and the Vulgate, seems to be rightly preferred by most editors to 'himself' (ἑαυτόν). This 'him' is the child of God spoken of in the first clause: who is it that 'keepeth him'? Not the child of God himself, as A.V. leads us to suppose and many commentators explain, but the Son of God, the Only-Begotten. On any other interpretation S. John's marked change of tense appears arbitrary and confusing. Recipients of the Divine birth are always spoken of by S. John both in his Gospel and in his Epistle in the *perfect* participle (ὁ γεγεννημένος or τὸ γεγεννημένον); iii. 9; v. 1, 4; John iii. 6, 8; also the first clause here. In the present clause he abruptly changes to the *aorist* participle (ὁ γεννηθείς), which he uses nowhere else (comp. Matt. i. 20; Gal. iv. 29). The force of the two tenses here seems to be this: the perfect expresses a permanent relation begun in the past and continued in the present; the aorist expresses a timeless relation, a mere fact: the one signifies the child of God as opposed to those who have not become His children; the other signifies the Son of God as opposed to the evil one. It is some confirmation of this view that in the Constantinopolitan Creed, commonly called the Nicene Creed, 'begotten of the Father' (τὸν ἐκ τοῦ Πατρὸς γεννηθέντα, is the same form of expression as that used here for 'begotten of God' (ὁ γεννηθεὶς ἐκ τοῦ Θεοῦ). Moreover this interpretation produces another harmony between Gospel and Epistle. Christ both directly by His power and indirectly by His intercession 'keepeth' the children of God: 'I *kept* them in Thy Name' (xvii. 12); 'I pray not that Thou shouldest take them out of the world but that Thou shouldest *keep them from the evil one*' (xvii. 15).

The Latin renderings are remarkable: *non peccat; sed generatio Dei conservat eum, et malignus non tangit eum* (Augustine, Jerome, Vulgate); and *peccatum non facit; quia nativitas Dei custodit illum, et diabolus non tangit illum* (Chromatius).

ὁ πονηρὸς οὐχ ἅπτεται αὐτοῦ. As R.V., **The evil** *one toucheth him* **not.** A.V. here as in i. 2 ('*that* eternal life') exaggerates the article into a pronoun. For ὁ πονηρός see on ii. 13: strangely enough the Genevan here has 'that wycked *man*'. 'Toucheth him not' is somewhat too strong for οὐχ ἅπτεται αὐτοῦ. "Ἅπτεσθαι, as distinct from θιγγάνειν (Heb. xi. 28; xii. 20), is 'to lay hold of'; and one may sometimes touch where one cannot lay hold. See on John xx. 17. The verb is very frequent in the Synoptists, elsewhere rare. In Col. ii. 21 the A.V. exactly reverses the climax by translating μὴ ἅψῃ 'touch not' and μηδὲ θίγῃς 'handle not'. Here the meaning is that the evil one may assault, but he gets no hold. 'No one shall snatch them out of My hand' (John x. 28). 'The ruler of the world cometh: and he hath nothing in Me' (John xiv. 30). Therefore whoever is in Christ is safe.

19. οἴδαμεν. The conjunction must be omitted on abundant authority. This introduces the second great fact of which the believer has sure knowledge. And, as so often, S. John's divisions are not sharp, but the parts intermingle. The second fact is partly anticipated in the first; the first is partly repeated in the second. Christians know that as children of God they are preserved by His Son from the devil. Then what do they know about the world, and their relation to the world? *They know that they are of God and the whole world lieth in* **the evil one**. It remains in his power. It has *not* passed over, as they have done, out of death into life; but it abides in the evil one, who is its ruler (John xii. 31; xiv. 30; xvi. 11), as the Christian abides in Christ. It is clear therefore that the severance between the Church and the world ought to be, and tends to be, as total as that between God and the evil one. The preceding verse and the antithesis to God, to say nothing of ii. 13, 14; iv. 4, make it quite clear that 'the evil' (τῷ πονηρῷ) is here masculine and not neuter. The Vulgate has *in maligno*, not *in malo*. Tyndale and Cranmer have 'is altogether set on wickedness', which is doubly or trebly wrong. Note once more that the opposition is not exact, but goes beyond what precedes. The evil one doth not obtain hold of the child of God: he not only obtains hold over the world, but has it wholly within his embrace. No similar use of κεῖσθαι ἐν occurs in N.T. Comp. Sophocles *Oed. Col.* 248.

20. οἴδαμεν δέ. This introduces the third great fact of which believers have certain knowledge. The first two Christian certitudes are that the believer as a child of God progresses under Christ's protection towards the sinlessness of God, while the unbelieving world lies wholly in the power of the evil one. Therefore the Christian knows that both in the moral nature which he inherits, and in the moral sphere in which he lives, there is an ever-widening gulf between him and the world. But his knowledge goes beyond this. Even in the intellectual sphere, in which the Gnostic claims to have such advantages, the Christian is, by Christ's bounty, superior.

The 'and' (δέ) brings the whole to a conclusion: comp. Heb. xiii. 20, 22. Or it may mark the opposition between the world's evil case and what is stated here; in which case δέ should be rendered 'but'. " Since the two preceding verses are opposed, as *asyndeta*, to the 20th, which is connected with them by δέ, we may at once infer that *vv*. 18,

19 contain two more or less parallel thoughts, to which *v.* 20 presents
one that corresponds to both. And so we find it. The preceding
verses stated that we know in what relation our Divine sonship places
us to sin and to the world. Here it is unfolded that we are conscious
of the *ground* of this relation to both " (Haupt).

ἥκει καὶ δέδωκεν. Just as ἥκει includes the notions both of 'hath
come' and 'is here', so δέδωκεν includes those of 'hath given' and 'the
gift abides'. It is the present result rather than the past act that is
prominent.

διάνοιαν. Intellectual power, the capacity for receiving knowledge.
The word occurs nowhere else in S. John's writings: γνῶσις does not
occur at all: σύνεσις occurs only Rev. xiii. 18; xvii. 9. Διάνοια indicates
that faculty of understanding and reflection which S. Peter tells his
readers (1 Pet. i. 13) to brace up and keep ever ready for use. Comp.
2 Pet. iii. 1 and a beautiful passage in Plato's *Phaedo* 66 A.

ἵνα γινώσκομεν. The force of this strange construction seems to be
'that we may continue to recognise, as we do now'. Such combina-
tions are not rare in late Greek. Comp. John xvii. 3; 1 Cor. iv. 6;
Gal. iv. 17. But in John xvii. 3 Westcott and Hort and the Revisers
retain γινώσκωσιν. It is possible that the construction is the result of
imperfect pronunciation. The subjunctive in certain cases was perhaps
pronounced like the indicative and then written instead of it. The
future indicative after ἵνα is comparatively common. Winer, 362.
Note that it is the *appropriation* of the knowledge that is emphasized
(γινώσκομεν), not, as at the opening of these three verses, the *possession*
of it (οἴδαμεν). In ἵνα γινώσκομεν τὸν ἀληθινόν we have another remarkable parallel with Christ's Prayer: ἵνα γινώσκουσίν σε τὸν μόνον
ἀληθινὸν Θεόν (John xvii. 3). For ἀληθινός see on ii. 8. Ὁ ἀληθινὸς
here is not equivalent to ὁ ἀψευδὴς Θεός (Tit. i. 2): the contrast is not
with the father of lies, but with the spurious gods of the heathen
(*v.* 21). What is the Gnostic's claim to superior knowledge in comparison to our certitude of such a fact as this? We know that we
have the Divine gift of intelligence by means of which we attain to the
knowledge of the *very* God, a personal God who embraces and sustains
us in His Son. Christianity is not, as Gnostics held, only one of
many attempts made by man to communicate with the Infinite. It
is in possession of 'the Truth'. The Christian *knows* (not merely
gropes after) his God and his Redeemer.

καί ἐσμεν ἐν τῷ ἀληθινῷ. Here, as in iii. 1, the Vulgate and many
other Latin authorities make καί ἐσμεν depend upon the preceding ἵνα
(*et simus*): wrongly in both cases. The new clause is a fresh statement clinching what precedes. Τῷ ἀληθινῷ means God, as in the
previous clause. It is needlessly arbitrary to change the meaning
and make this refer to Christ. ' The Son has given us understanding
by which to attain to knowledge of the Father'. Instead of resuming
'And we do *know* the Father', the Apostle makes an advance and
says: 'And we *are in* the Father'. Knowledge has become fellowship
(i. 3; ii. 3—5). God has appeared as man; God has spoken as man

to man ; and the Christian faith, which is the one absolute certainty
for man, the one means of reuniting him to God, is the result.
For ἐν τῷ ἀλ. the Thebaic has 'in the Life'.

ἐν τῷ υἱῷ αὐτοῦ. Omit 'even' which has been inserted in A.V. and
R.V. to make 'in Him that is true' refer to Christ. This last clause
explains how it is that we are in the Father, viz. by being in the Son.
Comp. ii. 23 ; John i. 18; xiv. 9; xvii. 21, 23. Tyndale boldly turns
the second 'in' into 'through'; 'we are *in* him that is true, *through*
his sonne Jesu Christ'. We have had similar explanatory additions
in *vv.* 13, 16. A and the Vulgate omit 'Jesus Christ'.

οὗτός ἐστιν ὁ ἀληθινὸς Θεός. It is impossible to determine with
certainty whether οὗτος refers to the Father, the *principal* substantive
of the previous sentence, or to Jesus Christ, the *nearest* substantive.
That S. John teaches the Divinity of Jesus Christ both in Epistle and
Gospel is so manifest, that a text more or less in favour of the doctrine need not be the subject of heated controversy. The following
considerations are in favour of referring οὗτος to *Christ*. 1. Jesus
Christ is the subject last mentioned. 2. The Father having been
twice called 'the true One' in the previous verse, to proceed to say of
Him 'This is the true God' is somewhat tautological. 3. It is Christ
who both in this Epistle (i. 2; v. 12) and also in the Gospel (xi. 25;
xiv. 6) is called the Life. 4. S. Athanasius three times in his
Orations against the Arians interprets the passage in this way, as if
there was no doubt about it (iii. xxiv. 4; xxv. 16; iv. ix. 1). The
following are in favour of referring οὗτος to the Father. 1. The
Father is the leading subject of all that follows διάνοιαν. 2. To repeat
what has been already stated and add to it is exactly S. John's style.
He has spoken of 'Him that is true': and he now goes on 'This
(true One) is the true *God and eternal life*'. 3. It is the Father who
is the source of that life which the Son has and is (John v. 26).
4. John xvii. 3 supports this view. 5. The Divinity of Christ has
less special point in reference to the warning against idols : the truth
that God is the true God is the basis of the warning against false gods:
comp. 1 Thess. i. 9. But see the conclusion of the note on ἀπὸ τ.
εἰδώλων in the next verse: also note *k* in Lect. v. of Liddon's *Bampton
Lectures*, and Winer, 195, 202.

21. FAREWELL WARNING.

21. τεκνία. As in ii. 1, 12, 28; iii. 7, 18; iv. 4, this address refers
to all his readers, and not merely the younger among them.

φυλάξατε ἑαυτά. As R.V., guard *yourselves*, to distinguish between
τηρεῖν (*v.* 18) and φυλάσσειν (2 Thess. iii. 3). Both verbs occur John
xvii. 12: comp. xii. 25, 47. The aorist imperative makes the command
sharp and decisive : 'once for all be on your guard and have nothing
to do with'. Comp. ἐκτινάξατε τὸν χοῦν (Mark vi. 11), ἐξάρατε τὸν
πονηρὸν ἐξ ὑμῶν αὐτῶν (1 Cor. v. 13). The difference between aorist
and present imperative is well seen in John ii. 16: 'Take these things
hence at once (ἄρατε) and do not go on making (μὴ ποιεῖτε)'. The use
of the reflexive pronoun instead of the middle voice intensifies the

command to use personal care and exertion. See on i. 8. This construction is common in S. John (iii. 3; John vii. 4; xi. 33, 55; xiii. 4; xxi. 1; Rev. vi. 15; viii. 6; xix. 7). For the reflexive of the third person with a verb of the second comp. 2 John 8; John v. 42. Winer, 178, 321. For ἑαυτά some authorities (אᴬ) have ἑαυτούς, which is the usual gender: the pronoun is rarely made to agree with a neuter form of address.

ἀπὸ τῶν εἰδώλων. Perhaps, *from the idols;* those with which Ephesus abounded: or again, *from your idols;* those which have been, or may become, a snare to you. This is the last of the contrasts of which the Epistle is so full. We have had light and darkness, truth and falsehood, love and hate, God and the world, Christ and Antichrist, life and death, doing righteousness and doing sin, the children of God and the children of the devil, the spirit of truth and the spirit of error, the believer untouched by the evil one and the world lying in the evil one; and now at the close we have what in that age was the ever-present and pressing contrast between the true God and the idols. There is no need to seek far-fetched figurative explanations of 'the idols' when the literal meaning lies close at hand, is suggested by the context, and is in harmony with the known circumstances of the time. Is it reasonable to suppose that S. John was warning his readers against "systematising inferences of scholastic theology; theories of self-vaunting orthodoxy...tyrannous shibboleths of aggressive systems", or against superstitious honour paid to the "Madonna, or saints, or pope, or priesthood", when every street through which his readers walked, and every heathen house they visited, swarmed with idols in the literal sense; above all when it was its magnificent temples and groves and seductive idolatrous rites which constituted some of the chief attractions at Ephesus? Acts xix. 27, 35; Tac. *Ann.* iii. 61, iv. 55. Ephesian coins with idolatrous figures on them are common. 'Ephesian letters' ('Εφέσια γράμματα) were celebrated in the history of magic, and to magic the 'curious arts' of Acts xix. 19 point. Of the strictness which was necessary in order to preserve Christians from these dangers the history of the first four centuries is full. Elsewhere in N. T. the word is *invariably* used literally: Acts vii. 41; xv. 20; Rom. ii. 22; 1 Cor. viii. 4, 7; x. 19; xii. 2; 2 Cor. vi. 16; 1 Thess. i. 9; Rev. ix. 20. Moreover, if we interpret this warning literally, we have another point of contact between the Epistle and the Apocalypse (Rev. ii. 14, 20; ix. 20; xxi. 8). Again, as we have seen, some of the Gnostic teachers maintained that idolatry was harmless, or that at any rate there was no need to suffer martyrdom in order to avoid it. This verse is a final protest against such doctrine. Lastly, this emphatic warning against the worship of creatures intensifies the whole teaching of this Epistle; the main purpose of which is to establish the truth that the Son of God has come in the flesh in the Man Jesus. Such a Being was worthy of worship. But if, as Ebionites and Cerinthians taught, Jesus was a creature, the son of Joseph and Mary, then worship of such an one would be only one more of those idolatries from which S. John in his farewell injunction bids Christians once and for ever to guard themselves.

Of course the figurative meaning of 'idols' is not excluded by maintaining the literal meaning as the primary one. Thus Cornelius à Lapide having first explained the passage of actual idolatry, *quia illo aevo hoc erat maxime periculosum,* adds *Mysticè, simulacra phantasiae hominum sunt prava dogmata, hæreses, phantasmata vana, avaritia, cupiditates honoris, pecuniae, voluptatis.* Comp. Bacon's *idola tribus, idola specus, idola fori, idola theatri* (*Nov. Org.* xxxix.—xliv.).

The final 'Amen' (KL and Vulgate) is the addition of a copyist, as at the end of the Second Epistle and the Gospel. It is omitted in אAB and most Versions. Such conclusions, borrowed from liturgies, have been freely added throughout N. T. Perhaps that in Gal. vi. 18 is the only final 'Amen' that is genuine; but that in 2 Pet. iii. 8 is well supported.

THE SECOND EPISTLE OF S. JOHN

The title, like that of the First Epistle and of the Gospel, exists in various forms both ancient and modern, and is not original: here again the oldest authorities give it in the simplest form. Ἰωάννου or Ἰωάνου β (אB). Ἰωάννου ἐπιστολὴ καθολικὴ β̄ (K). τοῦ ἁγίου ἀποστόλου Ἰωάννου τοῦ Θεολόγου ἐπιστολὴ δευτέρα (L). Θεῖος Ἰωάννης τάδε δεύτερα τοῖς προτέροισιν (f). In A the title has been torn off. In our Bibles the epithet 'Catholic' or 'General' is rightly omitted. The Epistle is addressed either to an individual, or to a particular Church, not to the Church at large.

1. For Ἐκλεκτῇ read ἐκλεκτῇ with all the best editors: the word is certainly not a proper name. For κυρίᾳ we should perhaps read Κυρίᾳ.

3. Omit Κυρίου before Ἰησοῦ with AB against אKL. A omits ἔσται μεθ' ἡμῶν.

4. B omits τοῦ before πατρός.

5. For γράφω read γράφων (אABKL), and with אA, Vulgate, and Memphitic place καινήν before γράφων σοι: but the other order (B, Thebaic) is very possibly correct. In the case of γράφω, as in many others, "Erasmus (1516) led the common editions wrong, where the Complutensian (1514) is correct" (Scrivener, p. 76).

8. For ἀπολέσωμεν and ἀπολάβωμεν (KL) read ἀπολέσητε and ἀπολάβητε (AB), and for εἰργασάμεθα (BKL) read εἰργάσασθε (אA and most Versions): the reading is doubtful.

9. For παραβαίνων (KLP) read προάγων (אAB). After the second διδαχῇ omit τοῦ Χριστοῦ with אAB against KL.

11. For ὁ γὰρ λέγων (KL) read ὁ λέγων γάρ (אAB). When γάρ appeared in the third place, the copyists frequently transposed it to the more usual second place.

12. For ἐλθεῖν (KL) read γενέσθαι (אAB). For ἀλλὰ ἐλπίζω (אBKL) A and the Vulgate have ἐλπίζω γάρ. For ἡμῶν (אKL) read ὑμῶν (AB).

13. For Ἐκλεκτῆς read ἐκλεκτῆς with the best editors as in v. 1 ἐκλεκτῇ. Omit ἀμήν with אAB against KL.

Excepting the omission of τοῦ in v. 4, B almost always, and perhaps quite always, has the right reading: אB may be implicitly trusted.

1—3. ADDRESS AND GREETING.

1—3. Like most of the Epistles of S. Paul, the Epistles of S. Peter, S. James, and S. Jude, and unlike the First Epistle, this letter has a definite address and greeting. In its fulness the salutation reminds us of the elaborate openings of the Epistles to the Romans, Galatians, and Titus.

1. ὁ πρεσβύτερος. This title was probably given to the writer by others before he adopted it himself. It indicates both age and office. It is a designation likely to be used of the last surviving Apostle; yet not likely to be chosen by a writer who wished to personate the Apostle, as being too indistinct. On the other hand an Elder, who did *not* wish to personate the Apostle, would hardly call himself '*The* Elder'. It is in addressing Elders that S. Peter calls himself ὁ συμπρεσβύτερος (1 Pet. v. 1). The omission of the name John is against the Presbyter John (if he ever existed) being the writer. "The use of the word in this Epistle shows that he cannot have understood this title in the usual ecclesiastical sense, as though he were only one among the many presbyters of a community. Clearly the writer meant thereby to express the singular and lofty position he held in the circle around him, as the teacher venerable for his old age, and the last of the Apostles" (Döllinger). "In this connexion there can be little doubt that it describes not age simply but official position" (Westcott). Comp. the use of πρεσβύτης (Philem. 9). See Appendix E. For the history of the title πρεσβύτερος see Bishop Lightfoot's *Philippians*, pp. 226—230.

ἐκλεκτῇ κυρίᾳ. *To an elect lady; electae dominae* (Vulgate). This is the most natural translation: but 'to *the* elect lady' may be right. All English Versions have the definite article. So also Luther: *der auserwählten Frau.* Comp. ἐκλεκτοῖς παρεπιδήμοις (1 Pet. i. 1). 'To the elect *Kyria*', is also possible, though less probable. The name existed; but if κυρία were a proper name here, we should have had Κυρίᾳ τῇ ἐκλ. like Γαΐῳ τῷ ἀγαπητῷ (3 John 1), ἀδελφῆς σου τῆς ἐκλ. (*v.* 13), Ῥοῦφον τὸν ἐκλ. (Rom. xvi. 13). If either word is a proper name, probably both are; 'To *Electa Kyria*': but this is not an attractive solution. 'To the lady *Electa*' may be safely dismissed, if only on account of *v.* 13. If ἐκλεκτή is a proper name here, it is a proper name there; which gives us two sisters with the same extraordinary name. 'Elect lady' is best, so as to leave open the question, which cannot be determined, whether the letter is addressed to an individual or to a community. In the one case τοῖς τέκνοις means the lady's children, in the other, the members of the community. Probability is largely in favour of the former hypothesis, which far better fits the somewhat informal designation, 'The Elder'. For the Church as a mother see Gal. iv. 26. But the Church *cannot* be meant here. Who is the Church's sister (*v.* 13)?

οὓς ἐγὼ ἀγαπῶ. The masculine οὓς probably covers both κυρίᾳ and τέκνοις: and this again would fit either a family or a Church. Comp. οἱ τρεῖς referring to three neuter words (1 John v. 8). However others may treat them, they may be assured of the Apostle's genuine affection. The emphatic ἐγώ implies that others are less truly affectionate.

ἐν ἀληθείᾳ. **In truth**: no article. Comp. 3 John 1; John xvii. 19; iv. 23; 1 John iii. 18. It means 'in all Christian sincerity', as opposed to nominal or hypocritical friendship: *vero amore diligo, illo videlicet qui secundum Deum est* (Bede). "What he means is that truth—truth of thought, truth of feeling, truth of speech and intercourse—was the very air in which his affection for this Christian lady had grown up and maintained itself" (Liddon).

ἀλλὰ καὶ πάντες οἱ ἐγνωκότες. As R.V., *but also all they that* **know**: literally, *that have come to know* (see on 1 John ii. 3). At first sight this looks like a strong argument in favour of the view that 'the elect Lady' is a Church. "How could the children of an individual woman be regarded as an object of the love of all believers?" The First Epistle is the answer to the question. Every one who 'has come to know the truth' enters that 'Communion of Saints' of which the love of each for every other is the very condition of existence. The Apostle speaks first in his own name, and then in the name of every Christian. "For all Catholics throughout the world follow one rule of truth: but all heretics and infidels do not agree in unanimous error: they impugn one another not less than the way of truth itself" (Bede). Here and in *vv.* 4 and 5 there is perhaps an allusion to the fact that some accused S. John of preaching new doctrine as to Christ's Person and commands. Ἡ ἀλήθεια is S. John's own term for the revelation of God in Christ: he learned it from his Master (John xiv. 7).

2. διὰ τὴν ἀλήθειαν. The repetition of ἀλήθεια is quite in S. John's style. For τὴν μενοῦσαν, *which* **abideth**, see on 1 John ii. 24. The change of construction, καὶ μεθ' ἡμῶν ἔσται (for ἐσομένην), indicates that the later clause is a kind of afterthought: comp. καὶ ἐσμέν (1 John iii. 1). Winer, 723. The μεθ' ἡμῶν is emphatic; *and with us it shall be*. For εἰς τὸν αἰῶνα see on 1 John ii. 17. Here again we have an echo of Christ's farewell discourses: 'He shall give you another Advocate, that He may *be with you for ever*, even the Spirit of *truth*' (John xiv. 16). Comp. 'I am...the Truth' (John xiv. 6) and 'The Spirit is the Truth' (1 John v. 6). The Apostle and all believers love the elect lady and her children on account of the ever-abiding presence of Christ in the gift of the Spirit.

3. ἔσται μεθ' ἡμῶν χ. ἐλ. εἰρ. *Yea,* **there shall be** *with us grace, mercy, and peace.* The preceding μεθ' ἡμῶν ἔσται has probably produced this very unusual mode of greeting. It is not so much a prayer or a blessing, as the confident assurance of a blessing; and the Apostle includes himself within its scope. This triplet of heavenly gifts occurs, and in the same order, in the salutations to Timothy (both Epistles) and Titus. The more common form is χάρις ὑμῖν καὶ εἰρήνη. In Jude 2 we have another combination ἔλεος ὑμῖν καὶ εἰρήνη καὶ ἀγάπη. In secular letters we have simply 'greeting' (χαίρειν) instead of these Christian blessings. Χάρις is the *favour* of God towards sinners (see on John i. 14); ἔλεος is the *compassion* of God for the misery of

sinners; **εἰρήνη** is the result when the guilt and misery of sin are removed. **Χάρις** is rare in the writings of S. John; elsewhere only John i. 14, 16, 17; Rev. i. 4; xxii. 21: ἔλεος occurs here only.

παρά...παρά... The repetition of the preposition marks the separate Personality of the Father and the Son. The doctrinal fulness of statement is perhaps in anticipation of the errors condemned in *vv.* 7 and 10. For *παρά* see on John i. 6; xvi. 27: it means 'from the presence of' or 'from the hand of'. In S. Paul's Epistles we usually have *ἀπό* (Rom. i. 7; 1 Cor. i. 3; 2 Cor. i. 2; &c.); and ℵ has *ἀπό* here.

ἐν ἀληθείᾳ καὶ ἀγάπῃ. These two words, so characteristic of S. John (see on 1 John i. 8; ii. 8; iii. 1), are key-notes of this short Epistle, in which 'truth' occurs five times, and 'love' twice as a substantive and twice as a verb. 'Εντολή is a third such word.

4.   THE OCCASION OF THE EPISTLE.

4.   The Apostle has met with some of the elect lady's children (or some members of the particular Church addressed), probably in one of his Apostolic visits to some Church in Asia Minor. Their Christian life delighted him and apparently prompted him to write this letter.

ἐχάρην λίαν. *I rejoiced greatly,* or, *I* have *rejoiced greatly,* or, perhaps, as R.V., *I* rejoice *greatly,* if it is the epistolary aorist, as in 1 John ii. 26; v. 13. The same phrase occurs 3 John 3 and Luke xxiii. 8. Χαίρω is cognate with χάρις in *v.* 3. Χάρις is originally 'that which causes joy': but there is no connexion between the two words here. Like S. Paul, the Elder leads up to his admonition by stating something which is a cause of joy and thankfulness: comp. Philem. 4; 2 Tim. i. 3; Rom. i. 8; &c.

ὅτι εὕρηκα. *That I* have *found,* or, **because** *I* have *found.* There is nothing in εὕρηκα to shew that there was any *seeking* on the part of the Apostle (John i. 44), still less that there had been any investigation as to the children's conduct.

ἐκ τῶν τέκνων. This elliptical expression occurs in classical Greek; συνηγυροῦσιν ἐκ τίνων (Aristoph. *Nub.* 1089); and therefore need not be classed as a Hebraism. Comp. LXX. in Ps. lxxii. 15. This ellipse of τινὲς or τινὰς is rather common in S. John (John i. 24; vii. 40; xvi. 17; Rev. ii. 10; v. 9; xi. 9; see on 1 John iv. 13). It is impossible to say whether the expression is a delicate way of intimating that only some of the children were walking in truth, or whether it merely means that the Apostle had fallen in with only some of the children. The expression of affection in *v.* 1 is in favour of the latter supposition; but the strong warnings against intercourse with heretical teachers favours the former; some of her children were already contaminated. Περιπατεῖν indicates the activity of human life (see on 1 John i. 7) and in this sense is found in all three Epistles, the Gospel, and the Apocalypse; elsewhere rare except in S. Paul: **ἐν ἀληθείᾳ** is in Christian truth, as in *vv.* 1 and 3; in Christian tone and temper.

6.]   *NOTES.*   135

καθὼς ἐντολὴν ἐλάβομεν. The changes made in R.V., **even as we received commandment,** are all improvements in the direction of accuracy. 'Even as' (καθώς) points to the completeness of their obedience; comp. 1 John ii. 6, 27; iii. 3, 7, 23; iv. 17. The aorist points to the definite occasion of their reception of the commandment: comp. ἠκούσατε 1 John ii. 7, 24; iii. 11; and ἔδωκεν iii. 23, 24. Ἐντολή is the third key-word of the Epistle, in which it occurs four times. Love, truth, and obedience; these are the three leading ideas, which partly imply, partly supplement one another. Obedience without love becomes servile; love without obedience becomes unreal: neither of them can flourish outside the realm of truth.

παρὰ τοῦ πατρός. As in *v.* 3, *from the hand of the Father,* who is one with the Son. The Divine command has come direct from the Giver. 'All things that I heard from My Father I have made known unto you' (John xv. 15), including the Father's commands.

5—11. We now enter upon the main portion of the Epistle, which has three divisions: *Exhortation to Love and Obedience* (5, 6); *Warnings against False Doctrine* (7—9); *Warnings against False Charity* (10, 11). As usual, the transitions from one subject to another are made gently and without any marked break.

5, 6.   EXHORTATION TO LOVE AND OBEDIENCE.

5. καὶ νῦν. As in 1 John ii. 28 (see note there), this introduces a practical exhortation depending on what precedes. 'It is my joy at the Christian life of some of thy children, and my anxiety about the others, that move me to exhort thee'.

ἐρωτῶ σε. S. John uses the same verb as that used of making request about 'sin unto death' (1 John v. 16). It perhaps indicates that he begs as an equal or superior rather than as an inferior. In both passages the Vulgate rightly has *rogo* not *peto*. In classical Greek ἐρωτῶ=*interrogo*, 'I ask a question', a meaning which it frequently has in N.T. S. Paul uses it very seldom, and always in the sense of 'I request': his usual word is παρακαλῶ, which S. John never employs. Only at the opening and close does the Apostle use the strictly personal σε (*v.* 16): in *vv.* 6, 8, 10, 12 he uses the second person plural. What meaning has this change, if the letter is addressed to a Church? It is natural, if it is addressed to a lady and her family. For ἐντολὴν καινήν see on 1 John ii. 7.

εἴχαμεν. Comp. ἐξῆλθαν in *v.* 7; 1 John ii. 19 (see note); 3 John 7. For ἀπ' ἀρχῆς see on 1 John ii. 7.

ἵνα ἀγαπῶμεν. It is doubtful whether this depends upon ἐρωτῶ or ἐντολήν: in either case ἵνα introduces the *purport* of the request or command, with perhaps a lingering notion of the *purpose* of it (see on 1 John i. 8 and comp. iii. 23).

6. καὶ αὕτη ἐστὶν ἡ ἀγάπη. *And the love is this:* the love which I mean consists in this (see on 1 John i. 5). In *v.* 5 obedience prompts love; here love prompts obedience. This is no vicious logical circle, but a healthy moral connexion, as is stated above on *v.* 4. Love divorced from duty will run riot, and duty divorced from love will starve. See on 1 John v. 3. The Apostle has no sympathy with a religion of pious emotions: there must be a *persevering walk according to God's commands.* In writing to a woman it might be all the more necessary to insist on the fact that love is not a mere matter of feeling.

αὕτη ἡ ἐντολή ἐστιν. As before, *The commandment is this*, i.e. consists in this. We had a similar transition from plural to singular, 'commandments' to 'commandment' in 1 John iii. 22, 23. For αὕτη ...ἵνα see 1 John v. 3.

In these verses (5, 6) S. John seems to be referring to the First Epistle, which she would know.

καθὼς ἠκούσατε. As R.V., **even as ye heard**, referring to the time when they were first instructed in Christian Ethics. See on καθὼς ἐντ. ἐλάβομεν in *v.* 4. R.V. is also more accurate in placing 'that' after, instead of before, 'even as ye heard'. But A.V. is not wrong, for 'even as ye heard' belongs to the apodosis, not to the protasis: still, this is interpretation rather than translation.

ἐν αὐτῇ. In brotherly love; not, in the commandment, as the Vulgate implies. S. John speaks of walking *in* (ἐν) truth, *in* light, *in* darkness; but of walking *according to* (κατά) the commandments. S. Paul speaks both of walking *in* love (Eph. v. 2) and *according to* love (Rom. xiv. 15). Neither speaks of walking *in* commandments: and in Luke i. 6 a different verb is used. Moreover the context here is in favour of ἐν αὐτῇ meaning in love.

7—9. WARNINGS AGAINST FALSE DOCTRINE.

7—9. The third element in the triplet of leading thoughts once more comes to the front, but without being named. Love and obedience require, as the condition of their existence, truth. It is in truth that 'the Elder' and all who love the truth love the elect lady and her children; and they love them for the truth's sake. Truth no less than love is the condition of receiving the threefold blessing of grace, mercy, and peace. And it was the fact that some of her children were walking in truth, while others seemed to be deserting it, which led the Apostle in the fulness of his heart to write to her. All this tends to shew the preciousness of the truth. Love of the brethren and loyal obedience to God's commands will alike suggest that we should jealously guard against those who by tampering with the truth harm the brethren and dishonour God and His Son.

7. ὅτι. Some would make this conjunction introduce the reason for *v.* 8: 'Because many deceivers have appeared......look to yourselves'. But this is altogether unlike S. John's simple manner; to say nothing of the very awkward parenthesis which is thus made of οὗτός ἐστιν...ὁ ἀντίχρ. 'For' or 'Because' points backwards to *vv.* 5 and 6, not forwards to *v.* 8. 'I am recalling our obligations to mutual love and to obedience of the Divine command, because there are men with whom you and yours come in contact, whose teaching strikes at the root of these obligations'.

πλάνοι. This word reaches the meaning 'deceivers' in two ways. 1. 'Making to wander, leading astray'. 2. 'Vagabonds', and hence 'charlatans' or 'impostors'. The former notion is predominant here: these πολλοί are *seductores* (Vulgate). The word is rare in N.T. S. John uses it nowhere else; but not unfrequently has the cognate πλανᾶν (1 John i. 8; ii. 26; iii. 7, &c.).

ἐξῆλθαν. *Are* gone forth (see on 1 John ii. 19). Here the English perfect idiomatically represents the Greek aorist, unless ἐξῆλθαν refers to a definite occasion, when these deceivers migrated from the communion to which they had belonged. This depends on the meaning of εἰς τὸν κόσμον. The κόσμος may mean either human society, or (in S. John's usual sense) that which is external to the Church and antichristian. See on 1 John ii. 2. The meaning may be that, like the many antichrists in 1 John ii. 18, they went out from the Church into the unchristian world. Possibly the same persons are meant in both Epistles. Irenaeus (A.D. 180) by a slip of memory quotes this passage as from the First Epistle (*Haer.* iii. xvi. 8).

οἱ μὴ ὁμολογοῦντες. As R.V., *even they that confess not:* the many deceivers and those who confess not are the same group, and this is their character,—unbelief and denial of the truth. 'Confess not' =deny. Note the μή: 'all who fail to confess, whoever they may be'; *quicunque non profitentur.* Winer, 606. In the rendering of ἐρχόμενον that of A.V., 'that Jesus Christ *is come* in the flesh', is not quite accurate; nor does R.V., 'that Jesus Christ *cometh* in the flesh', seem to be more than a partial correction. Rather, *that confess not Jesus Christ* **as coming** *in the flesh,* or possibly, *that confess not Jesus* **as Christ coming** *in the flesh.* See on 1 John iv. 2, where the Greek is similar, but with perfect instead of present participle. These deceivers denied not merely the fact of the Incarnation, but its possibility. In both passages A.V. and R.V. translate as if we had the infinitive mood instead of the participle. The difference is, that with the participle the denial is directed against the *Person,* 'they deny *Jesus*'; with the infinitive it is directed against the *fact,* 'they deny that He *cometh*' or '*has come*'. See Winer, 435. Note that Christ is never said to come *into* the flesh; but either, as here and 1 John iv. 2, to come *in* the flesh; or, to *become* flesh (John i. 14). To say that Christ came *into* the flesh would leave room for saying that the Divine Son was united with Jesus after He was born of Mary; which would be no true Incarnation.

οὗτός ἐστιν ὁ πλ. κ. ὁ ἀγτ. *This is* **the** *deceiver and* **the** *Antichrist:* a good example of inadequate treatment of the Greek article is here found in A.V. (see on 1 John i. 2). Luther is more accurate; 'Dieser ist *der* Verführer und *der* Widerchrist'. The transition from plural to singular (see on *v.* 6) may be explained in two ways: 1. The man who acts thus is the deceiver and the Antichrist; 2. These men collectively are the deceiver and the Antichrist. In either case the article means 'him of whom you have heard': 'the deceiver' in reference to his fellow men; 'the Antichrist' in reference to his Redeemer. This completes the series of condemnatory names which S. John uses in speaking of these false teachers; liars (1 John ii. 22), seducers (1 John ii. 26), false prophets (1 John iv. 1), deceivers (2 John 7), antichrists (1 John ii. 18, 22; iv. 3; 2 John 7). On the Antichrist of S. John see Appendix B.

8. βλέπετε ἑαυτούς. Comp. Mark xiii. 9. The use of ἑαυτούς κ.τ.λ. with the first (1 John i. 8) and second person (1 John v. 21; John xii. 8) is not uncommon. It occurs in classical Greek, even in the singular: οὐδὲ γὰρ τὴν ἑαυτοῦ σύ γε ψυχὴν ὁρᾷς (Xen. *Mem.* I. iv. 9).

The persons of the three verbs that follow are much varied in MSS. and Versions. The original reading is probably preserved in B and the Thebaic; ἀπολέσητε ἃ ἠργασάμεθα...ἀπολάβητε. This the Revisers adopt. To make the sentence run more smoothly some (A, Vulgate, Memphitic) changed ἠργασάμεθα to ἠργάσασθε, the reading adopted in the text, following Lachmann, Tischendorf and Tregelles: while others changed ἀπολέσητε and ἀπολάβητε to ἀπολέσαμεν and ἀπολάβωμεν. In 1 John ii. 14, 20 there are other instances of B and the Thebaic preserving what may be the original reading. For the construction comp. 1 Cor. xvi. 10. The meaning is, 'Take heed that these deceivers do not undo the work which Apostles and Evangelists have wrought in you, but that ye receive the full fruit of it'. He warns them against loss in both worlds.

μισθὸν πλήρη. Eternal life. The word 'reward' has reference to 'have wrought'. Comp. ὁ **μισθός** μου μετ' ἐμοῦ, ἀποδοῦναι ἑκάστῳ ὡς τὸ **ἔργον** ἐστὶν αὐτοῦ (Rev. **xxii.** 12). 'Apostles have done the work, and you, if you take heed, will have the reward'. Eternal life is called a *full* reward in contrast to real but incomplete rewards which true believers receive in this life; peace, joy, increase of grace, and the like. Comp. Mark x. 29, 30.

9. Explains more fully what is at stake; no less than the possession of the Father and the Son.

πᾶς ὁ προάγων. See on 1 John iii. 16. *Everyone that* goeth before, or, *that* goeth onwards. Προάγειν is fairly common in the Synoptists and the Acts, but occurs nowhere else in S. John's writings. It may be interpreted in two ways: 1. Every one who sets himself up as a leader; 2. Every one who goes on beyond the Gospel. The latter is perhaps better. These antichristian Gnostics were *advanced* thinkers: the Gospel was all very well for the unenlightened; but they knew something higher. This agrees very well with what follows; by advancing they did not abide. There is an advance which involves desertion of first principles; and such an advance is not progress but apostasy.

ἐν τῇ διδαχῇ. 'In the teaching', as R.V., is no improvement on ' in the doctrine'. Of the two words used in N.T., διδαχή (as here) and διδασκαλία (which S. John does not use), the former should be rendered 'doctrine', the latter, as being closer to διδάσκαλος and διδάσκειν, should be rendered 'teaching'. But no hard and fast line can be drawn.

τοῦ Χριστοῦ. The doctrine which He taught (John xviii. 19; Rev. ii. 14, 15), rather than the doctrine which teaches about Him.

Θεὸν οὐκ ἔχει. This must not be watered down to mean 'does not know God': it means that he has Him not as his God; does not possess Him in his heart as a Being to adore, and trust, and love.

ὁ μένων. The opposite case is now stated, and as usual the original idea is not merely negatived but expanded. Τοῦ Χριστοῦ in this half of the verse has been inserted in some authorities to make the two halves more exactly correspond. Καὶ τ. πατέρα καὶ τ. υἱὸν ἔχει shews that 'hath not God' implies 'hath neither the Father nor the Son'. See on 1 John ii. 23.

10, 11. WARNINGS AGAINST FALSE CHARITY.

10. εἴ τις ἔρχεται. As R.V., *If anyone cometh.* 'If there come any unto you' would require ἐάν with the subjunctive. It is implied that such people do come; it is no mere hypothesis: comp. 1 John v. 9; John vii. 4, 23; viii. 39, 46; xviii. 8. Ἔρχεται probably means more than a mere visit: it implies coming on a mission as a teacher; comp. 3 John 10; John i. 7, 30, 31; iii. 2; iv. 25; v. 43; vii. 27, &c.; 1 Cor. ii. 1; iv. 18, 19, 21; xi. 34, &c.

καὶ τ. τ. διδαχὴν οὐ φέρει. *And bringeth not this doctrine.* The negative (οὐ not μή) should be emphasized in reading: it "does not coalesce with the verb, as some maintain, but sharply marks off from the class of faithful Christians all who are *not* faithful" (*Speaker's Commentary* on 1 Cor. xvi. 22). The phrase διδαχὴν φέρει occurs nowhere else in N.T., but it is on the analogy of μῦθον or ἀγγελίην φέρειν (Hom. *Il.* x. 288; xv. 175, 202, &c.). Comp. Τίνα κατηγορίαν φέρετε κ.τ.λ.; (John xviii. 29).

μὴ λαμβάνετε...μὴ λέγετε. Present imperative forbidding a continuance of what is customary. 'Refuse him the hospitality which as a matter of course you would shew to a faithful Christian'. The severity of the injunction is almost without a parallel in N. T. Charity has its limits: it must not be shewn to one man in such a way as to do grievous harm to others; still less must it be shewn in such a way as to do more harm than good to the recipient of it. If these deceivers were treated as if they were true Christians, (1) their opportunities of doing harm would be greatly increased, (2) they might never be brought to see their own errors. "S. John is at once earnestly dogmatic and earnestly philanthropic; for the Incarnation has taught him both the preciousness of man and the preciousness of truth" (Liddon). The famous story respecting S. John and Cerinthus in the public baths is confirmed in its main outlines by this injunction to the elect lady, which it explains and illustrates. Both are instances of "that intense hatred of evil, without which love of good can hardly be said to exist" (Stanley). See the Introduction, p. xxxii.

The greatest care will be necessary before we can venture to act upon the injunction here given to the elect lady. We must ask, *Are the cases really parallel?* Am I quite sure that the man in question is an unbeliever and a *teacher* of infidelity? Will my shewing him hospitality aid him in teaching infidelity? Am I and mine in any danger of being infected by his errors? Is he more likely to be impressed by severity or gentleness? Is severity likely to create sympathy in others, first for him, and then for his teaching? In not a few cases the differences between Christianity in the first century and Christianity in the nineteenth would at once destroy the analogy between antichristian Gnostics visiting this lady and an Agnostic visiting one of ourselves. Let us never forget the way in which the Lord treated Pharisees, publicans, and sinners.

καὶ χαίρειν αὐτῷ μὴ λέγετε. 'And give him no greeting' is perhaps too narrow, whether as translation or interpretation. **And do not bid him God speed** will perhaps be a better rendering; and the injunction will cover any act which might seem to give sanction to the false doctrine or shew sympathy with it. Χαίρειν is used in a similar sense Acts xv. 23; xxiii. 26; James i. 1: comp. John xix. 3, &c.

11. ὁ λέγων γὰρ αὐτῷ χ. Much more, therefore, he that by receiving him into his house affords a home and head-quarters for false teaching. The reading ὁ γὰρ λέγων is an obvious correction.

κοινωνεῖ τ. ἔργοις αὐ. τ. πονηροῖς. As R.V., **partaketh in** *his evil* **works**: literally, with much emphasis on 'evil', *partaketh in his works, his evil (works)*. Κοινωνεῖν occurs nowhere else in S. John, but he uses the cognate κοινωνία, 1 John i. 3, 6, 7. The word for 'evil' (πονηρός) is the same as that used of 'the evil one', 1 John ii. 13, 14; iii. 12; v. 18, 19. What is involved, therefore, in having fellowship with such men is obvious. At a Council of Carthage (A.D. 256), when Cyprian uttered his famous invective against Stephen, Bishop of Rome,—Aurelius, Bishop of Chullabi, quoted this passage with the introductory remark, "John the Apostle laid it down in his Epistle": and Alexander, Bishop of Alexandria (c. A.D. 315), quotes the passage as an injunction of "the blessed John" (Socrates *H. E.* I. vi.). The change from 'deeds' to 'works' may seem frivolous and vexatious, but it is not unimportant. 'Works' is a wider word and better represents ἔργα: words no less than deeds are included, and here it is specially the words of these deceivers that are meant. Moreover in 1 John iii. 12 the same word is rendered 'works' of the ἔργα πονηρά of Cain. See on John v. 20; vi. 27, 29. Wiclif and the Rhemish have 'works' here.

At the end of this verse some Latin authorities add: *Ecce praedixi vobis, ut in die Domini non confundamini* (or *in die Domini nostri Jesu Christi*). Wiclif admits the insertion; the Rhemish does not: Cranmer puts it in italics and in brackets. It has no authority.

12, 13. CONCLUSION.

12, 13. The strong resemblance to the Conclusion of the Third Epistle seems to shew that the two letters are nearly contemporaneous, and it adds to the probability that both are addressed to individuals.

12. πολλὰ ἔχων. The First Epistle gives us some idea of what these many things were. **Γράφειν** is used in the wide sense of 'to communicate': just as our 'say' or 'tell' may include writing, γράφειν includes other modes of communication besides letters. In the **οὐκ ἐβουλήθην** we may perhaps trace a sign of the failing powers of an old man, to whom writing is serious fatigue. But what follows shews that the Apostle has not yet reached the state of feebleness recorded by Jerome, when he had to be carried to church.

'Paper' (χάρτης) occurs nowhere else in N.T.; but it occurs in LXX. of Jer. xxxvi. 23; and its diminutive (χαρτίον) is frequent in that chapter. In 3 Macc. iv. 20 we have a cognate word (χαρτήρια), which probably, like 'paper' here, means Egyptian papyrus, as distinct from the more expensive 'parchment' (μεμβράναι) mentioned 2 Tim. iv. 13. But both papyrus and parchment were costly, which may account for the Apostle's brevity. Augustine writes to Romanianus; "This letter indicates a scarcity of paper (*charta*) without testifying that parchment is plentiful here. My ivory tablets I used in the letter which I sent to your uncle. You will more readily excuse this scrap of parchment, because what I wrote to him could not be delayed; and I thought it would be absurd not to write to you for want of better material" (*Ep.* xv.). The very perishable nature of papyrus accounts for the early loss of the Apostolic autographs. See *Dict. of the Bible*, WRITING, and *Dict. of Antiquities*, LIBER.

'Ink' (μέλαν) is mentioned again 3 John 13; elsewhere in N.T. only 2 Cor. iii. 3: comp. LXX. of Jer. xxxvi. 18. It was made of lampblack and gall-juice, or more simply of soot and water.

ἀλλὰ ἐλπίζω. As R.V., *but I* hope: the verb is frequent in N.T., and there seems to be no reason for changing the usual rendering: comp. 1 Tim. iii. 14; Phil. ii. 19, 23. A.V. wavers needlessly between 'hope' and 'trust'.

γενέσθαι πρὸς ὑμᾶς. To appear before you: literally, 'to come to be in your presence, to become present with you, to be with you'. Comp. 1 Cor. ii. 3, xvi. 10. The phrase is used of words as well as of persons: πρὸς οὓς ὁ λόγος τοῦ Θεοῦ ἐγένετο (John x. 35); ἐγένετο φωνὴ πρὸς αὐτόν (Acts x. 13). In all these cases the coming is expressed with a certain amount of solemnity.

The 'you' (ὑμῖν, ὑμᾶς) in this verse includes the children mentioned in *v.* 1. This, when contrasted with 'thee' (σε, σοι) in *v.* 5, seems to be in favour of understanding the 'lady' literally. The change from 'thee' to 'you' seems more in harmony with a matron and her family than with a Church and its members.

στόμα πρὸς στόμα. In Num. xii. 8 we have στόμα κατὰ στόμα λαλήσω αὐτῷ: comp. Jer. xxxix. (xxxii.) 4. In 1 Cor. xiii. 12 the phrase is πρόσωπον πρὸς πρόσωπον: comp. Gen. xxxii. 31.

ἵνα ἡ χαρὰ ὑμῶν ᾖ πεπληρωμένη. As R.V., *that your joy may be* **fulfilled.** See on 1 John i. 4, and comp. Rom. i. 12.

13. ἀσπάζεταί σε. For the sake of uniformity with 3 John 14, **salute** *thee:* the same verb is used in both passages. That the elect sister herself sends no greeting is taken as an argument in favour of the 'elect lady' being a Church, and the 'elect sister' a sister Church, which could send no greeting other than that of its members or 'children'. But the verse fits the other hypothesis equally well. The lady's nephews may be engaged in business at Ephesus under S. John's Apostolic care : their mother may be living elsewhere, or be dead. It was perhaps from these children of a sister that the Apostle had knowledge of the state of things in the elect lady's house. Their sending a salutation through him may intimate that they share his anxiety respecting her and hers. It is impossible to give any reasonable interpretation of the sister and her children, if 'the elect lady' be taken as the Church at large.

THIRD EPISTLE OF S. JOHN

The title, like that of the Gospel and of the other two Epistles, is not original, and is found in various forms, the most ancient being the simplest. 'Ιωάννου or 'Ιωάνου γ̄ (אB). 'Ιωάννου ἐπιστολὴ γ̄ (C). ἐπιστολὴ τρίτη τοῦ ἀγίου ἀποστόλου 'Ιωάννου (L). As in the Second Epistle, the title in A is missing. Some authorities insert καθολική, which is manifestly inappropriate. The Second Epistle *may* be addressed to a local Church and be intended to be encyclical: beyond doubt this is addressed to an individual.

---

3. א, Vulgate, and Thebaic omit γάρ.

4. Before ἀληθείᾳ insert τῇ with ABC¹ against אKL. For χαράν (אACKL, Thebaic) B, Vulgate, and Memphitic have χάριν, which is very likely right.

5. For εἰς τούς (KL) read τοῦτο (אABC and Versions).

7. For ἐθνῶν (KL) read ἐθνικῶν (אABC).

8. For ἀπολαμβάνειν (KL) read ὑπολαμβάνειν (אABC¹). For ἀληθείᾳ (אBC) א¹A have ἐκκλησίᾳ.

9. After ἔγραψα insert τι with א¹ABC against KL. For ἔγραψα B has ἔγραψας. For τι א³ and Vulgate have ἄν. In the Vulgate *forsitan* is an obvious attempt to give a separate word to translate ἄν. See on 1 John ii. 19.

10. For βουλομένους (אAB and most Versions) C and Thebaic have ἐπιδεχομένους.

11. Before κακοποιῶν omit δέ with אABCK against L.

12. For οἴδατε (KLP) read οἶδας (אABC).

13. For γράφειν (KL) read γράψαι σοι (אABC): γράφειν is from 2 John 12. Similarly A and the Vulgate substitute ἐβουλήθην from 2 John 12 for θέλω. For γράψαι (KL) read γράφειν (אABC).

14. For ἰδεῖν σε (אKL) read σε ἰδεῖν (ABC).

For φίλοι (אBCKL) A has ἀδελφοί.

For ἀσπάζου (ABCKL) א has ἄσπασαι.

Once more the text of B is almost faultless, while every other authority admits serious errors.

---

1. The Address.

1. This Epistle, like the Second, and most others in N.T., has a definite address, but of a very short and simple kind: comp. James i. 1. It has no greeting, properly so called, the prayer expressed in *v.* 2 taking its place.

ὁ πρεσβύτερος. See on 2 John 1. From the Apostle's using this title in both Epistles we may conclude that he commonly designated himself thus. If not, it is additional evidence that the two letters were written about the same time: see on *vv.* 13, 14.

Γαΐῳ τῷ ἀγαπητῷ. **To Gaius the beloved**: the epithet is the same word as we have had repeatedly in the First Epistle (ii. 7; iii. 2, 21; iv. 1, 7, 11) and have again in *vv.* 2, 5, 11. The name Gaius being perhaps the most common of all names in the Roman Empire, it is idle to speculate without further evidence as to whether the one here addressed is identical with either Gaius of Macedonia (Acts xix. 29), Gaius of Derbe (Acts xx. 4), or Gaius of Corinth (Rom. xvi. 23). See Introduction, Chap. iv. sect. ii. p. lxxix.

ὃν ἐγὼ ἀγ. ἐν ἀληθ. *Whom I love* **in truth**: see on 2 John 1. This is not mere tautology after 'the beloved;' nor is it mere emphasis. 'The beloved' gives a common sentiment respecting Gaius: this clause expresses the Apostle's own feeling. There is no need, as in the Second Epistle, to enlarge upon the meaning of loving in truth. In this letter the Apostle has not to touch upon defects which a less true love might have passed over in silence. The emphatic ἐγώ again seems to imply that there are others who are hostile, or whose affection is not sincere. *In veritate, hoc est, in Domino qui est veritas* (A Lapide). Similarly Bede: *id est, vero amore diligo, illo videlicet qui secundum Deum est.*

2—4. Personal Good Wishes and Sentiments.

2. περὶ πάντων εὔχομαι. **I pray that in all respects**; literally, *concerning all things*. It might well surprise us to find S. John placing health and prosperity *above* all things, as A.V. has it; and though περὶ πάντων has that meaning sometimes in Homer (*Il.* i. 287), yet no parallel use of it has been found in either N.T. or LXX. It belongs to εὐοδοῦσθαι rather than to εὔχομαι, a word which occurs here only in S. John.

εὐοδοῦσθαι. The word occurs elsewhere in N.T. only Rom. i. 10 and 1 Cor. xvi. 2, but is frequent in LXX. Etymologically it has the meaning of being prospered in a *journey*, but that element has been lost in usage, and should not be restored even in Rom. i. 10.

ὑγιαίνειν. Bodily health, the chief element in all prosperity: Luke vii. 10; xv. 27; comp. v. 31. We cannot conclude from these good wishes that Gaius had been ailing in health and fortune: but it is quite clear from what follows that 'prosper and be in health' do not refer to his spiritual condition; and this verse is, therefore, good authority for praying for temporal blessings for our friends. In the

Pastoral Epistles ὑγιαίνειν is always used figuratively of faith and doctrine.

The order of the Greek is striking, περὶ πάντων at the beginning being placed in contrast to ἡ ψυχή at the end of the sentence: *in all things I pray that thou mayest prosper and be in health, even as prospereth thy soul.* The verse is a model for all friendly wishes of good fortune to others. Ἡ ψυχή here means the immaterial part of man's nature; and the well-being of the ψυχή is the measure of all well-being, in a far higher sense than the Aristotelian (*Nic. Eth.* I. vii. 15). *Ubi anima valet, omnia valere possunt* (Bengel). For a similar use of ἡ ψυχή as including the πνεῦμα comp. Matt. x. 28; 1 Pet. i. 9, 22.

3. ἐχάρην γὰρ λίαν. The γάρ has been omitted in some important authorities, perhaps under the influence of 2 John 4. It means 'I know that thy soul is in a prosperous condition, *for* I have it on good authority'. For ἐχάρην see on 2 John 4: but here it cannot so well be the epistolary aorist, but refers to the definite occasions when information was brought to the Apostle. Of course if ἐχάρην be rendered 'I rejoice' as epistolary aorist ἐρχομένων and μαρτυρούντων must be treated in like manner; as in R.V. margin.

ἐρχομένων. Imperfect participle of what happened repeatedly: so also μαρτυρούντων. **When brethren** (no article) *came and* **bare witness** (see on 1 John i. 2) **to thy truth** (see on *v.* 6). The whole, literally rendered, runs thus; *For I rejoiced greatly at brethren coming and witnessing to thy truth.* John v. 33 is wrongly quoted as a parallel. There the Baptist 'hath borne witness to the truth,' i.e. to the Gospel or to Christ. Here the brethren bare witness to Gaius's truth, i.e. to his Christian life, as is shewn by what follows. The σου is emphatic, as in *v.* 6; perhaps in contrast to the conduct of Diotrephes. Comp. Luke iv. 22. What follows, καθὼς σὺ κ.τ.λ., is part of what these ἀδελφοί reported, explaining what they meant by Gaius's truth.

4. μειζοτέραν τ. οὐκ ἔχω χαράν. The order is worth keeping, all the more so on account of the similar arrangement in John xv. 13; μείζονα ταύτης ἀγάπην οὐδεὶς ἔχει, ἵνα τις τ. ψυχὴν αὐτοῦ θῇ. **Greater joy have I none than this.** The Vulgate is barbarously exact: *majorem horum non habeo gratiam.* Comp. *majora horum* for μείζω τούτων (John i. 50). '*Gratiam*' implies the reading χάριν (B and Memphitic), which Westcott and Hort adopt. The double comparative μειζοτέραν is analogous to 'lesser' in English. In Eph. iii. 8 we have ἐλαχιστότερος. Such forms belong to the later stages of a language, when common forms have lost strength. Comp. καλλιώτερος, καλλιστότατος, *minimissimus, pessimissimus.* Winer, 81. The plural pronoun τούτων (corrected in some copies to ταύτης) may either mean 'these joys,' or 'these things,' viz. the frequent reports of the brethren: comp. μείζω τούτων ὄψει (John i. 50). Winer, 201.

ἵνα ἀκούω. There is no need either here or in John xv. 13 to suppose an ellipse of ἤ after the comparative. In both cases the ἵνα clause is epexegetic of the preceding genitive pronoun; and ἵνα ἀκούω = τοῦ ἀκούειν in apposition with τούτων. Winer, 745, 425.

τὰ ἐμὰ τέκνα. *My own children.* The emphatic ἐμά (contrast 1 John ii. 1; 2 John 4) perhaps indicates those who not only were under his Apostolic care, but had been converted by him to the faith.

περιπατοῦντα. See on 2 John 4. For the participial construction comp. ὅσα ἠκούσαμεν γενόμενα εἰς τὴν Καφ. (Luke iv. 23): ἀκούσας δὲ Ἰακὼβ ὄντα σιτία εἰς Αἴγυπτον (Acts vii. 12): and especially ἀκούομεν γάρ τινας περιπατοῦντας ἐν ὑμῖν (2 Thess. iii. 11). *To hear of my own children* walking *in the truth.*

5—8. GAIUS PRAISED FOR HIS HOSPITALITY : ITS SPECIAL VALUE.

5. ἀγαπητέ. The affectionate address marks a new section (comp. *vv.* 2, 11), but here again the fresh subject grows quite naturally out of what precedes, without any abrupt transition. The good report, which caused the Apostle such joy, testified in particular to the Christian hospitality of Gaius.

πιστὸν ποιεῖς. A.V., *thou doest faithfully.* So the Vulgate; *fideliter facis :* Wiclif, Tyndale, and other English Versions take the same view. So also Luther : *du thust treulich.* The Greek is literally, *thou doest* a faithful (thing), *whatsoever thou* workest (same verb as is rendered 'wrought' in 2 John 8) *unto the brethren:* which is intolerably clumsy as a piece of English. R.V. makes a compromise; *thou doest a faithful work in whatsoever thou doest;* which is closer to the Greek than A.V., but not exact. ' To do a faithful act ' (πιστὸν ποιεῖν) *possibly* means to do what is worthy of a faithful man or of a believer, *ostendens ex operibus fidem* (Bede); and 'to do faithfully' expresses this fairly well: *thou doest faithfully* in all thou workest towards *the brethren.* But this use of πιστὸν ποιεῖν is unsupported by examples, and therefore Westcott would translate *Thou* makest sure *whatsoever thou workest;* i.e. 'such an act will not be lost, will not fail of its due issue and reward.' The change of verb should at any rate be kept, not only on account of 2 John 8, but also of Matt. xxvi. 10, where 'she hath wrought a good work upon Me' (εἰργάσατο εἰς ἐμέ) is singularly parallel to 'thou workest toward the brethren' (ἐργάσῃ εἰς τοὺς ἀδελφούς). Cod. 80 has the singular reading μισθὸν ποιεῖς for πιστὸν ποιεῖς.

καὶ τοῦτο ξένους. And that strangers; i.e. towards the brethren, and those brethren strangers. Comp. 1 Cor. vi. 6; Phil. i. 28; Eph. ii. 8. The brethren and the strangers are not two classes, but one and the same. It enhanced the hospitality of Gaius that the Christians whom he entertained were personally unknown to him: *Fideliter facis quidquid operaris in fratres, et hoc in peregrinos.* Comp. Matt. xxv. 35.

6. οἳ ἐμαρτύρησάν σου τῇ ἀγάπῃ. As R.V., who bare witness to thy love. There is no sufficient reason here for rendering the aorist as the perfect; and certainly in S. John's writings (whatever may be our view of 1 Cor. xiii.) ἀγάπη must always be rendered 'love.' In a text like this, moreover, 'charity' is specially likely to be understood in the vulgar sense of almsgiving, with which it is contrasted in 1 Cor. xiii.

ἐνώπιον ἐκκλησίας. Probably at Ephesus; but wherever S. John was when he wrote the letter. Only in this Third Epistle does he use the word ἐκκλησία: viz., here, and in *vv.* 9 and 10 (and in some copies in *v.* 8, with or instead of ἀληθείᾳ). For the omission of the article before ἐκκλησίας comp. 1 Cor. xiv. 19, 35; as we say 'in church.'

οὓς καλῶς ποιήσεις προπέμψας. The order may as well be preserved: *whom* thou wilt do well to forward *on their journey*. Προπέμπειν occurs Acts xv. 3; xx. 38; xxi. 5; Rom. xv. 24; 1 Cor. xvi. 6, 11; 2 Cor. i. 16; Tit. iii. 13. There would be abundant opportunity in the early Church for such friendly acts; and in telling Gaius that he will do a good deed in helping Christians on their way the Apostle gently urges him to continue such work. Comp. Phil. iv. 14; Acts x. 33.

ἀξίως τοῦ Θεοῦ. Worthily of God (R.V.), or, in a manner worthy of God (Rhemish), or, *as it beseemeth God* (Tyndale and Genevan). 'Help them forward in a way worthy of Him whose servants they and you are.' Comp. 1 Thess. ii. 12; Col. i. 10.

7. ὑπὲρ γὰρ τοῦ ὀνόματος. For *for the sake of* the *Name :* the αὐτοῦ of some texts is a weak amplification followed in several versions. A similar weakening is found in Acts v. 41, which should run, 'Rejoicing that they were counted worthy to suffer dishonour for *the* Name.' 'The Name' of course means the Name of Jesus Christ: comp. James ii. 7. This use of 'the Name' is common in the Apostolic Fathers; Ignatius, *Eph.* iii., vii.; *Philad.* x.; Clem. Rom. ii., xiii.; Hermas, *Sim.* viii. 10, ix. 13, 28. Bengel, appealing to Lev. xxiv. 11, wrongly explains τ. ὀνόματος as *Nomine Dei:* so also Lücke, appealing to John xvii. 11.

ἐξῆλθαν. The word is used in the same absolute way Acts xv. 40; Παῦλος δὲ ἐπιλεξάμενος Σίλαν ἐξῆλθεν: i.e. on a missionary journey from a Christian centre.

μηδὲν λαμβάνοντες. The tense indicates that this was their custom, not merely that they did so on one occasion. Hence the greater necessity for men like Gaius to help. These missionaries declined to 'spoil the Egyptians' by taking from the heathen, and therefore would be in great difficulties if Christians did not come forward with assistance. We are not to understand that the Gentiles offered help which these brethren refused, but that the brethren never asked them for help. 'The Gentiles' (οἱ ἐθνικοί) cannot well mean Gentile *converts.* What possible objection could there be to receiving help from them? Comp. Matt. v. 47; vi. 7; xviii. 17, the only other places where the word occurs. There was reason in not accepting money or hospitality at all, but working for their own living, as S. Paul loved to do. And there was reason in not accepting help from heathen. But there would be no reason in accepting from Jewish converts but not from Gentile ones.

Some expositors render this very differently. 'For for the Name's sake they went forth from the Gentiles, taking nothing'; i.e. they were driven out by the heathen, penniless. But ἐξῆλθαν is too gentle a word to mean this; and the negative (μηδέν not οὐδέν) seems to imply that it was their *determination* not to accept anything, not merely that as a matter of *fact* they received nothing. For λαμβάνειν ἀπό in a similar sense comp. Matt. xvii. 25. Winer, 463.

8. ἡμεῖς οὖν. 'We' is in emphatic contrast to the heathen just mentioned. The Apostle softens the injunction by including himself; comp. 1 John ii. 1.

ὀφείλομεν ὑπολ. τ. τ. *Ought to* support *such*, to *undertake* for them: the verb (ὑπολαμβάνειν not ἀπολαμβάνειν) occurs elsewhere in N.T. only in S. Luke's writings, and there with a very different meaning. Comp. Xen. *Anab.* I. i. 7. There is perhaps a play upon words between the missionaries *taking* nothing *from* the Gentiles, and Christians being therefore bound to *undertake* for them.

ἵνα συνεργοὶ γινώμεθα. *That we* may become *fellow-workers with.* 'Fellow-workers' rather than 'fellow-helpers' on account of *v.* 5; see also on 2 John 11. Cognate words are used in the Greek, and this may as well be preserved in the English. 'Fellow-workers' with what? Probably not with the truth, as both A.V. and R.V. lead us to suppose; but with the missionary brethren. In N.T. persons are invariably said to be 'fellow-workers *of*' (Rom. xvi. 3, 9, 21; 1 Cor. iii. 9; 2 Cor. i. 24; Phil. ii. 25, iv. 3; [1 Thess. iii. 2;] Philem. 24), never 'fellow-workers *to*' or 'fellow-workers *with*'; those with whom the fellow-worker works are put in the genitive, not in the dative. The dative here is the *dativus commodi*, and the meaning is, *that we may* become **their** *fellow-workers* **for** *the truth.* Sometimes instead of the dative we have the accusative with a preposition (Col. iv. 11; comp. 2 Cor. viii. 23). In classical Greek those with whom the συνεργός works are more commonly in the dative than in the genitive.

9, 10. DIOTREPHES CONDEMNED FOR HIS ARROGANCE AND HOSTILITY.

This is the most surprising part of the letter; and of the internal evidence this is the item which seems to weigh most heavily against the Apostolic authorship. That any Christian should be found to act in this manner towards the last surviving Apostle is nothing less than astounding. Those who opposed S. Paul, like Alexander the coppersmith (2 Tim. iv. 14), afford only remote parallels (1 Tim. i. 20; 2 Tim. i. 15). They do not seem to have gone the lengths of Diotrephes: the authority of Apostles was less understood in S. Paul's time: and his claim to be an Apostle was at least open to question; for he was not one of the Twelve, and he had himself been a persecutor. But from the very first the N.T. is full of the saddest surprises. And those who accept as historical the unbelief of Christ's brethren, the treachery of Judas, the flight of all the Disciples, the denial of S. Peter, the quarrels of Apostles both before and after their Lord's departure, and the flagrant abuses in the Church of Corinth, with much more of the same kind, will not be disposed to think it incredible that Diotrephes acted in the manner here described even towards the Apostle S. John.

9. ἔγραψά τι τῇ ἐκκλησίᾳ. *I wrote somewhat to the Church;* i.e. 'I wrote a short letter, a something on which I do not lay much stress.' This was perhaps an ἐπιστολὴ συστατική respecting φιλοξενία.

The other reading (*I would have written to the Church*, ἔγραψα ἄν, *scripsissem forsitan*) is an obvious corruption to avoid the unwelcome conclusion that an official letter from S. John has been lost (comp. 1 Cor. v. 9). The reference cannot be to either the First or the Second Epistle, neither of which contains any mention of this subject: though some do consider that the Second Epistle is meant. There is nothing surprising in such a letter having perished: and Diotrephes would be likely to suppress it. That the brethren whom Gaius received were the bearers of it, and that his hospitality was specially acceptable on account of the violence of Diotrephes, does not seem to fit in well with the context. 'To the Church' probably means 'to the Church' of which Diotrephes was a prominent member: that he was in authority seems to be implied from what is stated *v.* 10.

ὁ φιλοπρωτεύων. The expression occurs nowhere else in N.T.; but it comes very close to "whosoever *willeth to be first* among you" (Matt. xx. 27). Φιλόπρωτος occurs in Polybius. Perhaps the meaning is that Diotrephes meant to make his Church independent: hitherto it had been governed by S. John from Ephesus, but Diotrephes wished to make it autonomous to his own glorification. Just as the antichristian teachers claimed to be first in the intellectual sphere (2 John 9), so the unchristian Diotrephes claimed to be first in influence and authority. This looks as if ecclesiastical government by a single official was in existence in Asia Minor in S. John's lifetime.

οὐκ ἐπιδέχεται ἡμᾶς. Such inhospitality was unheard of: Rom. xii. 13; xvi. 23; Heb. xiii. 2; 1 Pet. iv. 9; 1 Tim. iii. 2; v. 10; Tit. i. 8; Acts xvi. 15; xvii. 7; xxi. 8, 16. So also in the *Doctrine of the Twelve Apostles*: "Let every Apostle that cometh to you be received as the Lord" (xi. 4); where 'Apostle' is used in the generic sense of Rom. xvi. 7 for an itinerant Evangelist, such as are described by Eusebius (*H. E.* iii. xxxvii. 2—4). The passage throws much light on this Epistle, as also does what follows in the *Doctrine of the Twelve Apostles*. 'The Apostle is not to remain more than one day, or if need be two: but if he remains three, he is a ψευδοπροφήτης. And when he departs, he is to take nothing (μηδὲν λαμβανέτω) but bread to last him to his next night-quarters: but if he asks for money, he is a ψευδοπροφήτης.' These precautions shew that the hospitality, universally shewn to missionaries, was sometimes abused. The chapter ends thus: "Whoever says in the spirit, Give me money, or any other thing, ye shall not listen to him; but if for the sake of others who are in want he bid you give, let no one judge him."

10. διὰ τοῦτο. For this cause. See on 1 John iii. 1.

ὑπομνήσω. 'I will direct public attention to the matter'; equivalent to 'bear witness of it before the Church' (*v.* 6). For the construction comp. ὑπομνήσει ὑμᾶς πάντα (John xiv. 26). *I will* **call to remembrance** *his* **works** (see on 2 John 11).

λόγοις πονηροῖς. *With* **evil** *words:* the connexion with 'the evil one' must not be missed either here or in 2 John 11.

φλυαρῶν ἡμᾶς. The verb occurs nowhere else in N. T., and the construction with an accusative is quite exceptional. It is frequent in Aristophanes and Demosthenes, and means literally ' to talk nonsense.' Therefore ' prates against us,' *garriens in nos*, cannot well be improved: it conveys the idea that the words were not only wicked, but senseless. Comp. ' And not only idle, but *tattlers* (φλύαροι) also and busybodies, speaking things which they ought not' (1 Tim. v. 13). Other renderings are ' garringe, *or chidinge*, in to us' (Wiclif), ' chiding against us' (Purvey), ' jesting on us' (Tyndale and Cranmer), ' pratteling against us' (Genevan), ' chatting against us' (Rhemish), *plaudert wider uns* (Luther). ' Prating *about* us' may be right: comp. ἀλλάλαις λαλέοντι τεὸν γάμον αἱ κυπάρισσοι (Theocr. xxvii. 58).

The description of the ψευδοπροφήτης in the *Shepherd of Hermas* (*Mand.* xi. 12) illustrates this account of Diotrephes : " He exalts himself and wishes to have the chief seat (πρωτοκαθεδρίαν), and forthwith is hasty, and shameless, and talkative." Comp. 1 Pet. v. 3.

ἀρκούμενος ἐπὶ τ. The ἐπί is unusual. Both in N. T. and in classical Greek ἀρκεῖσθαι usually has the dative without a preposition : Luke iii. 14; 1 Tim. vi. 8; Heb. xiii. 5.

οὔτε...καὶ.... The combination οὔτε...τε... is not uncommon in classical Greek, but οὔτε... καὶ... is late. It seems to occur, however, in Eur. *I. T.* 591 εἰ γὰρ, ὡς ἔοικας, οὔτε δυσγενὴς καὶ τὰς Μυκήνας οἶσθα. Comp. οὔτε ἄντλημα ἔχεις καὶ τὸ φρέαρ ἐστὶν βαθύ (John iv. 11). Winer, 619.

ἐπιδέχεται. The word occurs nowhere in N. T. but here and *v.* 9, though common enough elsewhere. In *v.* 9 the meaning seems to be 'admits not our authority,' or 'ignores our letter.' Here of course it is ' refuses hospitality to.' But perhaps ' closes his doors against' may be the meaning in both places ; ' us' being S. John's friends. By saying ' us' rather than ' me,' the Apostle avoids the appearance of a personal quarrel.

ἐκ τῆς ἐκκλ. ἐκβάλλει. He excommunicates those who are willing to receive the missionary brethren. The exact meaning of this is uncertain, as we have not sufficient knowledge of the circumstances. The natural meaning is that Diotrephes had sufficient authority or influence in some Christian congregation to exclude from it those who received brethren of whom he did not approve. For the expression comp. John ix. 34, 35.

11, 12. THE MORAL.

11, 12. This is the main portion of the Epistle. In it the Apostle bids Gaius beware of imitating such conduct. And if an example of Christian conduct is needed there is Demetrius.

11. ἀγαπητέ. The address again marks transition to a new subject, but without any abrupt change. The behaviour of Diotrephes will at least serve as a warning.

μὴ μιμοῦ τ. κακὸν ἀ. τ. ἀγ. Imitate *not* the ill, *but* the good. Κακός, though one of the most common words in the Greek language to express the idea of 'bad,' is rarely used by S. John. Elsewhere only John xviii. 23; Rev. ii. 2; xvi. 2: in Rev. xvi. 2 both words occur. Perhaps 'ill' is hardly strong enough here, and the 'evil' of A.V. had better be retained. Nothing turns on the change of word from πονηρός in *v.* 10, so that it is not absolutely necessary to mark it. For μιμεῖσθαι comp. 2 Thess. iii. 7, 9; Heb. xiii. 7; the word occurs nowhere else in N.T.

ἐκ τοῦ Θεοῦ ἐστίν. He has God as the source (ἐκ) of his moral and spiritual life; he is a child of God. In its highest sense this is true only of Him who 'went about doing good'; but it is true in a lower sense of every earnest Christian. See on 1 John ii. 16, 29; iii. 8, 9; iv. 4, 6, 7.

οὐχ ἑώρακεν τὸν Θεόν. See on 1 John iii. 6. Of course doing good and doing evil are to be understood in a wide sense: the particular cases of granting and refusing hospitality to missionary brethren are no longer specially in question.

12. While Diotrephes sets an example to be abhorred, Demetrius sets one to be imitated. We know of him, as of Diotrephes, just what is told us here and no more. Perhaps he was the bearer of this letter. That Demetrius is the silversmith of Ephesus who once made silver shrines for Artemis (Acts xix. 24) is a conjecture, which is worth mentioning, but cannot be said to be probable.

Δημητρίῳ μεμαρτ. κ.τ.λ. Literally, **Witness** *hath been borne to Demetrius by all men and by the truth itself;* or less stiffly, as R. V., *Demetrius hath the* **witness** *of all men.* See on 1 John i. 2. 'All men' means chiefly those who belonged to the Church of the place where Demetrius lived, and the missionaries who had been there in the course of their labours. The force of the perfect is the common one of present result of past action: the testimony has been given and still abides.

καὶ ὑπ' αὐτῆς τῆς ἀληθείας. A great deal has been written about this clause; and it is certainly a puzzling statement. Of the various explanations suggested these two seem to be best. 1. 'The Truth' means "the divine rule of the walk of all believers"; Demetrius walked according to this rule and his conformity was manifest to all who knew the rule. Thus the rule bore witness to his Christian life. This is intelligible, but it is a little far-fetched. 2. 'The Truth' is the Spirit of truth (1 John v. 6) which speaks in the disciples. The witness which 'all men' bear to the Christian conduct of Demetrius is not mere human testimony which may be the result of prejudice or of deceit: it is given under the direction of the Holy Spirit. This explanation is preferable. The witness given respecting Demetrius was that of disciples, who reported their own experience of him: but it was also that of the Spirit, who guided and illumined them in their estimate. See note on John xv. 27, which is a remarkably parallel passage, and comp. Acts v. 32; xv. 28, where as here the human and Divine elements in Christian testimony are clearly marked.

καὶ ἡμεῖς δὲ μαρτ. As R. V., *yea, we also bear witness* (see on 1 John i. 2): the 'and' of A. V. is redundant. The Apostle mentions his own testimony in particular as corroborating the evidence of 'all men.' For καὶ...δὲ... see on 1 John i. 3.

καὶ οἶδας ὅτι κ.τ.λ. As R. V. *and thou knowest that our witness is true.* The evidence for the singular, οἶδας (אABC and most Versions), as against the plural, οἴδατε (KL), is quite decisive; a few authorities, under the influence of John xxi. 24, read οἴδαμεν: comp. John xix. 35. The plural has perhaps grown out of the belief that the Epistle is not private but Catholic. John xxi. is evidently an appendix to the Gospel, and was possibly written long after the first twenty chapters. It may have been written after this Epistle; and (if so) xxi. 24 may be "an echo of this sentence" (Westcott). The form οἶδας for οἶσθα is common in later Greek (John xxi. 15; 1 Cor. vii. 16), and occurs in Xenophon and Euripides. Similarly we have οἴδαμεν (John iii. 2, &c.), οἴδατε (Mark x. 38, &c.), οἴδασιν (John x. 5, &c.).

13, 14. CONCLUSION.

13, 14. The marked similarity to the Conclusion of the Second Epistle is strong evidence that the two letters were written about the same time. See notes on 2 John 12, 13.

13. πολλὰ εἶχον. Imperfect; at the time of his writing there were many things which he had to communicate to Gaius. οὐ θέλω. 'I do not care to.' See on John vi. 67; vii. 17; viii. 44.

διὰ μέλανος καὶ καλάμου. In 2 John 12 it is διὰ χάρτου καὶ μέλανος. Κάλαμος occurs nowhere else in the sense of 'reed for writing with, pen,' but only in the general sense of 'reed,' *calamus.* Quills were not used as pens until the fifth century. The earliest certain evidence as to their use is in the writings of Isidore, early in the seventh century. In LXX. of Ps. xliv. 1 κάλαμος is used of 'the pen of a ready writer.'

14. ἐλπίζω δὲ εὐθέως σε ἰδεῖν. *But I hope immediately to see thee.* The punctuation of this verse and of 2 John 12 should be alike. There is no reason for placing a comma before 'but I hope' in the one case and a full stop in the other. For στόμα πρὸς στόμα see notes there, and comp. the French *bouche à bouche.*

15. εἰρήνη σοι. This εἰρήνη takes the place of the ἔρρωσο in ordinary letters; comp. Gal. vi. 16; Eph. vi. 23; 1 Pet. v. 14. It is an ordinary blessing, suitable either for salutation or farewell, with a Christian fulness of meaning. Comp. John xx. 19, 26.

ἀσπάζονταί σε οἱ φίλοι. The *friends salute thee:* there is no authority for 'our' either as translation or interpretation. If any pronoun be inserted, it should be 'thy': the friends spoken of are probably the friends of Gaius. It is perhaps on account of the private character of the letter, as addressed to an individual and not to a Church, that S. John says 'the friends' rather than 'the brethren.' Comp. 'Lazarus, our *friend,* is fallen asleep' (John xi. 11); and 'Julius treated Paul kindly, and gave him leave to go unto *the friends* and refresh himself' (Acts xxvii. 3), where 'the friends' probably means '*his* friends,' just as it probably means '*thy* friends' here. In 'Lazarus, *our* friend' the pronoun is expressed in the Greek.

ἀσπάζου τ. φ. As R.V., Salute *the friends:* the same verb as in the previous sentence and in 2 John 13: 'greet' may be reserved for the verb used Acts xv. 23, xxiii. 26; James i. 1; comp. 2 John 10, 11 (χαίρειν). The former is much the more common word in N.T. to express salutation. For other instances of capricious changes of rendering in the same passage in A.V. comp. 1 John ii. 24; iii. 24; v. 10, 15; John iii. 31.

κατ' ὄνομα. The phrase occurs in N.T. in only one other passage (John x. 3); 'He calleth His own sheep *by name.*' The salutation is not to be given in a general way, but to each individual separately— ὀνομαστί. S. John as shepherd of the Churches of Asia would imitate the Good Shepherd and know all his sheep by name.

APPENDICES

A. The Three Evil Tendencies in the World.

The three forms of evil 'in the world' mentioned in 1 John ii. 16 have been taken as a summary of sin, if not in all its aspects, at least in its chief aspects. 'The lust of the flesh, the lust of the eyes, and the vainglory of life' have seemed from very early times to form a synopsis of the various modes of temptation and sin. And certainly they cover so wide a field that we cannot well suppose that they are mere examples of evil more or less fortuitously mentioned. They appear to have been carefully chosen on account of their typical nature and wide comprehensiveness.

There is, however, a wide difference between the views stated at the beginning and end of the preceding paragraph. It is one thing to say that we have here a very comprehensive statement of three typical forms of evil; quite another to say that the statement is a summary of all the various kinds of temptation and sin.

To begin with, we must bear in mind what seems to be S. John's purpose in this statement. He is not giving us an account of the different ways in which Christians are tempted, or (what is much the same) the different sins into which they may fall. Rather, he is stating the principal forms of evil which are exhibited 'in the world,' i. e. in those who are *not* Christians. He is insisting upon the evil origin of these desires and tendencies, and of the world in which they exist, in order that his readers may know that the world and its ways have no claim on their affections. All that is of God, and especially each child of God, has a claim on the love of every believer. All that is not of God has no such claim.

It is difficult to maintain, without making some of the three heads unnaturally elastic, that all kinds of sin, or even all of the principal kinds of sin, are included in the list. Under which of the three heads are we to place unbelief, heresy, blasphemy, or persistent impenitence? Injustice in many of its forms, and especially in the most extreme form of all—murder, cannot without some violence be brought within the sweep of these three classes of evil.

Two positions, therefore, may be insisted upon with regard to this classification.

1. It applies to forms of evil which prevail in the non-Christian world rather than to forms of temptation which beset Christians.

2. It is very comprehensive, but it is not exhaustive.

It seems well, however, to quote a powerful statement of what may be said on the other side. The italics are ours, to mark where there seems to be over-statement. "I think these distinctions, the lust of the flesh, the lust of the eye, and the pride of life, prove themselves to be very accurate and very complete distinctions in practice, though an ordinary philosopher may perhaps adopt some other classification of those tendencies which connect us with the world and give it a dominion over us. To the lust of the flesh may be referred *the crimes and miseries which have been produced by* gluttony, drunkenness, and the irregular intercourse of the sexes ; an appalling catalogue, certainly, which no mortal eye could dare to gaze upon. To the lust of the eye may be referred all worship of visible things, *with the divisions, persecutions, hatreds, superstitions, which this worship has produced in different countries and ages*. To the pride or boasting of life,—where you are not to understand by life, for the Greek words are entirely different, either natural or spiritual life, such as the Apostle spoke of in the first chapter of the Epistle, but all that belongs to the outside of existence, houses, lands, whatever exalts a man above his fellow,—to this head we must refer *the oppressor's wrongs*, and that contumely which Hamlet reckons among the things which are harder to bear even than the 'slings and arrows of outrageous fortune.' In these three divisions I suspect all the mischiefs which have befallen our race may be reckoned, and each of us is taught by the Apostle, and may know by experience, that the seeds of the evils so enumerated are in himself" (Maurice).

Do we not feel in reading this that S. John's words have been somewhat strained in order to make them cover the whole ground? One sin produces so many others in its train, and these again so many more, that there will not be much difficulty in making the classification exhaustive, if under each head we are to include all the crimes and miseries, divisions and hatreds, which that particular form of evil has *produced*.

Some of the *parallels* and *contrasts* which have from early times been made to the Apostle's classification are striking, even when somewhat fanciful. Others are both fanciful and unreal. The three forms of evil noticed by S. John in this passage are only partially parallel to those which are commonly represented under the three heads of the world, the flesh, and the devil. Strictly speaking those particular forms of spiritual evil which would come under the head of the devil, as distinct from the world and the flesh, are not included in the Apostle's enumeration at all. 'The vainglory of life' would come under the head of the world; 'the lust of the flesh' of course under that of 'the flesh'; while 'the lust of the eyes' would belong partly to the one and partly to the other.

There is more reality in the parallel drawn between S. John's classification and the three elements in the temptation by which Eve was overcome by the evil one, and again the three temptations in which

Christ overcame the evil one. 'When the woman saw that the tree was good for food (the lust of the flesh), and that it was pleasant to the eyes (the lust of the eyes), and a tree to be desired to make one wise (the vainglory of life), she took of the fruit thereof, and did eat' (Gen. iii. 6). Similarly, the temptations (1) to work a miracle in order to satisfy the cravings of the flesh, (2) to submit to Satan in order to win possession of all that the eye could see, (3) to tempt God in order to win the glory of a miraculous preservation (Luke iv. 1—12).

Again, there is point in the contrast drawn between these three forms of evil 'in the world' and the three great virtues which have been the peculiar creation of the Gospel (Liddon, *Bampton Lectures* VIII. iii. B), purity, charity, and humility, with the three corresponding 'counsels of perfection,' chastity, poverty, and obedience.

But in all these cases, whether of parallel or contrast, it will probably be felt that the correspondence is not perfect throughout, and that the comparison, though striking, is not quite satisfying, because not quite exact.

It is surely both fanciful and misleading to see in this trinity of evil any contrast to the three Divine Persons in the Godhead. Is there any sense in which we can say with truth that a lust, whether of the flesh or of the eyes, is more opposed to the attributes of the Father than to the attributes of the Son? Forced analogies in any sphere are productive of fallacies; in the sphere of religious truth they may easily become profane.

B. ANTICHRIST.

In the notes on 1 John ii. 18 it has been pointed out that the term 'Antichrist' is in N. T. peculiar to the Epistles of S. John (1 John ii. 18, 22; iv. 3; 2 John 7), and that in meaning it seems to combine the ideas of a mock Christ and an opponent of Christ, but that the latter idea is the prominent one. The false claims of a rival Christ are more or less included in the signification; but the predominant notion is that of hostility. The origin of the word is obscure; but S. John uses it as a term well known to his readers. In this respect the use of ὁ ἀντίχριστος is parallel to that of ὁ λόγος.

It remains to say something on two other points of interest. I. Is the Antichrist of S. John a person or a tendency, an individual man or a principle? II. Is the Antichrist of S. John identical with the great adversary spoken of by S. Paul in 2 Thess. ii.? The answer to the one question will to a certain extent depend upon the answer to the other.

I. It will be observed that S. John introduces the term 'Antichrist,' as he introduces the term 'Logos' (1 John i. 1; John i. 1), without any explanation. He expressly states that it is one with which his readers are familiar; 'even as ye heard that Antichrist cometh.' Certainly this, the first introduction of the name, looks like an allusion to a person. All the more so when we remember that the Christ was 'He that cometh' (Matt. xi. 3; Luke xix. 38). Both Christ and Antichrist had been the subject of prophecy, and therefore each might be spoken of as

'He that cometh.' But it is by no means conclusive. We may understand 'Antichrist' to mean an impersonal power, or principle, or tendency, exhibiting itself in the words and conduct of individuals, without doing violence to the passage. In the one case the 'many antichrists' will be fore-runners of the great personal opponent; in the other the antichristian spirit which they exhibit may be regarded as Antichrist. But the balance of probability seems to be in favour of the view that the Antichrist, of which S. John's readers had heard as certain to come shortly before the end of the world, is a person.

Such is not the case with the other three passages in which the term occurs. 'Who is the liar but he that denieth that Jesus is the Christ? This is the Antichrist, even he that denieth the Father and the Son' (1 John ii. 22). There were many who denied that Jesus is the Christ and thereby denied not only the Son but the Father of whom the Son is the revelation and representative. Therefore once more we have many antichrists, each one of whom may be spoken of as 'the Antichrist,' inasmuch as he exhibits the antichristian characteristics. No doubt this does not exclude the idea of a person who should have these characteristics in the highest possible degree, and who had not yet appeared. But this passage *taken by itself* would hardly suggest such a person.

So also with the third passage in the First Epistle. 'Every spirit which confesseth not Jesus is not of God: and this is the (spirit) of the Antichrist, whereof ye have heard that it cometh, and now it is in the world already' (iv. 3). Here it is no longer 'the Antichrist' that is spoken of, but 'the spirit of the Antichrist.' This is evidently a principle; which again does not exclude, though it would not necessarily suggest or imply, the idea of a person who would embody this antichristian spirit of denial.

The passage in the Second Epistle is similar to the second passage in the First Epistle. 'Many deceivers are gone forth into the world, even they that confess not Jesus Christ as coming in the flesh. This is the deceiver and the Antichrist' (*v.* 7). Here again we have many who exhibit the characteristics of Antichrist. Each one of them, and also the spirit which animates them, may be spoken of as 'the Antichrist'; the further idea of an individual who shall exhibit this spirit in an extraordinary manner being neither necessarily excluded, nor necessarily implied.

The first of the four passages, therefore, will have to interpret the other three. And as the interpretation of that passage cannot be determined beyond dispute, we must be content to admit that the question as to whether the Antichrist of S. John is personal or not cannot be answered with certainty. The probability seems to be in favour of an affirmative answer. In the passage which *introduces* the subject (1 John ii. 18) the Antichrist, of which the Apostle's little children had heard as coming, appears to be a person of whom the 'many antichrists' with their lying doctrine are the heralds and already existing representatives. And it may well be that, having introduced the term with the personal signification familiar to his readers, the Apostle goes on to make other uses of it; in order to warn them that, although the personal Antichrist has not yet come, yet his spirit and doctrine are already at work in the world.

Nevertheless, we must allow that, if we confine our attention to the passages of S. John in which the term occurs, the balance in favour of the view that he looked to the coming of a personal Antichrist is far from conclusive. This balance, however, whatever its amount, is considerably augmented when we take a wider range and consider— (a) The origin of the doctrine which the Apostle says that his readers had already heard respecting Antichrist; (b) The treatment of the question by those who followed S. John as teachers in the Church; (c) Other passages in the N. T. which seem to bear upon the question. The discussion of this third point is placed last because it involves the second question to be investigated in this Appendix;—Is the Antichrist of S. John identical with S. Paul's 'man of sin'?

(a) There can be little doubt that the *origin* of the primitive doctrine respecting Antichrist is *the Book of Daniel*, to which our Lord Himself had drawn attention in speaking of the 'abomination of desolation' (Matt. xxiv. 15; Dan. ix. 27, xii. 11). The causing the daily sacrifice to cease, which was one great element of this desolation, at once brings these passages into connexion with the 'little horn' of Dan. viii. 9—14, the language respecting which seems almost necessarily to imply an individual potentate. The prophecies respecting the 'king of fierce countenance' (viii. 23—25) and 'the king' who 'shall do according to his will' (xi. 36—39) strongly confirm this view. And just as it has been in individuals that Christians have seen realisations, or at least types, of Antichrist (Nero, Julian, Mahomet), so it was in an individual (Antiochus Epiphanes) that the Jews believed that they saw such. It is by no means improbable that S. John himself considered Nero to be a type, indeed the great type, of Antichrist. When Nero perished so miserably and obscurely in A.D. 68, Romans and Christians alike believed that he had only disappeared for a time. Like the Emperor Frederick II. in Germany, and Sebastian 'the Regretted' in Portugal, this last representative of the Caesars was supposed to be still alive in mysterious retirement: some day he would return. Among Christians this belief took the form that Nero was to come again as the Antichrist (Suet. *Nero*, 40, 56; Tac. *Hist.* II. 8). All this will incline us to believe that the Antichrist, of whose future coming S. John's 'little children' had heard, was not a mere principle, but a person.

(b) "That Antichrist is one individual man, not a power, not a mere ethical spirit, or a political system, not a dynasty, or a succession of rulers, was *the universal tradition of the early Church*." This strong statement seems to need a small amount of qualification. The Alexandrian School is not fond of the subject. "Clement makes no mention of the Antichrist at all; Origen, after his fashion, passes into the region of generalizing allegory. The Antichrist, the 'adversary,' is 'false doctrine'; the temple of God in which he sits and exalts himself, is the written Word; men are to flee, when he comes, to 'the mountains of truth' (*Hom. xxix. in Matt.*). Gregory of Nyssa (*Orat. xi. c. Eunom.*) follows in the same track." Still the general tendency is all the other way. Justin Martyr (*Trypho* XXXII.)

says "He whom Daniel foretells would have dominion for a time, and times, and an half, is even already at the door, about to speak blasphemous and daring things against the Most High." He speaks of him as 'the man of sin.' Irenaeus (v. xxv. 1, 3), Tertullian (*De Res. Carn.* xxiv., xxv.), Lactantius (*Div. Inst.* vii. xvii.), Cyril of Jerusalem (*Catech.* xv. 4, 11, 14, 17), and others take a similar view, some of them enlarging much upon the subject. Augustine (*De Civ. Dei*, xx. xix.) says "Satan shall be loosed, and by means of that Antichrist shall work with all power in a lying but wonderful manner." Jerome affirms that Antichrist "is one man, in whom Satan shall dwell bodily"; and Theodoret that "the Man of Sin, the son of perdition, will make every effort for the seduction of the pious, by false miracles, and by force, and by persecution." From these and many more passages that might be cited it is quite clear that the Church of the first three or four centuries almost universally regarded Antichrist as an individual. The evidence, beginning with Justin Martyr in the sub-Apostolic age, warrants us in believing that in this stream of testimony we have a belief which prevailed in the time of the Apostles and was possibly shared by them. But as regards this last point it is worth remarking how reserved the Apostles seem to have been with regard to the interpretation of prophecy. "What the Apostles disclosed concerning the future was for the most part disclosed by them in private, to individuals—not committed to writing, not intended for the edifying of the body of Christ,—and was soon lost" (J. H. Newman).

(c) Besides the various passages in N.T. which point to the coming of false Christs and false prophets (Matt. xxiv. 5, 24; Mark xiii. 22, 23; Acts xx. 29; 2 Tim. iii. 1; 2 Pet. ii. 1), there are two passages which give a detailed description of a great power, hostile to God and His people, which is to arise hereafter and have great success;—Rev. xiii. and 2 Thess. ii. The second of these passages will be considered in the discussion of the second question. With regard to the first this much may be asserted with something like certainty, that the correspondence between the 'beast' of Rev. xiii. and the 'little horn' of Dan. viii. is too close to be accidental. But in consideration of the difficulty of the subject and the great diversity of opinion it would be rash to affirm positively that the 'beast' of the Apocalypse is a person. The correspondence between the 'beast' and the 'little horn' is not so close as to compel us to interpret both images alike. The wiser plan will be to leave Rev. xiii. out of consideration as neutral, for we cannot be at all sure whether the beast (1) is a person, (2) is identical with Antichrist. We shall find that 2 Thess. ii. favours the belief that Antichrist is an individual.

II. There is a strong preponderance of opinion in favour of the view that *the Antichrist of S. John is the same as the great adversary of S. Paul* (2 Thess. ii. 3). 1. Even in the name there is some similarity; the Antichrist (ὁ ἀντίχριστος) and 'he that opposeth' (ὁ ἀντικείμενος). And the idea of being a rival Christ which is included in the name Antichrist and is wanting in 'he that opposeth,' is supplied in S. Paul's description of the great opponent: for he is a '*man*,' and he 'setteth himself forth as *God.*' 2. Both Apostles state that their readers had previously been instructed about this future adversary. 3. Both declare that his coming is preceded by an apostasy of many nominal Christians. 4. Both connect his coming with the Second Advent of Christ. 5. Both describe him as a liar and deceiver. 6. S. Paul says that this 'man of sin exalteth himself against all that is called God.' S. John places the spirit of Antichrist as the opposite of the Spirit of God. 7. S. Paul states that his 'coming is according to the working of Satan.' S. John implies that he is of the evil one. 8. Both Apostles state that, although this great opponent of the truth is still to come, yet his spirit is already at work in the world. With agreement in so many and such important details before us, we can hardly be mistaken in affirming that the two Apostles in their accounts of the trouble in store for the Church have one and the same meaning.

Having answered, therefore, this second question in the affirmative we return to the first question with a substantial addition to the evidence. It would be most unnatural to understand S. Paul's 'man of sin' as an impersonal principle; and the widely different interpretations of the passage for the most part agree in this, that the great adversary is an individual. If, therefore, S. John has the same meaning as S. Paul, then the Antichrist of S. John is an individual.

To sum up:—Although none of the four passages in S. John's Epistles are conclusive, yet the first of them (1 John ii. 18) inclines us to regard Antichrist as a person. This view is confirmed (*a*) by earlier Jewish ideas on the subject, (*b*) by subsequent Christian ideas from the sub-Apostolic age onwards, (*c*) above all by S. Paul's description of the 'man of sin,' whose similarity to S. John's Antichrist is of a very close and remarkable kind.

For further information on this difficult subject see the articles on Antichrist in Smith's *Dictionary of the Bible* (Appendix), and *Dictionary of Christian Biography*, with the authorities there quoted; also four lectures on *The Patristic Idea of Antichrist* in J. H. Newman's *Discussions and Arguments*.

C. The Sect of the Cainites.

The name of this extravagant Gnostic sect varies considerably in different authors who mention them: Cainistae, Caiani, Cainani, Cainaei, Cainiani, Caini, and possibly other varieties, are found. Cainites were a branch of the Ophites, one of the oldest forms of Gnosticism known to us. Other branches of the Ophites known to us through Hippolytus are the *Naassenes* (*Naash*) or 'Venerators of the serpent,' the *Peratae* (πέραν or περᾷν) 'Transmarines' or 'Transcendentalists,' the *Sethians* or 'Venerators of Seth,' and the *Justinians* or followers of Justin, a teacher otherwise unknown. Of these the Naassenes, as far as name goes, are the same as the Ophites, the one name being Hebrew, and the other Greek (ὄφις) in origin, and both meaning 'Serpentists' or 'Venerators of the serpent.'

All the Ophite sects make the serpent play a prominent part in their system, and that not out of sheer caprice or extravagance, but as part of a reasoned and philosophical system. In common with almost all Gnostics they held that matter is radically evil, and that therefore the Creator of the material universe cannot be a perfectly good being. The Ophites regarded the Creator as in the main an evil being, opposed to the Supreme God. From this it followed that Adam in disobeying his Creator did not fall from a high estate, nor rebel against the Most High, but defied a hostile power and freed himself from its thraldom: and the serpent who induced him to do this, so far from being the author of sin and death, was the giver of light and liberty. It was through the serpent that the human race was first made aware that the being who created them was not supreme, but that there were higher than he; and accordingly the serpent became the symbol of intelligence and enlightenment.

Logically carried out, such a system involved a complete inversion of all the moral teaching of the Old Testament. All that the Creator of the world (who is the God of the Jews) commands, must be disobeyed, and all that He forbids must be done. The negative must be struck out of the Ten Commandments, and everything that Moses and the Prophets denounced must be cultivated as virtues. From this monstrous consequence of their premises most of the Ophites seem to have recoiled. Some modified their premises and made the Creator to be, not an utterly evil being, but an inferior power, who through ignorance sometimes acted in opposition to the Supreme God. Others, while retaining the Ophite doctrine that the serpent was a benefactor and deliverer of mankind in the matter of the temptation of Eve, endeavoured to bring this into harmony with Scripture by declaring that he did this service to mankind unwittingly. His intention was evil; he wished to do a mischief to the human race. But it was overruled to good; and what the serpent plotted for the ruin of man turned out to be man's enlightenment.

The Cainites, however, accepted the Ophite premises without qualification, and followed them without shrinking to their legitimate conclusion. Matter and the Creator of everything material are utterly evil. The revolt of Adam and Eve against their Creator was a righteous act, the breaking up of a tyranny. The serpent who suggested and aided this emancipation is a good being, as worthy of veneration, as the Creator is of abhorrence. The redemption of man begins with the first act of disobedience to the Creator. Jesus Christ is not the redeemer of the human race. He merely completed what the serpent had begun. Indeed some Cainites seem to have identified Jesus with the serpent. Others again, with more consistency, seem to have maintained that Jesus was an enemy of the truth and deserved to die.

The moral outcome of such a system has been already indicated, and the Cainites are said to have openly accepted it. Everything that the God of the Old Testament forbids must be practised, and everything that He orders abjured. Cain, the people of Sodom, Esau, Korah, Dathan and Abiram, are the characters to be imitated as saints

and heroes; and in the New Testament, Judas. These are the true
martyrs, whom the Creator and His followers have persecuted. About
Judas, as about Jesus Christ, they seem not to have been agreed, some
maintaining that he justly caused the death of one who perverted the
truth; others, that having higher knowledge than the Eleven, he saw
the benefits which would follow from the death of Christ, and therefore brought it about. These benefits, however, were not such as
Christians commonly suppose, viz. the deliverance of mankind from
the power of the serpent, but the final extinction of the dominion of
the Creator. Irenaeus (*Haer.* i. xxxi. 1) tells us that they had a book
called the *Gospel of Judas.* In the next section he states the practical
result of these tenets. " They say, like Carpocrates, that men cannot
be saved until they have gone through all kinds of experience. They
maintain also that in every one of their sinful and foul actions an
angel attends them and listens to them as they work audacity and
incur pollution. According to the nature of the action they invoke
the name of the angel, saying, ' O thou angel, I use thy work. O
thou great power, I accomplish thy action.' And they declare that
this is ' perfect knowledge,'—fearlessly to rush into such actions as it
is not right even to name."

These are developments of those ' depths of Satan ' of which S. John
speaks in the Apocalypse (ii. 24) as a vaunted form of knowledge.
Into the fantastic details of the system it is not necessary to enter.
Suffice to say that, taking an inverted form of the Old Testament
narrative as their basis, they engrafted upon it whatever took their
fancy in the Egyptian rites of Isis and Osiris, the Greek mysteries of
Eleusis, the Phoenician cultus of Adonis, the speculative cosmogony
of Plato, or the wild orgies of Phrygian Cybele. *Purpurei panni* from
all these sources find place in the patchwork system of the Ophite
Gnostics. Christianity supplied materials for still further accretions,
and probably acted as a considerable stimulus to the development of
such theories. In several of its Protean forms we trace what appear
to be adaptations of the Christian doctrine of the Trinity.

" The first appearance of the Ophite heresy in connexion with
Christian doctrines," says Dean Mansel (*The Gnostic Heresies*, p. 104),
"can hardly be placed later than the latter part of the first century";
which brings us within the limits of S. John's lifetime. It is not
probable that the monstrous system of the Cainites was formulated as
early as this. But the first beginnings of it were there; and it is by
no means impossible that 1 John iii. 10—12 was written as a condemnation of the principles on which the Cainite doctrine was built.
Be this as it may, the prodigious heresy, although it probably never
had very many adherents and died out in the third century, is nevertheless very instructive. It shews us to what results the great Gnostic
principle, that matter is utterly evil, when courageously followed to
its logical consequences, leads. And it therefore helps us to understand
the stern and uncompromising severity with which Gnostic principles
are condemned, by implication in the Fourth Gospel, and in express
terms in these Epistles.

D. The Three Heavenly Witnesses.

The outcry which has been made in some quarters against the Revisers for omitting the disputed words in 1 John v. 7, and without a hint in the margin that there is any authority for them, is not creditable to English scholarship. The veteran scholar Döllinger expressed his surprise at this outcry in a conversation with the present writer in July, 1882: and he expressed his amazement and amusement that anyone in these days should *write a book* in defence of the passage, in a conversation in September, 1883. The Revisers' action is a very tardy act of justice; and we may hope that, whether their work as a whole is authorised or not, leave will before long be granted to the clergy to omit these words in reading 1 John v. as a Lesson at Morning or Evening Prayer, or as the Epistle for the First Sunday after Easter. The insertion of the passage in the first instance was quite indefensible, and it is difficult to see upon what sound principles its retention can be defended. There would be no difficulty in treating this case by itself and leaving other disputed texts to be dealt with hereafter. The passage stands absolutely alone (*a*) in the completeness of the evidence against it, (*b*) in the momentous character of the insertion. A summary of the evidence at greater length than could conveniently be given in a note will convince any unprejudiced person that (as Dr Döllinger observed) nothing in textual criticism is more certain than that the disputed words are spurious.

(i) *The External Evidence.*

1. **Every Greek uncial MS.** omits the passage.
2, *Every Greek cursive MS. earlier than the fifteenth century* omits the passage.
3. Out of about 250 known cursive MSS. only *two* (No. 162 of the 15th century and No. 34 of the 16th century) contain the passage, and in them it is *a manifest translation from a late recension of the Latin Vulgate.*

Erasmus hastily promised that if he could find the words in a single Greek MS. he would insert them in his text; and on the authority of No. 34 (61 of the Gospels) he inserted them in his third edition (1522); Beza and Stephanus inserted them also: and hence their presence in all English Versions until the Revised Version of 1881.

4. **Every Ancient Version of the first four centuries** omits the passage.
5. *Every Version earlier than the fourteenth century, except the Latin,* omits the passage.
6. **No Greek Father** quotes the passage in any of the numerous discussions on the doctrine of the Trinity. Against Sabellianism and Arianism it would have been almost conclusive.

It has been urged that the orthodox Fathers did not quote *v.* 7 because in conjunction with *v.* 8 it might be used in the interests of Arianism; in other words that they shirked a passage, which they saw might tell against them, instead of proving that it did not tell against them! And Cyril must not only have shirked but suppressed the disputed words, for he thrice quotes the passage without them. But in that case why did not the Arians quote *v.* 7? Had they done so, the orthodox would have replied and shewn the true meaning of both verses. Evidently both parties were ignorant of its existence.

Again, it has been urged that the Greek Synopsis of Holy Scripture printed in some editions of the Greek Fathers, and also the so-called *Disputation with Arius,* "*seem* to betray an acquaintance with the disputed verse." Even if this 'seeming' could be shewn to be a reality, the fact would prove no more than that the interpolation existed in a Greek as well as a Latin form about the fifth century. Can we seriously defend a text which does not even 'seem' to be known to a single Greek Father until 350 years or more after S. John's death? Could we defend a passage as Chaucer's which was never quoted until the nineteenth century, and was in no edition of his works of earlier date than that?—And the 'seeming' can *not* be shewn to be a reality.

7. *No Latin Father earlier than the fifth century* quotes the passage.

It is sometimes stated that Tertullian possibly, and S. Cyprian certainly, knew the passage. Even if this were true, it would prove nothing for the genuineness of the words against the mass of testimony mentioned in the first six of these paragraphs. Such a fact would only prove that the insertion, which is obviously of Latin origin, was made at a very early date. But the statement is not true. "Tertullian and Cyprian use language which makes it morally certain that they would have quoted these words had they known them" (Westcott and Hort Vol. II. p. 104).

Tertullian's words are as follows:—'*De meo sumet,*' inquit, *sicut ipse de Patris. Ita connexus Patris in Filio, et Filii in Paracleto, tres efficit cohaerentes alterum ex altero: qui tres unum sunt, non unus; quomodo dictum est, 'Ego et Pater unum sumus,' ad substantiae unitatem, non ad numeri singularitatem.* "He saith, *He shall take of Mine* (John xvi. 14), even as He Himself of the Father. Thus the connexion of the Father in the Son, and of the Son in the Paraclete, maketh Three that cohere together one from the other: which Three are one Substance, not one Person; as it is said, *I and My Father are one* (John x. 30), in respect to unity of essence, not to singularity of number" (*Adv. Praxean* xxv.).

S. Cyprian writes thus; *Dicit Dominus, 'Ego et Pater unum sumus'; et iterum de Patre et Filio et Spiritu Sancto scriptum est, 'Et tres unum sunt.'* "The Lord saith, *I and the Father are one;* and again it is written concerning the Father, Son, and Holy Spirit, *And three are one*" (*De Unit. Eccl.* vi.).

It is very difficult to believe that Tertullian's words contain any allusion to the disputed passage. The passage in S. Cyprian seems at first sight to look like such an allusion; but in all probability he has in his mind the passage which follows the disputed words; 'the spirit, the water, and the blood: and the three agree in one'; the Latin Version of which runs, *spiritus et aqua et sanguis; et hi tres unum sunt.* For the Vulgate makes no difference between the conclusions of *vv.* 7 and 8; in both cases the sentence ends with *et hi tres unum sunt.* That

S. Cyprian should thus positively allude to 'the spirit, the water, and the blood' as 'the Father, the Son, and the Holy Spirit' will seem improbable to no one who is familiar with the extent to which the Fathers make any triplet found in Scripture, not merely suggest, but *signify* the Trinity. To take an example from Cyprian himself: "We find that the three children with Daniel, strong in faith and victorious in captivity, observed the third, sixth, and ninth hour, as it were, for a sacrament of the Trinity, which in the last times had to be manifested. For both the first hour in its progress to the third shews forth the consummated number of the Trinity, and also the fourth proceeding to the sixth declares another Trinity; and when from the seventh the ninth is completed, the perfect Trinity is numbered every three hours " (*Dom. Orat.* xxxiv.).

But perhaps the most conclusive argument in favour of the view that Cyprian is alluding to 'the spirit, the water and the blood,' and not to 'the Three that bear witness in heaven, the Father, the Word, and the Holy Spirit,' is S. Augustine's treatment of the passage in question. *In all his voluminous writings there is no trace of the clause about the Three Heavenly Witnesses;* but about 'the spirit, the water and the blood' he writes thus:—"Which three things if we look at as they are in themselves, they are in substance several and distinct, and not one. But if we will inquire into the things signified by these, there not unreasonably comes into our thoughts the Trinity itself, which is the one, only, true, supreme God, Father, and Son and Holy Spirit, of whom it could most truly be said, *There are Three Witnesses, and the Three are One.* So that by the term 'spirit' we should understand God the Father to be signified ; as indeed it was concerning the worshipping of Him that the Lord was speaking, when He said, *God is spirit.* By the term 'blood,' the Son; because *the Word was made flesh.* And by the term 'water,' the Holy Spirit; as, when Jesus spake of the water which He would give to them that thirst, the Evangelist saith, *But this said He of the Spirit, which they that believed on Him were to receive.* Moreover, that the Father, Son, and Holy Spirit are witnesses, who that believes the Gospel can doubt, when the Son saith, *I am one that bear witness of Myself, and the Father that sent Me, He beareth witness of Me ?* Where, though the Holy Spirit is not mentioned, yet He is not to be thought separated from them" (*Contra Maxim.* II. xxii. 3). Is it credible that S. Augustine would go to S. John's Gospel to prove that the Father and the Son might be called witnesses if in the very passage which he is explaining they were called such? His explanation becomes fatuous if the disputed words are genuine. A minute point of some significance is worth remarking, that in these passages both S. Cyprian and S. Augustine invariably write 'the Son,' not 'the Word,' which is the expression used in the disputed passage.

Facundus of Hermiana in his *Defence* of the "Three Chapters" (c. A.D. 550) explains 1 John v. 8 in the same manner as S. Augustine, quoting the verse several times and evidently knowing nothing of v. 7. This shews that late in the sixth century the passage was not generally known even in North Africa. Moreover *he quotes the passage of S.*

Cyprian as authority for this mystical interpretation of *v.* 8. This shews how (300 years after he wrote) S. Cyprian was still understood by a Bishop of his own Church, even after the interpolation had been made. Attempts have been made to weaken the evidence of Facundus by asserting that Fulgentius, who is a little earlier in date, understood Cyprian to be referring to *v.* 7, not to *v.* 8. It is by no means certain that this is the meaning of Fulgentius; and, even if it is, it proves no more than that in the sixth century, as in the nineteenth, there were some persons who believed that Cyprian alludes to 1 John v. 7. Even if such persons were right, it would only shew that this corruption, like many other corruptions of the text, was in existence in the third century.

This may suffice to shew that the passage in Cyprian probably refers to 1 John v. 8 and gives no support to *v.* 7. And this probability becomes something like a certainty when we consider the extreme unlikelihood of his knowing a text which was wholly unknown to S. Hilary, S. Ambrose, and S. Augustine; which is absent from the earliest MSS. of the Vulgate (and consequently was not known to Jerome); and which is not found in Leo I.[1] Neither Codex Amiatinus, c. A.D. 541, "doubtless the best manuscript of the Vulgate" (Scrivener), nor Codex Fuldensis, A.D. 546, contains the passage, though the latter inserts the *Prologus*, which defends the interpolation.

The anonymous treatise *On Rebaptism* (which begins with a fierce attack on the view of S. Cyprian that heretics ought to be rebaptized, and was therefore probably written before the martyrdom of the bishop) twice quotes the passage (xv. and xix.), and in each case says nothing about the Three bearing witness in heaven, but mentions only the spirit, the water, and the blood. This confirms the belief that the words were not found in the Latin Version in use in North Africa at that time.

Lastly, the letter of Leo the Great to Flavianus in B.C. 449 (*The Tome of S. Leo*, v.), shortly before the Council of Chalcedon, "supplies positive evidence to the same effect for the Roman text by quoting *vv.* 4—8 without the inserted words" (Westcott and Hort, Vol. II. p. 104).

Therefore the statement, that *No Latin Father earlier than the fifth century quotes the passage*, is strictly correct. The words in question first occur in some Latin controversial writings towards the end of the fifth century, but are not often quoted until the eleventh. The insertion appears to have originated in North Africa, which at the close of the fifth century was suffering from a cruel persecution under the Arian Vandals. The words are quoted in part in two of the works attributed to Vigilius of Thapsus, and a little later in one by Fulgentius of Ruspe. They are also quoted in a confession of faith drawn up by Eugenius, Bishop of Carthage, and presented to Hunneric c. A.D. 484.

---

[1] The passage (sometimes quoted as from S. Cyprian) in the Epistle to Jubaianus may be omitted. 1. S. Augustine doubted the genuineness of the Epistle. 2. The important words *cum tres unum sunt* are not found in all, if any, early editions of the Epistle. 3. Even if they are genuine, they come from *v.* 8, not from *v.* 7.

But it is worth noting that in these first appearances of the text the wording of it varies: the form has not yet become set. Moreover, in the earliest MSS. which contain it, the Heavenly Witnesses come *after* 'the spirit, and the water, and the blood,' indicating that the insertion was originally a gloss: and one form of the reading introduces the gloss with a *sicut*, thus: *Quia tres sunt qui testimonium dant, spiritus et aqua et sanguis, et tres unum sunt. Sicut in caelo tres sunt, Pater Verbum et Spiritus, et tres unum sunt.* "This momentous SICUT explains how the words, from being a gloss or illustration, crept into the text" (Dobbin, *Codex Montfortianus*, p. 45). The *Prologus Galeatus* to the Catholic Epistles, falsely written in the name of Jerome, blames the Latin translators of the Epistle for omitting *Patris et Filii et Spiritus testimonium*, while the writer of it naively confesses that his contemporaries condemned him as *falsarium corruptoremque sanctarum scripturarum*. The date of it is certainly far later than Jerome. But not until some centuries later are the inserted words often cited even by Latin writers. Bede, the representative scholar of Western Christendom in the eighth century, omits all notice of them in his commentary, and probably did not know them; for he comments on every other verse in the chapter. Still later (A.D. 797) Alcuin was commissioned by Charles the Great to prepare a critical edition from the best Latin MSS. without reference to the original Greek; and he also omitted the passage.

The external evidence against them could not well be much stronger. If S. John had written the words, who would wish to expel such conclusive testimony to the doctrine of the Trinity from Scripture? If anyone had wished to do so, how could he have kept the words out of every MS. and every Version for four centuries? And had he succeeded in doing this, how could they have been recovered? Let us grant, for the sake of argument, that the passage was known to Tertullian, Cyprian, and some later Latin writers; is it therefore even *possibly* genuine? No reasonable hypothesis can be framed to account for a genuine portion of the Greek Testament being known to certain Latin authorities but to no others, whether Greek, Syriac, or Egyptian.

In short, we may use in this case the argument which Tertullian uses with such force in reference to the Christian faith. "Is it credible that so many and such important authorities should have *strayed* into giving unanimous testimony?" *Ecquid verisimile est ut tot et tantae ecclesiae in unam fidem erraverint?*

(ii) Internal Evidence.

But it is sometimes said that, although the external evidence is no doubt exceedingly strong, yet it is not the whole of the case. The internal evidence also must be considered, and that tells very powerfully the other way. Let us admit for the sake of argument that the internal evidence is very strongly in favour of the genuineness of the disputed words. Let us assume that the passage, though making sense without the words (as is indisputably the case), makes far better sense with the words. Let us suppose that the sense of the passage when thus enlarged is so superior to the shorter form of it, that it would be incredible that anyone to whom the longer form had occurred would ever write the shorter one. Can all this prove, in the teeth of abundant evidence to the contrary, that the longer and vastly superior passage was written, and not the shorter and inferior one ? If twenty reporters quite independently represent an orator as having uttered a very tame and clumsy sentence, which the insertion of a couple of short clauses would make smooth and far more telling, would this fact convince us that the orator must have spoken the two clauses, and that twenty reporters had all accidentally left just these two clauses out ? The fact that in a few out of many editions of the orator's collected speeches, published many years after his death, these two clauses were found, but not always in exactly the same words, would hardly strengthen our belief that they were actually uttered at the time. No amount of internal probability, supplemented by subsequent evidence of this kind, ought to shake our confidence in the reports of the twenty writers who took down the speaker's words at the moment. Where the external evidence is *ample, harmonious*, and *credible*, considerations of internal evidence are out of place. If the authorities which omit the words in question had united in representing S. John as having written nonsense or blasphemy, then, in spite of their number and weight and unanimity, we should refuse to believe them. But here no such doubts are possible ; and the abundance and coherence of the external evidence tell us that the internal evidence, whatever its testimony, cannot be allowed any weight.

And here it is very important to bear in mind an obvious but not always remembered truth. Although internal evidence by itself may be sufficient to decide what an author did *not* write, it can never by itself be sufficient to decide what he *did* write. Words may be in the highest degree appropriate to the subject and harmonious with the context ; but that does not prove that they were written. Without any external evidence we may be certain that S. John did not write 'The Word cannot come in the flesh'; but without external evidence we cannot know what he did write. And if the external evidence amply testifies that he wrote 'The Word became flesh,' it is absurd to try and ascertain from the internal evidence what (in our judgment) he must have written. So also in the present case it is absurd to say that the internal evidence (even if altogether in favour of the disputed words) can prove that S. John wrote the passage. In other words, although internal evidence alone may suffice to prove a passage *spurious*, it can never suffice to prove a passage *genuine*.

The case has been discussed on this basis for the sake of argument and to meet the extraordinary opinion that the internal evidence is in favour of the inserted words. But as a matter of fact internal considerations require us to expel the clauses in question almost as imperatively as does the testimony of MSS., Versions, and Fathers.

1.   The inserted words break the sense. In *v.* 6 we have the water, the blood, and the spirit mentioned ; and they are recapitulated in S. John's manner in *v.* 8. The spurious words in *v.* 7 make an awkward parenthesis ; which is only avoided when, as is sometimes the

case, *v.* 7 is inserted *after v.* 8. And in this position it betrays its origin, as having been in the first instance a comment on *v.* 8.

2. S. John nowhere speaks of 'the *Father*' and 'the *Word*' together. He either says '*God*' and 'the *Word*' (John i. 1, 2, 13, 14; Rev. xix. 13), or 'the *Father*' and 'the *Son*' (1 John ii. 22, 23, 24, &c. &c.). John i. 14 is no exception; 'father' in that passage has no article in the Greek, and should not have a capital letter in English. S. John *never* uses πατήρ for the Father without the article; and the meaning of the clause is 'the glory as of an only son on a mission from a father.' Contrast, as marking S. John's usage, John i. 1 with i. 18.

3. Neither in his Gospel, nor in the First Epistle, does S. John use the theological term ' the Word' in the body of the work: in both cases this expression, which is peculiar to himself in N. T., is confined to the Prologue or Introduction.

4. The inserted words are in the theological language of a later age. No Apostle or Evangelist writes in this sharp, clear-cut style respecting the Persons in the Trinity. The passage is absolutely without anything approaching to a parallel in N. T. If they were original, they would throw the gravest doubt upon the Apostolic authorship of the Epistle. As Haupt observes, "No one can deny that in the whole compass of Holy Writ there is no passage even approaching the dogmatic precision with which, in a manner approximating to the later ecclesiastical definitions, this one asserts the immanent Trinity. Such a verse could not have been omitted by inadvertence; for even supposing such a thing possible in a text of such moment, the absence of the words ἐν τῇ γῇ of *v.* 8 would still be inexplicable. The omission must then have been intentional, and due to the hand of a heretic. But would such an act have remained uncondemned? And were all our MSS. produced by heretics or framed from heretical copies?"

5. The incarnate Son bears witness to man; and the Spirit given at Pentecost bears witness to man; and through the Son, and the Spirit, and His messengers in Old and New Testament, the Father bears witness to man;—respecting the Sonship and Divinity of Jesus Christ. But in what sense can the Three Divine Persons be said to bear witness *in heaven?* Is there not something almost irreverent in making Them the counterpart of the triple witness on earth? The incongruity recalls that of the ignorant petition once seen placarded in a Roman Catholic Church, "Holy Trinity, *pray for us.*" And for whose benefit is the witness in heaven given? Do the angels need it? And if they do, what has this to do with the context? Nor can we avoid this difficulty by saying that the Three *are* in heaven, but *bear witness* on earth. It is expressly stated that the Three *bear witness in heaven*, while three *other* witnesses do so on earth.

6. The addition 'and these Three are one,' though exactly what was required by the interpolators for controversial purposes, is exactly what is not required here by the context. What is required is, not that the Three Witnesses should in essence be only One, which would *reduce* the value of the testimony; but that the Three should agree, which would *enhance* the value of the testimony.

On this part of the evidence the words of S. T. Coleridge and of

F. D. Maurice respecting the passage are worth considering. The former says, " I think the verse of the three witnesses spurious, not only because the balance of external authority is against it, as Porson seems to have shewn ; but also because, in my way of looking at it, it spoils the reasoning." (*Table Talk*, Jan. 6, 1823.) The latter writes, " If it was genuine, we should be bound to consider seriously what it meant, however much its introduction in this place might puzzle us, however strange its phraseology might appear to us. Those who dwell with awe upon the Name into which they have been baptized ; those who believe that all the books of the Bible, and St John's writings more than all the rest, reveal it to us ; those who connect it with Christian Ethics, as I have done ; might wonder that an Apostle should make a formal announcement of this Name in a parenthesis, and in connexion with such a phrase as *bearing record*, one admirably suited to describe the intercourse of God with us, but quite unsuitable, one would have thought, as an expression of His absolute and eternal being. Still, if it was really one of St John's utterances, we should listen to it in reverence, and only attribute these difficulties to our own blindness. As we have the best possible reasons for supposing it is not his, but merely the gloss of some commentator, which crept into the text, and was accepted by advocates eager to confute adversaries, less careful about the truth they were themselves fighting for,—we may thankfully dismiss it" (*Epistles of St John*, pp. 276, 277). Add to this the emphatic declaration of Sir Isaac Newton ; "Let them make good sense of it who are able: for my part I can make none."

We have, therefore, good grounds for saying that the internal evidence, no less than the external, requires us to banish these words from the text. They are evidence of the form which Trinitarian doctrine assumed in North Africa in the fifth century, and possibly at an earlier date. They are an old gloss on the words of S. John ; valuable as a specimen of interpretation, but without the smallest claim to be considered original. Had they not found a place in the *Textus Receptus*, few people not bound (as Roman Catholics are) to accept the later editions of the Vulgate without question, would have dreamed of defending them. Had the translators of 1611 omitted them, no one (with the evidence, which we now possess, before him) would ever have dreamed of inserting them. In Greek texts the words were first printed in the Complutensian edition of A.D. 1514, the addition being made, not from any Greek authority, but *by translation from the Vulgate*. Erasmus in his first two editions (1516 and 1518) omitted them ; but having given his unhappy promise to insert them if they could be found in any Greek MS., he printed them in his third edition (1522), on the authority of the worthless Codex Britannicus (No. 34). Yet even in his third edition, though he inserts the words in the text, he argues against their genuineness in the notes. Stephanus and Beza inserted them also: and thus they obtained a place in the universally used *Textus Receptus*. Luther never admitted them to his translation, and in the first edition of his commentary declared them to be spurious ; but in the second edition he followed the third edition of Erasmus and admitted the words. They first appear in translations published in Switzerland without Luther's name, as in the Zürich edition of Froschover (1529). They were at first commonly printed either in different type or in brackets. The Basle edition of Bryllinger (1552) was one of the first to omit the brackets. Perhaps the last edition which omitted the words in the German Version is the quarto of Zach. Schürer (1620). Among English Versions the Revised of 1881 has the honour of being the first to omit them. Tyndale in his first edition (1525) printed them as genuine, in his second (1534) and third (1535) he placed them in brackets, in the second edition with a difference of type. Cranmer (1539) follows Tyndale's second edition. But in the Genevan (1557) the difference of type and the brackets disappear, and are not restored in the Authorised Version (1611).

The following by no means complete list of scholars who have pronounced against the passage will be of interest. After Richard Simon had led the way in this direction towards the close of the seventeenth century he was followed in the eighteenth by Bentley, Clarke, Emlyn, Gibbon, Griesbach, Hezel, Matthaei, Michaelis, Sir Isaac Newton, Porson, Semler, and Wetstein. In the nineteenth century we have, among others, Ezra Abbott, Bishop Alexander, Alford, Bishop Blomfield, J. H. Blunt, S. T. Coleridge, Davidson, Döllinger, Düsterdieck, Bishop Ellicott, F. W. Farrar, Field, Haddan, Hammond, Haupt, Holzendorff, Horne, Hort, Huther, Lachmann, Bishop Lightfoot, Bishop Marsh, Macdonald, McClellan, F. D. Maurice, Meyrick, Oltramare, Plumptre, Pope, Renan, Reuss, Sanday, Schaff, Schmidt, Scrivener, Scholz, Tischendorf, Tregelles, Bishop Turton, Weiss, Weiszäcker, Westcott, De Wette, Bishop Chr. Wordsworth, and the Revisers. Even the most conservative textual critics have abandoned the defence of this text. As Dr Scrivener says, "to maintain the genuineness of this passage is simply impossible" (*Introduction to the Criticism of N. T.* 649). If this passage is possibly genuine, then scores of other passages are possibly or probably spurious, for the evidence in their favour is less weighty than the evidence against this passage. There is no escape from this conclusion.

Some will perhaps think that this Appendix is wasted labour : that it is a needlessly elaborate slaying of the slain. But so long as any educated Englishman, above all, so long as any English clergyman [1],

---

[1] An Essex Rector has recently (Feb. 1883) thought it worth while to publish a book restating most of the old and exploded arguments in defence of the disputed text: and a member of the York Convocation (April, 1883) denounced the Revised Version as most mischievous, because people now heard words read as Scripture in Church and then went home and found that the words were omitted from the new Version as *not* being Scripture; and he gave as an instance the passage about the Three Heavenly Witnesses, which had been read in the Epistle that morning. He afterwards stated in a published letter "that the last word had not been spoken on this text, and that he was quite content himself to read it in the A. V., as required in the Church Service.... Whether the text was expunged by the Arians (!), or interpolated by the Western Athanasians, is as much a question as ever." Jerome's famous hyperbole, "The whole world groaned and was amazed to find itself Arian," fades into insignificance compared with the supposition that long before Jerome's day the Arians had acquired influence enough to expunge a decisive passage *from every copy of the Bible in every language,* so that neither Jerome, nor any Christian writer of his time, or before his time, had any knowledge of its existence! Where was the

believes, and indeed publicly maintains, that the passage is genuine, or even possibly genuine, trouble to demonstrate its spuriousness will not be thrown away.

E. John the Presbyter or the Elder.

For some time past the writer of this Appendix has been disposed to doubt the existence of any such person as John the Elder as a contemporary of S. John the Apostle at Ephesus. It was, therefore, with much satisfaction that he found that Professor Salmon in the article on **Joannes Presbyter** in the *Dictionary of Christian Biography*, Vol. III. pp. 398—401, and Canon Farrar in *The Early Days of Christianity*, Vol. II. pp. 553—581, take a similar view. Dr Salmon's conclusion is this; "While we are willing to receive the hypothesis of two Johns, if it will help to explain any difficulty, we do not think the evidence for it enough to make us regard it as a proved historical fact. And we frankly own that if it were not for deference to better judges, we should unite with Keim in relegating, though in a different way, this 'Doppelgänger' of the apostle to the region of ghostland." Keim, with Scholten and others, would get rid of the second John by denying that John the Apostle was ever in Asia. This utterly untenable hypothesis has been discussed in the Introduction, chap. I. Dr Farrar, with more confidence, concludes thus; "A credulous spirit of innovation is welcome to believe and to proclaim that any or all of S. John's writings were written by 'John the Presbyter.' They were: but 'John the Presbyter' is none other than John the Apostle." Professor Milligan, Riggenbach, and Zahn are of a similar opinion, and believe that this *personnage douteux, sorte de sosie de l'apôtre, qui trouble comme un spectre toute l'histoire de l'Église d'Éphèse*[1], has no separate existence. Professor Charteris speaks of him as "leaving only vague and doubtful traces, not so much in the reminiscences of his contemporaries as in the half-imaginary historical notes of later ages" (*Canonicity*, p. 327).

The question mainly depends upon a quotation from Papias and the interpretation of it by Eusebius, who quotes it (*H. E.* III. xxxix.; Routh, *Rel. Sac.* I. 7, 8). Papias is stating how he obtained his information. "If on any occasion any one who had been a follower of the Elders came, I used to inquire about the discourses of the

---

passage lying hid all those centuries? How was it rediscovered? Those who have been endeavouring upon critical principles to obtain a pure text of the Greek Testament have been accused of unsettling men's minds by shewing that certain small portions of the common text are of very doubtful authority. But what profound uncertainty must be the result if we once admit, as a legitimate hypothesis, the supposition that an heretical party in the Church could for several hundred years rob the whole Church, and for many hundred years rob all but Western Christendom, of the clearest statement of the central doctrine of Christianity. What else may not the Arians have expunged? What may they not have inserted?

[1] Renan, *L'Antechrist*, p. xxiii. On the whole, however, Renan is disposed to believe in two Johns.

Elders—what Andrew or Peter *said,* or Philip, or Thomas or James, or John or Matthew, or any of the Lord's disciples; and what Aristion and the Elder John, the disciples of the Lord, *say.*"

Certainly the meaning which this at first sight conveys is the one which Eusebius adopts; that Papias here gives us two Johns, the Apostle and the Elder. But closer study of the passage raises a doubt whether this is correct. With regard to most of the disciples of the Lord Papias could only get second-hand information; he could learn what each *said* (εἶπεν) in days long since gone by. But there were two disciples still living at the time when Papias wrote, Aristion and John; and about these he had contemporary and perhaps personal knowledge: he knows what they *say* (λέγουσι). Of one of these, John, he had knowledge of *both* kinds; reports of what he said long ago in the days when Philip, and Thomas, and Matthew were living, and knowledge of what he says now at the time when Papias writes. If this be the meaning intended, we may admit that it is rather clumsily expressed: but that will not surprise us in a writer, who (as Eusebius tells us) was "of very mean intellectual power, as one may state on the evidence of his own dissertations." The title 'Elder' cuts both ways, and tells for and against either interpretation. It may be urged that 'the Elder' before the second 'John' seems to be intended to distinguish him from the Apostle. To which it may be replied, that it may quite as probably have been added in order to *identify* him with the Apostle, seeing that throughout the passage, Andrew, Peter, Peter, &c. are called 'Elders' and not Apostles. May not 'the Elder' be prefixed to John to distinguish him from Aristion, who was not an Apostle? In any case the first John is called 'elder' and 'disciple of the Lord'; and the second John is called 'elder' and 'disciple of the Lord.' So that the view of Eusebius, which *primâ facie* appears to be natural, turns out upon examination to be by no means certain, and perhaps not even the more probable of the two.

But other people besides Eusebius studied Papias. What was their view? Among the predecessors of Eusebius none is more important than **Irenaeus**, who made much use of Papias's work, and independently of it knew a great deal about Ephesus and S. John; and he makes no mention of any second John. This fact at once throws the balance against the Eusebian interpretation of Papias. **Polycrates**, Bishop of Ephesus, would be likely to know the work of Papias; and certainly knew a great deal about S. John and his later contemporaries. In the letter which he wrote to Victor, Bishop of Rome, on the Paschal Controversy (Eus. *H. E.* III. xxxi. 2; v. xxiv. 1—6) he proudly enumerates the 'great lights,' who have fallen asleep and lie buried at Ephesus, Smyrna, Hierapolis, Laodicea, and Sardis, as authorities in favour of the Quartodeciman usage. Among these the Presbyter John is not named. At Ephesus there are the graves of 'John who rested on the Lord's bosom' and of the martyred Polycarp. But no tomb of a second John is mentioned. And would not the reputed author of two canonical Epistles and possibly of the Apocalypse have found a place in such a list, had such a person existed distinct from the Apostle? Whether **Dionysius of Alexandria** (Eus. *H. E.* VII. xxv.)

knew Papias or not we cannot tell; but he had heard of two tombs at
Ephesus, each bearing the name of John. And yet he evidently knows
nothing of the Presbyter John. For while contending that the John
who wrote the Apocalypse cannot be the Apostle, he says that it is
quite uncertain who this John is, and suggests as a possibility 'John
whose surname was Mark,' the attendant of Paul and Barnabas (Acts
xii. 25, xiii. 5). The fragments of Leucius, writings of unknown date,
but probably earlier than Dionysius, contain many traditions respecting
S. John the Apostle, but nothing respecting any other John. The
fragments are sufficient to render it practically certain that the com-
piler of the stories which they contain knew no second John.

It would seem therefore that the predecessors of Eusebius, whether
they had read Papias or not, agreed in believing in only one John, viz.
the Apostle. Therefore those of them who had read Papias (and Irenaeus certainly had done so) must either have understood him to mean
only one John, or must have ignored as untrue his statement respecting a second. There is no independent evidence of the existence of a
second John. Papias, as interpreted or misinterpreted by Eusebius, is
our sole witness. Eusebius seems to have got the hypothesis of a
second John from Dionysius. But Dionysius never quotes Papias as
supporting it, and if he had read him must have believed him to mention only John the Apostle.

Indeed Eusebius himself would seem at one time to have held the
same view. In his *Chronicon* (Schoene, p. 162) he states that Papias
and Polycarp (to whom Jerome adds Ignatius) were disciples of John
the Divine and Apostle. That Papias was the disciple of another John,
is a later theory of his, adopted (as there is good reason for believing)
in order to discredit the Apocalypse. Eusebius was greatly opposed
to the millenarian theories which some people spun out of the Apocalypse; and in order to attack them the better he wished to shew that
the Apocalypse was not the work of the Apostle. But the Apocalypse
claims to be written by John. Therefore there must have been some
other John who wrote it. And as evidence of this other John he
quotes Papias, whose language is so obscure that we cannot be certain
whether he means one John or two.

The two tombs at Ephesus, each said to have borne the name of
John, need not disturb us much. Polycrates, writing on the spot
within a hundred years of the Apostle's death, seems to know nothing
of a second tomb. Dionysius, writing a century and a half after his
death and far away from Ephesus, has heard of two monuments, but
(much as it would have suited his theory to do so) he does not venture
to assert that they were the tombs of two Johns. Jerome, writing still
later and still farther away from the spot, says that a second tomb is
shewn at Ephesus as that of John the Presbyter, and that "some think
that they are two monuments of the same John, viz. the Evangelist"
—*nonnulli putant duas memorias ejusdem Johannis evangelistae esse*
(*De Vir. Illust.* ix.). The probabilities are that these people were
right. Either there were rival sites (a very common thing in topo-
graphy), each claiming to be the grave of the Apostle; or there were
two monuments commemorating two different things, e.g. the place of

his death and the place of his burial. Very possibly they were churches (Zahn, *Acta Johannis*, clxiv.).

The evidence, therefore, of the existence of this perplexing Presbyter is of a somewhat shadowy kind. It amounts simply to the statement of Papias, as conjecturally interpreted by Eusebius, and the two monuments. But the Eusebian interpretation is not by any means certainly correct, and the two monuments do not by any means necessarily imply two Johns. Moreover, Eusebius himself was not always of the same opinion, making Papias sometimes the disciple of the Apostle, sometimes the disciple of the supposed Presbyter. And in this inconsistency he is followed by Jerome. Assume the Eusebian interpretation to be correct, and it will then be very difficult indeed to explain how it is that Irenaeus and Polycrates know nothing of this second John, and how even Dionysius does not seem to have heard of him. Assume that Eusebius was mistaken, and that Papias mentions the Apostle twice over, and then all runs smoothly.

Does this hypothetical Presbyter explain a single difficulty? If so, let us retain him as a reasonable hypothesis. But if, as seems to be the case, he causes a great deal of difficulty and explains nothing that cannot be quite well explained without him, then let him be surrendered as a superfluous conjecture. *Personae non sunt multiplicandae.* We may heartily welcome the wish of Zahn (*Acta Johannis*, p. cliv.) that the publication of the fragments of Leucius will "give the *coup de grace* to the erudite myth created by Eusebius about 'the Presbyter John.' The latter has quite long enough shared in the lot of the undying Apostle. Had this doublet of the Apostle ever existed, he could not have failed to appear in Leucius : and in his pages the Apostle of Ephesus could never have been called simply John, if he had had at his side a second disciple of Jesus of this name." We, therefore, give up the second John as unhistorical. (See Salmon, *Historical Introduction to N. T.*, 109, 274, 330—334.)

It would seem as if 'Presbyter John' was destined to plague and perplex historians. A spectral personage of this name troubles, as we have seen, the history of the Church of Ephesus. Another equally mysterious personage of the same name confronts us in the history of Europe in the twelfth century; when the West was cheered with the news that a mighty Priest-King called Presbyter Johannes had arisen in the East, and restored victory to the Christian cause in the contest with the Saracens. For this extraordinary story, which appears first perhaps in Otto of Freisingen, see Col. Yule's article in the ninth edition of the *Encyclopaedia Britannica* and Baring Gould's *Myths of the Middle Ages*, p. 32. Probably in this case an unfamiliar oriental name was corrupted into a familiar name which happened to sound something like it.

F. The "Doctrine of the Twelve Apostles" and the Writings of S. John[1].

The date of the now famous Διδαχὴ τῶν δώδεκα ᾿Αποστόλων has still to be determined. But it can hardly be later than A.D. 140, and may easily be as early as A.D. 95. In other words it is almost certainly earlier than the Apologies of Justin Martyr, and may possibly be earlier than the Epistle of Clement. In any case, if it contains evidence of a knowledge of S. John's writings it is one of the earliest witnesses, or is perhaps the very earliest witness, that has come down to us.

The proof of its early date is negative rather than positive. There is an entire absence of all those features of which Church History between A.D. 140 and 200 is so full. There is no attempt at a Canon of the New Testament Scriptures. The Evangelists are still treated as one: their writings are "the Gospel." There are still only two orders in the Church, bishops and deacons, the former (as in N.T.) identical with presbyters, who are not mentioned. No outline of a Creed is given. No Christian festival is mentioned. No doctrinal errors are attacked; not even Gnosticism or Ebionism, which were in full bloom by A.D. 140. The only error which is attacked is the moral error of an evil life. The language of the treatise is Scriptural, not patristic. It has been ascertained that it has a vocabulary of 552 words, of which 504 occur in N.T., while of the remaining 48 about 17 are found in LXX. and others are compounds of N.T. words.

All these facts, with others pointing in the same direction, force on us the conviction, that in the Διδαχή we have a very early witness to whatever Books of N.T. were evidently known to the author.

Did he know the Epistles of S. John? A tabular arrangement of passages will help the student to decide this question for himself.

1 John	Διδαχή
iv. 18. ὁ δὲ φοβούμενος οὐ τετελείωται ἐν ἀγάπῃ.	x. μνήσθητι, Κύριε, τῆς ἐκκλησίας σου, τοῦ ῥύσασθαι αὐτὴν ἀπὸ παντὸς πονηροῦ, καὶ τελειῶσαι αὐτὴν ἐν τῇ ἀγάπῃ σου.
iv. 12. ἡ ἀγάπη αὐτοῦ τετελειωμένη ἐν ἡμῖν ἐστίν.	
iv. 17. τετελείωται ἡ ἀγάπη.	
ii. 5. ἐν τούτῳ ἡ ἀγάπη τοῦ Θεοῦ τετελείωται.	

The phrases "to be perfected in love" and "to have love perfected in" occur nowhere in Scripture but in these four passages. Comp. John xvii. 23.

1 John	Διδαχή
ii. 17. ὁ κόσμος παράγεται.	x. παρελθέτω ὁ κόσμος οὗτος.

---

[1] The substance of this Appendix appeared in the *Churchman*, July, 1884, and October, 1885.

The force of this instance is weakened by the similar passage 1 Cor. vii. 31, παράγει γὰρ τὸ σχῆμα τοῦ κόσμου τούτου: and the Διδαχή elsewhere exhibits traces of 1 Corinthians.

1 John	Διδαχή
iv. 1. δοκιμάζετε τὰ πνεύματα.	xi. πᾶς δὲ προφήτης δεδοκιμασμένος, ἀληθινός, κ.τ.λ.

The addition of ἀληθινός, which is one of S. John's characteristic expressions (see on 1 John ii. 8), strengthens the parallel in this case.

2 John	Διδαχή
10. εἴ τις ἔρχεται πρὸς ὑμᾶς, καὶ ταύτην τὴν διδαχὴν οὐ φέρει, μὴ λαμβάνετε αὐτόν.	xi. ἐὰν δὲ αὐτὸς ὁ διδάσκων στραφεὶς διδάσκῃ ἄλλην διδαχὴν εἰς τὸ καταλῦσαι, μὴ αὐτοῦ ἀκούσητε.

The weight of these instances from the Epistles is considerably augmented when we find apparent reminiscences of the Fourth Gospel and of the Apocalypse in the Διδαχή. It is almost universally admitted that evidence for S. John's Gospel may be accepted as evidence for his First Epistle, and *vice versâ*. They were very possibly published together, and the author of the Muratorian Canon seems to treat them as one book.

In the eucharistic thanksgiving (*Did.* x.) we have the address Πάτερ ἅγιε. This occurs in "the prayer of the Great High Priest" (John xvii. 11) and nowhere else in N.T. And there are several other expressions in the thanksgiving which look like echoes of Christ's prayer.

John xvii.	Διδαχή x.
δόξασόν σου τὸν υἱόν...ἵνα...δώσῃ αὐτοῖς ζωὴν αἰώνιον. αὕτη δέ ἐστιν ἡ αἰώνιος ζωή, ἵνα γινώσκωσί σε...καὶ ὃν ἀπέστειλας Ἰησοῦν Χριστόν. ἵνα ὦσιν καὶ αὐτοὶ ἡγιασμένοι.	ὑπὲρ τῆς γνώσεως καὶ πίστεως καὶ ἀθανασίας, ἧς ἐγνώρισας ἡμῖν διὰ Ἰησοῦ τοῦ παιδός σου. ζωὴν αἰώνιον διὰ τοῦ παιδός σου. τὴν ἁγιασθεῖσαν (ἐκκλησίαν).

The phrase ἐγνώρισας ἡμῖν διὰ Ἰησοῦ τοῦ παιδός σου occurs thrice in the eucharistic prayers and thanksgivings in the Διδαχή. Comp. καὶ ἐγνώρισα αὐτοῖς τὸ ὄνομά σου, καὶ γνωρίσω (John xvii. 26), and πάντα ἃ ἤκουσα παρὰ τοῦ πατρός μου ἐγνώρισα ὑμῖν (John xv. 15). Moreover, the prayer for unity in the Διδαχή (ix.), though very differently expressed, may easily be inspired by the similar prayer in John xvii. 11, 22, 23. "Just as this broken bread was scattered upon the mountains and being gathered together became one (ἐγένετο ἕν), so let Thy Church be gathered together from the ends of the earth into Thy Kingdom." Comp. 1 Cor. x. 17.

There are two other passages which look like reminiscences of the Fourth Gospel.

John	Διδαχή
xv. 1. ἐγώ εἰμι ἡ ἄμπελος ἡ ἀληθινή, καὶ ὁ πατήρ μου ὁ γεωργός ἐστιν.	ix. εὐχαριστοῦμέν σοι, πάτερ ἡμῶν, ὑπὲρ τῆς ἁγίας ἀμπέλου Δαβίδ.
i. 14. ἐσκήνωσεν ἐν ἡμῖν.	x. ὑπὲρ τ. ἁγίου ὀνόματός σου οὗ κατεσκήνωσας ἐν ταῖς καρδίαις ἡμῶν.

The source of "the holy vine of David" may be the Targum on Ps. lxxx. 18 and not John xv. 1; and God's "causing His Name to tabernacle within us" may come from Rev. vii. 15 or xxi. 3 rather than John i. 14. Σκηνόω used intransitively is a favourite term with S. John in allusion to the Shekina, the 'tabernacling' of Jehovah among His people in the Holy of Holies. But the idea of the Divine *Name* being enshrined in the heart at the reception of the heavenly food may have been suggested by Rev. ii. 17. 'I will give him of the hidden manna, and I will give him a white stone, and upon the stone a *new name written.*'

There are four other passages which may be connected with the Apocalypse.

(1) Σύ, δέσποτα **παντοκράτορ** (*Did.* x.). The epithet παντοκράτωρ occurs nine times in the Revelation and nowhere else in N.T., excepting 2 Cor. vi. 18, where it is a quotation from the LXX. For δεσπότης in an address to the Almighty comp. Rev. vi. 10.

(2) At the close of the eucharistic prayer we have Εἴ τις ἅγιός ἐστιν, ἐρχέσθω (*Did.* x.). Comp. ὁ ἅγιος ἁγιασθήτω ἔτι (Rev. xxii. 11); καὶ ὁ διψῶν ἐρχέσθω (Rev. xxii. 17).

(3) In chap. xi., respecting the ministry, we read Καὶ πάντα προφήτην λαλοῦντα ἐν πνεύματι οὐ πειράσετε, a use of πειράζειν in the sense of 'testing' ministers which may have been suggested by Rev. ii. 2; καὶ ἐπείρασω τοὺς φάσκοντας εἶναι ἀποστόλους, καὶ οὐκ εἰσί. For ἐν πνεύματι in the sense of 'in ecstasy' comp. Rev. i. 10; iv. 2; 1 Cor. xii. 3.

(4) Lastly, Κατὰ **κυριακὴν** δὲ Κυρίου (*Did.* xiv.) is probably the earliest instance of the use of κυριακή as a substantive in the sense of the Lord's Day or Sunday. In Rev. i. 10 it is still an adjective; ἐν τῇ κυριακῇ ἡμέρᾳ: where, however, some understand it as meaning, not the Lord's Day, but the Day of the Lord, i.e. the Day of Judgment.

These numerous coincidences in so short a treatise as the Διδαχή appear to constitute a fairly strong case. Not one of them can be considered decisive, although the first is certainly strong; and being from the First Epistle is of special interest in the present inquiry. Taken altogether they seem to justify the conclusion that the author of the *Doctrine of the Twelve Apostles* was acquainted with much of the teaching of S. John, either in a written, or at least in an oral form.

For a very full discussion of the phraseology of the Διδαχή, especially in connexion with the Canon of Scripture, see Dr Schaff's excellent edition, New York, 1885, from which one or two of the above parallels are taken. He entirely agrees with the conclusion just stated.

G. The Latin Versions compared in 1 John.

Critical editions of Latin Versions are among the *desiderata* in textual appliances: but excellent work is being done in this most promising and interesting field. See especially the valuable essays in *Studia Biblica* (Oxford, 1885) by Professors Wordsworth and Sanday, to the latter of whom this Appendix is much indebted.

The object of the Appendix is not to arrive at any conclusions (which would necessarily be premature), but merely to give some indication of the problems to be solved, and to show from the First Epistle of S. John the kind of facts which form materials for conclusions.

What was the origin of the Old Latin Version out of which Jerome formed the Vulgate? Was it originally one? And, if more than one, how many independent translations existed? In the Roman Empire the need of a Latin translation of the Scriptures would very soon be felt. And there would be nothing surprising in the fact, if fact it be, that several Latin Versions, i.e. translations for general use, were made in different parts of the Empire almost simultaneously.

The best working hypothesis at present seems on the whole to be, that there were *two* such original translations; and that the great variety of Latin texts that have come down to us are modifications of these caused (1) *by crossing of the two main stocks* and (2) *by local revision* of them. When the two translations came into contact, each would influence the other: and if the English of a Northumbrian miner is not easily followed by a Cornish one even in these days of railways and newspapers, we may be sure that a Latin Version made in one part of the Roman Empire might need a good deal of change in its vocabulary before it could become popular in another part. The two main classes of Latin texts are commonly distinguished as *African* and *European;* and the characteristics which have been already ascertained as belonging to each are so numerous and so definite, that it is unlikely that these two great families will eventually be traced to one parent.

But it does not necessarily follow that each of these two original translations covered the whole N.T. Both may have contained the Gospels, but only one of them the remainder. Both may have contained the Epistles of S. Paul, but only one of them the Catholic Epistles. It would be very rash to argue from phenomena found in the Gospels to conclusions respecting the Epistles, and perhaps even from phenomena found in the text of S. James to the text of the Epistles of S. John.

Still it is very interesting to notice that one of the conclusions reached by Professor Sanday with regard to S. James *does* seem to hold good of our Epistle. "What inferences are we to draw from all this as to the character of the Vulgate text in this Epistle (S. James)? *Extremely little is due to Jerome himself.* There is hardly a word that cannot be proved to have been in use before his time: in many cases where the evidence is slenderest as to the use of the word elsewhere the quotations in St Augustine and Ambrosiaster prove that it was already found in this Epistle" (*Studia Biblica*, 252). In the following tables, which were not drawn up with a view to eliciting this fact, it will be noticed that in the first passage (1 John ii. 1, 2) not a single word in the Vulgate text is Jerome's own; in the second (ii. 15 —17) only *superbia vitae;* in the third (iv. 2, 3) only the second *Christum*, which has no business to be there.

The passages were selected (1) because they are quoted by Cyprian, of whose works we now have a critical edition by Hartel; (2) because they each contain something of special interest in the way of reading or translation. The arrangement of the quotations in their respective columns is not intended to prejudge the question as to which writer gives an African, and which a European text. But we may safely consider Cyprian as having mainly the former, and the Vulgate as being, at any rate in its base, the latter. Tertullian is either omitted or placed below Cyprian, in spite of his priority. "The presence of a reading in Tertullian," says Dr Sanday, "does not, I believe, necessarily prove that it is African; for I strongly suspect that besides his own direct translations from the Greek, he also became acquainted with the European text during his stay at Rome, and made use of it together with the African. But I wish to speak on all points relating to Tertullian as yet with great reserve. Cyprian is our true starting point in the history of the African Version" (*S. B.* 245).

It is worth while observing that several renderings, which by evidence obtained in other parts of N.T. have been proved to be decidedly African in character, are in these passages found in Cyprian, or in Cyprian and Tertullian, and for the most part there alone. Thus *iste* for *hic* (*ista scribo*); *si qui* for *si quis* (*si qui deliquerit* and *si qui dilexerit*); *delinquere* for *peccare* (*ne delinquatis: et si qui deliquerit*); *delictum* for *peccatum* (*pro delictis nostris*); *quomodo* for *sicut* (*quomodo et ipse* [*Deus*] *manet*—four times). To such small points do the characteristic differences between the two main families of Old Latin texts extend.

These passages serve also to illustrate that *tendency to interpolation* which is one of the marked features of all Western texts. We have the insertion of *concupiscentia* in 1 John ii. 16 (*sed ex concupiscentia saeculi*) and the spurious addition to ii. 17 (*quomodo et ipse manet in aeternum*). Comp. the addition of *Dei* after *caritatem* (iii. 16) and after *caritati* (iv. 16); of *quod majus est* after *hoc est testimonium Dei* (v. 9); and (in some copies) of *ecce praedixi vobis ut in die Domini non confundamini* (2 John 11). From Wiclif's and Purvey's "The grace of God be with thee" (2 John 13) we infer that there also some Latin texts had a spurious addition to the text. Western interpolation reached a climax in the famous Latin addition to 1 John v. 7, 8.

LATIN VERSIONS OF 1 JOHN II. 1, 2.

CYPRIAN (Ep. lv. 18).

Filioli mei, ista scribo [scripsi Q] vobis ne de-linquatis: et si qui [quis BQR] deliquerit, advo-catum habemus apud patrem, Iesum Christum justum [suffragatorem Q], et ipse est deprecatio pro delictis nostris.

TERTULLIAN (De Pud. xix).

Filioli, haec scribo vobis, ne delinquatis, et si deliqueritis, advoca-tum habemus apud Deum patrem, Iesum Christum justum, et ipse placatio est pro delictis nostris.

VIGILIUS OF THAPSUS.

Haec vobis scribo ut non peccetis. Quod si peccaverimus, paraclitum habemus ad patrem.

Elsewhere Vigilius has advocatum.

VICTOR OF VITA.

Haec scribo vobis, ne peccetis. Sed et si quis peccaverit, paraclitum habemus apud patrem, Iesum Christum.

HILARY.

Ipse est placatio pro peccatis nostris.

AUGUSTINE (COMMENTARY).

Filioli mei, haec scribo vobis ut non peccetis: et si quis peccaverit, ad-vocatum habemus ad patrem, Iesum Christum justum, et ipse propitia-tio est peccatorum nos-trorum.

Elsewhere Augustine has et ipse est exoratio pro peccatis nostris; *and* et ipse est propitiatio pro peccatis nostris; *and et* ipse propitiator est pec-catorum nostrum.

JEROME (VULGATE).

Filioli mei, haec scribo vobis ut non peccetis: sed et si quis pecca-verit, advocatum habe-mus apud patrem, Iesum Christum justum, et ipse est propitiatio pro pecca-tis nostris.

So also Contra Jovin. II. 2 *two or three times.*

LATIN VERSIONS OF 1 JOHN II. 15—17.

JEROME (VULGATE).

Nolite diligere mundum neque ea quae in mundo sunt. Si quis diligit mundum, non est caritas patris in eo: quoniam omne quod in mundo est, concupiscentia carnis est et concupiscentia oculorum et **superbia vitae**, quae non est ex patre, sed ex mundo est. Et mundus transibit et concupiscentia ejus: qui autem facit voluntatem Dei, manet in aeternum.

Elsewhere Jerome has Omne quod in mundo est, desiderium carnis est et desiderium oculorum et superbia hujus vitae; quae non est de patre, sed de mundo. Et mundus praeterit et desiderium ejus. (Contra Jovin. I. 40.)

AUGUSTINE (COMMENTARY).

Nolite diligere mundum, neque ea quae sunt in mundo. Si quis dilexerit mundum, dilectio patris non est in ipso: quia omne quod in mundo est, desiderium est carnis et desiderium oculorum et ambitio saeculi: quae non sunt ex patre, sed ex mundo sunt. Et mundus transit et desideria ejus. Qui autem fecerit voluntatem Dei, manet in aeternum, sicut et ipse manet in aeternum.

Elsewhere Augustine has Et mundus transit et concupiscentia ejus. Qui autem facit vol. Dei, manet in aeternum, sicut et Deus m. in aeternum; *and again* Qui autem fecit.

LUCIFER.

Et mundus transit et concupiscentia ejus. Qui autem fecerit voluntatem Dei manet in aeternum quomodo et Deus manet in aeternum.

ZENO OF VERONA.

As Cyprian Test. III. xi, *with* si quis *for si* qui, *and Deus for ipse.*

VICTOR OF TUNUNA.

As Lucifer, but with vero *for autem.*

CYPRIAN (TEST. III. xi).

Nolite diligere [*ins.* huc A] mundum neque ea quae in [*ins.* hoc A] mundo sunt. Si qui [quis AMB] dilexerit [*ins.* hunc A] mundum, non est caritas patris in illo: quoniam omne quod in mundo est, concupiscentia carnis est et concupiscentia oculorum et ambitio saeculi, quae non est a patre, sed ex concupiscentia saeculi: et mundus transibit et concupiscentia ejus. Qui autem fecerit voluntatem Dei manet [*thus* WLMB, manebit rel.]in aeternum, quomodo et ipse [et Deus M; *omit* et LB] manet in aeternum.

Cyprian quotes this passage four times. Twice he has quia *for* quoniam, *twice* concup. mundi *for* concup. saeculi, *once* manebit *for* manet, *thrice* Deus *for* ipse.

LATIN VERSIONS OF 1 JOHN iv. 2, 3.

CYPRIAN (TEST. II. viii.).

Omnis spiritus, qui confitetur Iesum Christum in carne [carnem WB] venisse, de Deo est. Qui autem negat in carne [carnem B] venisse, de Deo non [natus non M] est, sed est de antichristi spiritu [est antichristus M].

Comp. TERTULLIAN (Adv. Marc. v. 16) *who combines either two readings or 1 John iv. 3 with 2 John 7*: Ioannes apostolus qui jam antichristos dicit processisse in mundum praecursores antichristi spiritus, negantes Christum in carne venisse, et solventes Iesum.

CODEX FRISINGENSIS.

Omnis spiritus qui confitetur Iesum [Christum] in carne venisse ex Deo est: et omnis spiritus qui non confitetur Iesum ex Deo non est; et hoc est illius antichristi.

FULGENTIUS.

Omnis spiritus qui non confitetur Iesum Christum in carne venisse ex Deo non est; et hic est antichristus.

Elsewhere he has Omnis spiritus qui solvit Iesum ex Deo non est; et hic est antichristus.

TRANSLATOR OF IRENAEUS.

Omnis spiritus qui confitetur Iesum [Christum] in carne venisse, ex Deo est. Et omnis spiritus qui solvit Iesum, non est ex Deo, sed ex [de] antichristo est.

TRANSLATOR OF ORIGEN.

Omnis spiritus qui solvit Iesum non est ex Deo.

LUCIFER.

Omnis spiritus qui destruit Iesum ex Deo non est; et hic est antichristus.

TICHONIUS.

Omnis spiritus qui solvit Iesum et negat in carne venisse de Deo non est, sed hic de antichristo est.

Conflation, as in Augustine.

JEROME (VULGATE).

Omnis spiritus qui confitetur Iesum Christum in carne venisse, ex Deo est: et omnis spiritus qui solvit Iesum Christum, ex Deo non est; et hic est antichristus.

The Clementine Vulgate omits the second Christum.

AUGUSTINE *reads* qui non confitetur *but explains both* qui non confitetur *and* qui solvit *without noting the change. Finally he combines the two like Tertullian, but in reverse order*: solvis Iesum et negas in carne venisse.

H. The English Versions derived from the Vulgate compared
    with it and with one another.

A comparison of the three English Versions which are based on the
Vulgate is interesting and instructive, not only in reference to the
history of the English Bible, but also as throwing light on the manner
in which the Vulgate was formed. Two centuries separate Wiclif's
work (c. 1380) from the Rhemish (1582), and much had taken place in
the way of translation of the Scriptures in the interval. Wiclif's
Version, even when revised by Purvey, was a mere translation from the
Latin without reference to the Greek. The Rhemish, while professing
to be the same, was influenced by Tyndale's translation from the
original. The precise Latin texts used by Wiclif and Purvey cannot
be ascertained; but their translation is much nearer to the ordinary
Vulgate of the Sixtine and Clementine editions than to the original
Vulgate of Jerome. This will be apparent from the tabular arrangement of the Second and Third Epistles given below. The Latin text
there printed is the Clementine, which in these Epistles agrees almost
exactly with the Sixtine, excepting as regards the spurious addition to
2 John 11, and some smaller points in 1 John ii. 4, 24 and v. 14.
The chief readings of the *Codex Amiatinus* (our best authority for the
text of Jerome) are added in brackets at the end of each verse; and the
chief readings of the Old Latin are added at the end of each Epistle.
It will be seen that neither Wiclif nor Purvey used texts that were
closely akin either to the Old Latin or to Jerome. Purvey tells us in
his Prologue (chap. xv.) that he "hadde myche travaile, with diverse
felawis and helperis, to gedere manie elde biblis, and othere doctouris,
and comune glosis, and to make oo Latyn bibel soumdel trewe." But
all these "old bibles," which he and his "fellows" collected, seem to
have had in the main the ordinary Vulgate text; and his "one Latin
bible somewhat correct" is of the same character. In a few cases he
appears to have had an older text than Wiclif: e.g. 1 John v. 10
in filio for *in filium;* 2 John 9 *praecedit* for *recedit:* but this is not
common. And in a few instances both Wiclif and Purvey seem to
have had the reading of Jerome rather than that of the Sixtine or
Clementine text: e.g. 1 John ii. 17 *transibit* and not *transit;* iii. 19
suademus and not *suadebimus.* But the large majority of instances are
the other way. In 1 John ii. 4 they read *Deum* for *eum;* ii. 24 *Quia si*
for *Si;* ii. 29 *et omnis* for *omnis;* iii. 11 *diligatis* for *diligamus;* iii. 12
qui ex for *ex;* iii. 13 *vos* for *nos;* iii. 17 *hujus mundi* for *mundi;* iv. 10
ipse prior for *ipse;* iv. 17 *charitas Dei* for *caritas;* iv. 19 *diligamus
Deum* for *diligamus,* or *dil. invicem;* v. 7 the great interpolation;
v. 13 *scribo* for *scripsi;* v. 14 *Deum* for *eum;* v. 16 *petat et dabitur* for
petit et dabit.

The MSS. of Purvey's Version do not exactly agree: those of Wiclif's
differ very considerably. The text adopted here is that of Forshall
and Madden. A slightly different text will be found in Lewis's edition
(1731) reprinted by Baber (1810); and yet another in Bagster's very
useful *English Hexapla* (1841). But neither Baber nor Bagster give

Wiclif's Version: they give Purvey's under the name of Wiclif. The variations between these three texts of Purvey's Version do not often in these Epistles go beyond spelling and punctuation. The spelling of Middle English being phonetic, differences of spelling are considerable even in the same document. Thus in one and the same text of 3 John we have 'brother' and 'brothir,' 'most' and 'moost,' 'welefuly' and 'welefuli,' 'wryte' and 'write,' 'Y' and 'I.' But the MSS. have no stops: the differences in punctuation are due to the editors. In the Clementine Vulgate and in the Rhemish Version the punctuation is sometimes very peculiar.

In the N.T. the work of Purvey is very analogous to that of Jerome. Both revisers had a complete translation, made by their predecessors, to work upon. Both knew of variations from that translation as sources whence improvements might possibly be drawn. In both cases many of the changes actually introduced by the reviser were already in existence as alternative renderings in commentaries or translations. Comparison of Old Latin texts tends to reduce within very narrow limits the amount of work on the N.T. done by Jerome that can justly be called original. And a study of the various readings given by Forshall and Madden under Wiclif's Version will shew how often the changes actually made by Purvey have been anticipated in some copy of the earlier translation. This is so frequently the case in the MS. styled by the editors V (New College 67), that one suspects this document of representing an early attempt at revision made by Purvey himself. In any case Purvey's merits are great. Out of existing materials he made numerous excellent selections and added many improvements which were entirely his own. And his work improved as he went on. The glosses which disfigure Wiclif's work, and which Purvey for the most part retains and sometimes adds to in the O.T., are dismissed from the N.T.[1] And the clumsy 'forsothe' and 'sotheli,' very frequent throughout the earlier translation, and still frequent in the first half of Purvey's recension, almost disappear in the last part[2]. Therefore in these Epistles we have the reviser at his best.

The alterations made by Purvey are not as a rule either emendations of the Latin text, or corrections of mistranslations, real or supposed. Some emendations and corrections no doubt occur: e.g. he rightly inserts 'Jhesu' before 'Crist' in iv. 2 and substitutes 'bileveth in the sone' for 'bileveth in to the sone' (*in filio* for *in filium*) in v. 10: and less well he changes 'for Crist is treuthe' into 'that Crist is treuthe' in v. 6. But far more often his alterations are *improvements in the English*, with a view to making a stiff and over literal translation more suitable for popular use as a Version. A few instances from the First Epistle will illustrate this.

[1] In 1 John i. 1; ii. 14; iii. 16, 20; iv. 3; v. 7, 21 Wiclif gives an alternative rendering or explanation. Purvey has nothing of the kind. Comp. 2 John 13; 3 John 10.
[2] See 1 John i. 7; ii. 2, 5, 11, 19, 23; iv. 20; v. 5; 2 John 6, 12; 3 John 14. In all these passages Purvey has changed Wiclif's 'sotheli' or 'forsothe' into some more suitable particle, or has omitted it altogether.

i. 8. Si dixerimus quoniam peccatum non habemus, ipsi nos seducimus.

Wiclif. If we shulen seie, for we han not synne, we oure silf deceyven us.

Purvey. If we seien, that we han no synne, we disseyven us silf.

ii. 1, 2. *Sed si* quis peccaverit, advocatum habemus apud patrem, Iesum Christum justum: et ipse est propitiatio pro peccatis nostris (*Am.* sed et si).

Wiclif. But and if ony man shal synne, we han avoket anentis the fadir, Jhesu Crist just, and he is helpyng for oure synnes.

Purvey. But if ony man synneth, we han an advocat anentis the fadir, Jhesu Crist, and he is the forȝyvenes for oure synnes.

ii. 6. Qui dicit se in ipso manere, debet, sicut ille ambulavit, et ipse ambulare.

Wiclif. He that seith him for to dwelle in him, and he owith for to walke, as he walkide.

Purvey. He that seith that he dwellith in hym, he owith for to walke, as he walkide.

ii. 21. Non scripsi vobis quasi ignorantibus veritatem, sed quasi scientibus eam.

Wiclif. I wroot not to ȝou as to men unknowinge treuthe, but as to knowinge it.

Purvey. Y wroot not to ȝou as to men that knowen not treuthe, but as to men that knowen it.

But a much fairer estimate of the amount and kind of difference between Wiclif and Purvey and between Purvey and the Rhemish Version will be formed from a continuous passage. After these verses selected from the First Epistle let us compare Wiclif with Purvey throughout the Second Epistle, and Purvey with the Rhemish throughout the Third; in each case placing the ordinary Vulgate text between the two English Versions.

WICLIF, c. 1380.	VULGATE.	PURVEY, c. 1388.
1. THE eldre man to the chosen lady, & to hir children, the whiche I love in treuthe; and not I aloone, but & alle men that knewen treuthe.	1. SENIOR Electae dominae et natis ejus, quos ego diligo in veritate, et non ego solus, sed et omnes qui cognoverunt veritatem,	1. THE eldere man, to the chosun ladi, & to her children, whiche Y love in treuthe; and not Y aloone, but also alle men that knowen treuthe;
2. for the treuthe that dwellith in ȝou, & with ȝou shal ben in to with outen ende.	2. propter veritatem, quae permanet in nobis, et nobiscum erit in aeternum.	2. for the treuthe that dwellith in ȝou, and with ȝou schal be with outen ende.
3. Grace be with ȝou, mercy, & pees of God the fadir, and of Jhesu Crist, the sone	3. Sit *vobiscum* gratia, misericordia, pax a Deo Patre et *a* Christo Jesu, Filio Patris,	3. Grace be with ȝou, merci, and pees of God the fadir, and of Jhesu Crist, the

WICLIF, c. 1380.	VULGATE.	PURVEY, c. 1388.
of the fadir, in treuthe and charite.	in veritate et charitate (*Am.* nobiscum: omits the second a).	sone of the fadir, in treuthe and charite.
4. I joyede ful miche, for I foond of thi sones goynge in treuthe, as we recey-veden maundement of the fadir.	4. Gavisus sum valde, quoniam inveni de filiis tuis ambulan-tes in veritate, sicut mandatum accepimus a Patre.	4. I joiede ful myche, for Y foond of thi sones goynge in treuthe, as we ressey-veden maundement of the fadir.
5. And now I preye thee, lady, not as writinge a newe maun-dement to thee, but that that we hadden at the bigynnynge, that we love eche other.	5. Et nunc rogo te, domina, non tanquam mandatum novum scribens tibi, sed quod habuimus ab initio, ut diligamus alterutrum.	5. And now Y preye thee, ladi, not as wri-tinge a newe maunde-ment to thee, but that that we hadden fro the bigynnyng, that we love ech other.
6. And this is cha-rite, that we walke up his maundementes. Sotheli this is the co-maundement, that as ȝe herden at the bi-gynnyge, in him walke ȝe.	6. Et haec est cha-ritas, ut ambulemus secundum mandata ejus. Hoc est *enim* mandatum, ut quem-admodum audistis ab initio in eo ambuletis (*Am.* omits enim).	6. And this is cha-rite, that we walke after his maundemen-tis. For this is the comaundement, that as ȝe herden at the bigynnyng, walke ȝe in him.
7. For many decey-vours wenten out in to the world, whiche knowlechen not Jhesu Crist for to have come in flesch; this is decey-vour and antecrist.	7. Quoniam multi seductores exierunt in mundum, qui non con-fitentur Jesum Chris-tum *venisse in carnem.* Hic est seductor, et Antichristus (*Am.* ve-nientem in carne).	7. For many dis-seyveris wenten out in to the world, which knoulechen not that Jhesu Crist hath come in fleisch: this is a disseyvere and ante-crist.
8. See ȝe ȝoure silf, lest ȝe leese the thinges that ȝe han wrought, but that ȝe receyve ful meede;	8. Videte vosmet ipsos, ne perdatis quae operatî estis: sed ut mercedem plenam ac-cipiatis.	8. Se ȝe ȝou silf, lest ȝe lesen the thingis that ȝe han wrouȝt, that ȝe resseyve ful mede;
9. witynge that ech man that goith awey, & dwellith not in the techinge of Crist, hath not GOD. He that dwellith in the tech-inge, hath and the sone and the fadir.	9. Omnis, qui rece-*dit,* et non *permanet* in doctrina Christi, Deum non habet: qui permanet in doctrina, hic et *Patrem et Filium* habet (*Am.* praecedit: manet: filium et pa-trem).	9. witynge that ech man that goith before, & dwellith not in the teching of Crist, hath not God. He that dwellith in the teching, hath bothe the sone and the fadir.
10. If ony man cometh to ȝou, & bringeth not to this	10. Si quis venit ad vos, et hanc doctrinam non affert, nolite reci-	10. If ony man cometh to ȝou, & bryngith not this tech-

WICLIF, c. 1380.	VULGATE.	PURVEY, c. 1388.
teching, nyle ȝe receyve him in to hous, nether ȝe shulen sei to him, Heyl.	pere eum in domum, nec ave ei dixeritis.	ing, nyle ȝe resseyve hym in to hous, nether seie ȝe to hym, Heil.
11. Sotheli he that seith to hym, Heyl, comuneth with his yvele werkis. Lo! I bifore seide to ȝou, that ȝe be not confoundid in the day of our Lord Jhesu Crist.	11. Qui enim dicit illi ave, communicat operibus *ejus* malignis (*Am.* illius). [Ecce praedixi vobis, ut in die Domini non confundamini.]	11. For he that seith to hym, Heil, comyneth with hise yvel werkis. Lo! Y biforseide to ȝou, that ȝe be not confounded in the dai of oure Lord Jhesu Crist.
12. I havynge mo thinges for to wrijte to ȝou, wolde not by parchemyn & ynke; sotheli I hope me to comynge to ȝou, & speke mouth to mouth, that ȝoure joye be ful.	12. Plura habens vobis scribere, nolui per chartam et atramentum: spero enim me futurum apud vos, et os ad os loqui: ut gaudium vestrum plenum sit.	12. Y have mo thingis to write to ȝou, & Y wolde not bi parchemyn & enke; for Y hope that Y schal come to ȝou, & speke mouth to mouth, that ȝour joye be ful.
13. The sones, or douȝtres, of thi systir chosen greten thee wel. The grace of God with thee. Amen.	13. Salutant te filii sororis tuae Electae.	13. The sones of thi chosun sistir greten thee wel. The grace of God be with thee. Amen.

The chief variations between the Vulgate and the Old Latin in this Epistle are the following (Sabatier, *Bibliorum Sacrorum Latinae Versiones Antiquae*, Remis, 1743, III. 981, 982):—

5. *Oro te domina, non sicut...ut diligamus nos* alterutrum.

6. *Hoc est mandatum, sicut* audistis ab initio, *ut* in eo ambuletis.

7. Quoniam multi *fallaces progressi sunt* in *saeculo...*venisse in *carne: isti sunt fallaces* et *antichristi.*

8. Videte *eos*, ne perdatis *quod...recipiatis.*

9. Non *manet...*qui *autem manet* in doctrina *ejus*, ille.

10. Si quis *venerit...et ave nolite dicere ei.*

Now we may go on to compare Purvey with the Rhemish in 3 John. But first it may be worth while to point out one or two characteristic renderings both in the Latin and in the English Versions. They shew the desire to keep very closely, in the one case to the Greek, in the other to the Latin, even at the risk of being scarcely intelligible, or at least very uncouth (comp. Wiclif's rendering of 2 John 6 quoted above). Thus we have the use of the genitive after a comparative; μειζοτέραν τούτων οὐκ ἔχω χάριν (as B and the Memphitic for χαράν), *majorem horum non habeo gratiam*, 'Y have not more grace of these thingis' or 'Greater thanke have I not of them' (v. 4; comp. μείζω τούτων, *majora horum*, John i. 50): the introduction of *quoniam* for ὅτι in the sense of 'that'; οἶδας ὅτι, *nosti quoniam* (v. 12; comp. 1 John i.

8, 10 ; ii. 5; iii. 2, 15; iv. 13, 14, 20; and with *quia* for ὅτι ii. 18 ; iii. 5; v. 15, 18): and the attempt to express the Greek particle ἄν by a separate word; ἔγραψα ἄν (as א³ and the Syriac Versions for ἔγραψά τι), *scripsissem forsitan*, 'I hadde write peradventure' or 'I had written perhaps' (*v.* 9: see note on μεμενήκεισαν ἄν, *permansissent utique*, 1 John ii. 19).

The italics in the Rhemish Version indicate renderings which seem to have come from Tyndale.

PURVEY, c. 1388.	VULGATE.	RHEMISH, 1582.
1. THE eldere man to Gayus, most dere brother, whom Y love in treuthe.	1. SENIOR Gaio charissimo, quem ego diligo in veritate.	1. THE seniour to Gaius the deerest, whom I love in truth.
2. Most dere brothir, of alle thingis Y make preyer, that thou entre, and fare welefully, as thi soul doith welefuli.	2. Charissime, de omnibus orationem facio prospere te ingredi, et valere, sicut prospere agit anima tua.	2. My deerest, concerning al thinges I make my praier that thou proceede prosperously, & fare wel, as thy soule doth prosperously.
3. Y ioyede greetli, for britheren camen, & baren witnessing to thi treuthe, as thou walkist in treuthe.	3. Gavisus sum valde venientibus fratribus, et testimonium perhibentibus veritati tuae, sicut tu in veritate ambulas.	3. I was exceding glad *when the brethren came*, & gave testimonie to thy truth, even as thou walkest in truth.
4. Y have not more grace of these thingis, than that Y here that my sones walke in treuthe.	4. Majorem horum non habeo gratiam, quam ut audiam filios meos in veritate *ambulare* (*Am.* ambulantes).	4. Greater thanke have I not of them, then that I may heare my children do walke in truth.
5. Most dere brother, thou doist faithfuli, whatever thou worchist in britheren, and that in to pilgrymys,	5. Charissime, fideliter facis, quidquid operaris in fratres, et hoc in peregrinos,	5. My deerest, thou doest faithfully whatsoever thou workest on the brethren, & that upon strangers.
6. which ʒeldiden witnessing to thi charite, in the siʒt of the chirche; which thou leddist forth, and doist wel worthili to God.	6. qui testimonium reddiderunt charitati tuae in conspectu Ecclesiae, quos, *benefaciens, deduces* dignè Deo (*Am.* benefacies ducens).	6. they have rendred testimonie to thy charitie in the sight of the church; whom, thou shalt doe wel, bringing on their way in maner worthie of God.
7. For thei wenten forth for his name, and	7. Pro nomine enim *ejus* profecti sunt, nihil	7. For, for his name did they depart, taking

PURVEY, c. 1388.	VULGATE.	RHEMISH, 1582.
token no thing of hethene men.	accipientes a gentibus (*Am.* omits ejus).	nothing of *the Gentiles.*
8. Therfor we owen to resseyve *siche*, that we be even worcheris of treuthe (Bagster, such manner men).	8. Nos ergo debemus suscipere hujusmodi, ut cooperatores simus veritatis.	8. We therefore ought to receive such: that we may be coadjutors of the truth.
9. I hadde write peradventure to the chirche, but this Diotrepes, that loveth to bere primacie in hem, resseyveth not us.	9. Scripsissem forsitan Ecclesiae: sed is, qui amat primatum gerere in eis, *Diotrephes*, non recipit nos (*Am.* Diotripes).	9. I had written perhaps to the church: but he that loveth to beare primacie among them, Diótrepes, doth not receive us.
10. For this thing, if Y schal come, Y schal moneste hise werkis, which he doith, chidinge aȝens us with yvel wordis. And as if these thingis suffisen not to hym, nether he resseyveth britheren, and forbedith hem that resseyven, and puttith out of the chirche.	10. Propter hoc, si venero, *commonebo* ejus opera, quae facit, verbis malignis garriens in nos: et quasi non ei ista sufficiant: neque ipse suscipit fratres: et eos, qui *suscipiunt*, prohibet, et de Ecclesia ejicit (*Am.* commoneam: cupiunt).	10. For this cause, if I come, I will advertise his workes which he doeth: with *malicious* wordes chatting against us, and as though these thinges suffise him not: neither him self doth receive the brethren, & them that do receive, he prohibiteth, and casteth out of the church.
11. Moost dere brothir, nyle thou sue yvel thing, but that that is good thing. He that doith wel, is of God; he that doith yvel, seeth not God.	11. Charissime, noli imitari malum, sed quod bonum est. Qui benefacit, ex Deo est: qui malefacit, non *vidit* Deum (*Am.* videt).	11. My deerest, do not imitate evil, but that which is good. He that doeth well, is of GOD: he that doeth il, hath not seen God.
12. Witnessing is ȝoldun to Demetrie of alle men, and of treuthe it silf; but also we beren witnessing, & thou knowist, that oure witnessing is trewe.	12. Demetrio testimonium redditur ab omnibus, et ab ipsa veritate, *sed* nos testimonium perhibemus: et nosti quoniam testimonium nostrum verum est (*Am.* omits sed).	12. To Demetrius testimonie is given of al, & of the truth it self, yea & we give testimonie: & thou knowest that our testimonie is true.
13. Y hadde many thingis to wryte to thee, but I wolde not write to thee bi enke and penne.	13. Multa habui *tibi scribere:* sed nolui per atramentum, et calamum scribere tibi (*Am.* scribere tibi).	13. I had many thinges to write unto thee: but I would not by inke and penne write to thee.
14. For Y hope	14. Spero autem	14. But I hope

Purvey, c. 1388.	Vulgate.	Rhemish, 1582.
soone to se thee, and we schulen speke mouth to mouth.	protinus te videre, et os ad os loquemur.	forthwith to see thee, and we wil speake mouth to mouth.
15. Pees be to thee. Frendis greten thee wel. Greete thou wel frendis bi name.	15. Pax tibi. Salutant te amici. Saluta amicos *nominatim* (*Am.* per nomen).	15. Peace be to thee. The freendes salute thee. Salute the freendes by name.

The chief variations between the Vulgate and the Old Latin in this Epistle are the following (Sabatier, *Bibliorum Versiones Antiquae*, III. 983, 984) :—

1. Senior Gaio *dilectissimo.*
4. *Majus autem* horum non habeo *gaudium...ambulantes.*
5. *quodcunque* operaris in *fratribus*, et hoc *peregrinis.*
6. *dederunt dilectioni* tuae *coram Ecclesia:* quos *optime facis, si praemiseris Deo digne.*
7. Pro nomine enim *Domini exierunt.*
9. *Scripsi etiam* Ecclesiae: sed *qui primatus agere cupit eorum.*
10. *Propterea cum venero, admonebo* ejus opera, quae facit, *malis verbis detrahens de nobis:* et *non sufficit ei,* quod *ipse non recipit* fratres ; *sed et volentes* prohibet.
12. Demetrio testimonium *perhibetur...et nos vero* testimonium perhibemus : et *scis,* testimonium nostrum verum est.
13. *Plura* habui *scribere tibi:* sed *nolo.*
14. Spero *enim* protinus te *visurum,* et os ad os *locuturum.*
15. Pax *tecum.* Salutant te amici *tui.*

Excepting *enim* in *v.* 14, and perhaps *in fratribus* in *v.* 5, there is no evidence that these readings were known to Purvey.

I. The Latin Correspondence between S. Ignatius and S. John.

This Appendix, with the exception of a few sentences, is taken almost *verbatim* from Bishop Lightfoot's great work on S. Ignatius and S. Polycarp, recently published.

The Latin Version of the Ignatian Epistles in their middle form has a special interest for Englishmen, as being a product of the remarkable but premature literary revival which distinguished the thirteenth century, and as giving the Ignatian letters in the only form in which they were known in this country till several years after the invention of printing. It does not seem to be quoted except by English writers, or to have been known out of England. It is with much probability conjectured to be a translation made by Robert Grosseteste, Bishop of Lincoln, c. A. D. 1250.

The collection comprises sixteen epistles in all besides the Acts of the Martyrdom, and it falls into two parts.

(1) The *first*, which ends with the Acts of Martyrdom and the accompanying Epistle to the Romans, includes twelve epistles. This portion is a translation from a Greek original. It corresponds exactly in arrangement and contents with the Greek collection represented by

the Medicean and Colbert MSS. and must have been translated by Bishop Grossteste or his assistants from some similar Greek MS. At the close of this part is a summary of the contents. This is the main indication in the Latin MSS. that the first part is separate from the second.

(2) The *second* part consists of the four short epistles, which make up the correspondence of the saint with the Virgin and S. John. These epistles appear never to have existed in the Greek, and therefore cannot have formed part of Grossteste's version. How they came to be attached to this version it is impossible to say; but inasmuch as they occur in both the MSS. L₁ L₂, in the same form and arrangement, though these two MSS. are independent of each other, they must have held this position at a very early date, and it is not improbable that they were appended soon after the version was made. They were very popular in the middle ages, and appear to have been much read about this time; so that no collection of the Ignatian Epistles would have appeared complete without them.

The great importance of this Anglo-Latin version of the Ignatian Epistles for textual criticism consists in its extreme literalness, to which the construction of the Latin is consistently sacrificed. This remark cannot of course apply to the correspondence with the Virgin and S. John which probably is not a translation and is comparatively unimportant. It is found in a considerable number of MSS. sometimes by itself, sometimes in connexion with the Epistles of the Long Recension. The various readings are very numerous, and the order of the four Epistles is different in different copies. Like so many other apocryphal writings, they help by contrast to confirm the authenticity of genuine writings. The wide difference between the two is fully accounted for by the fact that the one are spurious and the other not.

1.

Johanni Sancto Seniori Ignatius et qui cum eo sunt Fratres.

De tua mora dolemus graviter, allocutionibus et consolationibus tuis roborandi. Si tua absentia protendatur, multos de nostris destituet. Properes igitur venire, quia credimus expedire. Sunt et hic multae de nostris mulieribus Mariam Jesu videre cupientes et discurrere a nobis quotidie volentes, ut eam contingant et ubera ejus tractent, quae Dominum Jesum aluerunt, et quaedam secretiora ejus percunctentur eam. Sed et Salome quam diligis, filia Annae, Hierosolimis quinque mensibus apud eam commorans, et quidam alii noti referunt eam omnium gratiarum abundam et omnium virtutum foecundam. Et, ut dicunt, in persecutionibus et afflictionibus est hilaris; in penuriis et indigentiis non querula; injuriantibus grata; et molestata laetatur; miseris et afflictis coafflicta condolet, et subvenire non pigrescit. Contra vitiorum pestiferos insultus in pugna fidei discrepitans enitescit. Nostrae novae religionis est magistra; et apud fideles omnium operum pietatis ministra. Humilibus quidem est devota, et devotis devotius humiliatur. Et mirum ab omnibus magnificatur; cum a scribis et Pharisaeis ei detrahatur. Praeterea et multi multa nobis referunt de eadem: tamen omnibus per omnia non audemus fidem concedere, nec tibi referre. Sed sicut nobis a fide dignis narratur, in Maria Jesu humanae naturae natura sanctitatis angelicae sociatur. Et haec talia excitaverunt viscera nostra, et cogunt valde desiderare aspectum hujus (si fas sit fari) prodigii et sanctissimi monstri. Tu autem diligenti modo disponas cum desiderio nostro, et valeas. Amen.

2.

Johanni Sancto Seniori suus Ignatius.

Si licitum est mihi apud te ad Hierosolimae partes volo ascendere, et videre fideles sanctos qui ibi sunt; praecipue Mariam Jesu, quam dicunt universis admirandam et cunctis desiderabilem. Quem vero non delectet videre eam et alloqui, quae verum Deum deorum peperit, si sit nostrae fidei et religionis amicus? Similiter et illum venerabilem Jacobum qui cognominatur Justus; quem referunt Christo Jesu simillimum vita et modo conversationis, ac si ejusdem uteri frater esset gemellus; quem, dicunt, si videro, video ipsum Jesum secundum omnia corporis ejus lineamenta: praeterea ceteros sanctos et sanctas. Heu, quid moror? Cur detineor? Bone praeceptor, properare me jubeas, et valeas. Amen.

3.

Christiferae Mariae suus Ignatius.

Me neophitum Johannisque tui discipulum confortare et consolari debueras. De Jesu enim tuo percepi mira dictu, et stupefactus sum ex auditu. A te autem, quae semper ei familiarius fuisti conjuncta et secretorum ejus conscia, desidero ex animo fieri certior de auditis. Scripsi tibi et etiam alias, et rogavi de eisdem. Valeas; et tui neophiti, qui mecum sunt, ex te et per te et in te confortentur. Amen.

4.

Ignatio Dilecto Condiscipulo Humilis Ancilla Domini.

De Jesu quae a Johanne audisti et didicisti vera sunt. Illa credas, illis inhaereas, et Christianitatis susceptae votum firmiter teneas, et mores et vitam voto conformes. Veniam autem una cum Johanne te et qui tecum sunt visere. Sta et viriliter age in fide; nec te commoveat persecutionis austeritas, sed valeat et exultet spiritus tuus in Deo salutari tuo. Amen.

INDEX I

GREEK

INDEX II

GENERAL

homoeoteleuton, 32, 63, 93, 109
Huther quoted, 64, 86

idolatry, xvii, 129; how regarded
by Gnostics, 103, 107, 129
Ignatius, his silence respecting S.
John, xiii; on the last days,
55 ; on a Christian's knowledge,
61; coincidences with S. John's
Epistles, 79, 82, 83; Latin correspondence with the Virgin,
193
imperative aorist, 128
imperative present, 94, 139
imperfect participle, 145
indicative after ἵνα, 74, 127
indicative or imperative, 66, 69,
95
indicative or subjunctive, 107,111
infallibility of the Pope, 94
ink, 141
internal evidence, limits of, 168
internal evidence as to the authorship of the First Epistle, xlii;
of the Second and Third, lxxi;
as to 1 John v. 7, 167
interpolations in the Greek text,
70, 92, 96, 109
— in the Latin Versions, 53, 54,
84, 109, 140
intolerance of S. John, 139
Introduction to the First Epistle,
xxxvii
— — — Second, lxvi
— — — Third, lxxviii
Irenaeus on S. John and Polycarp,
xii; on the date of the Apocalypse, xxxvi; quotes the First
and Second Epistles, xl, lxviii,
96, 137; knows of no second
John at Ephesus, 173; on the
Cainites, 162

Jelf on the one error of the Apostles, 56; on the test of a state
of grace, 87, 88; on the value
of Christ's baptism and death,
116
Jerome on S. John's virginity,
xxxiv; on S. John's old age,

xxxv; on these three Epistles,
lxx; on the two tombs at
Ephesus, 174; character of his
Vulgate, 179; its divergences
from his own quotations, 39,
41, 78, 104, 106
John the Apostle and Cerinthus,
xxxii, 139; and the Parthians,
xliii; and the partridge, xxxii;
and Polycarp, xii; and the robber, xxxii; *ante Portam Lati-
nam*, xxx; his death, xxxv; his
tomb, 174; his relation to S.
Paul, lxii; his virginity, xxxiv,
xliii
John the Elder or the Presbyter,
lxxi, 132, 172
John Malalas on the Apostle's
death, xxxv
Judas, Gospel of, 162
Judgment, Day of, 105, 106
Justin Martyr on the Apocalypse,
xii; on Antichrist, 159; probably knew the First Epistle,
72, 79

key-words in the Second Epistle,
134, 135
knowledge of the Christian, 61,
124, 126; of the Gnostic, xxii,
21, 75, 127
Kyria, lxxv, 132

Lapide, Cornelius à, 130, 144
Latin interpolations, 53, 54, 84,
109, 140
Latin Versions, lxxxiv, 41, 52, 58,
75, 78, 102, 105, 107, 178
Leucian fragments on S. John's
death, xxxv; are silent as to a
second John at Ephesus, 174
Liddon on the title 'the Elder',
lxxi; on the elect lady, lxxv; on
S. John's view of Christianity,
61; on S. John's view of 'the
world', 98; on the witness of
the Spirit, 115; on loving in
truth, 133; on S. John's dog-
matism, 139
life, 16, 53

Thornapple Commentaries

Alexander, Joseph Addison
The Gospel According to Mark
The Gospel According to Matthew

Bernard, J. H.
The Pastoral Epistles

Henderson, Ebenezer
The Twelve Minor Prophets

Hodge, Charles
A Commentary on the Epistle to the Ephesians
An Exposition of the First Epistle to the Corinthians
An Exposition of the Second Epistle to the Corinthians

Lightfoot, J. B.
Notes on Epistles of St. Paul

Maier, Walter A.
The Book of Nahum

McNeile, Alan Hugh
The Gospel According to St. Matthew

Plummer, Alfred
The Epistles of St. John

Shedd, William G. T.
Commentary on Romans

Westcott, Brooke Foss
The Gospel According to St. John

Baker Book House, Box 6287, Grand Rapids, Michigan 49506